ANTHROGENESIS

ANTHROGENESIS

The Study of Humanity's
Ancient Beginnings:
Origins, Spirituality
And Mythology

A BOOK BY

JANET HIZAR HANSFORD, PH.D.

Cities of Light Publishing

Sedona, Arizona

Contents

Chapter Three: Formation Towards Planetary Life — 35

Chapter Four: Humanity Flourishes — 63

Chapter Five: Evolutionary Biology — 79

Chapter Eight: Western Hemisphere Migrations — 139

Chapter Twelve: North American Peoples — 237

Chapter Thirteen: The Triad Persists To The Present — 263

Chapter Fifteen: Humanity's Road Forward — 345

Janet Hizar Hansford

Acknowledgements

Anthrogenesis is the outcome of fifteen years of research and soul searching and a lifetime of inspiration from many sources including family, colleagues, and friends.

First, I wish to thank my husband and best friend, Michael, for his ongoing love and support of me, and for his encouragement in writing this book.

I am incredibly grateful to my mother and father for their patience with a little girl who was always asking, why does this happen? My earliest memories are full of love and support with all the curious questions that I asked—still ask!

My father once found me several houses down at our neighbor's home because I wanted to "See the kitty, daddy!" Mind you, I wasn't more than a toddler at the time. He was always my hero, especially so in times of need. My mother was a saint, who appreciated my adventuresome spirit, which she always cherished and guided. And that yearning for adventure continues to guide me. My parents were also instrumental in teaching me the importance of family, love, routine, and spiritual belief throughout my formative years.

I am thankful to my children, Andrew, and Kirstin, for being so precious because they taught me the virtue of patience in quintessential family life situations.

I especially want to thank Andrew because along with the godsend of motherhood, he presented me with the opportunity to develop marathon running, to catch him as a wee one when he thought of wandering from me!

I will never forget a vision that I had about 35 years ago, which forever changed the meaning of my life. I had a strong impression that I had been 'here' before as a 'healer.' As time passed, I learned to

i

welcome these intuitive experiences along with other meditative and contemplative events.

I must thank Lucis-Arcane and Georgia Lambert who were pivotal during my twenties and beyond for their spiritual understanding and illumination. HRH Dalai Lama inspired me with his overwhelming gift of compassion. Now, after many years of meditation and following the transcendental spiritual path, I am grateful for these influences.

I have had exceptional mentors over the course of my education and practice and wish to retrospectively thank Milton H. Erickson, M.D., the 'Grandfather of Clinical Hypnosis' whose work and indirect supervision sent me forth into my life's work, the psychologists Dr. John (Jack) G. Watkins at the University of Montana and his incredible wife, Helen H. Watkins for inspiring me in 'Ericksonian Hypnosis' during my doctoral studies and encouraging me in treating my patients with

Dissociative Identity Disorder (originally 'Multiple Personality Disorder'-American Psychiatric Association, DSM-III, 1980) and Earnest R. Hilgard, Ph.D., for his research in 'hidden observers' in hypnosis, which inspired me in my work.

I am grateful for the helpful counsel of Ralph B. Allison, M.D., to me while at CDC, San Luis Obispo, California and his support with the 'Inner Self Helper' or ISH in my research. Dr. Allison has incorporated spirituality into his work over the years and I can only hope to aspire to his level of mindfulness.

Also, I thank the countless patients across the years who have always been my teachers.

There are so many great internet and authors' sites that I must thank: sacredtexts.com, indians.org, hermetic.com, theosophy.net, binaryresearchinstitute.org, robertschoch.com, grahamhancock.com, jawest.net, blavatskytrust.org.uk, robertbauval.co.uk, lairdscranton. com, megalithomania.co.uk, ancient-wisdom.com, wisdomworld.org, theosociety.org, and Wikipedia and its inner groups- to name a few.

Without my editor, Lane Badger of Cities of Light Publishing, I couldn't have written this book.

Finally, there are undoubtedly many others who have been graciously helpful to me that go without mention. I thank you for your assistance to me.

Anthrogenesis

Preface

Recently, I was listening to a science program on cable and the speaker said, "We need science to be able to pave the way," and I thought, how many times have I said, either out loud or to myself, something like that? The scientific method is there for a reason; I do believe this, after receiving my Ph.D. and conducting post-doc studies to the present.

Conversely, over the course of my life I have practiced different world religions, prayed, meditated, chanted, and sometimes, became exasperated about why I am here and what am I missing. Depending on the period in my life, I might have sought forgiveness for irreverence or perhaps visualized 'white light' radiating throughout my body and centering me with the Universe…while chanting OM.

Yet, here I am writing a book utilizing Hermetic principles, innate to Theosophy, and other important spiritual streams, AND how science might figure into this unseemly mix of faith and reality!

A Note on Theosophy.

Over the course of expanding the Anthrogenesis concept, I studied a number of religious and philosophic tenets. I concluded that the optimum cultivation of the book, which commences with humanity's earliest history and culture, was to use Theosophy, mythology and spirituality within a philosophical construct that mainstream history has not yet been able to conceptualize. Theosophy alone takes mythology out of the realm of fantasy and into the sphere of understanding.

After being raised in a traditional Christian home, I stepped into the 'charismatic' experience with guitar-playing Sundays, full of worship and get-togethers. I borrowed the family car to drive to the 'special churches'—the ones that were quite popular in Southern California, sprouting up all over in the late '60s. The "sixties" have come to be considered one of our planet's most interesting times with famous phrases like 'Flower Power,' 'Consciousness,' 'Power to the People,' and 'Peace on Earth.' The 1960s were brought alive by amazing music, concerts, *love-ins, be-ins*…and a kind of brotherly love, which flooded our planet with spiritual energy, light, love, newness, and women's empowerment! Manly Palmer Hall discussed in "Flower Power"—one of his many lectures-originally from his book, *Secret Teachings of All Ages (1928)* that the 'Light' had begun to shine through the ethers—from the Great White Lodge on Sirius, around the end of World War II. It was a major factor in the development of the idealism and new vision of the 1960s in America and England and later spread globally.

Manly P. Hall conferred privately with F.D.R. during those most serious of times during WWII, when our world faced a depth of evil not seen for thousands of years. Perhaps, the last time evil reared its head to that degree was at the end of the Golden Age of Atlantis, when mankind operated by free will and material gain on the planet, ignoring the spiritual gifts of enlightenment, vision and spiritual wealth.

The educational experience exposes a student to many new ideas. While studying at California State University, Sonoma, I took a Psychology class, during which the instructor based our final grade on a project, in my case, it was study of the I Ching philosophy—throwing the sticks, not quite knowing how to read them, but putting my best foot forward in embracing the ancient spiritual experience with my lab partner!

The 1980s were filled with change, a newfound freedom with the Iron Curtain coming down and *Star Wars*. Our planet was in a technological expansion like never before. Over the course of that decade and the next, I followed my heart and continued on the path of enlightenment. I also traded my Macintosh SE for a newer Mac with more memory.

Funny how they say, a person attracts what they need, which is what happened to me. Over the course of years, I explored a number of transpersonal philosophies and as a therapist, I naturally incorporated spirituality into my work with patients. I found myself in Southwestern Vision Quest conferences, conducting studies on the soul's influence in healing, and giving women's workshops at the Unity Church on *"Women Who Run With The Wolves: Myths and Stories of The Wild Woman Archetype"* (Ballantine Books, NY, 1992), based upon the book by Dr. Clarissa Pinkola Estés, a Jungian analyst.

So, how does mainstream science connect with the universal collective unconscious?

The Origin of Consciousness: The Work of Julian Jaynes

One of my most treasured books is entitled, *The Origin of Consciousness in the Breakdown of the Bicameral Mind*, by Julian Jaynes, Ph.D., Professor of Psychology at Princeton University. (Houghton & Mifflin Company, Boston, MA, 1st Ed. 1976). I became fascinated by Jaynes' theory.

Jaynes contended that consciousness was learned as a byproduct of man's history and culture, being anchored to the brain's physiology. Jaynes described three forms of awareness as being (1) the bicameral or god-run man, (2) the modern problem-solving man, and (3) contemporary regressions of bicameralism which resembled religious states, schizophrenia and the poetic man—the more ancient brain-state of man.

Dr. Jaynes was considered bold and remarkable in that he had addressed the then poorly researched area of human consciousness in ways that heretofore were non-existent. Today, we understand that Jaynes' 'bicameral mind' connects more closely to the collective unconscious of transpersonal psychiatrist Carl Jung. Researcher's concurrent examination persists in consciousness, meditation and other states of mind within the brain's physiology to corroborate new theories.

In my private practice, I continued work with multi-consciousness with my patients, some of who had dissociative disorders and PTSD (Post Traumatic Stress Disorder), with many echoing Jaynes' work about the multitude of selves, but having no understanding as to what they were; where they came from; and what it meant. All of which brings me almost to the present.

After the new millennium, I found myself watching television, especially those airing variety in science, history, and new age programming. My interest was piqued and I started taking notes on programs, books, and other media that were intriguing to me.

These notes have become the basis of my book.

I have been on a journey that has changed my life, and hopefully, the lives of my patients for the past three decades. I continue this expedition by developing the book and the concept of *Anthrogenesis*.

Anthrogenesis opens the door to a more holistic understanding of human origins; a marriage of the left and the right brain, yin and yang, male and female— science and spirituality. Many outstanding sources are necessary to form a full concept of the human experience and human development from our ancient origins to the present day.

The Yugas and Precession

The Cycle of the Yugas within the ancient Vedic literature points to earth 'ages' that span vast periods of time. The Yugas reoccur time and time again, and bring in definite stages of human development and form an integral part in the blueprint of human consciousness. Swami Sri Yukteswar, a Vedic scholar of tremendous note, discussed the ages of the yugas in his book *The Holy Science*, written in 1894. Sri Yukteswar is best known in the West as the guru of Paramahansa Yogananda (1893-1952), his primary disciple, who upon first seeing his prophesied teacher exclaimed, "Gurudeva!" Yogananda went on to found the Self-Realization Fellowship (SRF) in America, authoring the classic, Autobiography of a Yogi in 1946. He is acclaimed as the bringer of the discipline of yoga to America.

Sri Yukteswar explains that each Yuga cycle has an ascending half and a descending half, each of which lasts 12,000 years. In the ascending half, humanity evolves through different ages of the Yugas, of varying length, becoming more spiritual and refined. I n t he d escending arc, humankind regresses into materialism and discord. The Yugas a re comprised of four phases from the Golden Age-Satya Yuga; Treta Yuga-the Silver Age; Dwapara Yuga- the Bronze Age; and finally, Kali Yuga, the Dark Age- most acrimonious age of all the Yugas.

The motion of the equinoctial points (reversed to the movement of the sun) around the zodiac has been observed for thousands of years and this phenomenon is called the 'precession of the equinoxes.' Astronomy currently explains that it takes 26,000 years to complete the zodiac. Yet, the Yugas calculate 24,000 years for completion of the cycle. So, this variable in time within the 'precession' is said to be an attributed to a 'dual star' which creates a gravitational wobble with the earth and causes the time discrepancy.

Sri Yukteswar enlightens us about the nature of this dual or binary star, saying that while the Earth's axis produces an elliptical motion, our Sun "takes some star for its dual and revolves around it in about 24,000 earth years–a celestial phenomenon which causes the reverse movement of the equinoctial points around the zodiac." From our terrestrial perspective, the precession of the equinox (also called 'the Platonic Year') is the observable singularity of the rotation of the heavens, a cycle which spans a period of about 24,000 years with our constellations appearing to slowly rotate around the earth, taking turns at rising behind the rising sun on the vernal (Spring) or autumnal (Fall) equinox. During these equinoxes, the length of day and night are equal.

In their book *The Yugas*, (2010) authors Joseph Selbie and David Steinmetz, cite Professor Giorgio de Santillana of MIT and historian W.K.C. Guthrie, about a "Golden Age" that appears to occur in many ancient cross-cultural mythologies. Ancient Greece had one of these ages, as Plato discusses in *Timaeus* and *Critias*. Stories and myths about a time of 'high culture; exist in many places across the globe, including the "Norse, Celtic, Hopi, Lakota, Persian, and ancient Egyptian" cultures. Also seen were "parallels" which looked like Kali Yuga (700 BCE to 1700 CE), when the "myth-tellers lived in the lowest" of times and recognized that "mankind has descended from a higher" civilization. In our ancient past, humanity delved into an early form of materialism, during the Atlantean Kali Yuga. The last sub-race of Atlantis, along with the Adepts (or 'Kings of Light'), were said to have colonized the Americas and Euro-Asia at that time, escaping the inevitable cataclysm.

According to Sri Yukteswar we are now in the ascending half of Dwapara Yuga and Helena P. Blavatsky indicates that humanity is now in the 5th Root Race, 6th Sub-race, called the "Austral-Americans."

However, the great adepts have always said that spiritual advancement can be realized by focusing one's attention on illumination, a day-to-day quest for peace, compassion and understanding of our fellow humanity, regardless of the Yuga that we are living in![1, 2, 3, 4, 5]

H.P. Blavatsky and the Ancient Wisdom

The Ancient Wisdom is the ancient spiritual teaching handed down from time immemorial and undiluted by the contemporary trends or culture of any particular period in human history. Correlated with Buddhism, Hinduism, Kabala and mystic Christianity, the Ancient Wisdom is thoroughly described in the writings of H.P. Blavatsky (1831-1891), also called 'H.P.B.' H.P. Blavatsky was to become the preeminent philosopher of Theosophical doctrine, furnished in her work and ultimately to become the world-renowned Theosophical teacher of the Ancient Wisdom.

Born in Russia, an adventurer at birth, Blavatsky travelled extensively, even before twenty-one years of age to Turkey, Egypt, and Greece, Canada, U.S.A, Mexico, South America and the West Indies, to the Cape of Africa and Ceylon and back to India. Her initial attempt to travel in Tibet failed, so Madame Blavatsky, as she would be called, went to Java and on to England with many years spent in India and later in Tibet, studying with her Master. In the fall of 1874, along with co-founders, Colonel Henry Steele Alcott and William Quan Judge, Madame Blavatsky founded The Theosophical Society with a mission, which included the following objectives: to "form a nucleus of the Universal Brotherhood of Humanity, without distinction of race, creed, sex, caste or color; to encourage the study of Comparative Religion, Philosophy and Science, and to investigate unexplained laws of Nature, and the powers latent in man."

Her first book in 1877, *Isis Unveiled*, discussed the 'scope and development of the Occult Sciences, the nature and origin of Hermetic practices, the roots of Christianity, the errors of Christian Theology and the fallacies of established orthodox Science', among other topics. She was taught by a number of Indian Mahatmas but chiefly the Master Morya and the Master Kuthumi who resided largely in Tibet.

Blavatsky and co-founder Alcott moved the Society to Adyar, Madras, India in 1879. Blavatsky wrote her codex maximus, *The Secret Doctrine*, in 1888, which was originally published by the Theosophical Publishing Company in India. This work covers the Ancient Wisdom; the creation of the universe, the evolution of humankind, and the primordial tradition underlying the various religions, mythologies and philosophies of the world, a deeply complex yet inspirational fountainhead of esoteric knowledge.

Esoteric Theosophy of Alice Bailey

Madame Blavatsky was a forerunner and mentor to both Alice A. Bailey (1880-1949) and her husband, Foster Bailey (1888–1977) who were disciples of the ageless Ancient Wisdom. She described this study of the Ancient Wisdom as a crucible of wealth, inherited over eons of time, which explores the deepest inquiries of the human mind, and the greatest insights into existence. Bailey furthered development in the impression of the 'Seven Rays.' Blavatsky referred to the Seven Rays: "The seven Builders (Creators) become the seven Prajapati, or the seven Rishis, in the same order as the Sephiroth become the Creators; then the Patriarchs, etc."

Bailey stepped into the public eye in 1925, with her first work, *Initiation, Human and Solar*, within which she recorded the dictation given to her telepathically from the Tibetan Master, Djwhal Khul or D.K. He, in turn, served the renowned Master Morya or 'M' and Master Kuthumi or 'K.H.' These two Masters of the Ageless Wisdom were considered part of the larger group of the Trans-Himalayan Brotherhood of Adepts.

Marriage of the Heart and Head

An important component of the Ancient Wisdom is the practice of harmlessness in all thought and deed. Gandhi resonated deeply with the practice of selfless action that influenced him throughout his life, with the parallels of service and selflessness quite clear. The Bhagavad Gita offers the path to salvation through devotion to Krishna, but Gandhi's view diverged from this as he thought that salvation comes from the aspiration to 'Krishna-like' thought and behavior. This is much like the Tibetan's teachings of the mystic becoming the occultist, but the work is only completed when the occultist merges with the mystic. In Alice Bailey's book, *The Light of the Soul*, (1927) the Tibetan tells us that "the devotee has to tread the Path of Raja Yoga- the mastery of the mental body over the emotional body, stemming from the solar plexus, and combine intellectual knowledge, mental control and discipline before the revelation can be truly made." The mystic, therefore, becomes the occultist, and the mind and heart qualities must be equally developed, for both are equally divine.

The Goddess Artemis, Mistress of Animals, Hunt and the Moon, unknown artist. Homer, Iliad xxi 470 f.

The Soul and Reincarnation

Central to the information presented by the Tibetan via Bailey is the knowledge of the existence of the soul and its reincarnation. The astronomy that Bailey's refers to is the 'soul consciousness of *all forms* including: constellations, individual stars, planets, and kingdoms (such as the human, animal, plant, and mineral) contained within a Planetary Life. Thus, the existence of the indwelling consciousness of all things, not just that of the human being becomes the proper territory for metaphysical inquiry.

Knowledge of one's astrological underpinnings is also very essential to every individual on the Path, as Bailey refers to the Path to Enlightenment. Understanding the *cosmic process* is key to *all* wisdom. This is known as esoteric wisdom and defined by Bailey as the soul or conscious side of life. In Bailey's book, *Esoteric Astrology* (1951), D.K., articulating through Bailey, indicates that the type of astrology he (D.K.) seeks to unveil is that of the soul, not of the personality, and that this astrology would be best understood by future astrologers. Esoteric astrology will help humanity to widen its horizons and realize its place in the much greater order. Specifically, he says, "The new soul astrology will have taken its place in mainstream thought by the end of the 20th century."

The Pleiades and the Great Bear

Djwhal Khul predicted that the constellation of the Great Bear, or Ursa Major, best known for its famous Big Dipper, would become very influential in the future. The Little Bear (Ursa Minor), or Little Dipper contains the most important navigational star in our sky, Polaris, North Star. And the star Sirius, the 'Heavenly Wolf,' is extremely important as the guardian of the celestial palace of the Great Lord, home of the Immortals. Alice Bailey, in *A Treatise on Cosmic Fire* (1925) discusses the importance of the Great Bear as one point in a *cosmic triangle* with the Pleiades and our Solar System. This cosmic triangle is also described as containing three centers, thought to be God or Brahma.

The ancient Greeks saw Artemis as the Great Bear as told in the story of Callisto. She is known as the She-Bear and rules the Arctic Pole. She is the Queen of the Virgin Meadow, Lady of Wild Mountains, and the Queen of the Crescent Moon. Moonlight reveals her being. It is Artemis that instigates wild animals and trees to dance.

A positive and negative polarity exists between the Pleiades and our Solar System. D.K. further points out that a previously hidden component of cycles (soon to be revealed) is to be found in the relationships of the Great Bear, the Little Bear, the Pole Star-Polaris, the Pleiades, Draco, Sirius, the constellation of Capricorn, and other constellations and stars of the Zodiac.

The Renaissance

The period of time referred to as the Renaissance (meaning *rebirth* in French), was a time of great social and cultural change in Europe, a rebirth in many different ways.

The time is c. 1350 CE, Northern Italy, following a macabre chapter of the Black Death, which wreaked havoc on society, sweeping through towns, killing a third to half the population of Europe. The Renaissance provided an ingenious return to the mysteries of the Greco-Roman era, the knowledge of Alexander's Library, and generally, a return to beauty, art, civility and the best of humanity. Let us not forget that the geniuses of the age like Galileo improved the telescope and made celestial calculations; Copernicus rediscovered our Sun's orbit; Leonardo Da Vinci's made impressive discoveries and rendered designs of futuristic inventions and wonders; Michelangelo's great art masterpieces returned to the classical techniques of realism within a three-dimensional perspective! There was also a remix of Greek and Latin influences in literature by masters such as Shakespeare…the list of greatness goes on and on. The Renaissance revitalized the study of human nature making it the center of intellectual interest. The world desperately needed a mini Golden Age just then to give some light back to the human spirit after the dark ages of ignorance, intolerance, and the plague.

Above, Beatrice explains to Dante that the Universe is a "Hierarchy of Being," with creatures devoid of reason in the early 'sea of being,'and heaven has 9 spheres ruled by the figure of Love. Painted by Giovanni di Paolo

Similarity of the Ancients

Another example is the intermingling of Old World cultures, which occurred throughout the Indus River Valley, Mesopotamia and Ancient Egypt. These were humanity's three earliest civilizations that share ancient roots. Out of these cultures came the first ancient writings—the Sanskrit of the Vedas, Sumerian cuneiform, and Egypt's hieroglyphics.

The Vedas are perhaps the most pervasive example of how science and consciousness bridge to explain the origin of man, spirituality and mythology. It is thought that the Vedas, particularly the Rig Veda, is the oldest book in the Indo-European language, which contains the initial construct of Sanskrit mantras that date back to 15,000 BCE -10,000 BCE. The Rig Veda traditions speak of a brotherhood of man, the importance of the cycles of the planet, the seasons, the sun and moon.

The Indus River Valley civilization began with Harappa culture, which grew into a vast society. Mohenjo-Daro and other cities along the Indus River were large populated centers of civilization. These vestiges of early city-states extended throughout today's Pakistan into northwest India and west into Afghanistan with a fully established culture by 1900 BCE. The Harappa language stems from an ancient dialect of unknown origin. Coincidentally, it is still spoken today in central and eastern India and Bangladesh.

What is known about the Indus River Valley culture is that it established vital trading routes to the northwest and into Central Asia, and west to Persia, Mesopotamia and the Arabian Sea. The diffusion of ideas and culture traveled with the goods to many countries with the trade routes.

The ancient Sumerians developed cuneiform writing about the same time as the Harappa culture was becoming established, and evolved a similar religion-based supplication of gods and goddesses responsible for the flooding of their respective river-oriented cultures, ultimately, developing an extraordinary trading cultures along their respective riverbanks. Egypt had similar practices revolving around the Nile River's annual flood of life-giving waters, enabling agriculture and becoming the central focus of their religious festivals.

The Indus River Valley city states like Harappa, and further afield in Sumer (between the Tigress and Euphrates rivers) and Egypt (Nile River Valley) had great similarities in developing writing systems and languages, which represented their large and flourishing agriculturally-based cultures with pantheons of fertility gods and goddesses, religious rituals, architecture and systems of governance through divine right and descent. Each of these cultures held belief systems that the goddesses and gods were intrinsically attached to cultural mores of their people and sustained life and prosperity.

The Hero Archetype

History has provided humanity with the archetype of the hero. It can be found in the archival past of Lemuria, a culture that was simple and operated by the Golden Rule. And throughout time, the great myth of the hero spread throughout cultures, religions and points of power and served to create control within society. The 'Aquarian Age' is seen as a post-Piscean interlude, during which an avatar, a bodhisattva, will reincarnate to assist humanity. History antedates 'the creation story' in many cultures with its father and mother symbols and the procreation of a son. The son is martyred only to resurrect and return to life as a savior to his people. In *The Hero With A Thousand Faces* (1949) Joseph Campbell explores archetypal constructs in myth, culture, psychology, and religion. "The usual hero adventure begins with someone from whom something has been taken, or who feels there is something lacking in the normal experience available or permitted to the members of society. The person then takes off on a series of adventures beyond the ordinary, either to recover what has been lost or to discover some life-giving elixir. It's usually a cycle, a coming, and a returning," according to Campbell. Without fail, most ancient cultures have evolved a similar story; the names are different, but the story remains the same.

Anthrogenesis in Humanity

Alice Bailey described humanity as being more spiritually inclined than ever and envisioned a universal new age belief; an amalgamation of philosophy, education, science, arts and music, culture, extending beneficence to the world at large. Now, the energies of our Dwapara Yuga period provides us time to contemplate many themes and separate the wheat from the chaff in our consciousness.

At this time, we extend compassion and goodwill to our fellow sisters and brothers who have lived through these great Yugas of time beside us. In *Anthrogenesis*, we will continue to explore the vast and marvelous expression of humanity. Now, as we live and envision the best of humanity, let's explore *Anthrogenesis* together!

Notes

1. Selbie, Joseph and Steinmetz, David, 2010. The Yugas, Crystal Clarity Publishers, Nevada City, CA.

2. https://www.ananda.org/clarity-magazine/2004/06/yugas-evolution-yogananda/

3. Yukteswar, Swami Sri, 1974. The Holy Science, International Publication Council of Self-Realization Fellowship, Los Angeles, CA.

4. Yogananda, Paramahansa, 1975. Autobiography of a Yogi, International Publication Council of Self-Realization Fellowship, Los Angeles, CA, pgs. 106-111.

5. https://vedanet.com/2012/06/13/keys-to-the-yugas-or-cycles-of-the-ages-subyugas-in-the-sri-yukteswar-yuga-cycle/

Anthrogenesis

Introduction

I am thrilled to now have the time to complete this book that I have been writing (in my mind) for a number of years! *Anthrogenesis* is more than a book; it is as an exploration of world origins as seen through the eyes of the contemporary scholar and mystic. We have been flooded with the richest, most exciting, and most far-ranging theories on our existence, far surpassing any other time in human history. From the distant past, the pages of the Vedas ring brighter and clearer than ever before, together with the most thought-provoking modern sciences of astrophysics, geology and spectrography, we have it all in one place, at one time. Not even the Renaissance came close to the wealth of knowledge that is just a Google search away today.

But how do we make sense of it all? How do we divine the Truth? Which theory of life do we choose—one or all? Or… is it about a unique fusion that puts it all together in an alchemical formula that transcends all the limitations of the conceptual mind and embodies the perfection of this magnificent Creation of Life on our planet?

In *Anthrogenesis*, I have incorporated is a *chronological perspective* of humanity by viewing the ancient past of this planet and moving forward in time with the themes of *origins, mythology* and *spirituality* and interesting theories that have arisen over the course of time in these fields. I have learned the importance of integrating both chronology and comparative methodology. Additionally, I will be using *references* that I consider to be essential for the reader's understanding.

I also integrate design elements in *Anthrogenesis* to bridge ideologies from the past with current scientific perspectives. Having respect for the method doesn't deter me from addressing what mainstream thought considers *on the edge* theories. I prefer to think that there are facts, history and knowledge that must be 'brought out into the light,' so to speak, in this book.

It's time for humanity to look at the reality of what *both* science and experience tell us about our planetary past. I think that as our society accepts new ideas and events, it will blossom and change. History, science, archaeology and religion may well be re-written! My hope is that when you read this compendium of knowledge—*Anthrogenesis*—you will have your own ideas and feel the motivation to develop your own theories and questions, as I have done.

Anthrogenesis Concept

At the outset, looking for a trusted anchor to construct the *Anthrogenesis* Concept required massive research materials from the fields of science, mythology, archeoastronomy, ancient culture, astrobiology, world religious writings and the nature of consciousness. These, I collected over the last decades of my life. In the course of my discovery regarding ancient humanity, it appears that evolution and other factors have influenced the course and development of human life, from the earliest stages of our infancy to the present. It is quite possible that the evolutionary history of our human tribe is intrinsic to what happens to life on our planet. It may be the same on other globes in our universe. Life has evolved with multiple influences within the framework of an inherently intelligent design. How does that happen?

Anthrogenesis, or humanity's ancient beginning, can be described as the spiritual science of life that rises out of matter. We understand our great history by overviewing scientific evidence and spiritual traditions, to explain the course of humanity's life in cycles of maturation and evolution.

Cellular Life

For example, in the late 19th century some scientists thought that *ontogeny* could uncover something about evolutionary history with continued step-by-step proof of that history. These researchers claimed that ontogeny recapitulates phylogeny. This phrase suggests that an organism's development will take it through each of the adult stages of its evolutionary history, or its phylogeny. At the time, some scientists thought that evolution worked by adding new stages on to the end of an organism's development. Thus its development would reiterate its evolutionary history—ontogeny, recapitulating phylogeny with the human at the top of the evolutionary scale.

This idea is a radical one because if strictly true, it would predict that in a chick's development, it would go through the following stages: a single-celled organism, a multi-celled invertebrate ancestor, a fish, a lizard-like reptile, an ancestral bird, and then finally, a baby chick. The form changes but the chick is still identified as a chick, it just has gone through stages of development, and evolved into a better, more adapted chick.

It was Haeckel who promoted the Lamarckian notion that evolution had a built-in direction towards *higher* forms, which was not so different from Darwinism. It is worth delving in a bit more into this thinking.

DNA, Epigenetics and the Path of Life

DNA has become an awesome tool in deciphering the human genome and other species of life in our world. When we add the DNA of genetics to *Anthrogenesis*, we observe that DNA mutates in all life forms and causation occurs by differing agents affecting growth, change, and change in other systems of the organism.

We see that adding, subtracting, slowing down or speeding up stages in the stream of life affects change. In Epigenetics, defined as the study of changes in organisms caused by modification of gene expression, rather than alteration of the genetic code itself, a biological perspective was the foundational source of study.

In the early 1930s Ernest E. Just (1883-1941) originally suggested the basic components of Epigenesis and refined it into an accepted

Discomedusae by Earnst H. Haeckel (1834-1919)

scientific theory. Later, the theory was expanded by zoological psychologist, Gilbert Gottlieb (1929-2006) who proposed 'Probabilistic Epigenesis,' which purports "that the emergent products of development are epigenetic, not just genetic, when considering the evolutionary process," and perhaps old-fashioned Neo-Darwinism has become limited by only considering chance in "genetic mutation, drift and recombination. Natural selection can result from a wide range of epigenetic processes contributing to individual ontogeny" such that change encompasses all of the possible developing factors in an organism and how they not only influence the organism, and each other, but also how the organism influences its own development. For example, developmental psychologist and analyst, Erik Erikson (1902-1994) used the term 'Epigenetics' to describe how human personality progresses in predetermined stages, as influenced by the contiguous environment and within the sociological components of culture.

Moving ahead with *Anthrogenesis*, we see that, as in 'Epigenetics,' there are distinct changes in the organism outside the realm of DNA, caused by nature, the environment, culture, social factors, ethnology and biology or disease, and perhaps even toxicology.

Discovery of our Ancestor, Denisova

In 2010, we discovered a new ancestor, *Denisova*, from a fossil found in Siberia. DNA revealed that our predecessor had a reversal of ancestral traits-*Denisovans* were more ape-like than *Neanderthals*. Initial genetic studies indicated that besides her 'sister' *Neanderthal, Denisova* was more prevalent in Melanesians than any other group, save for the Papua New Guineans and Aboriginal Australians. Melanesians were never thought to have been in Siberia so the *Denisovan* journey is still somewhat of a mystery. The *Denisovan* DNA has more recently been identified in Eurasians and Tibetans with ongoing research continuing with the associated DNA groups. It is possible that the *Denisovans* are relatives from our antediluvian past? Perhaps migratory patterns connected these ancestors to Oceania and South East Asia from the destruction of Atlantis that we distinguish in mythic lore found in all cultures.

I have more than a few ideas that will be presented in this book.

While most of our history is unobserved, DNA assists us in postulating a theory based upon a well thought-out methodology. All the factors in our world have caused it to unfold in the manner in which it has manifested. Our Universe is based upon a system with a plan, by that I mean that an intelligent design with a response occurring after something happens. Look at how long it would take if even now, we could have an exact answer to what causes dark energy, knowing that it comprises a great deal of space. NASA states, "Roughly 68% of the Universe is dark energy. Dark matter makes up about 27%. The rest, everything on Earth, everything ever observed with all of our instruments, is called 'normal matter'—adding up to less than 5% of the Universe."

Anthrogenesis explains important variables that orthodox science alone cannot explain.

Outside of our Earth realm, little 'truth' is known, save for what science has discovered. For example, what would science do if it discovered that our ancestors knew more than we do today? Would the 'truth' that lies hidden in dark warehouses and laboratories be made public?

The Causes of Life

Right now, we know that DNA designs human (and all organic life-forms, for that matter), along with aspects of epigenetics, as we have discussed. In psychology, we introduce the 'nature vs. nurture' debate, coined in 1869 by English scientist, Francis Galton (1822-1911). Briefly, the debate argues DNA and heredity over "tabula rasa"- the blank mind. German philosopher Immanuel Kant (1724-1804) proposed that a structure must exist in the mind in order to give meaning to experience.

Environment and biology both influence how human life is generated and evolves. I'm proposing that 'science' and 'experience' both affect and control humanity, along with the spiritual principles governed by the Universe. This concept is called *Anthrogenesis*.

The human being has come from a diversity of beginnings. Locked into Mythology, Science, Anthropology, Archeoastronomy, Transcendental Psychology, the Collective Unconscious, Evolution, and Physics, known History, Religion, Science and Philosophy. The true history of the human being reveals itself in depth and clarity, if we but take a holistic view.

In this book, I draw upon science, mythology, spirituality and philosophy to explain how humanity started, and I look at the stories told to explain and define the human timeline. To these I have added events currently unknown in the conventional story of human history.

To establish the paradigm of *Anthrogenesis*, we must examine the diverse components of human existence—worldwide.

Sir Galahad Discovers the Grail. Artwork by Edwin Austin Abbey, c.1890

Looking for the Holy Grail

We must have respect and reverence for our ancestors who shared with us important details of their existence in every medium available to them. I believe that our forbearers had much more wisdom than we now realize. Recognizing this leads us to being able to search for the *central paradigm of existence*, which begins to emerge through the study of sacred geometry, art and philosophy. Something numinous and essential to life fuels the Universe, evolution and expansion of consciousness.

We perceive this mystery in the nature of the Universe. We see this through ancient structures like Stonehenge, which have served to map our stars, connect with the gods, house our temples and spawn complex social systems. We discern the exquisite balance and beauty in nature of archaeoastronomy, with the awesome power with which these sacred places impact our lives.

Anthrogenesis Concept Ideas

In developing the specific concept of *Anthrogenesis*, we include areas of humanity that may not have been included in evolution, human origins, mythology or spirituality. Let's look at some ways to explore *Anthrogenesis* in more detail.

We have the impression that the ancients and their forefathers had access to complicated systems in philosophy, art, literature, architecture, and higher consciousness, for starters.

What did the ancients use in sacred construction?

Sacred Geometry is found in many of humanity's ancient structures, megaliths, and icons described in the Bible, i.e., the size of the Ark of the Covenant. The Ark of the Covenant was reported to have been constructed using the Fibonacci sequence (a Fibonacci sequence uses 0 then 1, with the next number found by adding up the two numbers before, so 0, 1, 2, 3, 5, 13, and 21...) and calculating a Golden Ratio (Phi is equal to 1:1.618). The Bible states, "Have them make a chest of acacia wood two and a half cubits long, a cubit and a half wide, and a cubit and a half high (Exodus 25:10)." The ratio of 2.5 to 1.5 is 1.666, which is as near to Phi as you get!

A New View of Paris

Let's take a look at the Eiffel Tower. The Eiffel Tower reminds us intuitively of a pyramid with its four-sided geometric shape. Why do we see this, you may say? A large half-circle is seen on each side of the tower, above the foundation. There are, what appears to be hundreds of triangles with lines and rectangles. There are also parallelograms (the 4-sided flat shapes with straight sides and the opposite sides are parallel) throughout the trellis and intricate metal design, with perfect rectangles in the railings.

It is an awesome sight and now we understand that Sacred Geometry was used in the design.

We feel a visual sense of enjoyment and peace looking at these works of arts, which cause us to feel their magnificence. We understand that these remarkable creations throughout our world, in art, culture, and philosophy, have a multifaceted yet untold sense of purpose.

How can we understand these mysteries that we dream about on the spiritual path? Here are a few questions to think about:

- *Is there more to our world than the eye can see?*
- *Is intuition better than logic?*
- *Is there a definition for the Soul?*
- *How long have we been here?*
- *What do dreams mean?*
- *What is the archaic wisdom of the feminine or Great Mother?*
- *Is mythology a way to see our past?*
- *Does a connection exist between the world religions?*
- *Is it possible to uncover new information about our origins?*
- *What spiritual practices did the ancients use?*
- *When will humanity begin the quest for enlightenment?*
- *What are some concepts that our ancestors contributed?*

Find ideas in our ancient philosophy that impact *Anthrogenesis*. The Triad is the eternal symbol of God, as understood by the ancients. The Triad is the basis for humanity's first religion so long ago. Rudolf Steiner stated that the higher triangle (and the triangle and the square) were made into symbols, especially in the Pythagorean School. Pythagoras taught the sacredness of the triad and the triangle, its symbol resulted from the creation of the monad and the dyad--the monad is the symbol of the Divine Father and the dyad of the Great Mother. The Monad moving into the dyad was able to become the parent of posterity, for the dyad was the womb of 'Mere' (Mother or the Gnostic-Sophia), inside of which the world was nurtured, and within which the world still lives 'in uteri'. God gave birth to His worlds out of Himself, and who, in His creative aspect, is always symbolized by the triangle.

Look at mainstream methods and theories to compare themes in *Anthrogenesis*:

Science, Anthropology, and Archeoastronomy can be used in conjunction with Precession to get more specific and diverse results in new studies. For example, the DNA double helix is thought to hold the keys to understanding the ancient sources and shared genes of life on Earth, possibly in life outside our planet. The possibility exists that the Ancient Mysteries, the World Scriptures, and the papyri of the 'Lost Scrolls' connected with the Giza Plateau, were used as the blueprint for construction of all antediluvian sacred structures. Were these relics left so that humanity could discover them in another time? Has that time now arrived?

Prana and Multi-Verses

Hinduism has dealt with etheric energy or prana of the cosmos, which is thought to consist of an elaborate web of light and energy. Perhaps the smallest indication is the *Nano* particle and the largest known element is a *Multi-Verse*, which may extend into *dark matter*, thought to be endless. We know that dark matter attracts and dark energy repels.

DM=27% or 21%
DE= 68% or 74%
Normal Matter= 4% or 5%

Each particle of prana is connected to another particle from the minute to the massive and everything in between. The chakras or energy centers of the human body are a connection to the etheric network for each human with the seven primary centers connecting to the larger network of the etheric network, comprised of light. The ethers of prana may hold a planet in an orbit and balance the electro-magnetic waves around the North and South Poles of Earth.

Binary Stars and Brahma

Researchers such as Walter Cruttenden and John Dering theorize that there are one or more stars, perhaps a white or red dwarf star, that provide the balance to Earth's cycles of rotation around the Sun, configure the precession of equinox and most probably affect the Earth's own axis rotation. The Earth's orbit around the Sun is the second celestial motion and the third celestial motion is the 'Precession of the Equinox,' based upon the timeline of Brahma, using the astronomical characters in conjunction with The Four Yugas; each Yuga calculated to 24,000 ± years, to allow for the chaos of the Universe which rectify the cycles into mathematical periods and a solid understanding for us.

Is Linear Time Real?

As we explore cosmology through the lens of the Anthrogenesis Concept, perhaps the etheric network is what we are call 'galactic glue,' the thing that holds the cosmos together. Maybe multiple dimensions called *Multi-Verses*, which exist in our Universe, play an important role in understanding advanced consciousness.

Linear Time and Precession

Time is one of the seven fundamental physical quantities in both the 'International System of Units' and 'International System of Quantities' so it is a circular definition, which is neutral. So, it may well be that linear time doesn't really exist. With that idea in mind, understanding how our cosmic-etheric system operates, may lead to understanding dimensional actions like time travel. Since the Industrial Revolution and even before during the Renaissance, humanity began to make use of the mind by logical thinking, advancing spiritual consciousness and for some, possible use of the 'Third Eye.' As humanity contemplates spiritual evolution and strives to move out of the Dark Ages, we will be able to use our minds to better investigate Precession, time and perhaps how the cosmic-ethers and prana impact our Universe.

Spiral as Sacred Geometry

Does our Solar System have one star or two? Is Sirius this configuration because of its spiritual connection to Earth? What energy balances the Universe? Does Precession play into the whole universal design? It could be that Dark Matter, currently invisible to us, plays an important part in the mechanism of our Universe. I think using the metaphor of the bell-shaped curve is a place to begin. I see this curve repeated in the mono-helix and intermeshed in the 'Double Helix' of our DNA. Ancient statuary seen in Mesoamerica, Egypt, Sumerian, Asia and elsewhere illustrate this helix. Perhaps this image is universal.

DNA Double Helix Molecule
Courtesy of the National Human Genome Research Institute

Anthrogenesis

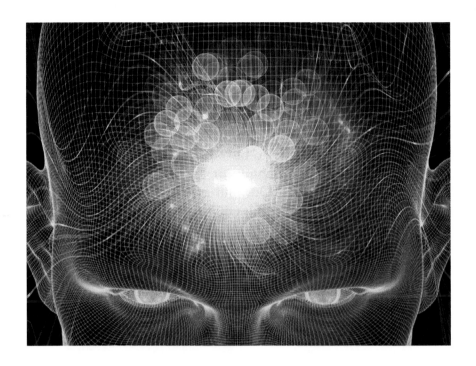

Chapter One

Our Universe Begins

Our Universe with Orthodox Underpinnings

After having reviewed the established scientific data available, the best estimate we have of the onset of our Universe is calculated at 13.798±0.037 billion years (Ga) in the Lambda-CDM concordance model. The Lambda-CDM model is the term used to describe the current and standard model of Big Bang cosmology because it is the easiest model that renders a good explanation of the properties of the cosmos, denoted by Lambda (Greek Λ), which is associated with dark energy, and cold dark matter (abbreviated CDM).[1]

Einstein's Theory of Relativity

Albert Einstein's Theory of Relativity, pertinent to our whole universe, describes the history of its expansion rate as related to how energy density in the universe varies over time. So, matter decreases as it spreads over increasing volume and, with radiation, the stretching of the electromagnetic waves causes the wavelengths to be longer and thus hold less energy. Both energy quantity and photon (or light) energy decrease as our Universe continues to expand. Our Universe initially was infinitely much smaller than a grain of sand, and it expanded from this extremely small volume with high mass and temperature.[2]

Courtesy of Carlos ZK

The Big Bang Theory

The Big Bang Theory is the most commonly accepted scientific theory of the origin of the Universe due to extraordinary evidence with logical assumptions. This theory changed the way we viewed our Universe by providing answers to some of its many mysteries. The Big Bang began with an expansion of space and this process continues today to stretch and expand. Note that we describe this process as *expansion*, not *explosion* because space itself commenced with the Big Bang, carrying matter along with it. Before the Big Bang theory, scientists had little information on the creation of the Universe, accepting religious explanations for its creation.[3]

In 1947 Sir Fred Hoyle landed upon the Steady State Theory, which expanded upon the Big Bang theory. The Steady State theory proposes that our Universe has always looked the same and always will. In 1951, the Catholic Church stated that the Big Bang theory was in accordance with the Bible, due to the results and quantity of pertinent scientific evidence.[4]

Planck and the Big Bang

In May 2009, the ESA (European Space Agency) launched "Planck" (named for German physicist Max Planck (1858–1947) who developed the formula for black-body radiation), an inter-galactic space mission with the Herschel infrared observatory. The objective of the mission was to measure Cosmic Microwave Background (CMB) which is the ancient radiation, originating from the Big Bang. The results from Planck indicated a more in-depth analysis of our cosmos such as the magnetic composition of the Milky Way, galaxy cluster formations, updated birthdates of stars and an ongoing mystery about gravity waves.[5]

Expansion of the Big Bang

The expansion of the Big Bang was demonstrated by the discovery that galaxies are rapidly moving away from us, suggesting that all the galaxies used to be incredibly close. Georges Lemaître, (1894-1966) considered the founder of the Big Bang Theory, suggested that, based on the current rate of expansion, the Universe had been densely packed into a small space and the entire Universe used to be one single particle. In a single explosion, this particle spewed chunks of rock, lava and elements- life-producing components- thus creating the Universe. The heated explosion explained the reason for the great quantity of helium in the galaxy.[6]

Hubble Observes an Expanding Universe

At Mount Wilson Observatory in 1929, the Big Bang expansion was illustrated by Edwin Hubble's discovery which proposed that the Universe is continuously expanding. Hubble used Mount Wilson's Observatory's 'Hooker' (named after the funder, John D. Hooker) telescope to make his observations by measuring the movement of the light coming from the galaxies. From this data he was able to calculate a galaxy's movement by illustrating that some galaxies were moving towards us but most were moving away from our galaxy. In so doing, Hubble theorized that the age of the Universe could be computed by measuring the rate of the expansion of the Universe.[7]

Blackbody Spectrum

Another piece of evidence supporting the Big Bang Theory is the radiation within the Universe. Scientists theorized that they could calculate the original strength of the radiation that was produced from the Big Bang. Then they could calculate how much the radiation would have weakened over time. The specific type of radiation that would have been produced by the Big Bang is called the Blackbody Spectrum. In the 1970s scientists confirmed that they had discovered a radiation with the Blackbody Spectrum; this was believed to have been from the Big Bang.[8]

The Big Bang and Matter

Stephen Hawking theorizes that "the Big Bang occurred less than 20 billion years ago, and based his theories and principles upon microwave conduction experiments that describe how matter expands. Professor Hawking describes the phenomena as a "contradictory dynamic" in illustrating the effect of the Big Bang on the 'static' Universe. "Why should stars suddenly turn on?" And, then he surprisingly states, "Any such lighting up time would have to be imposed by an intervention from outside the Universe."

"Later, it was realized that the Universe is not static but expanding. Galaxies are moving steadily apart from each other. In the Big Bang, all the matter in the Universe would have been piled on top of itself and the weight of this density would have been infinite. Professor Hawking states that it would have been what is called a "singularity." In a singularity, all the laws of physics would have broken down."[9]

The current study of Multi-verses along with thorough theoretical and applied research studies on dark matter and dark energy are still required to expand our knowledge of the cosmos. Most of our Universe contains about 5% of matter; the rest is about 27% dark matter and 68% dark energy. Dark matter has some shared properties, as does all ordinary matter; however, we have no ability to view dark matter. Based upon educated equations and observations, we can surmise about the properties of dark matter, which is understood to work as a negative pressure; electrons move fast and interact with a lot of atoms, creating a shower of positrons -anti-electrons- which speed up the expansion of the Universe.

One way that we have consistently measured distance in space is to make an educated guess in astrophysics, utilizing the principle of Occam's Razor, the speed of light and how this might correlate with the various galaxies, nebulae, and other cosmic phenomena. Over past decades, we have become skilled at compiling and discriminating the massive amounts of information collected from the Hubble Telescope (nasa.gov), the International Space Station (nasa.gov) and ongoing space missions with *JPL-NASA, that previously were unavailable, especially during the lifetime of Albert Einstein.[10, 11, 12]

JPL-NASA

Intelligent Life in Our Universe

While no specific scientific data exists to date, it has been speculated by scientists like Carl Sagan (1939-1996) that there is a strong possibility of other intelligent life in our Universe. His logic can be likened to the Occam's Razor, which states, "All other things being equal, the simplest solution is often the best." He theorized that the likelihood of intelligent life on other planets, in our vast galaxy, could not be denied. He pioneered exobiology and promoted the 'Search for Extra-Terrestrial Intelligence' (SETI).[13, 14]

Drake Equation

Frank Drake is credited with formulating the 'Drake Equation' which is the recognized method in the search for extraterrestrial intelligence and the speculative fields of Exobiology. Dubbed by various names and erroneously labeled the 'Sagan Equation,' Drake devised the equation in 1960, estimating the number of extraterrestrial civilizations that may exist in our galaxy. The purpose of the equation was to assist scientists in quantifying uncertainty in the factors that determine the number of such extraterrestrial civilizations. The mathematical formula provides a logical and predictable way of theorizing the existence of extraterrestrial life in our Universe, based upon several requirements necessary for the ability of life to form on a planet.

Dr. Drake has been Professor Emeritus of Astronomy and Astrophysics at the University of California, Santa Cruz, and most recently is searching for optical signals of intelligent origin, carried out with colleagues from Lick Observatory and the University of California at Berkeley, using the 40-inch Nickel telescope at Lick.[15]

Many Faces of Astrobiology

Astrobiology is the basic branch of biology that explores the existence of life on planets other than Earth and the bio-astronomy centered on searching for evidence of life; past or present and the evidence of bio-chemical life on our Solar System bodies. Also included is the search for planets in star systems, potential spectroscopic evidence of habitability, biological activity, intelligent signals of extraterrestrial origin, and the study of chemical life on comets, homogeneous asteroids and some meteorites. Exobiology focuses on study of the origin, evolution, distribution and the future of life in the Universe and exopaleontology is the search for evidence of past and current life on Mars and other bodies in our Solar System. This study also includes international coordination of effort in the establishment of collaborative, related scientific studies.[16, 17]

Archaeoastronomy

Anthrogenesis places importance on the study of Archaeoastronomy as a component of humanity's ancient legacy on Earth and evidence which encourage revelations in us and movement forward on our spiritual path. There has been much discussion over the last decade or so about the significance of archeoastronomy, especially in light of newly discovered megalithic sites and advances in understanding how the constellations factor into the science of architecture. It is essential for us to inquire about and examine our prehistoric civilizations in view of celestial and astronomical phenomena and the established seasons of the year.[18, 19]

"The singularity is what we think of and define when we discuss a black hole, which is an absence of matter."

-S. Hawking

Planet Magnetosphere

Pole Shifts and Geomagnetic Reversal

In 1958, Charles Hapgood published his book titled *Earth's Shifting Crust, A Key to Some Basic Problems of Earth Science*, with the collaboration of James H. Campbell and a foreword by Albert Einstein. He was perhaps the first researcher who conducted early 'pole shift' studies; needless to say, he was regarded as the pioneering theorist of his day. He suspected that 'true polar wander' was triggered by a 'mass distribution' throughout the planet accompanied by water movement, which may well prompt a pole shift. This evidence can be observed in volcanic ocean rock.[20]

Courtesy of JPL-NASA

A geomagnetic reversal is a change in the Earth's magnetic field such that the positions of magnetic north and magnetic south are interchanged. Walter Cruttenden has stated that, "Geophysicists have had mounting concerns due to wandering of the north magnetic pole by 700 miles in the last 200 years, with a 5% drop in the magnetosphere," which can be a signpost for reversal in the Earth's magnetic poles.[21]

We have acquired evidence that our Earth's magnetic field vacillates in its directionality, which in turn, governs polarity, such that we now understand Earth's magnetic field has undergone numerous reversals of polarity. The evidence shows that we have sustained 4 to 5 reversals per million years, throughout the last 10 million years. The actual length of a reversal of the field directions occurs in periods of thousands to tens of thousands of years. The last known complete geomagnetic reversal was the Laschamp Event, occurring 41,000 years ago, during the last glacial period. From the looks of our quoted references, it appears that some researchers definitely have their finger on the pulse of Earth's geomagnetism and it warrants further and extensive study.[22, 23]

Binary Systems and Precession

Life of a Star

I often ponder on the simple yet awesome nature of a star. As with our Sun, there is a progressive expansion requiring billions of years. The star depends upon hydrogen fusion, maintaining its incredible power through internal nuclear reactions and then at the end of its life, collapsing; the core energy ceases, having expended its fuel supply. Never fear, the slow deficit of resources causes the star to expand into a red giant before leaving a last vestige, a white dwarf star, surrounded by a ring of gases, dependent upon disintegrating compression for its livelihood. Fade out...to a black dwarf, although never observed, since a white dwarf takes time to decline—multiple billions of years.[24]

White Dwarfs and Precession

White dwarfs existing within a binary system may exist forever, speaking of which, Walter Cruttenden, of the Binary Research Institute, has a theory that our Sun has a companion star or stars, with the most likely candidate being a white or red dwarf. As Director of the Binary Research Institute (BRI), Cruttenden has been a pioneer in binary studies integrating them into the broader picture of the Ancient Wisdom, Precession, and the Yugas.[25]

Ancient Wisdom

"There were theosophists and Theosophical Schools for the last 2,000 years, from Plato down to medieval alchemists, who knew the value of the term. Theosophy transcends the Theosophical Society and was with humanity since its inception, not only in Western countries but also in the whole world. Since every great thinker and philosopher is a Theosophist, Buddha, Zoroaster, Lao-Tzu, Jesus Christ, Patañjali, Sankarâchârya, Nâgârjuna, and Rumi, among others, gave theosophical teachings, no matter how they labelled their teachings. According to the theosophical view, every world religion is based on, and comes from, one and the same ancient truth known in the past as the 'Wisdom-Religion.'

"This universal theosophy we are talking about 'is the body of truths which forms the basis of all religions, and which cannot be claimed as the exclusive possession of any.' However, the pure and original teachings of religions became, in time, more or less corrupted by human ambition and selfishness, and obscured by superstition and ignorance. Thus, universal theosophy became entangled in a mass of confusion, and over the course of the last hundred years, a special effort is ongoing to bring back the purity.

"One of the ongoing service activities of the Theosophical Society is to encourage investigation and discovery of one's spiritual truths that are often enshrined within the Ancient Wisdom itself. These eternal truths are found in the codes of differing religions, philosophies, and sciences, and the ability to offer Ancient Wisdom teachings to the public is presently in full swing."—Pablo D. Sender.[26]

Binary Star Systems

Speaking at the recent CPAK 2014 (Conference on Precession and Ancient Knowledge), Walter Cruttenden of the Binary Research Institute reported that a new dwarf planet was discovered by the research team of Trujillo and Sheppard on March 2014, called '2012 VP113', nicknamed 'Biden' from the 'VP' in the title. The scientists report that it is a pink dwarf, located in the Kuiper Belt and possibly contained in 'the inner Oort cloud' which corroborates that a conceivable similarity of this globe or a one-time presence of a much larger planet, often referred to as a super Earth, might be in orbit on the dark edges of our Solar System 'tugging' at the smaller dwarf planets.

Cruttenden asserts that in order to maintain the arc of gravitation and cycles of planetary rotation, it is necessary to confirm an additional and faraway stellar object, which keeps the elliptical motion of the earth in motion. The additional planet or planets are described in the Vedas, with the Yugas and 26,000-year cycles, keeping the equation in sync with four periods on a ratio of 4:3:2:1. Cruttenden theorizes that ancient cultures achieved levels of advancement during these Yugas far beyond those described in conventional timelines of history.

NASA corroborates this Great Year, also called a Platonic Year as coined by Plato in *Timaeus*. Precession was well known to Plato, who defined the "perfect year" as "the return of the celestial bodies (planets) and the diurnal rotation of the fixed stars (circle of the same) to their original positions."[27, 28, 29]

Sirius A and B by the Hubble Telescope. Courtesy of NASA and ESA, H. Bond- STSCI and M. Barstow- University of Leicester.

"The Great Center is the creative force that we call God. It is a triple system- Earth, Sirius and the Great Center."

- John Dering, October 19, 2014, CPAK Conference

Notes

1. http://astronomy.swin.edu.au/cosmos/c/concordance+model
2. http://www.space.com/17661-theory-general-relativity.html
3. Link 1.03: http://www.space.com/25126-big-bang-theory.html
4. http://www.aip.org/history/cosmology/ideas/bigbang.htm
5. http://www.esa.int/Our_Activities/Space_Science/Planck
6. http://www.amnh.org/education/resources/rfl/web/essaybooks/cosmic/p_lemaitre.html
7. https://cosmology.carnegiescience.edu/timeline/1929
8. https://www.ncbi.nlm.nih.gov/pmc/articles/PMC2669394/
9. http://www.hawking.org.uk
10. Jet Propulsion Lab, National Aeronautics and Space Administration
11. http://www.jpl.nasa.gov/
12. http://science.nasa.gov/astrophysics/focus-areas/what-is-dark-energy/
13. http://britannica.com/EBchecked/topic/424706/Occams-razor
14. http://www.seti.org
15. http://www.seti.org/drake
16. http://www.iau.org
17. http://jfarmer.asu.edu/pubs/pdfs/martianlife.pdf
18. http://www.binaryresearchinstitute.org/
19. http://www.terpconnect.umd.edu/~tlaloc/archastro
20. http://www.maar.us/crustal_displacement.html
21. Cruttenden, Walter, *Lost Star of Myth and Time*, 2006, St. Lynn's Press, POB 18680, Pittsburgh, PA, 15236, pg. 135-142.
22. http://www.geomag.bgs.ac.uk/education/reversals.html
23. Love, J.J., Mazaud, A., *Journal of Physics of the Earth and Planetary Interiors, A database for the Matuyama-Brunhes magnetic reversal,* Volume 103, Issues 3–4, 15 November 1997, Pages 207–245. doI – 10.1016/S0031-9201(97)00034-4.
24. http://map.gsfc.nasa.gov/universe/rel_stars.html
25. www.binaryresearchinstitute.org/
26. http://www.katinkahesselink.net/other/sender-theosophy.htm
27. http://www.Dwarf-Planets-Lead to Straight Roads, Walter-Cruttenden. CPAK-2014.pdf

28. http://www.nature.com/nature/journal/v507/n7493/full/
nature13156.html
29. http://www.ancient-wisdom.com/precession.htm#platonic year

Anthrogenesis

Chapter Two

Rocks Tell The Story

"How do we explain the ancient cosmology of the Hindus, Sumerians, and the Dogon? Hindu cosmology is based upon the Hindu Rig Veda, era 2000 BC, with the cyclical or oscillating Yuga Sutra system, ad infinitum. One cycle of existence is around 311 trillion years and the life of one universe around 8 billion years. This Universal cycle is preceded by an infinite number of universes and to be followed by another infinite number of universes. It includes an infinite number of universes at one given time. Being a scientist myself, the following dialogue may seem harsh but I think it must be said. Since the onset of the concomitant research and writing of this book, I have found differing explanations for antheogenesis; evolution, religious explanations, based upon a particular dogma's faith, intervention by the Gods and advanced life forms coming to Earth. The scientists have streamlined and simplified eons of artifacts and humanity into "The Three-Age System" of archaeology and physical anthropology, which has been the tool for dating mankind's periodization of human prehistory into three consecutive time periods, named for their respective tool-making technologies: the Stone Age, The Bronze Age and The Iron Age. In the apparent 'truth' of the evidence, arcane institutions continue to use nonchalance as avoidance. One striking contrast to this approach is the discovery and excavation of Gobekli Tepe, Turkey, where geologists report a civilization that was a minimum of "10, 000 to 12,000 years old." —Robert Schoch, Ph.D., Boston University[1, 2]

Ages of the Universe and Milky Way Galaxy

"Current calculations are (of) ~11 to ~13 Ga for the age of the Milky Way Galaxy (based on the stage of evolution of globular cluster stars) and the age of ~10 to ~15 Ga for the age of the Universe (based on the recession of distant galaxies)."[3]

Solar System and Earth Age

"Calculations result in an age for the Earth and meteorites, and hence the Solar System, of ~4.54 Ga with an uncertainty of less than 1 percent."[4]

Anthrogenesis progresses now with further chronology in the formation of the Milky Way and our Solar System. There continues to be a debate about the specific process in which Earth and the Solar System were formed. Some researchers believe that remaining materials are left over from the original nebula. Another hypothesis incorporates nebula research regarding the formation of the Orion constellation. In this premise, clouds of gas and dust called nebulae are scattered throughout the Universe. Within this nebula, new suns are forming as the dust cloud slowly condenses. The young star is surrounded by *proplyds*, which are pancake-shaped clouds of dust, which will potentially condense even further, to form planets or other globes around the star.[5, 6]

Some astrophysicists believe that fragmented meteorites from asteroids fell to Earth and were responsible in the formation of our Solar System. In this idea, there are more than 70 meteorites, of different types, whose ages have been measured, using radiometric dating (RD) techniques. The results show that the meteorites, and therefore the Solar System, formed between ~4.53 and ~4.58 Ga.[7]

Panspermia and Spores to Earth

Chandra Wickramasinghe, formerly a professor at Cardiff University in the UK, and more recently, with the Cardiff Centre for Astrobiology, developed the *Theory of Panspermia*. It contends that life on our Earth was seeded by contact with other life forms from our Solar System, the Milky Way and other galactic entities. As a result of the use of both radio and infrared astronomy, increasing numbers of complex organic molecules have been discovered in interstellar space. Over the past thirty years, evidence of this carbon-based bacterial life, found in cosmic dust, along with the discovery of extremophiles (life that is resistant to radiation breakdown) convey conclusions to us regarding the virus and its' ability to re-constitute in order to preserve life. This theoretical model purports that life may have originated elsewhere and those seeds have been scattered to begin life anew on planets such as Earth.[8, 9]

Life Forms of Panspermia

Moon Chronicles

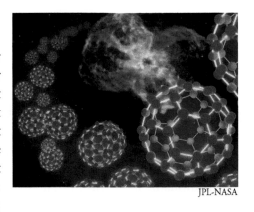

JPL-NASA

"The Moon may be older than prior estimates, even elder to our Earth or Sun. Dated at ~4.6 Ga, the Moon is abundant with rocks of different formations, dated anywhere from 4.4 to 5.3 Ga. While not subject to disturbance by plate tectonics, this phenomenon allows for rocks to 'lay upon the ancient dust where they were resting' possibly adding millions of years to these rocks.

"The dark spots we see on the Moon that create the image of the man in the moon are actually craters filled with basalt, which is a very dense material. 49 moons would fit inside the Earth, being about ¼ of Earth's diameter, having no global magnetic field. With only 59% of the Moon's surface visible from Earth, we always see the same side of the Moon; the other side is always hidden". So, from Earth, we always see the same side of the moon; the other side is always hidden. The moon is not a planet, but a satellite of the Earth. The surface area of the moon is 14,658,000 square miles or 9.4 billion acres. The moon rotates at 10 miles per hour compared to the earth's rotation of 1000 miles per hour. When a month has two full moons, the second full moon is called a blue moon. Another definition of a blue moon is the third full moon in any season (quarter of year) containing 4 total full moons."[10, 11]

The Life Atoms

"Life-Atoms are learning, evolving entities, each one a unit in one or other of the numberless hosts or hierarchies of them which exist. A life-atom is a vital individualized vehicle or body of a spiritual monad, which latter is the consciousness-center, the ultimate, noblest, highest, finest part of us. The heart of every life-atom is a spiritual monad. Life-atoms are young gods, embryo gods, and are, therefore, in a continuous process of self-expressing themselves on the planes of matter.

A life-atom may be briefly said to be the ensouling power in every primary or ultimate particle. An atom of physical matter is ensouled by such a life-atom, which is its pranic-astral-vital primary, the life-atom of it. The life-atom is not the physical atom, which latter is but its garment or vehicle and is compounded of physical matter only, which breaks up when its term of life has run, and which will return again in order to reimbody itself anew through the instrumentality and by the innate force or energy latent in its ensouling primary, the life-atom. In other words, the life-atom has a house of life, and this house of life is its body or physical atom; and the life-atom itself is the lowest expression of the monadic light within that atomic house."[12]

Radioactive Age Dating

The results from RD occur over the 'deep time' in geology of our Earth and past time has been organized into various units according to events occurring within each period. This is the method used by geologists to determine the ages of rocks because atoms in the rock spontaneously change into different atoms over time, through radioactive decay. By

using this method, scientists can work out how many years have passed since the rock formed, which is determined by using RD methods.[13]
See: Appendix I – Earth Age Estimation

Archaic Rocks

Our ancient rocks, as stated earlier, have been dated by several RD methods and the consistency of the results give scientists confidence that the ages are correct to within a few percent. Our Earth is ~4.5 Ga. and this age is based on research from the Canyon Diablo Meteorite, at Barringer Meteor Crater in Arizona. Single zircon crystals from Western Australia indicate young sedimentary rocks with ages of ~4.4 Ga, making these tiny crystals the oldest materials found on Earth to date. While Earth's oldest rocks show Earth at ~4.4 Ga, there is no data to explain the exact age of Earth's formation, however, ancient rocks exceeding ~3.5 Ga are found on all of Earth's continents. Earth's next oldest rocks are found in Acasta Gneiss, in northwestern Canada, dated at ~4.03 Ga. with the Isua-Supracrustal rocks in West Greenland dated at ~3.7 to ~3.8 Ga.

More rocks, virtually as old as the latter, are found in the Minnesota River Valley and northern Michigan, dated at ~3.5-~3.7 Ga, as well as in Swaziland, dated at ~3.4-~3.5 Ga, and in Western Australia, dated at ~3.4-~3.6 Ga.[14, 15]

Back to the Past

"The Earth is very old—4.5 billion years or more according to scientific estimates. Most of the evidence for an ancient Earth is contained in the rocks that form the Earth's crust. The rock layers themselves—like pages in a long and complicated history—record the events of the past and buried within them are the remains of life—the plants and animals that evolved from organic structures that existed 3 billion years ago. Also contained in rocks once molten are radioactive elements whose isotopes provide Earth with an atomic clock. Within these rocks, "parent" isotopes decay at a predictable rate to form "daughter" isotopes. By determining the relative amounts of parent and daughter isotopes, the age of these rocks can be calculated. Thus, the scientific evidence from rock layers, from fossils, and from the ages of rocks as measured by atomic clocks attests to a very old Earth."[16]

Geologic Time Scale

The Geologic Time Scale (GTS) is a system of chronological measurement that connects stratigraphy (a branch of geology dealing with the classification, nomenclature, correlation, and interpretation of stratified rocks) to time, and is used by geologists, paleontologists, and other Earth scientists to describe the timing

JPL-NASA

and relationships between events that have occurred throughout Earth's history. For example, the Cretaceous–Paleogene Extinction event or K-T, defines the boundary between the Cretaceous period and the Paleogene period. This event brought about the demise of non-avian dinosaurs and other life forms. The older time spans, which predate the reliable fossil record, or before the Proterozoic Eon, are defined by the absolute age. The GTS time spans represent the terminology, dates and standard color codes set forth by the International Commission on Stratigraphy (ICS), whose responsibility is to precisely define global units (systems, series, and stages) of the International Chrono-Stratigraphic Chart that in turn, are the basis for the units (periods, epochs, and age) of the International Geologic Time Scale; thus setting global standards for the fundamental scale for expressing the history of the Earth.

Blavatsky's chronology is thought to be quite different than this modern standard of time. GTS describes the timing and relationships between events that have occurred throughout Earth's history while the International Commission on Stratigraphy (ITS) defines the global standards for periods, epochs, and ages. It has been under renovation over the last decade.[17]

See: Appendix II – Radiometric Dating Methods
Appendix III – Geologic Time Scale
Appendix IV – Global Boundary Stratotype Section

The Precambrian by Helena P. Blavatsky

"With regard to the 320 million years assigned to sedimentation, it must be noted that an even a greater time elapsed during the preparation of this globe for the Fourth Round previous to stratification."

—Blavatsky, H.P., *The Secret Doctrine, Vol. II.*

"Blavatsky stated that esoteric teachings agree with some scientific statements, but clarification is required on the '300,000,000 years of vegetable life' preceding the planetary Lords or progenitors of human life. There were traces of life on Earth besides 'the Eozoon Canadense' during primordial times and vegetation belonged to this Fourth Round, but other animal life were remnants of the past Third Round."[18]

"The drama enacted on our planet is at the beginning of its Fourth Act-the Fourth Round...For this verse belongs to the general Cosmogony given in the archaic volumes, whereas Book II (*The Secret Doctrine,* Vol. II) will give a detailed account of the "Creation" or rather the formation, of the first human beings-the First Root Race, followed by the second humanity-the Second Root Race and then by the third- the Third Root Race, the 'Emirians' or, as they are called, "the first, second, and the third Root-Races." As the solid Earth began by being a ball of liquid fire, of fiery dust and its protoplasmic phantom, so did man." Blavatsky adds that Theosophy and science share some basic division methods, such as the fact that science divides Earth into five main periods starting at the beginning of life on Earth. But Theosophy only divides *human life* into the Seven Root Races and expounds on all life within the four kingdoms- mineral, plant, animal, and human."[19]

Grand Canyon National Park. Courtesy of Michael L. Hansford©

Earth's Ancient Rocks and Continents

Earth's Eons

The Precambrian Supereon from ~46 Ga to ~542 Mya measuring Earth's ancient time into three eons: the Hadean, Archean and Proterozoic with the Phanerozoic Eon, calculated ~542 Mya to the present. The Hadean, being the oldest interval of time, dated from ~4.6 to ~4 Ga, represents the time before the known fossil record of life on Earth. No known rock record dating from the Hadean Eon are known to exist, save the Acasta Gneiss rocks at ~4.03 to ~2.5 Ga in Canada's Northwest Territories. The Isua Greenstone Belt, Greenland is the oldest rock in the world at ~3.8 Ga. Different spans of time on the GTS are typically defined by changes in strata makeup because matching each which will reveal major geological or paleontological events, such as mass extinctions. An interesting feature of these ancient rocks is that they were not formed from 'primordial crust'-they consist of lava flows and sediments deposited in shallow water, an indication that Earth history began well before these rocks were deposited.[20, 21]

See:
Appendix V – Acasta Gneiss Rock Formation
Appendix VI – Isua Greenstone Belt
Appendix VII – Continent: Vaalbara

Earth's Continents during the Archean Eon

Primordial rocks began forming on Earth during the Archean Eon from ~4 Ga to ~2.5 Ga with continents emerging, beginning with Vaalbara, Ur, Kenorland and Arctica- between ~3.8 to ~2.1. The oldest rocks known on Earth were deposited with archaic life-forms found in the rocks. Some were sedimentary rocks deposited in the oceans, containing microscopic life-forms with bacterial characteristics. These organisms were among the only living things on Earth for over one billion years.[22]
See: Appendix VIII – Continent: Ur
Appendix IX – Continent: Kenorland
Appendix X – Continent: Arctica

Metal Spheres Found in South Africa

At the Wonderstone Silver Mine in the Western Transvaal, South Africa, excavations of deep rock had produced several strange metallic spheroids made of a nickel-steel alloy, which does not occur naturally, with 200 found to date. Various RD techniques date the spheres at · 2.8 to 3 Ga.[23]
See: Appendix XI – Stromatolites

Complex Life Evolves

During the Proterozoic Eon, oxygen accumulated with the first complex cellular life evolving on Earth. Between ~2.1–1.8 Ga continents Columbia-Nena emerged, later enclosing continent Laurentia from ~1.8 to ~1.5 Ga.[24]
See:
Appendix XII – The Proterozoic Eon
Appendix XIII – Continent: Columbia-Nena
Appendix XIV – Continent: Atlantica

Lord Rama Asks Hanuman to Deliver His Ring

Legend has it that while Lord Rama entrusted his ring to Hanuman, the monkey god was unable to deliver the ring to Sita, his wife, having been apprehended and imprisoned in route by Ravana, the demon king. Lord Rama subsequently looked to Hanuman's monkey army and a high-ranking officer, Nala, for assistance.[26, 27]

Sister Nivedita (1867-1911) and Ananda K. Coomaraswamy (1877-1947)

Lemuria, a Large Pacific Continent

Oceania is thought to have consisted of one large Pacific Continent, believed to be Lemuria, with numerous small islands surrounding it, but these islands are currently scattered across the ocean. The Malayan

Archipelago consists of detached segments; the western partition includes the Indo-Malayan Archipelago-Borneo, Java, and Sumatra. On the eastern flank, the Malay Archipelago (island groups within the Indian and Pacific Oceans, between Asia and Australia) encompasses Sulawesi, the Spice Islands, New Guinea, and Solomon's Islands, historically connected to Australia. These two land masses were allegedly two continents separated by a strait, in the past.[25]

Ancestors of All Living Things

At the closing of the Proterozoic Eon, life had spread throughout Earth, evolving to a higher degree and becoming the ancestors of all Earth's living things. Supercontinent Rodinia emerged from ~1.1 Ga to ~750 Mya to later include Laurentia. Then, at ~750 Mya, Rodinia split into three continents moving towards an 'early African pre-continent.' Continent Laurentia was later to encompass the continents of today's Northern Hemisphere.[28]

See:
Appendix XV – End of the Proterozoic Eon
Appendix XVI – Continent: Rodinia
Appendix XVII– ContinentPannotia-Vendian
Appendix XVIII – Continent: Laurasia

The Fourth Round Begins

"It was during the time of the Laurentian that the Fourth Round began, some ~320 Mya towards the end of the Precambrian era, a period marked by tremendous geological upheaval."[29]

See:
Appendix IXX – Continent: Laurentia
Appendix XX– The Paleozoic Era

Theosophy on Early Paleozoic

Blavatsky reports, "A few living entities, mostly or entirely marine, managed to exist in and survive the great disturbances during the dawning of the opening drama of the Fourth Round with their fossils found in the earliest periods of the *Paleozoic Era*, associated with the rather more advanced forms which gradually superseded the tremendous cataclysms and the general transformations of the Earth's crust that took place at the end of the Third Round- greater than any of the revolutions that have happened since, and which destroyed nearly all traces of the Third Round forms of life." [30]

See:
Appendix XXI – The Ordovician Period
Appendix XXII – The Carboniferous Period
Appendix XXIII – The Permian Period
Appendix XXIV – Continent: Pangaea

Permian Highlights

During the Permian Period, from ~299 to ~252 Mya, fossil evidence of sail backed reptiles have been confirmed by mainstream anthropology. Pangea appeared from ~300 to ~210 Mya, located in the Southern Hemisphere and was enclosed by the colossal Panthalassa super-ocean. [31]
See: Appendix XXV – Tethys Ocean

Earth's Five Mass Extinctions

In the last 500 million years, Earth has undergone five mass extinctions, including the event 66 million years ago that wiped out the dinosaurs, which according to mainstream science, resulted from a giant asteroid. Less consensus exists on the Permian extinction, called 'The Great Dying,' considered Earth's most severe mass extinction in history, annihilating 90 percent of marine and terrestrial species, including snails and small crustaceans to early lizards and amphibians. Possible reasons include volcanic eruptions, de-oxygenation in the oceans, and an asteroid collision. [32]
See: Appendix XXVI – Continent: Gondawana

The First Root Race

"The First Root Race (the Sons of Yoga) of humanity, was of astral-etheric entities and appeared at or around 130 to 150 million years ago in the Silurian or Devonian Period, or possibly in the Carboniferous period of the Paleozoic era, and ended in the Permian period."[33]

(Author's Note: If we make an educated date based upon Blavatsky's time frame, it seems that the First Root Race would have appeared in the late Jurassic or early Cretaceous period, which encompasses 130 to 150 Mya, in the current time scale.)

The Geological Time Scale (GTS) describes the timing and relationships between events that have occurred throughout Earth's history while the International Commission on Stratigraphy (ITS) defines the global standards for periods, epochs, and ages. Blavatsky's chronology is thought to be quite different than this modern standard of time.

David Pratt (davidpratt.info) details his "rough guide to the geological periods as used by H.P.B. (SD 2:710, 314fn, 395): the Primordial Age (comprising the Laurentian, Cambrian, & Silurian) began 320 million years ago; the Primary Age (comprising the Devonian, Carboniferous, & Permian) began about 148 million years ago; the Secondary Age (comprising the Triassic, Jurassic, & Cretaceous) began about 44 million years ago; the Tertiary (comprising the Eocene, Miocene, & Pliocene) began about 8 million years ago; and the Quaternary began about 870,000 years ago. These figures differ from the 'scientific' figures derived from radiometric dating – a method that fails to take account of the process of condensation and materialization which predominated during the arc of descent, up to the middle of the fourth round, when the ascending arc of etherealization began."

The Second Root Race

"The Second Root Race, the Lanoo, lived at the ancient North Pole, having originated in the late Carboniferous to early Permian, and ending in the late Triassic or early Jurassic of the Mesozoic (Secondary) era." We have calculated this time to be c. 25 to 30 million years ago. H.P.B. said that "the actual duration of the first two and one-half races is withheld from all but the higher Initiates."[34]

See: Appendix XXVII, The Mesozoic Era

Age of Reptiles

Appearance of the Third Root Race

"The Third Root Race appeared during the Age of Reptiles; the Triassic, the Jurassic and Cretaceous." Using Madame Blavatsky's time frame, this is approximately 44 million years ago. The GTS period for the Age of Reptiles currently covers 252 to 66 Mya. We are left with perhaps some mystery about the actual dates and times of humanity's history. Blavatsky was cautioned by her Masters not to reveal excessive knowledge, since the veil of mystery had already been in place for millennia.

Achelousaurus, Late Cretaceous Period, North America, dated at ~74.2 Mya, courtesy of Mariana Ruiz

"During the earlier sub-races of the Lemurian Race, Blavatsky stated that "humans shared many characteristics with the animal kingdom such as instinctual awareness. In the later Lemurian sub-races, the individuals are said to have been practiced and adept in Hatha yoga to enable their spirituality to be in tune with their Father, the Creator."[35]

Fifth Sub-Race of Lemuria

"The Lemurian middle sub-races produced a division of the sexes and developed a conscious mind among the karmically-ready beings, during the late Mesozoic, which H.P.B. said was c. 18 ½ million years ago." Current GTS periods place this event in the Miocene; from ~23 to ~5.3 Mya.[36]

See: Appendix XXIII, The Cretaceous Period

Origin of the Brotherhood of Adepts

Self-conscious individuals began to appear in the First, Second, and early Third Root Races. Prior to the descent of the Manas, these spiritually-conscious forerunners of the race assembled to form an association of like-minded humans. With advancement in spiritual and intellectual gifts, these individuals made a commitment to spiritual consciousness and Light, under the guidance of Sanat Kumara—the Silent Watcher (Lord of the World) of our globe.

This was the founding of the Brotherhood of Adepts, which has been in existence ever since. The Masters are the guides and helpers of the human race and the custodians of the Ageless Wisdom.[37]
See:
Appendix XXIX, The Cenozoic Era
Appendix XXX, The Paleogene Period

India Subduction: Himalayas

Between ~40 to ~50 Mya, the large landmasses of India and Eurasia collided, due to the subduction from plate tectonics, eventually forming the Himalayas.[38]
See: Appendix XXXI, the Pliocene Epoch

Vaivasvata Humanity in the Secondary Age

Blavatsky cited 'Vaivasvata' as the phase in humanity's linking with the 'Soul' and a distinct division of the sexes from androgyny. She said humanity had its onset within these first humans, where our particular interest lies, which began advanced development from 18-19 Mya.[39]

Atlanteans at Mid Root Race

Beginning ~5 Mya, the Atlanteans were at the midpoint of the Fourth Round and past the middle of the Fourth Race, at ~4.5 Mya.[40]

Humans Split from Apes

With research and DNA studies pending, it is thought that at ~6 Mya, hominins split off from the other apes, which included the gorillas, bonobos and chimpanzees.[41, 42, 43, 44]

The Dark Lords Conspire in Atlantis

"The Fourth Root Race, the Atlanteans, were past mid-race at 4.5 Mya, when Atlantis was cast into the descent-with matter. The average Atlantean was left with little or no spiritual direction unless one was attached to the 'Kings of Light' and the Adepts of the White Brotherhood. Ultimately, many of the citizens of Atlantis became self-driven, with the onslaught of destruction reaching its full encroachment."[45]

The bulk of Atlantis was submerged and destroyed in the Quaternary Period, and all that remained were fragments of land.

Isthmus of Panama Emerges

At ~3 Mya, "The reemergence of the land bridge between North America and South America at the Isthmus of Panama about 3 Mya allowed migration of species and mixing of gene pools in subspecies." Also, at the same time, a cooling trend causes year-round ice to form at the North Pole.[46]

Kansan Glaciations

At ~450,000 years ago, the 3rd most recent glacial period, the Kansan glaciations, began during which ice sheets reached their maximum extent in the Pleistocene, down through the terrains within the state of Kansas and Slovakia.[47]

Aryan Root Race Begins

In Atlantis, 100,000 years ago, an early sub race of the Aryan Root Race came into incarnation.[48]

Lake Toba Eruption

Between 69,000 to 77,000 years ago, Lake Toba, located inside the Toba caldera complex in Northern Sumatra, was the site of a massive super volcanic eruption, adjacent to the town of Amanita, at Samosir, on Lake Toba. The '*Toba Catastrophe Hypothesis*' holds that this event caused a global volcanic winter of 6–10 years and possibly a 1,000-year-long cooling episode.[49]

Last Glacial Maximum

At near 21,000 years ago, the 'Last Glacial Maximum' occurred, with the ice sheets moving down the Great Lakes, the mouth of the Rhine, and covering the British Isles.[50]

Atlantis Continues to Sink

The Pleistocene Period, from ~2.5 Mya to ~11,700 years ago included a number of geological occurrences to the present day. In Atlantis, the island of Ruta, in the Pacific Ocean, finally sank ~850,000 years ago along with the island of Daitya, in the Indian Ocean, sinking ~270,000 years ago.[51]

Worldwide Flooding

The Holocene, c. 9,700 BCE, witnessed the Younger Dryas, a warming trend resulting in worldwide flooding explained as solar activity by Robert Schoch, Ph.D., who attributes this change to a solar "plasma event", which is evidenced in samples from the Greenland ice cores. Graham Hancock in *The Magicians of the Gods* (2015), cites a comet as the cause.[52]

Holocene Period Sees Island Poseidon Submerge

The Holocene Period, from 11,700 years to the present, saw Poseidonis, the last island of Atlantis submerge in the Atlantic Ocean, at 11.5 thousand years ago.[53]

Notes

1. Robert Schoch, Ph.D., Boston University, © 2014
2. http://www.www.robertschoch.com
3. http://pubs.usgs.gov/gip/geotime/age.html
4. http://pubs.usgs.gov/gip/geotime/age.html
5. http://mysteriesofouruniverse.weebly.com/what-are-proplyds.html
6. https://www.spacetelescope.org/news/heic0917/
7. http://pubs.usgs.gov/gip/geotime/age.html
8. http://www.panspermia.org
9. http://www.arxiv.org/ftp/arxiv/papers/1101/1101.4295.pdf
10. http://www.moonconnection.com/moon_facts.phtml
11. http://moon.nasa.gov/moonfacts.cfm
12. http://www.theosophy-nw.org/theosnw/ctg/l-ln.htm
13. http://geomaps.wr.usgs.gov/parks/gtime/radiom.html
14. *Voice of the Rocks: A Scientist Looks at Catastrophes and Ancient Civilizations*, by Robert M. Schoch, Ph.D. and Robert Aquinas McNally, Harmony Books, NY, NY, a subsidiary of Crown Publishing Group and Random House, 1999, Pgs. 150-155.
15. *The Purposeful Universe: How Quantum Theory and Mayan Cosmology Explain the Origin and Evolution of Life* by Carl Johan Calleman, Ph.D., Inner Traditions & Bear & Co, 2009. P. 22
16. http://pubs.usgs.gov/gip/2008/58/
17. http://www.stratigraphy.org
18. http://www.theosociety.org/pasadena/sd/sd2-3-05.htm
19. Blavatsky, H.P., *Secret Doctrine*, II.
20. http://geology.com/usgs/geologic-time-scale/
21. http://www.ucmp.berkeley.edu/help/timeform.php
22. http://www.ucmp.berkeley.edu/precambrian/archean_hadean.php
23. Cremo, Michael A. and Thompson, Richard L., 1993, *Forbidden Archeology: The Hidden History of the Human Race*, Bhaktivedanta Book Publishing, and p. 813.
24. http://www.ucmp.berkeley.edu/precambrian/proterozoic.php
25. http://www.sacred-texts.com/atl/tll/tll02.htm
26. Jogi, Dr. Sunil, *Lord Hanuman*, 2014, Diamond Pocket Books Pvt., Ltd., Chapter 19, Spiritual and Blessed One.
27. http://www.rense.com/general30/nasa.htm

28. http://www.fossilmuseum.net/Paleobiology/Preambrian_ Paleobiology.htm

29. http://www.sacred-texts.com/the/sd/sd2-3-05.htm

30. Blavatsky, H.P., *The Secret Doctrine,* vol. II.

31. http://paleobiology.si.edu/geotime/main/permian2.html

32. http://news.mit.edu/2011/mass-extinction-1118

33. Blavatsky, H.P., *The Secret Doctrine,* vol. II.

34. Blavatsky, H.P., *The Secret Doctrine,* vol. II.

35. Blavatsky, H.P., *The Secret Doctrine,* vol. II.

36. Blavatsky, H.P., *The Secret Doctrine,* vol. II.

37. http://www.sacred-texts.com/eso/ihas/ihas07.htm.

38. http://pubs.usgs.gov/gip/dynamic/himalaya.html

39. Blavatsky, H.P., *The Secret Doctrine,* vol. II.

40. Blavatsky, H.P., *The Secret Doctrine, I.*

41. http://jhered.oxfordjournals.org/content/92/6/469

42. R. L. Stauffer, A. Walker, O. A. Ryder, M. Lyons-Weiler, and S. Blair Hedges

43. Human and Ape Molecular Clocks and Constraints on Paleontological Hypotheses

44. J. Hered (2001) 92 (6): 469-474 doI – 10.1093/jhered/92.6.469

45. Blavatsky, H.P., *The Secret Doctrine,* vol. II.

46. http://www.encyclopedia.com/topic/Pliocene_epoch.aspx

47. http://www.kgs.ku.edu/Publications/PIC/pic28.html

48. Blavatsky, H.P., *The Secret Doctrine,* vol. II.

49. http://www.oba.arch.ox.ac.uk/project.htm

50. http://onlinelibrary.wiley.com/doi/10.1029/1999JD900084/epdf

51. Blavatsky, H.P., *The Secret Doctrine,* vol. II.

52. Schoch, Robert, *Forgotten Civilization, The Role of Solar Outbursts in Our Past and Future,* 2012, Inner Traditions, VT., Pgs. 87-91

53. Blavatsky, H.P., *The Secret Doctrine, II.*

Anthrogenesis

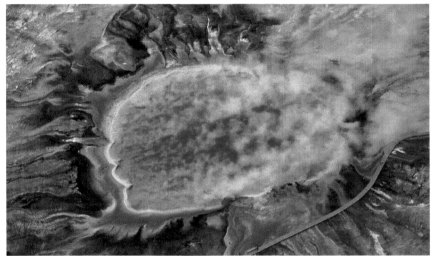

Grand Prismatic Spring, Yellowstone National Park, courtesy Jim Peaco, NPS

Chapter Three

Formation Towards Planetary Life

The Parents of Man on Earth

"Behold the beginning of sentient formless life. First the divine, the one from the MOTHER-SPIRIT; then the spiritual; the three from the one, the four from the one, and the five from which the three, the five, and the seven. These are the three-fold, the four-fold downward; the "Mind-Born" Sons of the First Lord; the Shining Seven. It is they who are thou, me, him, oh' Lanoo. They, who watch over thee, and thy MOTHER EARTH." Book of Dzyan, Stanza VII, Verse I [1]

Vedic stories recounting of the beginning of the Universe begin with Brahman, the impersonal, supreme and unrecognizable 'Principle of the Universe' with the 'Cosmic Egg' which is the Universe, and in the

35

Puranas, this objective 'Principle of the Universe' drops a seed, which becomes the 'Golden Egg', from which Brahma is produced.'[3]

The Rig Veda

The Rig Veda, taught in Indian oral tradition, was ultimately written during 15th to 12th Century BCE. The text describes the Brahmanda- the Cosmic Egg encompassing the totality of our Universe; the Solar System and galaxies, spreading out from a fixed locus, called a Bindu. The Universe infinitely cycles between expansion and contraction. Lemaître, as stated in Chapter One, also believed that one single particle exploded to become our Universe.[4]

Brahmanda and The Cosmic Egg

Shared Aspects of Theosophy and Vedic Traditions

Helena Petrovna Blavatsky accomplished extensive studies in India with her 'Mahatmas' (Yogis), various Eastern scholars and her Masters, affording her an extraordinary depth in spiritual mastery and philosophy. She relied profoundly on Vedic literature, Hindu beliefs, Kabbalah, Zoroastrianism and Tibetan Buddhism. Blavatsky

Pixabay

described the Universe as a manifestation of the Logos (the Life Principle and Evolutionary Energy radiating from Absolute Brahman, Parabrahm, Adi-Buddhi or Ein-Soph), commencing at the onset of the Great Cycle or Manvantara, becoming the living Universe. In Theosophy, a Manvantara is the term used to describe the Universe expanding its powers and structure by alternating periods of world manifestation and world rest; the Father of all Mankind, the 'Creator' who answers to Brahma. Lasting 311,040,000,000,000 human years, the Universe is comprised of millions of galaxies, solar systems and other Matter. This may include dark matter or other phenomena we haven't identified.[5]

Three Basic Principles

Blavatsky's canon employed the Vedic principles, such as the Septenary (seven) Elements because it precisely corroborates the occult teaching in line with the Three Basic Principles described in *The Secret Doctrine*:
"1 – The ONE Absolute, Infinite, Omnipresent, Eternal, Divine Principle, 2 – The cyclic appearance and disappearance of the Universe and everything in it and, 3 – The Law of Karma and Reincarnation and the fact that the ongoing evolutionary journey of each spiritual entity is inevitably governed by this Law."[6]

There are '12 Great Orders of Spiritual Beings' which are interconnected with the 12 Signs of the Zodiac: Aries, Taurus, Gemini, Cancer, Leo, Virgo, Libra, Scorpio, Sagittarius, Capricorn, Aquarius, and Pisces. "The hierarchy of Creative Powers is divided into seven (or 4 and 3) esoteric, within the 12 Great Orders, recorded in the twelve signs of the Zodiac; the seven of the manifesting scale being connected, moreover, with the Seven Planets. All this is subdivided into numberless groups of divine Spiritual, semi-Spiritual, and ethereal Beings."[7]

Spiritual Evolution in the Universe

There are cosmic-etheric planes of manifestation within our cosmos. Think multiple dimensions. Blavatsky describes the spiritual evolution of life within the Universe in cycles of 7, divided across the labyrinth of physical and spiritual dimensions in this cosmic plane. This all-embracing Path of the Soul, from primordial atoms of life to an Initiate on the Path of Discipleship and then perhaps an advanced Monad, speak of the evolution of life in our Universe. One observes that humanity advances through service and compassion, taking on an advanced esoteric state of being, within this complex of cosmic etheric existence. Humans occupy just a few of these lower levels of consciousness, along with the Elementals (3 kingdoms of small etheric lives) minerals, plants and animals.[8, 9, 10]

More discussion on this topic a bit later.

Our Solar System

After the Cosmic Egg is released, the Universe manifests into galaxies, and later, in a Solar System, the designation of Matter, having its origin in Spirit as prime, seeking the best expression of the Logos. The Sun represents the physical body of the Solar Logos; His ring-pass-not or influence is encompassed within Solar System. His seven Schemes are comparable to the cycles of our Solar Logos; progression is achieved by advancing through His Solar scheme of the Seven Chains.[11]

The Lunar Chain

The 3rd of these 7 Chains is known as the "Lunar Chain" or "Moon Chain." What is now our Moon, was at one time the former living Planet Earth, on which we ourselves were evolving in much lower kingdoms of nature. This was, of course, untold billions of years ago and is virtually incomprehensible to us.[12]

A Septenary Kosmos

The cosmic Septenary begins with the largest manifestation of life, which is named a Scheme, which represents a Globe and a Chain of planetary life, contained within 7 Globes, within a Chain and 7 Chains within a Scheme. The present Earth Chain, the fourth Earth Chain, began a billion years ago. In this Fourth 'Earth' Round, there are a total of 7 Rounds of life on the Earth that will incarnate over the millennia.[13]

The Absolute, Infinite Logos

The LOGOS is "The Absolute is the One Infinite Eternal Divine Principle, the Supreme and Ultimate Reality, which is beyond all definition, description, and comprehension. It is the One Life, the One Element, the One Immutable Essence and Energy, which is Existence Itself, and which is itself entirely unmoved and unaffected by anything, regardless of whether the Universe is in existence at the time or not. It is the true Divine Self or Higher Self of all because 'It' is really the one and only Reality."[14]

"Now, when the Universe comes into being, the One Absolute Infinite Divine Principle – which is usually called by the Hindu term of 'Parabrahm,' 'Parabrahman,' or Brahman in Theosophical teachings, radiates forth from Itself what is called the Logos. This is the Universal Energy, the all-ensouling Light and Life of the Universe. This Logos, the Universal Logos, is the Living Universe itself."[15]

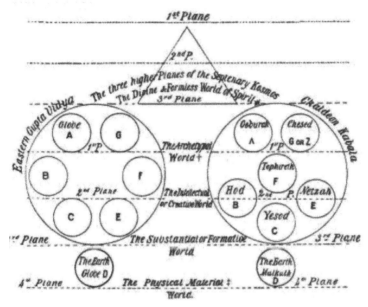

A Septenary Kosmos, courtesy of *The Secret Doctrine*, by H.P. Blavatsky, Vol. I., page 200.

The Seven Rays are derived from the Great Central Spiritual or Universal Sun.

"The Universal Logos or Brahman emanates seven distinct universal forces or energies and these are the Seven Rays. The Seven Rays actually comprise the essence of the Universal Logos and they are themselves the entirety of the seven "occult forces" of the manifested Universe. Perhaps the term "occult" should be clarified, seeing as it appears frequently in the writings of H.P.B., the writings of the Master Kuthumi and the Master Morya in "The Mahatma Letters," and many other books on Theosophy."[15]

Seven Chains in the Seven Rounds

The evolutionary Life-Wave passes through each of the Chains 7 times and these are referred to as the 7 Rounds. Each Round sees humanity reaching a significantly higher level of evolution, both inward and outward, but the inward or spiritual evolution is the most important. A Round begins on the 1st Globe of a Chain and causes that Globe to become active and alive.[16, 17]

Seven Globes in a Round

Each Planet is a sevenfold system, consisting of seven Globes with only one in physical incarnation. So, each physical globe has 6 non-physical globes that exist close together, a united bond and linking which happens as an objective of evolution. These 6 other globes, such as Saturn, Neptune, Mars, Mercury, Venus or Jupiter are part of the planetary Chain (none of these Globes are in physical incarnation) so if a Life-Wave of physical evolution and human expression is currently taking place on one of these, we will never be able to perceive it, find it, or know anything about it. The Master K.H. wrote that the physical Globe of Mars is currently in a state of total inactivity (not in physical incarnation) because the Life-Wave has passed on to one of the non-physical Globes and that Life-Wave is just beginning a new Round on the planet Mercury, after that planet being in "a state of obscuration."[18]

The Earth Chain

The Earth was to be populated by beings from its parent, the Moon. The Life Cycle of Earth is fueled by the principles and energies of the Lunar or Moon Chain, which eventually resulted in the formation of a new planetary chain, our Earth Chain, the successor of the Moon Chain. The result of the Moon Chain was death, with gradual disintegration and ultimate absorption into the cosmos.[19, 20]

Treading the Spiritual Path

The Words of Lord Buddha

The Lord Buddha elaborated on the importance of spiritual training, to respect our reason, our intuition, and to avoid the danger of spiritual practices simply because one thinks the teacher wishes it so. The following excerpt is a direct quote from the Master D.K. (also called Djwhal Khul) in 1922.

"We must not believe a thing merely because it is said; nor traditions because they have been handed down from antiquity; nor rumors, as such, nor writings by sages, because sages wrote them; nor fancies that we may suspect to have been inspired in us by a Deva (that is, in

From the book Paintings of Buddha Meditating.

presumed spiritual inspiration); nor from inferences drawn from some haphazard assumption we have made; nor because of what seems an analogical necessity; nor on the mere authority of our teachers or masters. But we are to believe when the writing, doctrine or saying is corroborated by our own reason and consciousness. For this, I have taught you not to believe merely because you have heard, but when you believed of your consciousness, then to act accordingly and abundantly." -Alice A. Bailey, *Initiation, Human and Solar*. Lucis Trust Publishers, 1922.

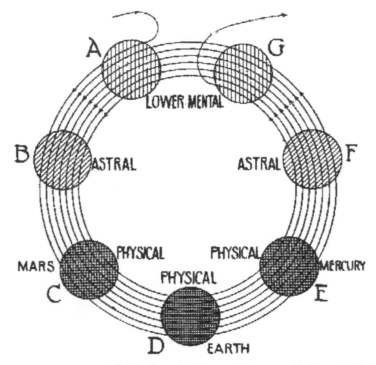

The Solar System, by AP Sinnett, 1930, courtesy of the Theosophical Society, UK

The Seven Rounds of the Earth Chain

"The Chain that we are currently in is called the 'Earth Chain.' It is the 4th of the 7 Chains. The preceding 3 Chains of our evolutionary scheme have already run their course and have ceased to be. 3 Chains have not yet come into existence, but they will do so in the future, successively, as each chain is the product of its predecessor. We are currently on the 4th Globe of the 4th Chain and in the 4th Round. This current period of our Earth civilization is in its fifth successive major epoch, termed the 5th Root Race. The 1st Root Race on our globe during this 4th Round was called the *Sons of Men*, as termed in the 'Ancient Wisdom,' the 2nd Root Race was called the *Hyperboreans*. The 3rd Root Race was the *Lemurian* Root Race, the 4th Root Race was the *Atlantean* Root Race, and the 5th Root Race, our current humanity, is named the Aryan/Indo-Caucasian Root Race. Two further Root Races will ensue prior to the end of this 4th Chain."[21]

Root Races and Sub-Races

"The seven major Root Races of civilization evolve and pass, during each of these Rounds. Each Root Race exhibits a new major Race- type- of humanity by evolving, dominating and therefore, coming to the forefront during that Root Race. Each Root Race consists of 7 sub-races. The 6th sub-race of the 5th Root Race is gradually beginning to develop through the Californians, and the Australians, throughout the next few hundred years. The onset of the 6th Root Race is a very long way off indeed. Most of us who are humans today were animals on the Moon Chain and those who are currently animals today will be humans on the next chain (the 5th Chain), as every Monad-every "Divine Spark" which has been sent forth from the Absolute-evolves progressively and gradually through the mineral kingdom, vegetable kingdom, animal kingdom, into the human kingdom and beyond. LIFE is always moving, developing and evolving, ever onward, ever upward, and ever heaven-bound. By the time the 5th Chain begins, we who are humans today will have entered into a far higher and more spiritual state of existence."[22]

The Seven Principles of Man

In the great evolutionary scheme, each Round of the Life-Wave through our Earth Chain – and to a lesser extent, each Root Race during each Round – is intended to develop one of the 7 Principles in the human constitution to perfection. The 7 principles are divided into The Lower Quaternary-the Lower, basic self and The Upper Triad-the Spiritual aspect.[23]

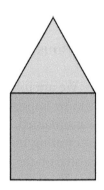

A simple way to visualize this concept is the triangle upon a square, as depicted here, Blavatsky's Lower Quaternary and Upper Triad.

The Lower Quaternary

Excerpted from H.P. Blavatsky's *The Key to Theosophy*, 1889:

1st- Rupa, the Physical body, is the vehicle of all the other "principles" during life.

2nd- Prana, Life or Vital principle, is the vehicle the physical body, the astral- emotional body and the seat of animal desire.

3rd- Linga Sharira, or Astral body, is the emotional vehicle (referred to as the double).

4th- Kam rupa, seat of animal desires and passions, is the center of our animal being.

The Upper Triad

5th- Manas, a dual principle in its functions; Mind, Intelligence- the higher human mind, whose light links the MONAD during the present lifetime-the future state and Karmic destiny of the person varies if Manas gravitates downward to Kama rupa, the seat of the animal passions or upward to Buddhi, the Spiritual Ego. In the latter, the higher consciousness of the human's Spiritual aspirations of mind-Manas merge with Buddhi-soul, forming the Ego- moving into Devachan.

6th- Buddhi- the Spiritual Soul, the vehicle of pure universal spirit.

7th- Atma or Spirit- One with the Absolute, as its radiation. The idea of the Absolute suggests the ONE, the ALL, comparable to Brahman and the source of Law and Life in the Universe and represents the ultimate reality.[24]

Previous Life on the Planets

We are told that in order for the Manu and the Beings who aided him to improve the physical type of humanity, a process of evolution was ordained. The most evolved physical being who assisted the Manu in creating mankind on Earth was a huge ape-like creature, who had existed on the three physical planets of Mars, Earth and Mercury during the Third Round. Upon the arrival of human life in Earth's Fourth Round, these ape-like creatures, the residuum left on Earth during obscurity, joined the in-coming human stream as soon as the race became fully physical. Their bodies may have been utilized for purposes of reincarnation for some of the entities. This was most easily achieved by the Manu, who used the archetype originally formed in the mind of the Planetary Logos, working within the astral plane.[25]

Astral Envelope Releases Pre-Adamite Prototypes

The planetary Manvantara of the Earth-Chain began about 2 billion years ago. 320 million years passed before Earth's sedimentation was achieved but not all the kingdoms, especially the Elementals or Devas were complete in their evolutionary stage. Animal life existed from the previous Round (Third Round) but they were contained within the ethereal casing, which grew denser over time, until the final phase was in place. Only vegetation was created during this Fourth Round, encased in its astral sheath, as well.

Nevertheless, in order to commence with the First Root Race, the awakening of the mineral, plant and animal kingdoms was necessary. The Primary Period encompassed the Devonian, Coal and Permian Ages and the first sub-race, the Pre-Adamite prototypes, were then released out of their astral envelope. The higher mammals in the Fourth Round followed the humans with some of these mammals assuming a portion of the first human life during the First Root Race.[26]

One Cosmic Day of the Creator Brahma

Vedic philosophy sees one cosmic day in the life of the Creator, Brahma, is equal to 80,640,000,000 years. The Cosmos are acting and guiding from 'within' with an 'outward' direction in the manifestation of all form and life; there is no beginning in the past, there is no end to the future and the flow of Time is eternal. Creation and Dissolution are simply two events in a long cyclic succession of cosmic events. Creation is a manifestation in concrete terms of the Absolute or Brahma. Dissolution is when the entire created universe merges in the Absolute. And that is when the period of non-manifestation begins. The periods of manifestation and of non-manifestation alternate from one to the other.[28]

Brahma's Life Cycle

The lifespan of Brahma, the Creator god is 100 Brahma years, 72,000 kalpas or 311.04 trillion human years (a year of Brahma). Both a 'Day' and 'Night of Brahma' each equal 4.32 billion human years (or 14 Brahma hours) totaling 8.64 billion years or 2 kalpas. Each kalpa is composed of 1,000 Maha Yugas equaling a Day of Brahma. Life only occurs during the Day of Brahma. When the 'Night of Brahma' begins, the Universe succumbs to total destruction and darkness. Life begins anew at the next 'Day of Brahma'.

Over and again, without beginning or end... the Vedic philosophy reveals the unending cycle of the Universal Mind that begins with a Day of Brahma; this is the duration of the Manu and all associated divinities, and it equals 852,000 divine years, or 306,720,000 calendar years.[29]

Manvantara

The Vedic idea of a Manvantara is in Sanskrit, called a sandhi, a combination of words Manu and Antara, Manu-antara or Manvantara. A Manvantara also refers to a Manuvantara or Age of a Manu, the Hindu progenitor of humanity. It is an astronomical period of time measurement meaning the duration of a Manu or his life span. Each Manvantara is created and ruled by a specific Manu, who in turn is created by Brahma, the Creator himself. Manu creates the world and all its species during that period of time and each Manvantara lasts the

Brahma Riding On His Goose, unknown artist, c. 1850. Victoria and Albert Museum, London, UK

lifetime of a Manu, upon whose death, Brahma creates another Manu to continue the cycle of Creation or Shristi. Every Manvantara contains the Four Yugas, time periods described at length in the Puranas of Sanskrit literature. A Manvantara equals 306,720,000 human years. The smallest Yuga cycle is called a *Maha Yuga* and equals 4,320,000 human years. Each Maha Yuga is subdivided into the following Four Great Ages, with lengths that follow a ratio of 4:3:2:1. We are currently in the 7th Manvantara according to Vedic reckoning. Each Manvantara is divided into 71 Maha-Yugas. We are in the 28th Maha-Yuga of this Manvantara.[30]

Cycle of Brahma's Creation

Vishnu takes a new Avatar and a new Indra and a Saptarishis are appointed. Eventually it takes 14 Manus and their respective Manvantaras to create a Kalpa or a 'Day of Brahma,' according to the Hindu Time Cycles and also the Vedic timeline. Thereafter, at the end of each Kalpa, there is a period – same as Kalpa – of dissolution or Pralaya, wherein the World, the Earth and all its' life forms, but not the entire Universe itself, is destroyed and lies in a state of rest, which is called the, 'Night of Brahma.' Then, Brahma starts his cycle of creation, destruction and rest all over again.[31]

The Four Yugas

Each Yuga cycle contains 4 Yugas. Satya Yuga or Golden Age equals 1,728,000 human years. This Yuga, called the Age of Truth, is endowed with many qualities that will be developed during the Yuga and include virtue reigning supreme; human stature is set at 21 cubits or approximately 31.5 feet with a lifespan equivalent to a 'lakh' or 100,000 years with death transpiring only when willed.

Treta Yuga or Silver Age totals 1,296,000 human years. This age includes humanity's virtue at three quarters strength and one quarter indulgence or materialistic drive, with the human height equal to 14 cubits or 21 feet tall and the life cycle amounting to 10,000 years.

Dvapara Yuga or the Bronze Age computes at 864,000 human years, human virtue is at one half virtue, and one half self-driven or the impetus towards power and control, 7 cubits or 10 ½ feet tall with a life expectancy of 1,000 years.

Kali Yuga or Iron Age lasts 432,000 human years. This is our current Yuga and its characteristics are only one-quarter righteousness and three quarters indulgence, with our human stature at 3.5 cubits or 5.25 feet in height with a life cycle of 100 to 120 years.[32, 33]

Kingdoms of Universal Life

In the beginning of the new Universe, there are seven groups of our Universal Life with the Seven Rays at the top of the evolutionary group (also referred to as Dhyani-Chohans). Between the manifestations of each kingdom (each accomplishing its seven inherent cycles), there is a brief rest period (obscurity), which ends when the next kingdom arrives. Each of the seven kingdoms which subsequently succeed, can be referred to as kingdoms, classes of Monads or life-waves.

In descending order of appearance, first are the three kingdoms of Elementals, with their seven phases. The predecessors of the Mineral kingdom next appear, complete their seven cycles and leave the globe. The Plant kingdom begins precisely as did its forbearers and completes the seven cycles, with obscurity in between the next class, the forerunners of the animals. Next come the animals, who share limited time with the human kingdom. Humanity then appears, successively completing the seven Root Races, within which are the seven Sub-Races. At this time, the human kingdom leaves the planet followed by a brief hiatus. After this obscurity, the Dhyani-Chohans, classes of Monads, and life-waves, come to the globe to recommence this process of life on the globe. Historically, Dhyani-Chohans were depicted as an Archangel or high spiritual Being charged with the supervision of the Cosmos. Such are the Kumaras and the Root-Manus of a Race having been referred to as 'Lords of Light' or the 'Sons of Wisdom' or one of the Seven intelligent, conscious, and living 'Principles of the Logos.'[34, 35]

H.P. Blavatsky notes that an exact date for the incarnation of any specific life-forms, on any one planet, whether it be etheric, physical or cosmic ether, will not be given to seekers on the Path. This is wisdom that comes with many incarnations and the development of 'chelaship' and being able to use the knowledge for the betterment of the Master's direction and human betterment as a whole. The details of ancient origins are not revealed, because this data pertains to the Mystery of Initiation, the secrets of the Ancient Mystery School. She adds that Mercury, Venus, Mars, Jupiter, Saturn, are as visible to us as our Earth may be to any beings residing there, due to the reality that we are all on the same cosmic plane. Other such planets remain obscured from us because of the high level of spiritual evolution they have attained, so we are not able to sense them unless humanity reaches a similar level of consciousness.[36]

Life in the Cosmos

Theosophy teaches that the Globes, Planets, Stars of our Solar System throughout the Universe exist for the purpose of habitation and evolution. H.P.B. adds, "Still the fact remains that most of the planets, as the stars beyond our system are inhabited, a fact which has been admitted by the men of science themselves." Mars supported life over billions of years, but is currently in obscuration or inactivity, known in Sanskrit as a pralaya, which means essentially a transitory paralysis and lifelessness until the evolutionary life-wave of Mars again passes onto the physical level, while the life-wave of its chain is active in other non-visible globes. Since Mars lost most of its magnetic field about 4 billion years ago, the Martian ionosphere is unable to stop the solar wind or radiation, and it interacts directly with exposed soil, making life, as we know it, impossible to exist. Also, liquid water, necessary for life and for metabolism, cannot exist on the surface of Mars with its present low atmospheric pressure and temperature, except at the lowest shaded elevations for short periods and liquid water never appears at the surface itself.[37, 38]

Follow the Water

Water on our world has been in a concomitant scheme with the continents and movement of land. Haeckel's 18th century summation of water tends to describe this phenomenon quite astutely…

"Thus, ever since liquid water existed on the earth, the boundaries of water and land have eternally changed, and we may assert that the outlines of continents and islands have never remained for an hour, nay, even for a minute, exactly the same. For the waves eternally and perpetually break on the edge of the coast, and whatever the land in these places loses in extent, it gains in other places by the accumulation of mud, which condenses into solid stone and again rises above the level of the sea as new land. Nothing can be more erroneous than the idea of a firm and unchangeable outline of our continents, such as is impressed upon us in early youth by defective lessons on geography, which are devoid of a geological basis."

Oxygen and hydrogen commingle to make water, which is believed to have come to Earth via the comets and asteroids, and both contain ice particles. The most popular trend is the vote for asteroids, due to chemical compatibility, which could have easily filled the vast bodies of water on Earth.

"Follow the Water," was the prior science theme of the Mars Exploration Program, JPL NASA which guided missions such as 2001 Mars Odyssey, Mars Exploration Rovers, Mars Reconnaissance Orbiter, and the Mars Phoenix Lander, with one of the Fundamental Questions for exploration of Mars being: "What are, and where are, the reservoirs of water and carbon dioxide on Mars?" Without water, life as we understand it, is impossible!

The discovery of water in Mars surface layers was made in September of 2013, from NASA's rover, 'Curiosity,' as part of its mission to explore Mars. Considered a significant step in the Mars' program, everyone breathed a sigh of relief.[39, 40]

The Night of the Universe

"The eternal parent, wrapped in her ever invisible robes, had slumbered once again for seven eternities."

– *Book of Dzyan*, Stanza I, Verse I.

"The "Parent Space" is the eternal, ever present cause of all – the incomprehensible DEITY, whose "invisible robes" are the mystic root of all matter, and of the Universe."

'Thus, the "Robes" stand for the noumenon (phenomena) of undifferentiated Cosmic Matter. It is not matter as we know it, but the spiritual essence of matter, and is co-eternal and even one with Space in its abstract sense. Root-nature is also the source of the subtle invisible properties in visible matter. It is the Soul, so to say, of the ONE infinite Spirit. The Hindus call it Mulaprakriti, and say that it is the primordial substance, which is the basis of the Upadhi or vehicle of every phenomenon, whether physical, mental or psychic. It is the source from which Akasa radiates."

"The Seven Eternities meant are the seven periods, or a period answering in its duration to the seven periods, of a Manvantara, and extending throughout a Maha-Kalpa or the Great Age -100 years of Brahma – making a total of 311,040,000,000,000 of years."[41]

Xt'actani, The Moon Goddess

The Moon Goddess, Xt'actani, a popular figure in the Maya mythology, is connected to Mars. As of yet humanity does not have a fully developed and synthesized brain, which comes with the evolution of consciousness, so we are not able to see many of the planets in this Solar System.

Origin of the Stanzas of Dzyan

The Stanzas of Dzyan is an ancient text of Tibetan origin. The Stanzas formed the basis for *The Secret Doctrine* (1888), one of the foundational works of the Theosophical movement. Blavatsky reported that the Book of Dzyan belonged to a group of esoteric Tibetan writings, known as the Books of Kiu-Te. Before beginning her public mission, Madame Blavatsky spent two years living with the Masters in the Ladakh area, and near Shigatse, Tibet. The Masters Morya of Kashmir and Kuthumi of India were not Tibetan themselves, but were associated with a Gelug Buddhist monastery, Tashilhunpo at Shigatse–the seat of the Panchen Lama of the "yellow hat" order of Tibetan Buddhism, which is the order of the Dalai Lama.[42]

Six Previous Attempts

Six attempts to establish life on Earth were undertaken by the Ancient Ones. Blavatsky espoused that the first types of life on Earth began billions of years ago and were maintained within an astral-ethereal status. The seventh finally resulted in the first Root Race of humankind, which was an astral-etheric race.[43]

Sons of Men Work with the Devas

The previous Rounds left Earth with certain life forms and the Third Round afforded the opportunity for life to finally evolve with success. The Fourth Round began some 320 million years ago towards the end of the Precambrian era, a period marked by tremendous geological upheavals. The beginnings of our first root race, the Sons of Men, was a race of astral entities, emerging in the mid Mesozoic Era, 150 million years ago.

They were created with the help of the Elemental kingdom, also called Devas. Thus this First Root race later evolved into the second root race or Hyperborean, the third, the Lemurian, the fourth, the Atlanteans and finally into our current fifth root race, the Aryan race. The root races also have "sub-root races," which can be differentiated by certain evolutionary attributes—physical, emotional, mental, personality and soul aspects that change over the evolutionary course of each root race. We are currently in the Fifth sub-race; the 'Austral-Americans.'[44]

"Theosophical literature teaches that upon the death of a human being, the physical body is discarded together with the linga-sharira (etheric double or matrix body). The consciousness is now lodged in the desire-body (kama-rupa), which is still attached to the mental, spiritual and atmic principles of the human being. The soul then enters into a temporary state of unconsciousness during which it undergoes a gestation period. After a period of sleep that varies in length according to the individual circumstance, the soul undergoes a second death whereinthe kama-rupa (desire body) is similarly discarded, the latter drawing towards it the gross portions of the human mind (manas). On the other hand, the Monad, that is, the Atma-Buddhi, assimilates to itself the "good, pure and holy" part of the mind. The Ego then, after discarding the body, etheric double, prana, desire body, and the gross elements of the mind, enters into devachan. The "Mahatma Letters" state that "no sensual, material or unholy recollection can follow the purified memory of the Ego to the region of Bliss."[45]

The Kalevala, Rune I, Birth of Wainamoine

In primeval times, a maiden,
Beauteous Daughter of the Ether,
Passed for ages her existence in the great expanse of Heaven,
Seven hundred years she wandered,
Seven hundred years she labored,
Ere her first-born was delivered.
Ere a beauteous duck descending,
Hastens toward the water-mother.
Lightly on the knee she settles,
Finds a nesting-place befitting,
Where to lay her eggs in safety,
Lays her eggs within, at pleasure,
Six, the golden eggs she lays them,
Then a Seventh, an egg of iron...[46]

Mother's First Attempt

The first attempts made by the Mother turned out to be water men, "terrible and bad" … Mother had not asked for Wisdom from the Great Ones but had created them from her breast. There were goat-men, dog-headed men and men with fish bodies, all of which had two and four heads. It was a disappointment for Mother. The Dhyani came and were not pleased. Later, the Lhasa from above and the Lhamayin ended the lives of these unfortunate beings. Egyptians remember the stories of these creature so that in their art and history, they can be found: the chimera and many animals with differing body parts, also, the Sphinx with the body of a lion, wings of a bird and the head of a woman; or the head of a lion, the body of a goat and a serpent's tail.[47, 48]

Sons of Yoga, the Self Born

The Lhasa, the Spirits of Life, were obligated to be born in the bodies of the first human root race, the Sons of Yoga as it then existed. Their creation came from the Lords, Fathers and Sons of Twilight. The text reads, "Make thy calculations, O' Lanoo, if thou wouldst learn the correct age of thy small wheel."[49]

Early Races of Humanity

The first lives were more astral in nature than physical, guided by spiritual instinct and cocooned within a dreamy-sleep state. They were born by osmosis from the parent being very massive in size. Physical man had developed from double-sexed to single-sexed—separated into male and female. In this way man has become a spiritual being of the kind which he is now. These first races did not eat as we do today—they took sustenance into the body by osmosis, much like breathing in air. Death was 'a melting into' the next race until the end of the second race when individuals fell asleep and faded out. The Lemurians made death a decree, since bodies were solid and they died when vital energy ended.[50, 51]

Pixabay

Forerunners of the Human Race Arrive

Self-conscious human-like individuals began to appear even in the First, Second, and early Third Root Races. In the middle of the Third Race, the Adepts from the Venus chain came, and then, the Lunar Pitris came later. Adepts and the higher Devas, the self-conscious forerunners of the human race, came under the influence of the 'silent watcher' of our globe, and gathered together to form a focus of spiritual and intellectual light. This was the origin of the Brotherhood of Adepts, which has been in existence ever since. The Adepts or Mahatmas are the guides and helpers of the human race, and the custodians of the Ageless Wisdom.[52]

Budding of Humanity

Our Second Root Race, the Hyperborean, was a continuation of the First Root Race- still partially in a causal body, growing dense and opaque with time. Towards the end of the Second Race, the Hyperborean body became more gelatinous, with filament developing within structure, slowly evolving the rudimentary beginnings of bones and organs, hair and skin, along with an ovoid form, which would later come to resemble the human form.

Anthrogenesis

In upcoming sub-races, a distinction transpired, between a Light and Dark dream-like state; the onset of waves of light, used to sense the Soul. The body had a single eye, which no longer exists today. The legend of the Cyclops with one eye is a recollection of these conditions. There was a Kama-body of wishes and the Soul had a place internally in Man, even though the 'spark of the Monad' had not descended yet into humanity.[53]

Hermaphrodites

In Lemurian times, our Third Race developed the division of the sexes. On one side, the human body became receptive only to fertilization by another human being; the other side developed the archaic-physical 'soul organs'-the nervous system, through which the sense impressions of the outside world were mirrored in the soul. An entry of the thinking spirit into the human body had then been prepared.

In the first section of the book, *Anthrogenesis*, we discussed the development of the chicken from fertilization to birth. This explanation of the race is analogous to Ernst Haeckel's description of common evolution stages of all species; plant, animal, human. First, the two eyes developed when the soul began to connect with the light impressions from the outside more intimately with its own life. With this, the capacity for the perception of the soul in the environment disappeared. Thus, over time the soul became the mirror of the external world. The outside world was replicated within the soul, as an image and also within the human body; the arrangement of atoms, fibers, tissues, vessels, organs, muscles, bones…the Fibonacci sequence that we observe throughout nature. In the etheric junctures, life flourished with early life shedding cells to share with other ancient human life or possibly to an animal species, remembering this was in a different cosmic-plane. Karma was a magnet to life then as it is today.

"Evolution is an eternal cycle of becoming, we are taught; and nature never leaves an atom unused," says Madame Blavatsky in *The Secret Doctrine*, Vol. II.[54, 55]

Workshop of Sostratos-Alexandria, Hermitage Museum, Russia

The Myth of Hermaphroditus

In Greek mythology, Hermaphroditus was the son of Hermes and Aphrodite, the gods of male and female sexuality. He fused with the nymph, Salmacis. This union resulted in his possessing both male and female attributes: female thighs, breasts, and style of hair, and male genitalia. He was accorded a new station and was counted among the Erodes or 'winged' love gods.

The term "hermaphrodite" derives from the name 'Hermaphroditos' and refers to one who bears the physical traits of both sexes. The mythological figure of Tiresias that figures in both the life of Odysseus and during the Odyssey, and could be called a sequential hermaphrodite having changed from a man to a woman and back again by the gods.[56]

The Lemurian Spiritual Path

Millions of years pass during Lemuria, but now there occurred an event pregnant with consequences, perhaps the most momentous in human history. Full of mystical import, this event brings into view beings who belonged to entirely different systems of evolution, and who nevertheless came to Earth during Lemurian times to be associated with our humanity.

It was decided then that humanity would be endowed with the Monad, or the 'divine soul' that would allow humanity to follow a spiritual path to Initiation. The Lemurian humanity existed primarily on the lower etheric levels and the first half of the root race was moving into the physical plane from the astral plane. Many cultures talk about the Ancient Ones; Fohats, Arhats and other Great Beings that had come to Earth to overshadow the creation of the Third Root Race.

The Lemurians, under their guidance, rapidly advanced in mental growth. The stirring of their minds mixed with feelings of love and reverence for those infinitely wiser and greater than themselves, resulted in imitation, and then, an advance in their own mental growth. There was the subsequent transformation of the mental sheath into a higher vehicle capable of carrying over the human characteristics from lifetime to lifetime. This advancement brought forth an outpouring of Divine Life, and the endowment of individual immortality.[57]

Notes

1. http://www.sacred-texts.com/the/sd/sd1-1-02.htm – page 33. The Cosmic Egg

2. http://www.theosociety.org/pasadena/fso/fso9.htm

3. http://www.sacred-texts.com/the/sd/sd1-2-07.htm

4. http://www.physicsoftheuniverse.com/cosmological.html

5. Blavatsky, H.P., *The Secret Doctrine, I.*

6. http://blavatskytheosophy.com/the-seven-rays/

7. http://www.sacred-texts.com/the/sd/sd1-1-11.htm

8. http://blavatskytheosophy.com/the-three-logoi/

9. http://www.baharna.com/karma/yuga.htm

10. http://www.katinkahesselink.net/blavatsky/articles/v13/ph_020.htm

11. http://www.lucistrust.org/books/the_beacon_magazine/reprinted_from_the_beacon/the_solar_angel

12. Blavatsky, H.P., *The Secret Doctrine, II.*

13. Bailey, Alice, A Treatise on Cosmic Fire, 1973, Theosophical Publishing Company, N.Y., p. 402-17.

14. http://blavatskytheosophy.com/understanding-the-logos/

15. http://blavatskytheosophy.com/the-seven-rays/

16. http://blavatskytheosophy.com/chains-globes-rounds-and-root-races/

17. http://www.sacred-texts.com/the/tot/chap09.htm

18. http://blavatskytheosophy.com/chains-globes-rounds-and-root-races/

19. Blavatsky, H.P., *The Secret Doctrine, II.*

20. Sinnett, A.P., *The Solar System*, 1930, Theosophical Publishing Society, UK.

21. Blavatsky, H.P., *The Secret Doctrine, II.*

22. http://blavatskytheosophy.com/chains-globes-rounds-and-root-races/

23. http://www.sacred-texts.com/the/sd/sd1-2-05.htm

24. http://www.theosociety.org/pasadena/key/key-6.htm

25. http://www.blavatskytheosophy.com/the-men-from-other-planets

26. http://www.theosociety.org/pasadena/sd/sd2-3-05.htm

27. http://www.theosociety.org/pasadena/sd/sd2-1-02.htm

28. http://hinduism.stackexchange.com/questions/229/what-is-the-life-span-of-lord-brahma-according-to-vedas

29. http://baharna.com/karma/yuga.htm

30. http://www. katinkahesselink.net/blavatsky/articles/v13/ph_020.htm

31. http://katinkahesselink.net/blavatsky/articles/v13/ph_020.htm

32. http://www.stephen-knapp.com/timings_of_the_four_yugas.htm

33. http://www.veda.harekrsna.cz/encyclopedia/time.htm

34. Blavatsky, H.P., *The Secret Doctrine, II.*

35. http://www.theosociety.org/pasadena/dialogue/dial32s.htm

36. http://www.sacred-texts.com/the/sd/sd1-1-08.htm

37. http://www.sacred-texts.com/the/sd/sd2-3-04.htm

38. http://mars.nasa.gov/files/resources/MAVEN_PressKit_Final.pdf

39. Ernst Haeckel's History of Creation, 2nd ed., 1876, Vol. I., pp. 360-62.

40. http://www.mars.jpl.nasa.gov/programmissions/science

41. http://www.sacred-texts.com/the/sd/sd1-1-02.htm pages: page 27.

42. http://blavatskytheosophy.com/the-secret-book-of-dzyan/

43. Blavatsky, H.P., *The Secret Doctrine, II.*

44. Bailey, Alice. *A Treatise on Cosmic Fire*, 1973. Lucis Trust Publishing, Albany, N.Y.

45. https://archive.org/stream/mahatmaletters032210mbp/mahatmaletters032210mbp_djvu.txt

46. http://www.sacred-texts.com/neu/kveng/kvrune01.htm

47. http://www.sacred-texts.com/the/sd/sd2-1-03.htm

48. http://www.theoi.com/Ther/Khimaira.html

49. http://www.sacred-texts.com/the/sd/sd1-1-10.htm

50. http://www.sacred-texts.com/the/sd/sd2-1-06.htm

51. Besant, Annie, *Extracts From the Vahan, Including Answers by Annie Besant… and Others*, Edited by Sarah Corbett, The Theosophical Publishing Society, London And Benares, 1904, pages 682-685.

52. Steiner, Rudolf, *Compiled Lectures*, 1969, Health Research Books, Pomeroy, WA.

53. Steiner, Rudolf, *Cosmic Memory*, Rudolf Steiner Publications, Inc., Great Barrington, MA, 1959.

54. http://www.evolution.berkeley.edu/evolibrary/article/history_15

55. http://icb.oxfordjournals.org/content/46/4/349.full
56. http://www.theoi.com/Ouranios/ErosHermaphroditos.html
57. Blavatsky, HP, *The Secret Doctrine: II.*

Anthrogenesis

Chapter Four

Humanity Flourishes

"There was a lapse in the upward gathering of our Earth Mother, and 'She' was unable to meet the requirements of etheric-physical needs of the Planetary Logos. Many millions of years elapsed."

Blavatsky, H.P., *The Secret Doctrine*, Vol. II.

The Lhasa Begin

Lhasa (Blavatsky uses 'Lhas') is an ancient Himalayan word referring to the Spiritual hierarchies of superhuman beings, including the Hyannis and Archangels. Lhasa, Tibet, is named after these Great Spirits.[1]

Lucis, the Light Bearer from Venus

The system of Venus has a very close connection with our Earth system. H.P.B. tells us in *The Secret Doctrine* that Venus and the Earth are referred to in Esoteric Science as "twin sisters" but "the Spirit of the Earth is subservient to the "Lord of Venus." She continues, "Venus is the most occult, powerful, and mysterious of all the planets; the one whose influence upon, and relation to the Earth is most prominent." It's also taught that Venus is "the Guardian Spirit of the Earth and Men" and that "according to the Occult Doctrine, this planet (Venus) is

our Earth's primary, and its spiritual prototype. We are told that every change that takes place on Venus is felt by, and reflected on, the Earth. The planet Venus, adds H.P.B., "is the LIGHT-BEARER of our Earth, in both its physical and mystical sense." Venus is "the bright and morning star," which is an appellation applied to both Lucifer and the Christ in the Bible.[27]

Cover of *Lucifer*, Theosophical Monthly Magazine, c. 1895

Lhasa Assume Limited Physical Vehicles

The Lhasa had to physically incarnate into the bodies of the race versus assuming its use; much like a Bodhisattva. Incarnating entailed developing generational bodies to contain the Lhasa more effectively. It would have been easier for both the Lhasa and the Lemurians if there had been no delay on the part of the Lhasa initiating their Karmic task, because subsequent consequences could have been avoided. The Lemurians had chosen physical bodies that were below the cosmic-physical criterion needed by these higher evolved spiritual entities, the Lhasa. Their task entailed acting as guides and teachers, improving the race-type from the existing half-human, half-animal form. Time was nigh, for the physical body and humanity's transformation had arrived.[2]

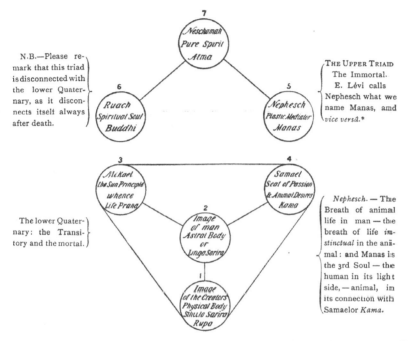

Helena Petrovna Blavatsky, *The Secret Doctrine, Vol. I.*

Early Groupings of Adams

Anthrogenesis anticipates a new perception of Genesis by providing more details about Adam and his kin. Blavatsky says that Adam essentially was a prototype for all the Root Races. The creation of Adam, Cain, Seth, Enoch and Noah are only Biblical names assigned to evolutionary groups, to designate the first men, within their stages of evolution. In her book, *Isis Unveiled* (1877), Blavatsky elaborates on these first men named 'Adam,' which is a Hebrew name meaning "to be red, ruddy," and used in Genesis for 'man,' the original mankind. The Kabbalah describes four 'Adams.' First, there was the *archetypal*, or heavenly man- 'Adam Qadmon' and the prototype for the second Adam. From these comes the third Adam; pre-terrestrial and innocent and quite removed from the first Adam Qadmon. The fourth Adam is the post-Eden; after the '*The Fall*,' an earth-bound sexual being.[3]

"Adam Qadmon—Hebrew, ['ādām—'mankind' + qadmōn— 'to be before, precede'] Primordial man, Adam Primus; in the Qabbalah macrocosmic man in contrast to the earthly Adam, the microcosm. Often called the Heavenly Man because symbolically he is the Sephirothal Tree of Life, each of the Sephiroth having its correspondence with a part of the body, the head being Kether (or Crown), and the feet standing for Malchuth (Kingdom).' Adam Qadmon corresponds mystically to the Hindu Purusha: both are generalizing terms used to represent the cosmic Logos or hierarch of their respective hierarchies. Blavatsky compares 'Adam Qadmon to the first Manu, Svayambhuva, "the synthesis of the fourteen Manus." (TG 206—*Theosophical Glossary*, by H. P. Blavatsky); also to the Greek Prometheus and the divine Pymander of the Hermetica — the power of the thought divine "in its most spiritual aspect." (*Isis Unveiled*, 1:298).[4]

Beings Refuse The Provided Etheric Sheaths

Some of the Lemurians were unwilling to reconcile with the level of physical matter they were endowed with by the Dzyan Masters. During this time, other unidentified Beings not associated with the current incarnating race attempted to take over humanity's evolutionary process but wanted to focus on a materialistic and lower functioning style of human development, not in-line with evolution of spiritual consciousness, as envisioned by our Sirius planetary Masters. The dharma of these beings later became associated with a Hebrew tradition, since they had no true homeland and fit an adage oft referred to as the "Wandering Jew." These Lemurians had no space to move into and some reincarnated before the expected time, resulting in mutations of matter and consciousness while others were preoccupied with undesirable activities.

The Lhasa were a highly evolved humanity from a system of evolution that had run its course, at a period in the infinite ancient past. They had reached a high stage of development on their chain of worlds and since dissolved, having passed the intervening ages in bliss of a 'nirvana state.' But their karma then necessitated a return to a useful field of action and development on the physical plane, as they had not yet fully learned the lesson of compassion. So, their temporary task lay in becoming guides and teachers of the Lemurian race.[5, 6]

Divine Beings from Venus

Edward Robert Hughes (1851-1914)

Divine Beings from Venus Assist Humanity

During the Lemurian period on Earth, human beings were on the verge of attaining true spiritual virility. Needing additional help from advanced beings, the Divine Beings from Venus were called upon to assist in their education. Under their guidance and influence of these Venusian teachers, the Lemurians rapidly advanced in mental growth. The positions occupied by these beings were naturally those of rulers, instructors in religion, and teachers of the arts and it is in this latter capacity that a reference to the arts taught by them comes to our attention.

The Venusians came from the Planetary Chain in which Venus is incarnated as the physical planet. Having already reached the Seventh Round in its Fifth Manvantara, the Venusians had attained a higher spiritual evolution than humanity on Earth. They were 'divine' while we were 'human.' The stirring of human minds with feelings of love and reverence for those whom they felt to be infinitely wiser and greater than themselves, naturally resulted in efforts of imitation, so the necessary advance in human mental growth was achieved. Higher mental sheaths became vehicles capable of carrying over the human characteristics from life to life, thus warranting that outpouring of the Divine Life, which endowed the recipient with individual immortality.

A distinction must be made between the coming of exalted Beings from Venus and that of those described as the Lhasa, a highly evolved humanity from a previous planetary evolution. The former, as we have seen, were under no karmic impulse. They came to live and work among the humans, not requiring a physical vehicle because they were able to provide an advanced vehicle for themselves. At some later time in the distant future we humans may be called to help a neophyte race striving towards adulthood on an evolving planet and lovingly return the favor by giving a helping hand to these beings aspiring to humanity, on the Jupiter or perhaps, the Saturn Chain.

It must be remembered that up to this time, the Lemurian race consisted of the second and third groups of the Lunar Pitris. But now that they were approaching the level reached on the Lunar Chain by the first group of Pitris. They needed to reincarnate, and did so throughout the Fifth, Sixth and Seventh sub-races with some births extending into the Atlantean Race. The Lunar Pitris, who were evolved from these lunar groups were essentially enlisted from the animal kingdom from that Lunar Manvantara (Round).[7, 8]

Lemuria in the Age of Reptiles

The Lemurians originally emerged with a flexible, jelly-like constitution, with the onset before Blavatsky's mid-point of 18 ½ million years (Madame B. does not provide an exact time due to discretion by the Masters), employing androgyny as had their predecessors of the Second Root Race. With a long road ahead for these humans, the bisexual forefathers with reproductive organs of both sexes, continued to evolve. These early ovoid forms, with filament stemming, grew more cartilaginous, transforming into bones, muscles and later, a nervous system with blood vessels. Cellular nuclei remaining from the Second Race, evolving into true organs. And evolution continued with physical humans forming out of the earlier astral-etheric races.

While the First Root Race was astral-etheric in nature, the Second Root Race gained a translucent physical form with massive bodies. A later 3rd sub-race of the Second Root Race arrived with enormous gelatinous bodies, which solidified over time into soft-boned limbs within a bony structure. Early Lemurians were embryonic by design and finally able to stand upright and walk backwards, with two eyes in the face becoming basic organs of physical sight. They had the 'Third Eye,' an actual organ of physical sight, adding psychic vision well into the late Lemurian sub-races and into Atlantis. The Lemurians evolved solid bodies with sexual division, causing the third eye to lose its power and gradually recede from the outward anatomy by the time of the 3rd sub-race of Atlantis. This gland gradually moved into the skull, known today as the pineal gland, located beneath the posterior part of the *corpus callosum*. The pineal gland is thought to be the physical seat of the Soul.

A Lemurian Described

By the 5th Lemurian sub-race, humanity was quite tall, averaging 12-15 feet in height. Blavatsky says that Lemurians "had already made their appearance, as during the Triassic." The appearance of our relative may remind us of a Hobbit, so pleasant a character, popularized in J.R.R. Tolkien's *Lord of the Rings* trilogy. So, think 'Bilbo Baggins' as you read this description, only taller.[9]

The fellow had a yellowish brown skin, with a long lower jaw. His eyes radiated the Love of his Father, the Great Being we call God, with Brotherhood and friendship, epitomized by the Golden Rule. His eyes were keen; he could see quite a distance with the added help of 180-degree vision. His face was sloping and smoothed to an even level, with the aid of his Third Eye located at the back of his head. Our ancestor had fine hair, with no real neck, his skull met his head and to adorn himself, a fancy piece of skin was at the location of his forehead. He was strong with firm, unbending extremities, long, with large hands and feet, like Bilbo's. The only difference is that our fellow's feet were reversed. A loose robe of skin cloaked our ancestor's frame, with a circular headband containing bright red and blue tassels. Being a warrior of his age, our Bilbo would train a small, domesticated reptile, like a Plesiosaurus; kept in check with a twisted lead. He carried a long, honed rod in the opposite hand. Our Lemurian was very calm, kind and devoted to love. A picture of what appears to be a Lemurian is carved into rock in an African cave along with another drawing of a group of Lemurians. I was unable to recruit the photo but it is in the West African Museum, as recalled.[10, 11]

Lemurians Evolve into Modern Humans

So, a group of peaceful, unencumbered simple humans evolved the DNA of the most ancient, revered people alive because they united humanity as a *One People* worldwide. The Lemurian race existed in the early physical-etheric plane and was not human, as we understand modern man to be. The body became densely physical after the sexes had achieved separation and slowly over the millennia, the body achieved a more modern appearance.

Humanity's descendants of the Lemurians still inhabit our Earth today in cultures with vague, remnant DNA such as indigenous Australians, indigenous forefathers of the Andaman Islanders, the indigenous successors in the mountains of India, which include the Todas people, the Kostas descendants, the Kurumbas families, the Badagas indigenous people, the Tierra-del-Fuegan people, and the indigenous and most revered Africa Bushmen.[12]

Giants of the Races

Genesis refers to the now legendary episode regarding early days of humanity when "Sons of God" took as their wives the daughters of men, resulting in "giants in the land." Humans are said to have been 'Giants' of titanic size during the first races, gradually reducing stature in succeeding ages-a process also occurring in the animal and plant kingdoms. The Bible reports 'Giants' as being present in the book of Genesis, Ch.14. Additionally, throughout many chapters of the first chapters in Genesis, there are very antiquated humans, such as Adam, who lived to 930 years, in Genesis 5:4, Noah lived 950 years, in Genesis 9:29, Enoch lived 365 years in Genesis 5:23, and Methuselah was 969-years old when he died, Genesis 5:27.[13, 14]

The Lemurians of Easter Island

The Secret Doctrine sites Easter Island's massive statues, with some standing at 27 feet in height by 8 feet across the shoulders, as representative of features and height of our ancestors. They are reportedly the stature of the last Lemurian artisans who erected them and close to Oceania, where Lemuria was thought to endure.

Blavatsky reports that the height of the first two Lemurian races was a reported 100-feet tall, gradually shortened over the ages, with the last Lemurians at 60-feet tall, tapering down to 20-25 feet at Lemuria's

A View of the Monuments of Easter Island, Rapanui,
c. 1775-1776 by William Hodges

destruction. Blavatsky said that that the so-called 'mythological' tradition about giants in all cultures, have their origin and basis in archaic fact.[15]

The Collective Unconscious

Is it possible that our collective unconscious is one area where we can access our archaic memories? Have we had dreams or even déjà vu experiences in which we see ourselves living in different times? Practices such as meditation can assist us in transcending the daily human experiences and promote spiritual enlightenment.

Carl Jung described the collective unconscious as that segment which holds residues of ancestral life, containing specific images or archetypes, known as mythological images. "Cut into the vestige of ancestral life, the mythological images are awakened: these are the archetypes. An interior spiritual world whose existence we never suspected opens out and displays contents that seem to stand in sharpest contrast to all our former ideas."[16]

No Fossils Remain

As is the way of the Ancient Mysteries, the veil of secrecy remains intact. While it was possible for some fossils to be found from earlier races, due to the tremendous volcanic activity and continental shifts, tectonic plate movement, flooding, lava flows and massive upheaval, it is virtually impossible to find the remnants of our ancestors.[17]

Expansion of the Late Lemurians

The last two sub-races of the Lemurians, the Lemuro-Atlanteans, built cities, cultivated the arts and sciences, and sowed far and wide the first seeds of civilization under the guidance of their divine instructors and their own awakened minds. Lemuria was centered in the Pacific Ocean and we know it as Mu. Mu sank 8 million years ago at the end of the Tertiary period. Hermaphroditism ended in the middle period of this Third Race and correlates with the awakening of our self-conscious minds and human bodies that were fully developed with the predominant characteristics of one of the sexes.[18]

Mesozoic Animal Interbreeding

The Ape Race arose from naïve interbreeding between early sub-races of non-conscious beings and a high order of ape animals, during the Mesozoic; the Age of Reptiles. These apes had been present on Earth at the beginning of the Fourth Round and separation of the sexes had already happened with animals and later, within the human kingdom. The humans were still instinctual and devoid of self-consciousness; thus this reproduction was not troublesome.[19]

When the 4th Root Race of Atlantis came into being, animal breeding multiplied throughout these islands in the Atlantic Ocean. At the mid-point of the Atlantic Root Race, the *"door into the Human Kingdom"* was closed for the entire duration of the evolutionary cycle of our planetary chain. Millions upon millions of years must pass before evolution of entities from the animal kingdom transitioning into the Human Kingdom can occur, with the numbers of humanity already established during the middle of Atlantis.[20]

The Truth about Lucifer

In retrospect, why is it that the Old Testament was altered from the original text of Moses, the Chaldeans, and Zarathustra to veil aspects of mankind? This original canon was altered concerning the story of the angels' fall to Earth, i.e. being cast out of Heaven and thrust down to Earth. As far as Lucifer (the word means 'light bearer') goes, he was one of the Light Bearers with the Beings from Venus; the word has no other meaning.[21]

H.P.B. reports that the angels descent represented the result of man's knowledge, for his "eyes were opened." In each of us therein lies the 'golden thread' of continuous life–periodically broken into active and passive cycles of existence on Earth with affective events in Devachan, from the beginning of our appearance upon this Earth. It is the strata (Sanskrit) or luminous thread of immortal, impersonal, monad-ship on which our earthly lives are strung as so many beads.[22]

The Provocative Book of Enoch

Our church fathers such as Irenaeus, Origen, Tertullian and Jerome held the *Book of Enoch* (c. 200 BCE) in great reverence. However, perhaps in 'veiling truth,' the Book of Enoch was removed from the Holy Bible after wide use before the church's purge of apocryphal materials. Speculation for this may be due to Enoch's discussion of "fallen angels," documentation of extraterrestrials, Satan's evil origin and an angel teaching "secrets of their wisdom" (Chapter 69:8-12). Only the Ethiopians had access to the book until the 20th century. English translations were later made from the Ethiopian copy, found again by Scotsman James

Bruce in 1773. The Dead Sea Scrolls contained a copy of Enoch discovered in 1948.[73] [74]

Role of the Angels

Esoterically, the role of the Guardian Angel was made possible by the sacrifice of the Venusian Beings; the Solar Angels, in their preservation of the principle of mind (occult fire) through persistent repeated incarnations in form until animal man became thinking man and finally began to awaken to his true spiritual heritage: the human-divine man.

Thus, the Solar Angel creates the form for the incarnating soul principle—the causal body—and it also withdraws that body at the fourth initiation, when the link between form and spirit has been permanently fused and the causal body is shattered. We are reminded that the Solar Angels submitting to the Law of Duality so that human evolution could ultimately be dependent upon mental discrimination and free will and thus, upon the capacity to have options, and hopefully, to choose the higher path. It is a choice for each human being to be guided by free will. There is always a choice of two paths.[25, 26]

Senses of the Root Races

The First Race had no speech, living in a daydream while the Hyperborean used chant-like vowel sounds. The Lemurian sounds mimicked nature's sounds and speech slowly developed through the races while some psychic thought transference continued. Each Root Race brought a distinct sense into activity: a sense of hearing, a sense of touch, a sense of sight, a sense of taste, and a sense of smell. Now, humans have five senses. Sound calculation is at eleven octaves with sight at one octave of light. Hearing took the lead with speech following. The last races will develop the senses to a fine degree. Manas, the awakening of Mind began in Lemuria about 18 million years ago with this fifth principle. Manas is awaiting completion at the end of the Fifth Round. By the end of the Seventh Round, our lower human monads will have become higher human monads, and will enter the lowest of the three Dhyani-Chohan kingdoms, assuming that we run the race successfully. It will then be our duty to act as Manasaputras for the human monads in the next Manvantara, which are currently the animal monads.[27, 28]

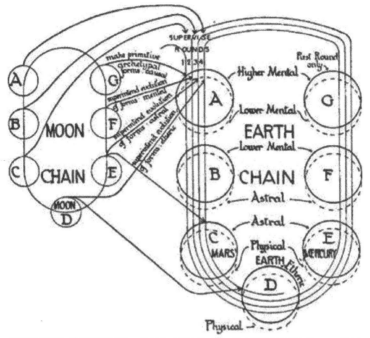

DIAGRAM XXXVII.—The Work of the Barhishads in the Earth Chain.

A Lunar Pitri Defined

Lunar means "belonging to the moon," while Pitri is a Sanskrit word meaning "father." Beings who have attained a high position in evolution on the preceding Lunar Chain are now able to 'father' the evolution of humanity on this Terrene Chain. The term with this definition, includes the Barhishads and the Lower Dhyanis or Solar Pitris but does not include the less advanced entities from the Lunar Chain, constituting the bulk of our present races, the seven classes of "Lunar Pitris" often spoken of by Mme. Blavatsky. For these Mrs. Besant has suggested the apt phrase "Ex-lunar Monads" as avoiding confusion with the true Pitris."[29]

75

Notes

1. Blavatsky, HP, *The Secret Doctrine: II.*
2. Blavatsky, HP, *The Secret Doctrine: II.*
3. http://www.theosociety.org/pasadena/etgloss/a-adh.htm
4. http://www.theosociety.org/pasadena/etgloss/a-adh.htm
5. Blavatsky, HP, *The Secret Doctrine: II.*
6. http://www.hinduwebsite.com/divinelife/annie/7principlesofman. asp
7. http://www.sacred-texts.com/atl/tll/tll18.htm
8. https://books.google.com/books?isbn=0835631095
9. Blavatsky, HP, *The Secret Doctrine: II.*
10. Scott-Elliot, William, 1925. The Story of Atlantis and The Lost Lemuria, p. 28.
11. http://tolkiengateway.net/wiki/Bilbo_Baggins#Personality
12. http://www.everyculture.com/South-Asia/Hill-Tribes. html#ixzz3Q3MziAWB
13. http://www.answersingenesis.org/bible-characters/giants-in-the-old-testament
14. http://www.jewishencyclopedia.com/articles/6658-giants
15. http://www.blavatskytheosophy.com/human-evolution-in-the-secret-doctrine
16. http://wenshuchan-online.weebly.com/carl-jung--buddhism-part-i.html
17. http://wenshuchan-online.weebly.com/carl-jung--buddhism-part-i.html
18. http://www.blavatsky.net/index.php/37-topics/atlantis/55-atlantis-found
19. http://www.blavatskytheosophy.com/lucifer-the-lightbringer
20. http://www.blavatskytheosophy.com/human-evolution-in-the-secret-doctrine
21. http://www.blavatskytheosophy.com/lucifer-the-lightbringer
22. H.P.B., SD, Vol. II, p. 512-13.
23. Charles, R.H., *The Book of Enoch*, Introduction by R.A. Gilbert, 2003, Red Wheel/Weiser, LLC, ME, page viii.
24. http://www.theosophy-nw.org/theosnw/teachers/te-gdp8.htm

25. http://www.lucistrust.org/en/arcane_school/talks_and_articles/ descent_and_sacrifice

26. http://www.lucistrust.org/en/books/the_beacon_magazine/ reprinted_fromthe_beacon/the_solar_angel

27. http://www.theosociety.org/pasadena/forum/f21n05p193_ evolution-into-the-human-kingdom.htm

28. http://www.hiddenlighthouse.wordpress.com/category/lemuria/

29. *A Dictionary Of Some Theosophical Terms*, Compiled by Powis Hoult. The Theosophical Publishing Society, London (1910). p. 75.

Anthrogenesis

Chapter Five

Evolutionary Biology

"Ontogeny Recapitulates Phylogeny"

by Ernst Haeckel, 1866.

"The theory of recapitulation, also called the biogenetic law or embryological parallelism, and often expressed as ontogeny recapitulates phylogeny, was first put forward in 1866 by German zoologist Ernst Haeckel. Haeckel proposed that the embryonic development of an individual organism or ontogeny followed the same path as the evolutionary history of its species or phylogeny."[1]

"Man is descended from a hairy, tailed, quadruped; probably arboreal in its habits."

- Charles Darwin, *The Descent of Man* (1871)

Gigantopithecus

Does the ape species, *Giantopithecus* still survive and live in our present world? Is it the Yeti of the Tibetans?

Giantopithecus is a larger version of hominid and possibly a predecessor to the Aryan Root-Race, or a hominid evolutionary link. The remains of humans measuring 12 feet tall have been discovered recently with reports of semi-human or apelike creatures 7 to 15 feet tall existing in remote areas, in the present day. But, eventually, all of the lower animals will gradually die out, as evolution returns to the next Manvantara.

Scientific Explanations for Life

Charles Darwin brought a scientific genesis to the physical sciences when he discussed his theories about natural selection after returning from his voyage on the HMS Beagle in 1836, during which he noted his observations in journals with a book following some 20 years later, *On the Origin of Species*. Born in Shrewsbury, Shropshire, Charles Robert Darwin lived from February 12, 1809 to April 19, 1882 and was trained as an English naturalist. His book *On the Origin of Species* (1859), provided evidence that evolution has taken place and proposed the theory of natural selection which explains how evolution works. Evolution by natural selection is the key to understanding biology, and the diversity of life on Earth.[2]

Natural selection is the process wherein organisms with constructive traits are more likely to reproduce and pass on these traits to the next generation. Over time this process allows organisms to adapt to their environment. This is because the incidence of genes for favorable traits increases in the population. However, the families in a species are not all alike due to differences in genetic makeup which selects for one organism being superior in survival and reproduction than others in a particular environment. During reproduction the life form passes along its genes, giving advantage to its offspring. Some adaptations may be long-lasting and useful in multiple habitats while others may be short lived in a consistent ecosystem, but other life form may 'be selected' if the environment modifies for longer intervals.[3]

Ancient Biology

See: Appendix XXXII – Ancient Biology

Classification of Kingdoms of Life

Carl Linnaeus, a Swedish botanist, physician, and zoologist, laid the foundations for the modern biological naming scheme of binomial nomenclature, thereby developing a system for classifying plants and animals, based on a hierarchy of categories ranging from kingdom down to species, during the year of April, 1732. He is also known as the father of modern taxonomy and considered one of the fathers of modern ecology. This table shows the classification of modern humans, *Homo sapiens*[4]:

Linnaean Classification of Human or *Homo sapiens*[5]:

Domain: Eukaryota

Kingdom: Animalia

Phylum: Chordata

Subphylum: Vertebrata

Class: Mammalia

Subclass: Theria

Infraclass: Eutheria

Order: Primates

Suborder: Haplorrhini

Superfamily: Hominoidea

Family: Hominidae

Subfamily: Homininae

Tribe: Hominini

Genus: Homo

Species: *H. sapiens*

Subspecies: *H. s. sapiens*

New World Hominids: It's In The Teeth

See: Appendix XXXIII

Paleontology

"Dr. Louis Leakey, a major figure in paleontology stated that he believed three hominins were alive at the same time, perhaps with interbreeding; *Australopithecus, Neanderthal* and *Homo sapiens*, at 3 million years, 2 million years and 1 million years, respectively."[6, 7]

Michael Cremo wrote of apes evolving alongside with men. It is no accident that humanity has found so many species of hominin apes with the inherent difficulty of tracing lineage back to ape and evolving forward to *H. sapiens*. Between all of the ape descendants, none seem to be really connected to the current *H. sapiens*. Dr. Michael Cremo contends that these beings lived together with several types of hominin, which would make some sense due to the mixture of genetic qualities, i.e. height, body structure, jaw and tooth arrangement, and hair color.[8]

Is it possible that 'Lilith, with her long, hairy body' in mythological allegories may have been one of these many ape progenies? H.P. Blavatsky says "These beings in female forms (Lilith is the prototype of these in the Jewish traditions) are called in the esoteric accounts "Khado" (Dakini, in Sanskrit). Allegorical legends call the chief of these Liliths, Sangye Khado, (Buddha Dakini, in Sanskrit); all are credited with the art of "walking in the air," and the greatest kindness to mortals; but no mind, only animal instinct."[9, 10, 11]

The Monkeys, Apes And Hominins

See: Appendix XXXIV

Humanity's Hidden History

Humans and apes did indeed have a common ancestor who was perhaps man himself, in his earlier, more primitive form. Darwinian primatology theory is contradicted by abundant evidence of stone tools, incised bones, and skeletal remains showing that human beings existed in the Pleistocene, millions of years before our supposed apelike ancestors are thought to have appeared. This evidence is currently ignored or suppressed by the scientific community.[12]

"There is evidence that humans were present before, during, and after the age of the dinosaurs. Human footprints alongside dinosaur footprints were found in Texas and a modern human skeleton was found in a 300-million-year-old layer of slate rock in Illinois." -Michael Cremo in "*The Hidden History of the Human Race.*"[13]

See:
Appendix XXXV – Splits in Old World Monkeys
Appendix XXXVI – Orangutans and Gibbons
Appendix XXXVII – Hominid Fossil Record

Longer Time Scale for Human Evolution

In his article (*Longer Time Scale for Human Evolution*), Dr. Hawks cites widespread re-sequencing of primate species and direct comparisons of parent and offspring genomes followed by subsequent analysis of whole genomes in parent–offspring trios, which while shoring up the missing links to corroborate theory, it has shown that wild chimpanzees and gorillas have "Long generations, with few genetic mutations in each, meaning that the clock of genetic substitutions has ticked very slowly during the evolution of humans and apes." He adds that for paleontologists, this will be a relief because new hominin species are being excavated in the present and future. Dr. Hawks sees that hominin species have a newfound increase in evolutionary time.[14]

Toumai, the Divider

Between July 2001 and March 2002, *Sahelanthropus tchadensis*, (nicknamed *Toumai*), an extinct hominin species was discovered in Djurab Desert of Chad, Africa, by a team of four researchers led by Michel Brunet and three Chadians, Adoum Mahamat, Djimdoumalbaye Ahounta and Gongdibé Fanoné, and Frenchman, Alain Beauvilain. The hominin dates to about 7 million years ago, considered closer to the time of the chimpanzee and human divergence. Since that time, there has been strong debate as to the reliability of the specimen to the split between humans and apes.[15]

Debate Continues On Ardipithecus Ramidus

Left: image courtesy of Scientific Paleo artist Jay Matternes

There continues to be debate in the field of paleoanthropology about the 4.4 million-year-old hominid *Ardipithecus ramidus*, who opened up a new chapter on human evolution because it is as close as we have ever come to finding the last common ancestor of chimpanzees and humans.[16]

From Ardi to the Greeks

Taking a more abridged look at human evolution, between our 4.4 million-year-old hominin *Ardi* or *Ardipithecus ramidus*, and the Lower Paleolithic beginning in the Lower Pleistocene some 2.5 million years ago, there was the appearance of *Homo habilis. Homo erectus* later appeared by about 1.8 million years ago, via the interim hominin, *Homo ergaster.* The Lower Paleolithic throughout the Upper Paleolithic, then into Baradostian times with arrival in the Holocene, has revealed findings that enthuse us and illustrate the many hominin diversities.

Homo neanderthalensis, Neanderthal was active between 350,000 to 40,000 years ago. Culture and evolution made for swift progress through the Neolithic, with humanity becoming apparently quite proficient with tools and farming of the land and sea. By the Upper Paleolithic-Baradostian times humanity seems to be better yet. We ultimately arrive much later in the Bronze Age as we develop better tools and survive the Younger Dryas. This may have provided a strong push for advancement in home and hearth. By now, humanity has reached the Aegean times, our Cycladic culture, in bed with the ancient Greeks.

We shall discuss more of the mythologies of the ancients in the chapters to come.[17, 18]

Humans, Chimps and Bonobos

"Two African apes are the closest living relatives of humans: the chimpanzee (*Pan troglodytes*) and the bonobo (*Pan paniscus*). Although they are similar in many respects, bonobos and chimpanzees differ strikingly in key social and sexual behaviors and for some of these traits they show more similarity with humans than with each other. This is a report of the sequencing and assembly of the bonobo genome to study its evolutionary relationship with the chimpanzee and human genomes. We find that more than three per cent of the human genome is more closely related to either the bonobo or the chimpanzee genome than these are to each other. It is known that whereas DNA sequences in humans diverged from those in bonobos and chimpanzees five to seven million years ago, DNA sequences in bonobos diverged from those in chimpanzees around two million years ago. Bonobos are thus closely related to chimpanzees. These regions allow various aspects of the ancestry of the two ape species to be reconstructed. In addition, many of the regions that overlap genes may eventually help us understand the genetic basis of phenotypes that humans share with one of the two apes to the exclusion of the other."[19]

The Legacy of DNA

The 1962 Nobel Prize in Medicine was awarded to James Watson and Francis Crick who in 1953 proposed what is now accepted as the first correct double-helix model of DNA (deoxyribonucleic acid) structure in the journal *Nature* which included the double-helix, molecular model of DNA based on a single X-ray diffraction image of "Photo 51" taken by Rosalind Franklin and Raymond Gosling in May, 1952. DNA, with its double helix shape molecule, is found in each cell and contains the genetic code that transmits cellular information about proteins and enzymes to make animals, plants, protozoa, algae and lower forms of life. DNA is inherited by offspring from the parents combined DNA so shared traits will be observed such as skin, hair and eye color.[20]

The DNA Chromosome

Progress in mitochondrial (maternal DNA) and Y chromosome (paternal DNA) DNA advanced the understanding of human origins with the application of the molecular clock principle, revolutionizing the study of molecular evolution. Vincent Sarich and Allan Wilson measured the immunology of blood serum albumin between humans and African apes, with the reaction strength expressed as an *'immunological distance,'* which was related to differences in the amino acid among similar proteins in different species. An adjustment curve of the identification of the species' chromosome pairs was developed, with known variance times in the fossil record, which allowed data to be used as a 'molecular clock' to estimate the times of the pair separation, with poorer or unknown fossil records.

In the journal, *Science*, in 1967, Sarich and Wilson estimated the divergence time of humans and apes at four to five million years ago during a time when standard interpretations of the fossil record gave this divergence of 10 to 30 million years. Later fossil discoveries, like Lucy, and reinterpretation of older fossil materials such as *Ramapithecus*, showed the younger estimates to be correct and validated the blood serum method.[21, 22]

The Smart Gene

In the *Journal of Molecular Psychiatry*, February, 2014, the lead study author, Dr. Sylvane Desrivières-King's College London, Institute of Psychiatry reported that subjects in the NPTN gene study performed better in intelligence tests and ascertaining structural differences in the brain's differences in intellectual ability of over fifteen hundred, 14-year-old teens who had willingly participated with parental agreement by submitted DNA and MRI scans with verbal and non-verbal intelligence exams. One particular gene variant indicated a thinner cortex in the left cerebral hemisphere, in the frontal and temporal lobes, and subjects performed less well on tests for intellectual ability.[23, 24]

On September 9, 2014 Australian researchers reported that they had discovered four 'Smart' genes that influence cognitive performance of particular pathways in the brain related to the central cellular mechanism for learning and memory associated with human intelligence for the first time. The hypothesis suggested an increase in the Stanford-Binet Intelligence Test tool, and scoring by these subjects increased by 2 points. The standard deviation on this intelligence test is 15 points, with average intelligence scoring at a total of 100 points.[25, 26]

The God Gene

"Geneticist Dean Hamer, the director of the Gene Structure and Regulation Unit at the U.S. National Cancer Institute reported his hypothesis regarding genetic inheritance and DNA appearance of the *'God gene'* in people who responded with (1) spirituality that can be quantified by psychometric measurements; (2) the underlying tendency to spirituality is recorded as partially heritable; (3) part of this heritability is attributed to the gene VMAT2, (4) this gene alters monoamine levels; and (5) spiritual individuals are favored by natural selection because they are provided with an innate sense of optimism, the latter producing positive effects at either a physical or psychological level. Dr. Hamer's study results appears to be correlated with the attributes of 'spiritually-minded' individuals. The complete study was described in his book published in 2005."[27]

Public Domain

Awesome is the Creator

Notes

1. http://www.ucmp.berkeley.edu/history/haeckel.html
2. http://darwin-online.org.uk/timeline.html
3. http://www.darwin-online.org.uk
4. http://www.teara.govt.nz/en/document/12130/classification-of-humans
5. Groves, C.P. (2005). Wilson, D.E.; Reeder, D.M., eds. Mammal Species of the World: A Taxonomic and Geographic Reference (3rd ed.). Baltimore: Johns Hopkins University Press. OCLC 62265494. ISBN 0-801-88221-4.
6. Leakey, Louis S. B., *By The Evidence: Memoirs*, 1932-1951, Harcourt Brace Jovanovich, N.Y. 1974.
7. http://anthro.palomar.edu/hominid/australo_1.htm
8. Cremo, Michael, Thompson Richard L., *Forbidden Archaeology*, Bhaktivedanta Institute, San Diego, CA, 1993.
9. http://lilithgate.atspace.org/essays/lilith2.html
10. Duke University. *"New Fossil Tying Humans, Apes And Monkeys Is Full Of Surprises."* ScienceDaily.
11. http://www.sciencedaily.com/releases/2007/05/070514174240.htm (accessed October 23, 2015).
12. http://www.jstor.org/stable/3629782
13. http://www.social-consciousness.com/2013/01/the-hidden-history-of-human-race.html
14. *Longer Time Scale for Human Evolution*, John Hawks, Published online before print September 14, 2012, doI – 10.1073/pnas.1212718109, PNAS September 25, 2012 vol. 109 no. 39 15531-15532.
15. http://www.nature.com/nature/journal/v418/n6894/pdf/nature00879.pdf
16. http://www.sciencemag.org/content/326/5949/60.1.full.pdf
17. http://www.nature.com/nature/journal/v505/n7481/full/nature12886.html
18. http://www.iranicaonline.org/articles/paleolithic-age
19. http://www.nature.com/nature/journal/v486/n7404/full/nature11128.html

20. http://www.chemheritage.org/discover/online-resources/ chemistry-in-history/themes/biomolecules/dna/watson-crick-wilkins-franklin.aspx

21. http://www.genome.gov/27555170: National Human Genome Research Institute, National Institute of Health, United States Government

22. http://www.sciencemag.org/content/158/3805/1200 : *Immunological Time Scale for Hominid Evolution.* Vincent M. Sarich and Allan C. Wilson. Science 1 December 1967: 158 (3805), 1200-1203. [DOI – 10.1126/science.158.3805.1200]

23. Journal of Molecular Psychiatry (2015) 20, 263–274; doI – 10.1038/mp.2013.197. Published online February 11, 2014:

24. http://www.nature.com/mp/journal/v20/n2/pdf/mp2013197a. pdf:

25. Proceedings of the National Academy of Sciences (PNAS), January 27, 2015. Vol. 112, No. 4.

26. http://www.pnas.org/cgi/doi/10.1073/pnas.1424631112

27. Hamer, Dean, *The God Gene: How Faith is Hardwired into our Genes*, Anchor Publishing, N.Y. 2005.

Anthrogenesis

Chapter Six

Spirituality Of Divine Love

"Before it became Earth, the Earth, with all the beings which belong to it, passed through the three conditions of the Saturn, Sun, and Moon existence. Saturn, Sun, and Moon are, as it were, the three incarnations of the earth in primeval times. What in this connection is called Saturn, Sun, and Moon no more exists today as a physical planet than the previous physical incarnations of a human being continue to exist alongside his present one."

- Rudolf Steiner, *Cosmic Memory* (1959)

Divine Love, The Great Source of Mu

At the destruction of Mu, Ra Mu, the King and High Priest of the Motherland, addressed the pleading crowds saying: "You shall all die together, you and your servants and your riches. From your ashes new nations shall arise and if they forget they are superior, not because of what they put on but what they put out, the same will befall them."

James Churchward, *Sacred Symbols of Mu*, Ch. II.[1]

Mu, an Intrinsic Part of Nature

The Mu were an intrinsic part of nature, which taught humans the Origin of Life, the connection with the Great Source and the origin of Great Cosmic Forces that control the Universe with science being the twin sister of religion; man could not comprehend the Cosmic Forces without embracing Great Divine Love which rules the Universe."[2]

The original Naacal teachings are an account of Creation which include man and woman, movement of celestial bodies and the forces governing this movement in the Universe. The source of these forces, along with what Life is, the Origin of Life and necessary changes in life formed during Earth's development including the geological occurrences. The ancient Naacal Masters also called the Naacal, used their Spiritual Forces to assist humanity in ruling the Earth; there were no miracles.

The Adept, the Naacal, spread teachings of Sacred Inspired Religion and formed colleges for educating the priests in religion and science. The Maya and Egyptian writings of the Sacred Mysteries were only entrusted to the high priesthood and were safeguarded in secret places to current times. Some of these Mysteries have been revealed with others waiting for humanity to rise to the times, which will initiate the Great Truths. Naacal writings, also referred to as Neferit, state that there was a Supreme Being–infinite and all powerful–the Creator who created all things above and below. This Almighty was humanity's Heavenly Father.[2]

Fatherhood of God, the Creator

This Fatherhood of God was described as the Creator, who put an eternal soul in man's body; his material body had to return to Earth when the body died. The released soul then went into the great beyond to wait until it was called for to occupy another material body. The soul had a task to rule the material body by transcending materialistic yearnings to completion and the soul would return to the Great Source to live in perfect joy and happiness; due to the briefness of material life to overcome the material desires, the soul reincarnated until the task was completed.[3]

The Great Love is 'The Heavenly Father'

The Heavenly Father was The Great Love. This 'great love' ruled the Universe throughout infinity; the love of the Heavenly Father was greater than the love of one's worldly father, seen as a reflection of Him. All humanity was created by the Heavenly Father. Humanity's duties on Earth were to follow Truth, Love, Charity (specifically to thoughts AND acts of goodwill to others), Chastity, and to have perfect love and confidence in the Heavenly Father, so as to ready himself to pass into the great beyond when called.

Right: Mu's Cosmogonic Diagram

The Construction of the Diagram

"In the center is a circle within two crossed and interwoven triangles. Being interwoven or interlaced, these triangles form but one figure. These two triangles are enclosed within a second circle, thus leaving twelve divisions. Beyond this circle is a third, leaving a space between the two. On the outside of this third circle are 12 scallops. Falling from the outside of the scallops is a ribbon which has 8 divisions."[4]

Mu's Illustrated Prayer

"The young Naacals had to memorize the above drawn picture, Mu's Cosmogonic Diagram and the following sums up the translation: "I believe there are eight roads to travel to reach Heaven. My soul will first arrive after travelling these roads at the gates to the world beyond. To enter these my soul must show that my earthly body overcame the twelve great earthly temptations. Having shown that it had done so, my soul will be allowed to pass into the world beyond. This I must traverse until I reach the Gates of Heaven. Here my soul must prove that my earthly body possessed the twelve great virtues. Having shown that it did, my soul will then be passed through the Gates into Heaven to the Throne of Glory, where sits the Heavenly Father waiting to receive it." The Naacals made the Golden Rule and the Lord's Prayer, comprising the Sacred Naacal mantras, later being adopted by many world religions.

No further specifics are available about their religion, however we must remember that our Lemurian forefathers were much less evolved than we, especially in their mental body and speech; the visual symbols typified what the meaning and importance was for them.[5, 6, 7, 8]

Ancient Symbols of Cosmic Forces

The Old Testament's first chapters were meant to teach humanity how Nature illustrates the origin of life. This Great Source and the Great Cosmic Forces control the Universe. Moses explained the Sacred Teachings of Mu, while at the Mount Sinai's temple as the High Priest. Biblical translators were unable to translate these Mosiac* teachings which were in the Naacal mother tongue. Subsequently, as each region developed changes were made to this doctrine and new laws were issued without including Mu's original sacred teachings.[1]

*Mosaic (məʊˈzeɪk) or Mosaical, (adj.) are Ecclesiastical terms of or pertaining to Moses or the writings, laws, traditions or principles attributed to him.[9]

Megaliths of Sulawesi

We observe the statues in Bada Valley, Isle of Sulawesi, Indonesia as an indication of our quest for Anthrogenesis. These mysterious, magnificent statues are testaments to the skill and genius of a civilization that science is still unable to explain. They are beautiful stone megaliths reminiscent of the Easter Island Moai.[18, 19]

Egypt Standardizes Lemurian Beliefs

At the time of Mu's submersion all symbols retained their original meanings and up to Egypt, many of the original symbols had survived, but were assimilated into Egyptian hieroglyphic form, pattern and design. Many new symbols were added with esoteric meanings as time went on. When Upper and Lower Egypt merged into one kingdom, two sets of symbols were combined and the sacred Naacal meaning was further lost. So, there were two symbols for every concept, which caused great confusion.

Freemasonry is thought to have incorporated many of these ancient symbols. Belief in a great Designer and Maker was said to have been retained together with ceremonies implementing ancient symbols although the original meanings may have been changed or forgotten. Symbols were sacred, moral in meaning, derived from the first religion of humans or the 'First Time' from the Egyptians.

The ancient Lemurians of the Seventh Sub-Root Race began to populate the area we know as West Nigeria, embracing the Cape of Good Hope and western Africa. These ancestors, thousands of years before Homer, worshipped an unseen being under the name of the Light. The Vedas called it Dyaus Pitar, the Greeks called it Zue Pater and the Romans called it Jupiter. These three languages (Sanskrit, Greek and Latin) term for the Heavenly Father were very similar. Greek philosophers traveled to Egypt, most notably Solon, and were schooled in the Egyptian Sacred Mysteries. Upon returning to Greece this knowledge became mixed into their own sacred mysteries, resulting in new names, myths and theology which resembled the teachings of Egypt and India.[10, 11]

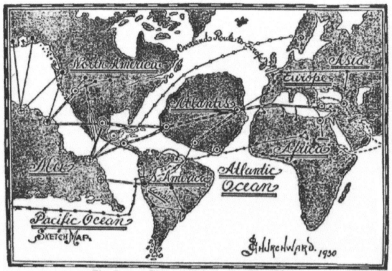

The Eastern Lines of Colonization from Mu.

bibliotecapleyades.net

Lemurian Migration

Oceania, India, Egypt, Africa, Asia, Australia

Referring to the map of Lemuria (above), migrations from Mu spread out through the Americas, South Pacific, Oceania, Easter Island, Asia, China, India, Africa, Australia and New Zealand. We see the similarities among the indigenous populations from all these lands. The Olmec, for example, have five or more races symbolized in their sculpture, pottery and artifacts. Orthodox anthropology speculates that the migration from Africa to the west coast of current day Mexico occurred about two million years ago. Wishar S. Cerve's book *Lemuria, The Lost Continent of the Pacific* tells us that the Lemurians "dispersed themselves" first into Africa, which at the time was still connected to Lemuria. Water levels began to rise, submerging portions of Africa, forcing the Lemurians to migrate to Sumatra, Java, Borneo, New Guinea, Australia and New Zealand.[12]

The End of Lemuria

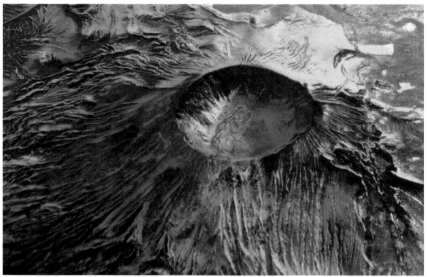

United States Geological Service

South Pacific and Oceania

Oceania, Australia, New Zealand, Melanesia, Indonesia, Easter Island,
Micronesia, New Guinea, Japan

Blavatsky's Oceania

Blavatsky described Oceania as a group of islands that were once a single continent, Lemuria. It's as if a silken thread runs through the islands and continents of Oceania. She said that the continent of Lemuria perished by volcanic action. It was raked by the burning ashes and the red-hot dust from numerous volcanoes. One place in Lemuria, an extensive mountainous region consisted of five active volcanic mountains. The seismic cataclysms which followed the volcanic eruptions caused such wide-spread damage that part of the continent submerged. The Lemurians met their doom by fire or suffocation as the land was slowly eaten away by internal fires.

All of the islands from the Malayan archipelago to Polynesia are thought to be fragments of that once immense submerged continent. One of the most ancient legends of India, preserved in the temples by oral and written tradition, relates that several hundred thousand years ago there existed in the Pacific Ocean an immense continent which was destroyed by geological upheaval, and the fragments of which must be sought in Madagascar, Ceylon, Sumatra, Java, Borneo, and the principal isles in Polynesia. The three summits of this continent, the Sandwich Islands, New Zealand and Easter Island are fifteen to eighteen hundred leagues (4,500 to 5,400 miles) from each other and the groups of intermediate islands, Viti, Samoa, Tonga, Foutouna, Ouvea, the Marquesas, Tahiti, Poumoutou and the Gambiers, are seven or eight hundred to one thousand leagues (2,100 or 2,400 to 3,000 miles) distant themselves from these extreme points.

Post-Lemuria essentially, although not specifically, began when lands after the volcanic eruptions ceased. By that age, the last of the Lemurians and the first Atlanteans had begun to travel to their new locations.[13, 14]

Creation Story of Australia

The Aboriginals believe that 'Dreamtime' was when spirit beings formed creation and that a culture of heroes-gods traveled across a land without form and created sacred sites and other significant places, and gave language to people.

In the beginning, there was only darkness and bare land- no life on Earth, no animals, no plants, no trees and no humans. Wandjina, the creator, was a spirit god, with many gods who had big black eyes, no mouth, and a halo. Wandjina walked on Earth and created everything from rivers and mountains to plants and animals bringing the ancestors from within the earth and over the seas, and life began. Some ancestors were like men and others were like animals and the ancestors could shape shift and became man or animal. The god, Baiame, then arrived from the skies with his wife Birrahgnooloo-Emu the goddess of fertility. They made a son named Darramulum. Baiame gave the first rules to humans, forbidding them to eat the animals. The gods spent time with the ancestors, schooling and assisting the ancestors to advance. Later, the ancestors began to kill and eat animals and they were seized then chastised by the god, Baiame. Next, the other gods appeared from the sky with powers and created humans who fought each other and were then punished by the gods.[15]

Maori Creation Story of New Zealand

At Creation, the Earth goddess, Papa, and her husband Rangi, the sky god, were very much in love, hugging each other and not wanting to let go, meaning the earth and the sky were always joined solidly together, but no light could come into the world. Papa bore several children, but they were stuck between their parents, unable to escape. The children decided they had to leave, so one child, Tane, suggested forcing their parents apart. All the children agreed that this was a good idea. Each child tried without success to separate their parents until Tane tried by folding himself small, slipping between his parents with feet against Rangi and shoulders against Papa. Tane pushed for many hours, days, weeks and for many years until very slowly Tane uncurled and straighten himself, finally pushing his parents apart.

Pixabay

Light then entered the world for the first time since creation and the plants grew. But Rangi and Papa were very sad to be separated and they cried and cried until Rangi's tears ran into rivers, becoming a sea to threaten the world with flooding. Something had to be done, so one child turned Papa over, so Rangi could not see her face. Then, Rangi didn't cry so much but you could still see his tears every morning; they are the dewdrops on the grass and Papa's sighs were the mists rising from the ground.[16]

Indonesian Creation Story

The goddess Sideak Parujar escaped from her lizard-like husband-to-be, descended on spun-thread from the world of gods-the sky, to the middle world made only of shapeless waters. It was uncomfortable there but Sideak Parujar committed to stay and her kind grandfather sent a handful of earth.

Mistakenly, she spread the earth on the head of a horrific dragon called Naga Padoha who lived in the underworld water. The monster was upset and attempted to rid himself of the earth by rolling around and making the goddess very miserable. But she was ingenious, thrusting a sword to the hilt into the monster, thus stopping him. Every time Naga Padoha writhed with his resistance, an earthquake reverberated throughout the land. But, unknown to Sideak Parujar, her suitor in lizard disguise, stalked her to the Earth and the goddess married him and they were blessed with two twin children, a boy and a girl. When the children grew up, their divine parents departed back to the god's sky world and the children formed a happy marriage, making many humans to inhabit the Earth. Later, the couple moved to the volcano named Pusut Buhit, located on the western shore of Lake Toba, where they founded the village of Si Anjur Mulamula. Si Raja Batak, an ancestor of the couple is considered the mythological ancestor of the Batak people.[17]

Difference between Hominin and Hominid

"Hominin–the group consisting of modern humans, extinct human species and all our immediate ancestors (including members of the genera *Homo, Australopithecus, Paranthropus* and *Ardipithecus*)."

"Hominid–the group consisting of all modern and extinct Great Apes (that is, modern humans, chimpanzees, gorillas and orangutans plus all their immediate ancestors)."[20]

Archeogenetics of Melanesia
and the Denisovans

History of Melanesia

In Melanesia, an area comprised of 2,000 islands, the history of its people stems from antiquated times when Australia and New Guinea were connected, some 70,000 years ago. Geographically, Melanesia sits within a 'ring' of Pacific Ocean volcanoes called the "Pacific Rim of Fire, where volcanism runs rampant. Ancient tales of Lemuria entice us to appreciate Pele, the Hawaiian goddess of fire, residing in the southernmost island of Hawai'i, within the volcano Kilauea, central to this volcanic ring. Blavatsky spoke of the South Pacific as being the home of Lemuria or 'Mu,' as it is called.

Melanesia is encompassed by Oceania, a region centered within the islands of the tropical Pacific Ocean, comprised of many peoples, languages and lifestyles. Opinions of what constitutes Oceania range from its three sub-regions of Melanesia, Micronesia, and Polynesia to the entire insular region between Asia and the Americas, including Australasia and the Malay Archipelago. The reality is that the 'ocean,' thus Oceania, is the context for shared geography and economy.[21]

Ethno-Cultural Definition of Melanesia

A study found a high rate of genetic differentiation and diversity among the groups living within the Melanesian islands, with the peoples distinguished by island, language, topography, and geography among the islands. Such diversity developed over tens of thousands of years of settlement before the Polynesian ancestors ever arrived at the islands. For instance, populations developed differently along the coasts than in more isolated valleys.[22]

Melanesians

Melanesians are the dominant inhabitants of Melanesia with many speaking one of many Papuan languages, though a few groups such as the Moluccans, the Motu and Fijians speak Austronesian languages. The

Melanesians appear to have occupied islands from Eastern Indonesia to as far east as the main islands in the Solomon Islands, including Makira and possibly the smaller islands farther to the east.[23]

Denisovans Appear in Melanesia

Using DNA extracted from a finger bone found in 2010 in the Denisova Cave, southern Siberia, we have sequenced the genome of an archaic hominin. This archaic individual is from a group that shares a common origin with Neanderthals. While the population was not involved in the gene flow from Neanderthals into Eurasia, the data suggests that it contributed 4-6% of its genetic material to the genomes of present-day Melanesians. The evidence from Melanesia suggests their territory extended into South Asia, where ancestors of the Melanesians developed. Ancestral Australians also have proportional Denisovan DNA.

The hominin population is named Denisova (after the cave where the tiny finger was discovered) and suggest that it may have been widespread in Asia during the Late Pleistocene epoch from an ancient ancestor who interbred in Africa with Neanderthal and later in Asia. Neanderthals are understood to have migrated out of Africa into Europe and the Denisovans headed east about 400,000 years ago.

This genetic evidence originated from the original fossil found in Siberia where Neanderthals and Denisovans were both found in this unique cave in the Altai Mountains on the border between Russia, China, Mongolia and Kazakhstan. A tooth was also found in Denisova Cave carrying a mitochondrial (mt or maternal) genome highly similar to that of the finger bone. This tooth shares no derived morphological features with Neanderthals or modern humans, further indicating that Denisovans have an evolutionary history distinct from Neanderthals and modern humans.[24, 25, 26]

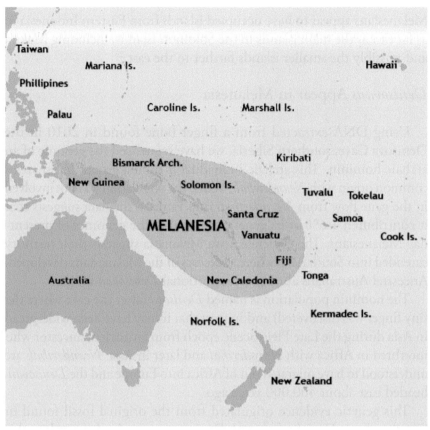

Migration Patterns of *Denisovans, Neanderthals* and *Homo heidelbergensis*

Melanesians not in Siberia

Ancestors of Melanesia were thought to never have been in Siberia. So, how is it that our archaic hominin *Denisova* arrived in Melanesia? Outside of the Asian discovery, the *Denisovan* DNA is present only in Ancestral Aborigines, Papua New Guineans and Melanesians, to date. The *Denisova* hominin is different than other hominins in that 'the *Denisova* individual and the population to which it belonged carry some exceptionally archaic molecular mitochondrial DNA (mtDNA) as well as morphological dental features, i.e., 'large teeth.' Besides the idea that *Denisova* is somewhat of a 'sister to *Neanderthals*, the scientists give more reasons to explain the archaic DNA results in conjunction with a theory about the evolutionary status of *Denisova*.[27]

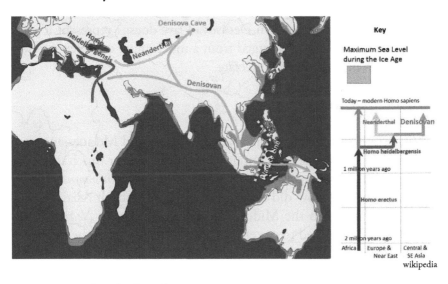

wikipedia

Denisovan Study Implications

Denisova is a sister group to *Neanderthals*. Three possibilities could account for how such features have come to be present in Denisovans. 1) One possibility is that these features were retained in *Denisovans* but became lost in modern humans and *Neanderthals*, 2) A second but not mutually exclusive possibility is that they entered the *Denisova* population through gene flow from some even more diverged hominin. Although such gene flow cannot be detected with the current mtDNA and nuclear DNA data, further sequencing of other hominin remains may allow testing for *Denisova* in the future and finally, 3) A third possibility that could account for the apparently archaic dental morphology, but not the mtDNA, is a reversal to ancestral traits.[28]

Dr. John Hawks has stated that "teeth, types of arrangement and molars versus incisors, etc. are features that indicate a more advanced ape or monkey. Further results have shown that *Denisova* progenitors possess a distinctive population background, a hominin category shared with the *Neanderthal* ancestry. Like *Neanderthal*, the *Denisovans* evolved during lengthy seclusion or at least limited contact from each other and from the sub-Saharan Africans."

Dr. Hawks said: "Maybe *Denisovans* didn't live in South or Southeast Asia at all. If not, that demands that we explain how Australians got their genes, maybe the population was geographically extensive and diverse, but the genome from Denisova Cave doesn't represent it well, maybe African diversity emerged from a much more complex series of interactions than we now appreciate."[29]

Neanderthals and *Denisovans*

Ancestral Australians, Papua New Guineans and Melanesians were wide spread in the past, with an unknown root race or timeframe. The *Neanderthals* were in Africa and Europe and the *Denisovans* were in Siberia and Asia. How did *Denisova* wind up in South Asia? African humans migrated to the Middle East and mixed with *Neanderthals*. *Neanderthal* continued to eastern Siberia, being found in the Denisova Cave, Russia. They bred and migrated to the Pacific and disappeared. Currently, in the Middle East and outside of Africa, DNA is 25% *Neanderthal* and Pacific Islanders are 50% *Denisovan*.[30]

Denisovans Resided in Western Europe

In 2013, mtDNA was discovered in the femur of a 400,000-year-old hominin excavated from the Sima de los Huesos Cave in Spain. Researchers had earlier presumed that this bone was either *Neanderthal* or *Homo heidelbergensis* but further studies found the DNA to be closer to *Denisovan* mtDNA than to *Neanderthal*. One aspect of this study indicates that *Denisovans* lived in Western Europe, where *Neanderthals* were previously thought to be the only inhabitants.[31, 32]

Tibetan *Denisovan* Genome

According to a study published in the journal *Nature*, July 2014, Tibetans have a DNA gene component (haplotype) that supports adaptation to low oxygen levels at high altitude apparently inherited from *Denisova* mtDNA from this region.[33]

Thoughts on the *Denisovan* Discovery

Were our ancestors Denisova progenitors from millennia past?
Did a continental shift, floods, volcanic activity or other geological changes occur that affected the *Denisovan* migration?

Vladivostok, Siberia is not so far from the waters of the Pacific Ocean; what if *Denisova* migrated south to ancient Oceania? Could *Denisova* then migrate east to South America?

5-7 Mya humans, bonobos, gorillas and chimps shared DNA. 2.5 Mya humans shared DNA with *Neanderthal* and about 8 Mya humans and *Denisovans* shared DNA. And 640,000 years ago *Denisovans* shared DNA with *Neanderthal*. We understand currently that *Denisovans* ranged from Siberia to Southeast Asia, lived and interbred with ancestors of some present-day modern humans. About 3% to 5% of DNA from Melanesians, Papua New Guineans and Aboriginal Australians is deriving from Denisovan.[34]

What Are the Implications of *Denisova*?

It appears that many types of hominins, not just from Africa, have an important position in our human evolution. In developing the Anthrogenesis theory, we observe that a possibility exists that Melanesians may have ancestors from Lemuria and possibly Atlantis, since their DNA seems to be localized in Oceania. *Neanderthal* and *Denisova* DNA together are found in Western Europe, and Asia, to date.[35]

How are Humans and *Neanderthals* Related and Studied?

Humans and their close *Neanderthal* relatives began diverging from a common ancestor about 700,000 years ago, and the two groups split permanently some 300,000 years later, according to two comprehensive analyses of *Neanderthal* DNA in 2006. *Neanderthal* genomes and ours were 99.5 percent identical, based on DNA extracted from three Croatian fossils, from a study by Dr. Svante Pääbo, a geneticist with the Max Planck Institute for Evolutionary Anthropology, in Leipzig, Germany.[36]

Anbangbang Rock Shelter, Kakadu National Park, Australia

The Ancient Continent, Australia

With Australia leading as the most archaic continent, proximal to Melanesia, perhaps the Denisova DNA studies will expand as resources increase, moving forward with *Anthrogenesis*. The study of geology and paleoanthropology in former Gondwanaland continents like Africa, South America, India and Australia may ultimately require major revision as well as Oceania, in our history and geography foundations.[37]

Why Human Origins Are Chiefly in Africa?

The reason we find so many hominin fossils in Africa is because it was a "file cabinet" of ape evolution. Current knowledge states that fossils don't survive on continents that historically underwent massive subduction with volcanic activity in the past. Nature's unique design of the Rift Valley in Africa over the last 20 million years allowed sedimentation beds to form and encase millions of fossils beside an elongated section of land, pulling away from the East African tectonic plate. Moisture retained by the Kenyan and Ethiopian mountains mandated that the Rift would dry out, with savanna replacing the humid equatorial forests. With the forests disappearing, the pre-hominin and ape originators were destined to stay close to the valley, leave the trees and evolve within the open country.[38]

Micronesia's Nan Madol

Nan Madol may have been one of the seven cities of ancient Lemuria as postulated by historian James Churchward. Comprising a set of almost 100 stone and coral fill platforms, sitting atop simulated islands and separated by narrow channels with an enclosed outer seawall, Nan Madol is an engineering wonder. Yet, the mystery remains as to why it was such a massive undertaking in the building of this city, because no records exist as to the exact time it was built, where the enormous rocks came from, how they were transported there, and for what reason it was constructed on top of a reef. The stone city of Nan Madol, in Pohnpei, is today part of the Federated States of Micronesia and the only known ancient city ever built on top of a coral reef, thought to have been erected by the Saudeleur people, who built the 92 islands at the edge of a mangrove swamp. The stacks of the cut stone logs were a massive engineering feat of genius, with each log weighing up to 50 tons. Construction is thought to have started 1,500 years ago, with the buildings of this mysterious 1,000-year-old site, the ceremonial seat of an ancient empire.[39, 40]

Sacred Feminine in Nan Madol

Leila Castle, traveler of sacred sites-especially the sacred feminine-has written extensively about her magical experiences in various cultures throughout the world. In the book, *Earthwalking Sky Dancers: Women's Pilgrimages to Sacred Places, Issue 56* (1996), under the section titled, *"Journey to Mu,"* contributing author Caroline Hadley

Nervig pursues a discourse on the effluent by mainstream, in acknowledging the sacred feminine of Nan Madol. She cites an antediluvian history of its islanders, who honor the feminine in all aspects of life, thus "achieving the ideal of balance" in their culture. This feminine approach includes accepting and receiving what the moment gives, so consistent with the spiritual posture of synchronicity with the Universe, Godhead, "being in the moment," use of the intuition, and being content with what life brings, thus defying Western practices of time-keeping and materialism. Hadley Nervig adds that spiritual advisors encourage Western culture to find harmony over the imbalance of a masculine hierarchy; resulting from the Kali Yuga influence in the spectrum of time, as discussed earlier in *Anthrogenesis*.

In response to the ancient Saudeleur dynasty, Hadley Nervig says: "Legend states *clearly* that Nan Madol was built by two twin brothers named Olsihpa and Olsohpa, possibly giants, who came from the outside. By using a special kind of magic, they were able to *fly* the heavy basalt logs into position. Their Pohnpeian helpers also learned these *mwanamwan* techniques and were able to use them during the construction process to make things lighter and easier to move them. There are Pohnpeians today who possess this ability, although it is said that they have forgotten the more difficult aspects of the actual levitation.

"Nan Madol is many miles from the quarries of columnar basalt thought to be the source of its stone. How could a bamboo raft (the only explanation given by outsiders for how the rock logs could have been transported) float ten-to-fifty-ton stones over a shallow reef that is less than four feet deep most of the time? The extraordinary high tides (approximately five feet) that occur only a few times a year would still not accommodate the displacement by the huge stones."

"It is an insult to Pohnpeians that their history is not taken more seriously. Why have researchers ignored the magic factor and not done serious research how it might have worked, especially when there are still sources that are alive! This could be much more than an anthropological study, providing an invaluable source of information on the human mind and its capabilities in relation to the law of physics, as well as a better understanding of past civilizations."

In *Anthrogenesis*, we intend to enlighten the community to voyage into research hitherto sidestepped by mainstream sources. In his book, *Sacred Places* (Inner Traditions/Bear & Co, Santa Fe, NM., 1990), James

Swan, Ph.D., has chronicled sacred mysteries, citing shamanic rituals of the Indigenous Native Peoples (Hopi and Navajo), the healing techniques of Stanislov Grof, M.D. and the mythology of Joseph Campbell, to mention a few, classified as phenomena which conventional archaeology has ignored.

"The Pohnpeians tell a story of Isokelekel, a son born from a Kosraean (local island of Kosrae) mother, with his father being the god Nahnsapwe. Exacting a 'warrior's revenge' for his father's exile by the bequeathed Saudeleur sovereign (said to be descended from Olsihpa and Olsohpa), Nahnsapwe assembled 333 warriors to Pohnpei, effectively forestalling succession of the insidious monarchs, ultimately liberating Nan Madol. But, a question arose by the three chiefs of the city; how to choose the next king. Eventually, a wooden outrigger canoe was spotted hovering over the island of Temwen. An attempted inspection was thwarted by the chiefs because they were raised into the airborne canoe, where waited the God Luhk. He came to establish a royal system in Pohnpei, naming Isokelekel as king, which instituted the royal lineage of Nahnmwarkis, which has endured to current times."

"Most Pohnpeians believe that Nan Madol began with the arrival of the twin sorcerers, Olsihpa and Olsohpa, from the mythical Western Katau. The twins, said to be much taller than native Pohnpeians, sought a place to build an altar, so they might worship Nahnisohn Sahpw, the god of agriculture. The brothers were successful and built an altar at Nan Madol, where they performed rituals to levitate the huge stones with the aid of a flying dragon. When Olsihpa died of old age, Olsohpa became the first Saudeleur."[40, 41]

The Yonaguni Mystery

Blavatsky said that Lemuria was destroyed by volcanoes which triggered explosions all through the South Pacific. The Yonaguni Monument, located off the coast of Yonaguni, in the westernmost portion of the Ryukyus, was discovered in 1986 at Yonaguni Island, west of Japan, and may be a remnant of Lemuria. An archaic looking structure, it is described as a stepped-pyramidal edifice and is close in proximity to the island remnants of ancient Lemuria, Yonaguni's assemblies are thought to be much older than 4,000 years, says discoverer and diver Kihachiro Aratake.

He consequently began working in tandem with Professor Masaaki Kimura of the College of the Ryukyus, a marine geologist at Ryukyu University in Okinawa, who has conducted numerous studies on the Yonaguni relics and site.

Stones recovered from the site have been Carbon-14 dated to over 3,000-years-old. Plate tectonics and shifting caused what Dr. Kimura refers to as a temple, to fall beneath the waters. He attributes the masonry to ancestors who understood the methods of carving these huge underwater structures. One observes a rock, carved in the shape of a human face, as well as stepped structures; one with a facsimile of a turtle on its top.

Graham Hancock and Robert Schoch examined the Yonaguni ruins some years ago, finding evidence of very ancient human habitation, including tombs and other structures artificially carved from the bedrock. The pyramid, a rectangular stone ziggurat, completes a portion of the underwater complex of stone structures which bear a resemblance to ramps, steps and terraces. Hancock and Schoch date the site on a spectrum of between 5,000 to 8,000 years old.

High above, on Yonaguni Island, hidden within the forest, is another carved face, situated at the apogee of the island, reported by islanders to be a 'sacred icon,' left by the ancestors to protect the underwater site. It is exceptionally evocative of the underwater face.[42, 43]

Micronesia Creation Myth

"Regarding the creation of the world, they say that Puntan was a very ingenious man who lived in an imaginary place which existed before earth and sky were made. This good man, being about to die called his sister who, like himself, had been born without father or mother. Making known to her the benefit he wished to confer upon humanity, he gave her all his powers so that when he died she could create from his breast and back, the earth and sky, from his eyes, the sun and the moon, a rainbow from his eyebrows, and thus adjusting everything else."[44]

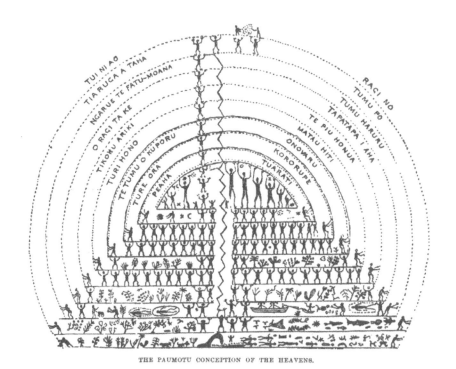

THE PAUMOTU CONCEPTION OF THE HEAVENS.

The Paumotu Conception of the Heavens of Creation

Notes on the Drawing

It is explained by the natives that the lowest division represents a period when the world was inhabited by animals not known to the Islanders, and when the sky hung low over earth and sea. In the third division are shown the first homicide, the first burials, and the first canoe.

In the fourth the first coconut tree, pandanus tree, Puatea (Tourne-fortia) tree, and Tou (Cordia Subcordata) tree.

In the ninth, on right side, the Constellation Scorpio, and on the left side, the moon and a star and a man making an offering or sacrifice at a fire. The names written outside each circle are as follows:

113

Outer Circle left side	'Iui ni ao
Second	Tia ruga a taha
Third	Garu te fatumoana
Fourth	O ragi te ke
Fifth	Tikohu ariki
Sixth	Turi hono
Seventh	Te tumu o Kuporu
Eighth	Ture Ora
Ninth	Peaha
Outer Circle right side	Ragi no
Second	Tumu no
Third	Tumu haruru
Fourth	Tapatapa i aha
Fifth	Te piu honua
Sixth	Matau hiti
Seventh	Onovaru
Eighth	Kororupe
Ninth	Tuarati

The canoes are those built by Rata; the inscription above the sail of the middle one is "Tutu nei tere a tetoira"—"Sailing with a light easterly breeze to the westward." Note the ladder-like masts which were those used on the Tuamotu sea-going pahi canoe of old.

I am doubtful as to the value of this drawing, as I think that the author was probably influenced by missionary teachings and by pictures which he had seen.

For instance, the figures of the Ass and the Ape in the lowest division: the homicide in the third suggests Cain and Abel: the offering (if it was intended to signify such) in the ninth suggests Abraham and Isaac.

Nevertheless, the general idea is that of ancient tradition: the raising of the heavens by human or rather superhuman effort. The names of the heavens are also interesting.

Paiore, the Artist

The artist, Paiore drew the representation of how his people view their ancient times and cosmology. The following statement reflects Paiore's thoughts on the drawing.

"The likeness is of things made known to the people of ancient times. The form of this our World and the account of our ancestors, and of the beginning of the movement of animal life. This is the true and succinct description (literally a bundle tied up with a knotted string) of mankind which was confined in narrow spaces, and of the origin of things and of the various trees (or vegetation) and of the bringing forth of animals which suckle their young, such as four-footed animals. These are to be seen in this sheet of paper as understood by the writer, I, Paiore, 1869."[45, 46]

Papua New Guinea Creation Myth

"The idea that there was a sky world which was a replica of this one was fairly widespread in Papua New Guinea. The Ayon pygmies of the interior tell how Tumbrenjak climbed down to earth to go hunting and fishing. When he attempted to return, he found the rope cut. He cried and his wife looked down and cried. His wife threw down fire and all the fruits and vegetables, including four cucumbers. As soon as the man walked off into the bush, these turned into four women. When he returned he found all his work done and heard the women's laughter. The offspring of this man and his four wives are the ancestors of the different tribes."[47]

Post-Apocalyptic South Pacifica

Master Kuthumi clarifies in the *Mahatma Letters*, written primarily to Madame Blavatsky that "Lemuria can no longer be compared with Atlantis any more than Europe with America." Lemuria was destroyed by volcanoes, Atlantis sustained floods, subsequently sinking, and most of the population were drowned with their high civilizations and gods. Between these two catastrophes, only a short period of about 700,000 years had elapsed. Blavatsky envisioned Lemuria as "covering a vast area, stretching from "the foot of the Himalayas, which separated it from the inland sea, rolling its waves over what is now Tibet, Mongolia, and the great Gobi Desert; from Chittagong, westward to Hardwar, and eastward to Assam. From thence, it stretched South across what is known to us as Southern India, Ceylon, and Sumatra; then embracing on its way, as we go South, Madagascar on its right hand and Australia and Tasmania on its left, it ran down to within a few degrees of the Antarctic Circle; from Australia, an inland region on the Mother Continent in those ages, it extended far into the Pacific Ocean."

The Master Morya explains that "the Asian races stem from the 7th and final sub-race of Atlantis, called "Mongols" which include most of the northern Asian peoples. The indigenous peoples of Africa and Australia originate from earliest Atlantean sub-races as well as the Seventh and final sub-race of the Lemurian Root Race."[48]

Polynesian Creation Story

"Ku, the Creator, began to chant over the great watery chaos.
"Things born from darkness are darkness."
"Things born from light are lightness."

As the chant continues Po, the earth was born, and Ao, the sky was born. And from the watery chaos Ku chanted out Kanalos, the great squid, the sea god, and Kane-the human and Hina, the earth mother. Kane made many animals, many plants and fresh water in many forms. But he wanted to have a being which looked and acted like him. So he took some soft red clay from Hawaiki- the home land and created Hine-hau-ona;

Pixabay

the Earth-born woman. Kane and Hine-hau-ona had a child named Hine-titama- the dawn woman.

Then Kane did great wrong. He mated with Hine-titama, not telling her who he was and as soon as she did learn it she went screaming to her mother's domain, Po, the earth, and the land of the Dead. Hine-titana cried out, "You have broken the cord to the earth," and henceforth, Kane could not touch the Earth. And so it is that humans live on the Earth, and when they die they return to Po, the land of dreams, lovemaking, and spirit, so they can never be touched by Kane."[49]

The Lost Island of Mu in the South Pacific

Many 'Children of the Sun" are said to have migrated from latter day Lemuria and Atlantis to the South Pacific islands and continents. In Hawaii, the 'heiaus' are similar to faraway temples of Okinawa, with stone walkways, wooden carvings and shrines, and are said to have been built by the 'Menehune,' a fair-haired race of very small statured, but excessively strong ancestors. On Kauai, there is a tale of the great island of 'Mu' having disappeared in the flood, with migrants bringing the culture of ancestors to Hawaii.

Japan Creation Myth

"Long ago all the elements were mixed together with one germ of life. This germ began to mix things around and around until the heavier part sank and the lighter part rose. A muddy sea that covered the entire earth was created. From this ocean grew a green shoot. It grew and grew until it reached the clouds and there it was transformed into a god. Soon this god grew lonely and it began

Inari and Her Foxes, Courtesy of Dreolin

to create other gods. The last two gods it made, Izanagi and Izanami, were the most remarkable.

"One day as they were walking along they looked down on the ocean and wondered what was beneath it. Izanagi thrust his staff into the waters and as he pulled it back up some clumps of mud fell back into the sea. They began to harden and grow until they became the islands of Japan.

"The two descended to these islands and began to explore, each going in different directions. They created all kinds of plants. When they met again they decided to marry and have children to inhabit the land. The first child Izanami bore was a girl of radiant beauty. The gods decided she was too beautiful to live in Japan, so they put her up in the sky and she became the sun. Their second daughter, Tsuki-yami, became the moon and their third and unruly son, Sosano-wo, was sentenced to the sea, where he creates storms."[50]

The goddess Amaterasu, born from the left eye of her father, Izanagi, herself later bore a son who would become the first emperor of Japan and all following emperors since then claimed descent from her.

Creation Stories of Easter Island

Rapa Nui or Easter Island is the world's most isolated, inhabited island, separated by thousands of miles of water from any continent, with Pitcairn Island being the closest stop. On Easter, 1722, Dutch explorer, Jacob Roggeveen discovered the island. It was then inhabited by three distinct races of humanity- "Dark-skinned, Red-skinned, and very Pale-skinned People with red hair." The Moai statues, standing at 30 feet, weighing 82 tons or so, tell a story of a people who wanted to leave a legacy. It is said that a battle ensued between the indigenous peoples, the 'Short' and 'Long Ears' which legend says were enemies and fought to the death. The 'Short Ears' were the victors.

Theosophical literature says that the Lemurians built these Moai as replicas of themselves upon arriving to Rapa Nui after the fiery end of their island. Perhaps there is some truth to this because the oldest name for the island is 'Te Pito o Te Henua, which means 'the center of the world.'. Both Blavatsky and Scott-Elliot describe the 'Cyclopean' statues as corresponding to the actual size of the Lemurians, with, if we stay the literary course, enormous bodies erected at "27 feet tall by 8 feet across the shoulders."

The sanctuary at Ahu Akivi, thought to have been built in the 14th century CE, is a sacred, celestial observatory reconstructed by archaeologists, who found the statues face down to the ground. The mysteries lie in its location, far inland with the seven Moai, their closely matched size, positioned in a single line and looking outward to the sea- aligned to the equinox. Legend holds that the seven statues represent ancient Polynesian ancestors who traveled from far away islands to the Moai's new homeland.

There are many questions surrounding the origins, myths and spiritual practices of the indigenous peoples prior to the known migrations from South America. While there are differing theories about the actual date of settlement by the South Pacific peoples, the statues seem to tell a story that perhaps the island is very, very ancient, given that many of the statues are deeply buried, some up to the chest, which would take a millennium to condense the earth piled around these massive structures. Some say that the statues were moved with ropes but that seems a bit foolish in light of new research that indicates heavy stones cannot be moved with a rope and pulley system. The people have an ancient hieroglyphic script, 'rongorongo', which resembles the archaic style seen throughout the Mesoamerican, the American Southwest, Göbekli Tepe and other worldwide sites with petroglyphs portraying stick humans, birds, lizards and symbols. Robert Schoch, Ph.D. of Boston University, reports that these glyphs may relate to a worldwide solar outburst responsible for deluges and lost cultures. Is it possible that the flora and fauna which may have been prevalent on Rapa Nui at one point in time have disappeared with an inundation from our past? The island today is essentially barren of complex plant and animal life save for those which were imported to the island. Easter Island continues to hold a mystery that only time can explain.[51, 52]

Notes

1. Churchward, James, *Sacred Symbols of Mu*, 1988, CW Daniel Co, LTD, Essex, England and The Brotherhood of Life, Inc., Albuquerque, NM.

2. http://www.sacred-texts.com/atl/ssm/ssm05.htm

3. http://www.sacred-texts.com/atl/ssm/ssm05.htm

4. http://www.sacred-texts.com/atl/ssm/ssm05.htm

5. Churchward, James, *Sacred Symbols of Mu*, 1988, CW Daniel Co, LTD, Essex, England and The Brotherhood of Life, Inc., Albuquerque, NM.

6. https://docs.google.com/file/d/0B17t2HhTjZgFcnMzaW4wanRYc1U/edit

7. Wilcock, David, *Shift of the Ages, Convergence, Volumes I-III*, 2002.

8. http://www.divinecosmos.com/: Website of David Wilcock.

9. http://www.thefreedictionary.com/mosaic

10. Scott-Elliot, W. 1972. *The Story of Atlantis and The Lost Lemuria*, Theosophical Publishing House, Fletcher & Son, LTD., Norwich, Great Britain.

11. Churchward, James, *Sacred Symbols of Mu*, CW Daniel Co, LTD, Essex, England and The Brotherhood of Life, Inc., Albuquerque, NM, 1988.

12. S. Cerve, Wishar, *Lemuria, The Lost Continent of the Pacific*, Supreme Grand Lodge of the Rosicrucians, San Jose, CA, 1984.

13. http://www.lemuria.net/

14. *Journal of Polynesia Science*, Volume 58, 1949, Volume 58, No. 1, The Polynesian Collection of Trinity College, Dublin; and the National Museum of Ireland, by J. D. Freeman; Contents, Paper and p. 1-18.

15. http://www.ancient-origins.net/human-origins-folklore/australian-aboriginals-creation-myth-00229

16. http://www.history-nz.org/maori9.html

17. http://www.australianmuseum.net.au/creation-story-from-lake-toba-sumatra-indonesia

18. http://www.sulawesi-experience.com/news/bada-valley.html

19. http://www.sacred-texts.com/pac/om/om06.htm

20. http://australianmuseum.net.au/hominid-and-hominin-whats-the-difference

21. http://www.newworldencyclopedia.org/entry/Melanesia

22. Friedlaender, Jonathan, *Genome Scans Show Polynesians Have Little Genetic Relationship to Melanesians*, Press Release, Temple University, 18 January 2008.

23. http://www.sciencemag.org/content/309/5743/2072

24. http://www.nature.com/nature/journal/v468/n7327/full/nature09710.html

25. http://www.nature.com/nature/journal/v505/n7481/full/nature12886.html

26. http://www.ucmp.berkeley.edu/quaternary/pleistocene.php

27. http://www.nature.com/nature/journal/v468/n7327/pdf/nature09710.pdf

28. http://www.nature.com/nature/journal/v468/n7327/pdf/nature09710.pdf

29. http://johnhawks.net/weblog/reviews/denisova/denisova-high-coverage-2012.html

30. http://www.nature.com/nature/journal/v468/n7327/pdf/nature09710.pdf

31. http://www.nature.com/news/hominin-dna-baffles-experts-1.14294

32. http://www.nature.com/nature/journal/v505/n7481/full/nature12886.html

33. http://www.nature.com/nature/journal/v512/n7513/full/nature13408.html

34. http://www.nature.com/nature/journal/v505/n7481/full/nature12886.html

35. http://www.livescience.com/7944-mysteries-neanderthals.html

36. http://www.livescience.com/1122-neanderthal-99-5-percent-human.html

37. http://earthsci.unimelb.edu.au/Joyce/heritage/EHarticletext.html

38. http://humanorigins.si.edu/research/east-african-research/adventures-rift-valley-interactive

39. http://www.davidhatcherchildress.com/lost-cities-ancient-lemuria-pacific

40. http://www.newdawnmagazine.com/articles/the-lost-lands-of-mu-and-lemuria-was-australia-once-part-of-a-sunken-continent

---

40. Castle, Leila, editor, *Earthwalking Sky Dancers: Women's Pilgrimages to Sacred Places*, Issue 56, Journey to Mu, by Carol Hadley Nervig, 1996, Frog Books, Berkeley, CA, pp. 95-110.
41. Swan, James, Ph.D., *Sacred Places*, 1990, Inner Traditions/Bear & Co, Santa Fe, NM.
42. http://www.grahamhancock.com
43. http://www.robertschoch.com/yonagunicontent.html
44. http://www.janeresture.com/micronesia_myths
45. http://www.jps.auckland.ac.nz/document?wid=1094&page=0&action=null :
46. *JPS, Volume 28* 1919, Volume 28, No. 112, The Paumotu Conception of the Heavens and of Creation, by J. L. Young, p. 209-211.
47. http://www.janeresture.com/melanesia_myths/png.htm
48. http://www.blavatskytheosophy.com/articles
49. http://www.mythome.org/creatpoly.html
50. http://dept.cs.williams.edu/~lindsey/myths/myths_17.html
51. http://www.geographia.com/chile/easterisland.htm
52. Schoch, Robert, Forgotten Civilization, *The Role of Solar Outburst in Our Past and Future,* 2012, Inner Traditions, VT.

Olmec La Venta Stele 19, Courtesy Audrey and George Delange Taube, Karl A., Olmec Art at Dumbarton Oaks,
Dumbarton Oaks Research Library and Collection, 2004, Trustees for Harvard University, Washington, D.C.

Chapter Seven

The Feathered Serpent

"Not for the first time I felt myself confronted by the dizzying possibility that an entire episode in the story of mankind might have been forgotten. Indeed, it seemed to me then, as I overlooked the mathematical city of the gods from the summit of the Pyramid of the Moon, that our species could have been afflicted with some terrible amnesia and that the dark period so blithely and dismissively referred to as `prehistory' might turn out to conceal unimagined truths about

123

our own past. What is prehistory, after all, if not a time forgotten – a time for which we have no records? What is prehistory if not an epoch of impenetrable obscurity through which our ancestors passed but about which we have no conscious remembrance? It was out of this epoch of obscurity, configured in mathematical code along astronomical and geodetic lines, that Teotihuacan with all its riddles was sent down to us. And out of that same epoch came the great Olmec sculptures, the inexplicably precise and accurate calendar the Mayans inherited from their predecessors, the inscrutable geoglyphs of Nazca, the mysterious Andean city of Tiahuanaco and so many other marvels of which we do not know the provenance. It is almost as though we have awakened into the daylight of history from a long and troubled sleep, and yet continue to be disturbed by the faint but haunting echoes of our dreams." – Graham Hancock, *Fingerprints of the Gods: The Evidence of Earth's Lost Civilization*, October, 2015.

Olmec Provenance

Anthrogenesis continues exploration on the underpinnings of the gifted Olmec, true artisans of this land. The Olmec sites are located in the Mexican states of southern Veracruz and Tabasco on the Isthmus of Tehuantepec. The isthmus provided the shortest land trade route between Atlantic and Pacific ports since transoceanic trade may have been extensive for millennia. Their most important sites in order of importance were La Venta, San Lorenzo Tenochtitlan and Tres Zapotes. Olmec lands covered the Gulf of Mexico's south coast, coastal plains of southern Veracruz and territories divided by the Coatzacoalcos River basin system, too. But the Olmec cultural influence is thought to have extended over vast areas of Central America, from Guatemala and El Salvador to Nicaragua and Costa Rica. By c. 1750 BCE, the Olmec civilization was well-established in Mesoamerica, until 400 BCE.[1]

And the history of this magnificent people is truly enigmatic. Is it possible that they were ancestors of the Lemurians or perhaps the subsequent Atlanteans? The Aztecs walked their sacred streets and lived in their ancient cities. The Mayans were credited with their glyphs. Current people treasure their artifacts. But how the Olmec originated then vanished without a clue continues to remain a mystery.

Blavatsky points out in *The Secret Doctrine* that there were adjoining lands between the coast of Chile and Polynesia, called 'Pacificus.' This is where the Pacific portion of Lemuria is said to have existed in prediluvian times. Along with dialogue from anthropologist Dr. Charles Carter Blake (1840-1897), Blavatsky adds, "The voyage of the 'Challenger' has proved the existence of three long ridges in the Atlantic Ocean, one extending for more than three thousand miles, and lateral spurs may, by connecting these ridges, account for the marvellous similarity of the fauna of the Atlantic islands." (*Secret Doctrine.* Vol II, page 782)

The Olmec homeland was conceivably a cosmopolitan center where worldwide cultures intermingled. The Olmec art, with its many faces may well reminisce this multinational civilization.[2]

Advanced Resources and Trade

Olmec city-centers were spaced such that they ruled their population and domain, distributing prized natural resources throughout the Olmec society. San Lorenzo Tenochtitlan was centrally based in Olmec territory and along with La Venta and Laguna de Los Cerros, stretched from east to west with the ability to manage the vast flood plain area and fertile land of the Coatzacoalcos River Basin, thus controlling the river trade routes. San Lorenzo Tenochtitlan architecture featured public-ceremonial buildings, elite residences, and houses of commoners. The Olmec incorporated basalt drainage systems in their sites, covered with capstones they served as aqueducts. La Venta provided rich inlets for harvesting coastal sea life and potential for trading with other sea based cultures very early on, which would have included cacao, rubber, and salt. Laguna de Los Cerros, close to the Tuxtlas Mountains has basalt reserves, a stone needed to manufacture stone monuments and buildings.

The bountiful coastal areas of the Gulf of Mexico afforded the Olmec cultivation of corn and beans. They certainly would have gathered the vegetable-plant sources such as palm nuts. With the ocean so close, sea-life was invaluable in the form of clams and turtles.[3, 4]

Heart of the Olmec People

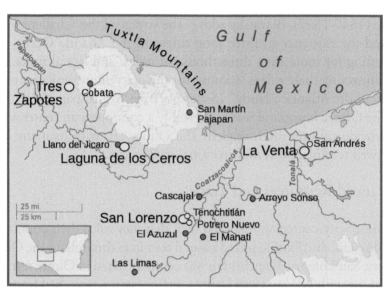

Madman2001

Olmec Colossal Heads

The Olmec colossal heads are the most renowned symbol of the Olmec civilization. No known pre-Columbian text exists which explains the origin or meaning of these impressive monuments. The largest head is about *twice the height of an average human male*. A total of seventeen heads have been discovered to date, thought to represent warrior-chieftains, perchance a ruling dynasty. The frequency of African and Asian facial features on the stone heads fuels evidence of both Asian and African connections with Pre-Columbian American, with finds ranging from linguistics, plant geography to skeletons and terracotta figures, synonymous with ancient North African Tifinagh inscriptions found in the Virgin Islands.[5]

In 1862, Jose Melgar unearthed the first colossal Olmec head in Tres Zapotes, the third Olmec capital, while the remaining colossal heads were retrieved chiefly in La Venta and San Lorenzo Tenochtitlan.

Monument Q is an exquisitely carved head displaying 'Ethiopian' style braided hair at the back of the head, with African features. The colossal head of 'The Grandmother' at Monument 5 illustrates the finest in legendary Olmec art. The heads were carved from single blocks or boulders of volcanic basalt, quarried at the Tuxtlas Mountains, 50 miles from La Venta.[6]

The Olmec Indigenous People

Notice that the figures have enlarged skulls. Mainstream explains this as headdress but Blavatsky mentions very large heads and bodies of the ancient third and fourth races.

The Many Faces of the Olmec

Olmec Colossal Head   Olmec Asian Figurine

San Lorenzo Colossal Head 6 Photo courtesy of Unwiredben

"One of the most intriguing aspects of the Olmecs is their lifelike portrayal of different racial types in their art. From the earliest discoveries of the huge carved-stone African heads, to the extraordinary similarity to the Chinese Shang culture in art and text, the Olmecs appear to have been influenced by several racial types, making them possibly one of the earliest true multi-cultural societies in the Americas. There has been much debate over this issue, although the evidence is in favour of the probability of contact with old-world cultures from both the Pacific and the Atlantic, it is yet to be officially accepted by academia. It is perhaps no coincidence that the Gulf of Mexico is the narrowest continental separation between the two oceans."[7]

"Ancient Olmec artefacts give the theory further substance. The written language found on the Olmec jars, pottery, and statues reveals what could be the actual influence of Chinese culture. Professor Xu points out that various words found on these decorative objects match exactly with those used in Shang China: Sun, Mountain, Artist, Water, Rain, Sacrifice, Health, Plants, Wealth, and Earth. In fact, the majority of the 146 characters used by the Olmec are exactly the same as primitive Chinese writing. When Xu showed the Olmec artefacts to university students involved in analyzing primitive Chinese culture, they actually believed it was ancient Chinese script"[8] – Dr. Mike Xu, Professor of Chinese Studies, University of Central Oklahoma

Caucasoid Carvings of Spanish Conquistadores?

A stela discovered in Monte Alban highlights the African featured Olmec, carved together with bearded Caucasoid men. How and when did these two races migrate and live together in this great culture?

A multitude of different sculptures, carvings and structures led anthropologists to attribute them to the Maya, until the large Olmec heads were later discovered along with the bearded Caucasoid art. Neither beard nor moustache had ever been seen in the Amerindians. As far as that goes, the African and Asian peoples portrayed in Olmec art have little to no facial hair.

Besides differing physical features and culture, there must be a significant residual amount of history which exists between the Olmec and Maya, if we compute their timelines. Mainstream science hasn't settled on an explanation of their oppositional details, with chronological impediments, yet retention of common household geography.

Lest we now add the Caucasoid individuals, explained as 'Spanish conquistadores,' before their recorded time of arrival in Mesoamerica, a contrariwise case in point is the Caucasoid individuals, explained as 'Spanish conquistadores,' appearing long before their recorded time of arrival in Mesoamerica. Therefore, with the presence of carved Caucasoid stelae, we now must enlarge upon Olmec culture to include these Caucasoid individuals. But, all we really know about the Olmec origins is that they were an intelligent, creative society that appeared in Mesoamerica for several thousand years, then vanished without a trace.

So, the carved Caucasoid-looking heads indicate that the Olmec culture must have had contact or even included Caucasoid individuals. But, all we really know about the Olmec origins is that they were an intelligent, creative society that appeared in Mesoamerica and existed for several thousand years, then vanished without a trace. Who were the Caucasians and where did they come from? Were they colonists from Mu, the island destroyed by volcanoes and earthquakes, located in the South Pacific area? Blavatsky says that Lemuria influenced migration throughout the South Pacific to the Americas, and beyond.[9, 10]

La Venta Sacred Pyramid and Temple

"Archaeoastronomical investigation has shown that the pyramid at La Venta was intentionally aligned toward the polar area of the sky and to specific stars in the Big Dipper. The level of precision in these alignments is quite impressive. However, the effects of precession inevitably caused these alignments to "go out of sync," and the Olmec astronomers and temple-builders responded by periodically reorienting the pyramid. Their solution, however, was bound to be temporary, for precession would once again cause a misalignment between the stars and the pyramid. Nevertheless, the realignments of La Venta's pyramid provide evidence that Olmec astronomers were aware of precession." – John Major Jenkins, *Maya Cosmogenesis*, 1998.

At La Venta, seemingly constructed as a sacred city, one observes the 'Great Pyramid,' built c. 1000 BCE, the oldest pyramid in the New World. Within the plaza are altars and stelae positioned with the mounds in the 'Ceremonial Court,' which is surrounded by basalt columns, north of the Great Pyramid. The midline construction of the site was oriented 8° west of north, with this alignment echoed in the central avenue, pointing to the principal mountain.

"The site was aligned towards the stars of both Ursa Major (the Big Dipper) and Sadr (gamma Cygni) the central star in Cygnus, calculated by archeologist Marion Popenoe Hatch in the '70s. Andrew Collins in *The Cygnus Mystery* also addressed this observation. Her (Hatch's) astronomical analysis found they were both used to determine the time of the summer solstice, a tradition she traces back to 2000 BCE through computer calculations. The symbol in Maya texts used to represent Cygnus she has identified as the cross bands glyph, which appears also on much earlier Olmec statues of the 'were-jaguar."[11, 12]

The stars were studied by the Olmec to an excellence which undoubtedly set the foundation of their Long Count Calendar. The 'Mosaic Pavements' of polished serpentine, incorporate the bar-and-four-dots design, with central bars in each, illustrating the four elements of the quincunxes, strategically located at inter-cardinal points. This astrological significance gives credence to Olmec knowledge in the ritual practice of cosmology.

Reminiscent of the Egyptian antiquities and temples complexes, discoveries made beneath the main plaza, by the archaeology team of Stirling and Drucker, included polished jade, elaborate paintings, clay floors and several royal burials including a sarcophagus carved like a crocodile. Additional graves were discovered in a tomb chamber constructed from basalt columns with burials offerings of stunning greenstone figures, jewelry, and ax tools.[13, 14]

Antiquity of the Olmec

The Olmec are the mother culture of Mesoamerica. Their civilization is now thought to be at least 3,200 years old, exemplifying an impressive and exquisite society from city-plans organized around sacred geometry and astronomy, to the magnificent colossal heads and artistic crafting of stelae and mosaics, a hallmark in our Anthrogenesis Concept as seen worldwide in ancient, prosperous cultures.

Stonework produced within Olmec culture echo Egypt's finest sculptures. Olmec artists carved

La Venta, Monument 5

large man-jaguar warriors that are similar to the Egyptian sphinxes on display showing lions with the heads of gods or kings. The seated statue of an Egyptian scribe carved between 2465 BCE and 2323 BCE shows stonework and attention to detail that parallels a seated stone sculpture of an Olmec lord. There is no evidence the Olmec and Egyptians ever met.[15]

Illustrated by their royals wearing heavenly symbols, the Olmec created a belt or sky-band comprised of sky gods symbols: the Sun God and the Moon, the Sun, Venus, day, night and the star views. Their kings are depicted carrying bars decorated as sky-bands to indicate their heavenly mandate, designed with ornate jaguar pelt attire; the spots were understood to signify the stars, encircled by the sky-band, giving the ruler a halo of celestial authority.

"The jaguar is America's largest and most powerful cat and for more than three thousand years it has been Mexico's most enduring symbolic animal. The jaguar's image, sometimes appearing alongside the smaller ocelot and the plain-coated puma, prowls the art of most ancient Mexican civilizations, from the Olmec to the Aztec." – Dr. Nicholas Saunders, Department of Archaeology and Anthropology, School of Arts, University of Bristol.[16, 17]

The Ball Games

Rubber ball games were rampant throughout Mesoamerica. This ball game was used for recreational and religious purposes by many tribes from the region. The word "Olmec" is translated from Nahuatl to mean "rubber people." Archaeologists working at La Venta found what remained of a ball court, thus advancing the game theory with

Courtesy of Wikiwand

Olmec ball courts providing the missing link. So with the early discovery of rubber balls at the Olmec site, El Manati in Tenochtitlan by San Lorenzo, the antiquity of Olmec ball games was confirmed.[18, 19]

Olmec Had The Wheel!

Archaeologist Matthew Stirling excavated the bottom half of Stela C at Tres Zapotes in 1939. The carved basalt stele exhibiting an Olmec style had a jaguar on one side. The opposite side was inscribed with Mesoamerican 'Long Count' calendar, indicating a date later calculated to 7.16.6.16.18-September 3, 32 BCE. Besides the stela, he also found a small jaguar mounted on wheels, quelling the long held belief that Pre-Columbia had no wheels![20]

And It's Called Epi-Olmec Script

"Among one of the most important was the discovery of an inscribed slab found under the waters of the Acula River near the village of La Mojarra in 1986 in the Mexican state of Veracruz. Dubbed Stela 1 of La Mojarra, this monument was inscribed with 465 glyphs arranged in 21 columns, and the image of a ruler. The writing on it is nothing like any other writing system in Mesoamerica, such as Maya, Zapotec, Mixtec, or Aztec; although like the Maya it also used the Long Count."[21]

The Olmec had already begun to use a true zero, a shell glyph; several centuries before Ptolemy, by the fourth century BCE. Now termed 'Epi-Olmec,' we see they were the earliest users of the 'bar and dot' system of recording time. The Epi-Olmec script is also known as 'La Mojarra script' after the discovery's location. Discovery of artifacts in scripted with Epi-Olmec or close facsimiles are found in range of the Isthmus of Tehuantepec. Various examples of artifacts with Epi-Olmec have been excavated but none are as significant as Stela I. This glyph later became an integral part of the Maya numerals.[22, 23]

Olmec Devise the Mesoamerican Calendar

The Olmecs were clever mathematicians and astronomers that we now believe made the Mesoamerican calendars.

"Tres Zapotes is famous for Stela C, a rectangular stone block with a post-Olmec Izapa-style mask on one side, and a Long Count date expressed in bars and dots on the other. The date, 7.16.6.16.18 6 Eznab (31 BCE), was at the time, the Mesoamerica's oldest 'Mayan' Long

132

Count inscriptions. What was shocking about this was that Tres Zapotes was not a Maya site—not in any way at all. It was entirely, exclusively, unambiguously Olmec. This suggested that the Olmecs, not the Maya, must have been the inventors of the calendar, and that the Olmecs, not the Maya, ought to be recognized as 'the mother culture' of Central America."[24]

Olmec and the 12 Tribes of Israel

It appears that the Olmec made twelve migrations to the New World. A famous Mayan historian, Ixtlixochitl, records that the Olmec came to Mexico in 'ships of bark' and landed at Pontochan, which they then commenced to populate. These people are frequently depicted in the Mayan books/writings carrying trade goods. The tree depicts seven branches and twelve roots. The seven branches may represent the seven major clans of the Olmec. The twelve roots extending into the water from the boat might signify the "twelve roads through the sea," mentioned by Friar Diego Landa—or possibly the 12 Tribes of Israel.[25, 26]

Our Olmec Forefathers

The Olmec culture established a civilization with industry, art and religion, agronomy, while constructing sacred cities with pyramids, colossal heads and temples, and an oligarchy consistent with later Mesoamerican peoples. The hottest news is that along this course, the Olmec instituted their complex yet artistic script-language, in conjunction with their astronomically precise Mesoamerican calendar. This wealth of cultural heritage is only now beginning to gain acceptance among Mesoamerican academia.

San Lorenzo Tenochtitlan was an age-old, sophisticated Olmec municipality long before relocation was initiated in the course of La Venta's magnificent construction. Thus, the importance of ceremonial complexes far outlasted many of the generations to come. Successive cultures became established within former Olmec lands, most notably the Maya to the east, the Zapotec to the southwest and the Teotihuacan culture to the west. Olmec instituted sacred spiritual belief, fathoming the heavens in their conclusions, fashioned in ways, during the course of their reign, which today cannot be fully understood.[77]

Olmec Hatha Yoga Masters

Are these Olmec Practicing Postures of Hatha Yoga?

According to H.P. Blavatsky, Lemurians practiced Hatha Yoga as a part of their worship of the Father who taught them that brotherhood and simple compassion is god-like.[28]

Beginning in 2400 BCE, the Mesoamerican yoga practice called Chi' is cited in the ancient tongue of Ch'orti.' The phrase "ah wa' ch'a' ban" means "the one being in a good horizontal (position)" in Ch'orti.'[29, 30, 31, 32, 33, 34, 35, 36]

Two-Legged King Pigeon Pose
– Reverse Rajakapotasana
Source unknown

One-Legged King Pigeon Pose –
Reverse Eka Pada Rajakapotasana
Source unknown

King Pigeon Pose-reverse,
chin up – Kapotasana. Photo
courtesy of Michel Zabe

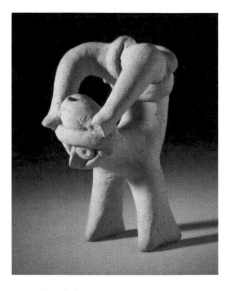

Vrischikasana, Scorpion pose
LACMOA, Colima, Mexico

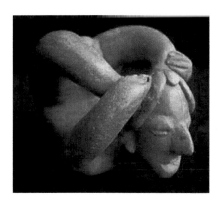

Body Roll, Limbs to head
Source unknown

Mesoamerican Glyph For
Yoga Meditation: *Chi'* – Tim
Lohrentz

Notes

1. http://www.latinamericanhistory.about.com/od/TheOlmec/p/The-Olmec.htm

2. http://www.sacred-texts.com/the/sd/sd2-3-09.htm

3. http://www.assatashakur.org/forum/they-all-look-like-all-them/33241-olmec-civilization-print.html

4. http://www.ancient.eu/Olmec_Civilization/

5. http://www.whenweruled.com/?p=52

6. http://www.ancient-wisdom.com/mexicotreszapotes.htm

7. http://www.ancient-wisdom.com/olmecs.htm

8. http://www.ancient-wisdom.co.uk/olmecs.htm

9. Hart, Will, *The Genesis Race: Our Extraterrestrial DNA and the True Origins of the Species*, Inner Traditions /Bear & Co. 2003.

10. Blavatsy, H.P. SD, II, 1977.

11. http://grahamhancock.com/newmanh1/#edn_22

12. Collins, Andrew, *The Cygnus Mystery*, Watkin USA, Dist.-Penguin Random House Publishers, 2010, (p.61)

13. Hancock, Graham, 1995, *Fingerprints of The Gods*, Three Rivers Press, NY, pages 118-35.

14. http://www.assatashakur.org/forum/they-all-look-like-all-them/33241-olmec-civilization-print.html

15. http://www.crystalinks.com/quetzalcoatl.html

16. http://www.mexicolore.co.uk/aztecs/flora-and-fauna/jaguar

17. http://www.Grahamhancock.com/fingerprints

18. http://www.ancient.eu/article/604/

19. http://research.ua.edu/2005/10/rubber-people-the-americas-first-civilization/

20. http://anthropology.si.edu/olmec/english/sites/tresZapotes.htm

21. http://www.ancientscripts.com/epiolmec.html

22. http://www.archive.archaeology.org/online/news/la.mojarra.html

23. Childress, David Hatcher, 2011. *The Mystery of the Olmec's*, SCB Distributors.

24. http://www.ancient-wisdom.com/mexicotreszapotes.htm

25. http://www.academia.edu/4897595/JMIS_Joachim_of_Fiore_ the_Jews_Diego_de_Landa_and_the_Maya

26. Blavatsky, H.P. SD, II, 1977.

27. http://www.ancient.eu/Olmec_Civilization/

28. Blavatsky, H. P., *The Secret Doctrine,* vol. II, *1977.*

29. http://www.mesoweb.com/pari/publications/news_ archive/30/olmec_sculpture.html

30. Jeffrey P. Blomster (2002). *WHAT AND WHERE IS OLMEC STYLE? Regional perspectives on hollow figurines in Early Formative Mesoamerica.* Ancient Mesoamerica, 13, pp 171-195. doI – 10.1017/ S0956536102132196.

31. Jeffrey P. Blomster (1998). *Context, Cult, and Early Formative Period Public Ritual in the Mixteca Alta.* Ancient Mesoamerica, 9, pp 309-326. doI – 10.1017/S0956536100002017.

32. http://inclusivebusiness.typepad.com/indigenous_ elsalvador/2013/12/pre-classic-maya-meditation- and-science.html —Tim Lohrentz

33. https://en.wiki2.org/wiki/Olmec_figurine

34. Blavatsky, H. P., *The Secret Doctrine,* Vol. *II, 1977.*

35. Men, Hunbatz, *Secrets of Mayan Science/Religion,* 1990, Inner Traditions/Bear & Co, VT.

36. http://inclusivebusiness.typepad.com/indigenous_ elsalvador/2013/12/pre-classic-maya-meditation- and-science.html

Anthrogenesis

Rudolph

Chapter Eight

Western Hemisphere Migrations

The Mayan Ancestors

In researching the Maya, an indigenous people of Central America, we see innovative and amazing sciences. Blavatsky gave clues regarding the origins of civilizations on Earth. She says in *The Secret Doctrine, Vol. I*, "The Watchers reign over man during the whole Satya Yuga and the smaller subsequent Yugas, down to the beginning of the Third Root Race in Lemuria; after which it is the Patriarchs, Heroes, and the Manes-the Egyptian Dynasties enumerated to Solon, the incarnated Dhyani-Chohans of a lower order up to King Menes and the human kings of other nations; all were recorded carefully."

The term 'Maya' traveled thousands of miles from Mesoamerica to Egypt, to India and beyond. Theosophy defines Maya as, "The creative power by which the universe comes into manifestation. Maya is conceived as a cosmic entity, a universal substance or sum of forces comprehending all conditioned powers, causes and effects. In itself it is unreal, opposed to the Real or Absolute Thought which informs it." [1]

Mayan Adepts Aid Humanity

It is said that the Mayan priests were adepts of the Ancient Wisdom and that they descended from the White Brotherhood on Sirius, arriving in the early Root Races on Earth. They incarnated to provide a spiritual base on Earth and spread the Ancient Wisdom throughout the early continents—from Lemuria throughout the South Pacific to the Americas and Africa, across oceans to Sumer, Egypt, throughout the Middle East and onward to Asia, India and Africa. Cambodia's Angor Wat stone personages illustrate remarkable similarity to Olmec/Mayan stelae faces. Yonaguni Monument, off the south coast of Ryukyu Islands, Japan, is said to be a vestige from Lemuria, located within the Pacific Rim.

In Mesoamerica, the adepts assisted Atlantis' fourth sub-race, the Toltec in grounding the Ancient Wisdom, passing it throughout the America right through to Asia and the Middle East.

The great wealth of stelae and extraordinary edifices of the Yucatan speak to contact with ancients who, as we now understand, migrated from Mu, diffusing and incorporating the structure of that Root Race flourishing in Mesoamerica. These ancestors were a tall and massive people, keeping in mind that Blavatsky states Lemurians (and later Atlanteans) were contemporaneous with the Mesozoic, possessing small dinosaurs which were trained for the hunt. Were these not their 'dragons?' In the Yucatan and Asia, comprising myth throughout Earth, we see the dragon as the enigmatic figure in artwork and lore. Perhaps these myths have a basis in truth after all!

At Chichen Itza, the stelae revealed bearded men with Caucasoid features. Perhaps the Carthaginians to whom the Maya paid tribute, traveled back and forth to the Yucatan. And visa-versa; Herodotus discusses the wars in India with the Maya. The Carthaginians and Phoenicians (two different peoples) were known sea cultures with sea routes extending all over the Mediterranean, including large portions of Spain and Sicily. The civilizations of Mesopotamia may be humanity's earliest connection between Mesoamerica and Egypt and the rest of the

Middle East for teachings of the sacred Ancient Wisdom and history of mankind in written form.[2, 3]

Feathered Vision Serpent of Kukulkán

The Sacred Earth Birds

The South Pacific-Oceania-is comprised of three ethno-geographic groups: Melanesia, Micronesia, and Polynesia. Easter Island's bird symbol contains various animals with a bird head, each with an egg in its claws, much the same as in Hawaii, showing the great diffusion of symbolic forms of communication, common to cultures of the region. The Mesoamericans have the god, Quetzalcoatl, epitomized as an exquisite plumed serpent and sacred bird combined. The Maya refer to him as Kukulkán. The North American Indians have a special love for bird symbolism. For example, the Thunder Bird of the Southwest represents the 'creative forces' of the Great Spirit.

This symbol is seen around the world in diverse cultures. Examples are found in Hittite art forms. Birds also appear among the Babylonian and Chaldean art forms as one of the Sacred Four Creative Forces. The Assyrian Genii are illustrated with the wings of birds, also the Egyptian god, Horus, the sky-god. The Alaskan totem pole of the Haiden Indians of Queen Charlotte Island, is sacred indeed, as stated by their chief, to which the totem pole belongs: "The winged creature which crowns the totem pole is the Thunder Bird and represents the Great Creator."[4]

History of the Sacred Bird

1.   2.   3.   4,

James Churchward's *The Sacred Symbols of Mu* (1933) states, "There was just one step between the original cross and the winged circle, unless we accept the Mexican butterfly winged circle as a step: 1.) is the Original Cross, 2.) is the Dhyan (Dhyani) Chohans, Ancient, Oriental, and Mexican, 3.) is the Mexican Butterfly Winged Circle and, 4.) is the Hindu Bird Winged Circle."[5]

Above: Mexican Butterfly Winged
Cross
Right: Lemurian Cosmological
Symbol

See the 'Winged Disk from Assyria' below, as it is comparable to the Mu's ancient symbol. Refer to *Anthrogenesis*- Chapter Six, Section: Mu's Illustrated Prayer, for more details.[6]

Evolution of the Winged Disk

All of the winged circles below have feathered wings except the one from ancient Sumer (bottom). The wings seem to have evolved from the original symbol attributed to Mu.[7, 8, 9]

1. Winged Disk – Ancient Egypt – Curve lost before onset of the New Kingdom.

2. Winged Disk – Ur

3. Winged Cardinal Cross – "Hindu Bird winged Circle"- Churchward (1933)

4. Winged Disk – Egypt – Horus

5. Winged Disk – Assyria – Body of wing quite similar to Mu's cosmological symbol.

6. Winged Disk – Sumer

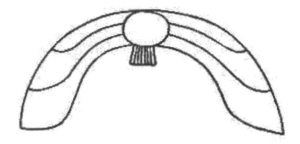

Popol Vuh Sacred Creation

The *Popol Vuh* or *Popol Wuj*, in the K'iche' language means "Book of the Community" and contains the Maya Creation Story. The scope and depth of this work is an intoxicating view of a culture enmeshed with traditions. This old history was recorded as an act of preservation by the royal K'iche' lineage, rulers of the highlands of Guatemala, in the 16th century. Spanish colonial domination resulted in major portions of the masterpiece being burned by Catholic missionaries; never again to be restored to its original eminence.

The Maya account commences with, "This is the beginning of the ancient traditions of this place called K'iche'..., this is the account of when all is still silent and placid. Hushed and empty is the womb of the sky...." It contains tales of the Hero Twins, and the K'iche' genealogies and land rights. In this story, the Creators, Heart of Sky and six other deities including the Feathered Serpent, wanted to create human beings with hearts and minds who could "keep the days." But their first attempts failed. When these deities finally created humans out of yellow and white corn who could talk, they were satisfied. In another epic cycle of the story, the Death Lords of the Underworld summon the Hero Twins to play a momentous ball game where the Twins defeat their opponents. The Twins rose into the heavens, and became the Sun and the Moon. Through their actions, the Hero Twins prepared the way for the planting of corn for human beings to live on Earth, and for the Fourth Creation of the Maya."[10]

Hiking Quirigua Pyramid and Temple Grounds with Dr. Hansford ©Michael L. Hansford

Cultures Bridged Across Time

The *Popol Vuh* paints the landscape of a culturally exquisite people, the Maya, who were 'living in this happy land in great peace speaking one language.' In her book, *Isis Unveiled*, Blavatsky says, "...in the fragments left of the original *Popol Vuh*, there is sufficient evidence that the religious customs of the Mexicans, Peruvians, and other American races are nearly identical with those of the ancient Phoenicians,

Babylonians, and Egyptians." -Blavatsky, H.P., 1877. *Isis Unveiled*, I, Theosophical University Press, Pasadena, CA.[11, 12]

Creation Effort Similarities

The stages of conception illustrated in the '*Popol Vuh*' portray indistinguishable similarities to creation transcribed in the *Stanzas of Dzyan*. Stanza II – Earth-Mother and Fathers" (SD) and "She Who Has Borne Children and He Who Has Begotten Sons" or simply "Mother" and "Father" (*Popol Vuh*).[13, 14]

Both accounts of creation include several attempts to create both animals and humans in vain. "Our flesh is not there…they slew the forms, which were two and four faced…They fought the men with fishes bodies." -*Stanzas of Dzyan*, Stanza II, 7-8.[15]

Mother and Father made the animals, "They did not speak like people. Their speech was unrecognizable. The speech of the animals could not be understood. Because of the way they were made, they were not successful. They were not able to speak our names. The animals that were on the face of the earth were eaten and killed." (*Popol Vuh*)[16]

Fathers Give Life But No Mind

In *The Secret Doctrine, Vol II* Blavatsky writes, "The Fathers, the boneless, could give no life to beings with bones. How… are minds made? …The fathers called, …the fire that burns in earth, the earth spirit called the Solar Fire,… they produced a good shadow, … it needed a body, … the Fathers gave it form, the Solar Lhasa gave it spirit of life, the Dhyani-Chohans gave it the mirror of Its body, the 'Drainer of Waters' gave it a vehicle of desires: but Breath needs a Mind. We cannot give that, we never had it… said the Fathers. Thus, have the boneless given life to those who became men with bones in the third". (*Stanzas of Dzyan*, Stanza IV, 15-17.)

They Spoke but without Knowledge

"Let us try again to make one who will honor us, respect us; one who will be a provider and a sustainer…Mother and Father had already conceived the animals of the mountains, the guardians of the forest and all that populate the mountains…the deer and the birds, the puma and the jaguar, the serpent and the rattlesnake, the pit viper and all that to live in meadows, orchards, tops of trees and multiply in forests, branches of trees bushes …and all the animals were given homes. They spoke but without knowledge and understanding. After their inability to speak was realized by Father and Mother: You shall be replaced because you were not successful."(*Popol Vuh*)[17]

Humans Created a Speechless Race

"The animals separated the first. They began to breed. The two-fold man separated also. He said: Let us as they; let us unite and make creatures. They did." The newly born race was created to house the souls of men from a previous Round that had come from the Moon, with ape-like, bodies, unable to support a 'Soul' or to support a Mind." The Lemurians, the Third Race progressed slowly from the Second Race, with the two root races sharing the physical vehicle for many millions of years. It wasn't until later, during the Fourth Race of Atlantis that they knowingly reproduced with animal beings to use for power and material gains.(SD)[18]

They Walked Without Purpose

Mother and Father wanted to create people capable of speech to sustain the gods, to worship them, and in this creation, it was the 'effigies of wood.' "They had the appearance of people and spoke like people and populated the world. But, they walked without purpose and were not capable of understanding those who had given them birth and hearts. This was the end of the effigies carved of wood. A vengeance came from all kingdoms in the world to these effigies of carved wood; the animals, the stones on which they grind their corn and wheat, the pots, the vessels, turned against these people and the Moon and Sun eclipsed." (*Popol Vuh*)[19]

And the Lhasas Wept…

"Seeing which, the Lhasa, who had not built men, wept, saying: "The Amanasa (Sanskrit – Mindless) have defiled our future abodes. This is karma. Let us dwell in the others. Let us teach them better, lest worse should happen. They did … Then all men became endowed with Manas. They saw the Sin of the Mindless. The Fourth race developed speech. The one became two; also all the living and creeping things that were still one, giant fish-birds and serpents with shell-heads."(SD)[20]

Our World Mother

Mother of the World by Nicholas Roerich (1874-1947), NYC Museum

The worship of the female goddess in Mesoamerica moved forward across subsequent migrations and world-wide, from corner to corner. This includes the Mayan goddesses such as Ixchel, Alaghom-Naom and

Ixazalvoh, along with the goddesses Isis, Iannes, Ishtar and Oannes across the seas.[21]

In *Anthrogenesis*, we investigate this idea further, discussing the feminine hierarchy of rulers, starting at the beginning of time, so many eons ago. Mother of a thousand names, it is she, whom the culture revered and worshiped because she bore new life. Mother Earth consciousness seems to have been somewhat forgotten in our current Kali Yuga, but it has always been Mother that brought life, as observed in countless societies throughout our planet. Even in the primordial stages of cell division by the Olano and later, the Hermaphrodites who employed budding; all had Mother! Later, as recorded in song and verse by the indigenous Indians of the Americas, we again witness the matriarchal underpinnings of our Mother Earth.[22]

By Leaps and Bounds

In their open-ended endurance, Lemurian sub-races, where the physical body was concerned, amassed incredible progress throughout the eras, coming into realization at the door step of Atlantis, the next backdrop for those of the Fourth Root race. These 'first true humans,' as Blavatsky said, had forged ahead, materializing a solid and reproduction-ready physical body and used it! Now humanity had a body, a mind and emergent vitality of spirituality. Their physical and spiritual capabilities would bloom, with traits tantamount to the gods, inherent in the future Atlanteans.[23]

Late-Race Lemurians Migrate

Blavatsky points out that each Root Race initiates its manifestation in the previous Race. And so it was with Lemuria. Previous to concomitant geographical events, migration had begun from Mu with inhabitants relocating to Africa, however overlapping sections of Africa then attached to Lemuria were unusable wetlands. Much of the populace headed east to Sumatra, Borneo, Java, New Guinea, Oceania and Australia, with similar dialects and words a dead giveaway for their origins. The Lemurians root strains later incarnated in Atlantis. The early Atlantean sub-races journeyed in numerous directions, with many sub-races advancing into

Africa, such as the Rmoahals, Atlantis' first sub-race, which had what we call a black complexion.[24]

Atlantis

Many souls from our solar system and beyond incarnated during Atlantis, befitting the imperative to build humanity's population. The life of an Atlantis citizen was a superlative experience. At its height, the Golden Yuga offered sublime opportunities in spirituality, expansive sensory and mental capabilities, and amazing beauty in the arts and sciences, such as we cannot imagine! The Library at Alexandria must have contained many of its mystical papyri and relics. Solon's astute narrative from Egypt eludes to the totality of Atlantis. It is told that there were a multitude of brilliant gemstones, gold and crystals with acoustical healing properties; children were schooled in multi-sensory systems; love, and kindness, caring for all humans were all part of the curriculum. Immense, extravagant structures glistened with precious metals and colossal statuaries. One can only speculate about what other amazing things were apart of this ancient culture.[25, 26]

Life in Utopia

In the earlier sub-races of Atlantis, life was simple. Many of the genuine aspects of Lemuria had rolled over into Atlantis, save the tall, massive body structure, which had now shortened to a mere height of 20 to 30 feet by mid-race (diminishing further to 15-10 feet during Persia-Iran, our third sub-race of the contemporaneous Aryan Root Race), with continued decline in height by the end of Atlantis. Plato discusses Atlantis under pretext in his late dialogues: "On the north side they (the Atlanteans) had dwellings in common and had erected halls for dining in winter, and had all the buildings which they needed for their common life, besides temples, but there was no adorning of them with gold and silver, for they made no use of these for any purpose; they took a middle course between meanness and ostentation, and built modest houses in which they and their children's children grew old, and they handed them down to others who were like themselves, always the same."[27, 28, 29]

And time passed with Atlantis transforming amidst the years: Plato discusses in *Critias*, an amazing island, noting "the combatants on the other side (Atlantis) were commanded by the kings of Atlantis" "And at the very beginning they built the palace in the habitation of the god's and of their ancestors, which they continued to ornament in successive generations, every king surpassing the one who went before him to the utmost of his power, until they made the building a marvel to behold for size and for beauty."[30]

One common thread with the ancients was the use of the colors red, black and white, which esoterically relate to the sacred myths of Lemuria by the Naacals, who were also the Ancient Masters of Atlantis, the Mayans and the Egyptians. "One kind was white, another black, and a third red, and as they quarried, they at the same time hollowed out double docks, having roofs formed out of the native rock."[31]

The royal palace of the Atlantean king purportedly had walls overlaid with silver and points topped in gold and "in the centre was a holy temple dedicated to Cleito and Poseidon, which remained inaccessible, and was surrounded by an enclosure of gold; this was the spot where the family of the ten princes first saw the light, and thither the people annually brought the fruits of the earth in their season from all the ten portions, to be an offering to each of the ten."[32]

The lands of the three main islands described by Solon were fertile and luscious: "The surrounding mountains were celebrated for their number and size and beauty, far beyond any which still exist, having in them also many wealthy villages of country folk, and rivers, and lakes, and meadows supplying food enough for every animal, wild or tame, and much wood of various sorts, abundant for each and every kind of work."[33]

Plato ostensibly took note of emerging barbarism in Atlantis calling it "...an island greater than both Libya and Asia together, a colossal warlike power, rushing from the Atlantic Sea and spreading itself, with aggressive ferocity over all Europe and Asia." Greece was ultimately victorious over Atlantis.[34]

Sadko in the Underwater Kingdom, Ilya Repin (1844-1930)

Atlantis Populations Amass

Already established within the reproductive patterns of the Atlanteans were the seeds of the Fifth or Aryan Root Race, ready to expand the human form. Each sub-race contributed ancestral traits consecutively throughout each Root Race. The Atlantean sub-races were as follows: 1st sub-race, the Rmoahals, 2nd sub-race, the Tlavatli, 3rd sub-race, the Toltec, 4th sub-race, the Primal-Turanians (wherein the mastery of the life force and the concentrated misuse of earthly powers occurred), 5th

Primal-Semites, the originators of a basic form of logical thinking, 6th sub-race, the Akkadians, who developed the faculty of thought even further than their predecessors—the 5th sub-race and, the 7th sub-race, the Mongols, who besides being nomadic, were the last Atlantean family sub-race in development.[35]

Atlantis Shares Phonetics

Atlantis has been ascribed with the introduction of hieroglyphics, bequeathing both Egypt and Ur with this 'writing of the Gods' because both civilizations were thought to be Atlantean colonists. Having the prize in their pocket, so to speak, the colonists transported phonetics and writing, along with other untold treasures of their day. Ignatius Donnelly in, *Atlantis, the Antediluvian World*, 1882, states, "ONE of the most marvellous inventions for the advancement of mankind is the phonetic alphabet, or a system of signs representing the sounds of human speech. Without it our present civilization could scarcely have been possible. No solution of the origin of our European alphabet has yet been obtained: we can trace it back from nation to nation, and form to form, until we reach the Egyptians, and the archaic forms of the Phoenicians, Hebrews, and Cushites, but beyond this the light fails us.

The Egyptians spoke of their hieroglyphic system of writing not as their own invention, but as "the language of the gods." (Lenormant and Cheval, *Ancient History of the East*, vol. ii., p. 208.) "The gods" were, doubtless, their highly civilized ancestors--the people of Atlantis--who, as we shall hereafter see, became the gods of many of the Mediterranean races. "According to the Phoenicians, the art of writing was invented by Taautus, or Taut, 'whom the Egyptians call Thouth,' and the Egyptians said it was invented by Thouth, or Thoth, otherwise called 'the first Hermes,' in which we clearly see that both the Phoenicians and Egyptians referred the invention to a period older than their own separate political existence, and to an older nation, from which both peoples received it." (Baldwin's *Prehistoric Nations*, p. 91.)

The Atlanteans Journey

The fifth and sixth sub-races of Atlantis, the Semites-Kabyle (the Phoenicians) and Akkadians were nomadic peoples like their forbearers, the Tlavati—Cro-Magnon—the second sub-race progenitors. They traveled with the Turanian-fourth sub-race, leading migrations from east of Atlantis to present Morocco and Algeria while the Semites progressed to North America, becoming immersed within the indigenous Indian peoples, henceforth journeying to Europe, Egypt, Africa and Asia. The Akkadians passed through the Mediterranean area and Sardinia, with Basque culture advancing their heritage to Persia and Arabia. Add to this the Etruscans, Phoenicians and the Carthaginians.

The sculpture (on page 155) was discovered in Tuscany, a very rare find since many ancient relics were destroyed by past cultures out of fear.[38]

Atlantis Begins Its Downfall

At c. 4.5 million years ago, the Atlanteans had developed fully organic physical bodies, since matter achieved full manifestation in this Kali Yuga, the midpoint of the Seven Root Races. Their downfall got underway by humans breeding with the mindless human-beings, all the time consciously aware of these intentional actions. Krita Yuga initiated its downward cycle and this reproduction went into full swing, not conducive to a part-human part-animal race. Humans and animals were simply too close genetically to prevent a fertile union. Only the least progressed of these apes were allowed to live. Consequently, the Atlanteans' most evolved human apes died out because when they realized the actions of the less evolved humans, they waged vigorous wars of extermination towards the end of this Fourth Root Race, in the late the Miocene epoch. The apes of today are their descendants, a resultant combination of interbreeding, evolution and DNA.[39]

Tuscany Anthropomorphic Statue. Archaeological Museum of Massa
Marittima, Vado all'Arancio, Massa Marittima,
Grosseto Province, Tuscany, Italy, courtesy of Sailko.

The Spiritual Bond Was Severed

The spiritual bond was severed, initiating the destruction of Atlantis.
The relationship of Atlantean humanity to the Spiritual Kingdom was
consequently halted; the Antahkarana was ultimately torn, breaking
humanity's connection between the Spiritual Hierarchy and humanity
at large. This action, on a higher cosmic plane, set in motion the actions
that resulted in the ultimate destruction of Atlantis. This unfortunate

155

chapter of malevolence finally culminating with the first land masses plunging the kingdom into the sea.[40]

The Antahkarana

The Antahkarana is a Sanskrit word derived from 'antah' meaning inner, and 'karana' meaning instrument. It is the spiritual or "Rainbow Bridge' that connects humanity with the Ancient Ones." "The science of the Antahkarana is the new and true science of the mind, which will utilise mental substance for the building of the bridge between personality and soul, and then between soul and spirit. It concerns the substance of the three higher levels of the mental plane."

"The science of meditation can be applied to every possible life process. It is a subsidiary science preparatory to the science of the Antahkarana. This is the means of building between the personality and the soul. It is the true science of bridging in consciousness. It relates the individual mind eventually to the higher mind and later to the Universal Mind. It will eventually dominate the new educational methods in schools and colleges. The science of service grows normally and naturally out of the successful application of the other two sciences. Service is the true science of creation and is a scientific method of establishing continuity."[41]

Atlantis Spirals Downward

A minor offset with migration was set in motion to Oceania and the Americas. The culture without Spirit persisted, out of sync with the Elders of the Race, manifesting a dark nature-worship lifestyle devoted to attaining excess in all ways; material gains, misusing potent astral-psychic faculties and dominance over less evolved souls. As humanity approached the 'midnight hour,' greed and power accumulated its hold over the culture and mankind was soon to be doomed with this agenda. But, the ongoing struggle for survival endured, a keynote of those times, amplifying excessive population density towards annihilation.[42]

The Flying Carpet (1880) by Viktor M. Vasnetsov (1848-1926), Art Museum of Nizhny Novgorod, Russia

Priest Kings Ready Escape from the Floods

The priest-kings exemplified the Ancient Wisdom and directed the migrations from the doomed Atlantis. Each time an air ship was ready, a priest-king managed the people for transport out of Atlantis. Individual groups left at varying times. The Tvali moved spatially outward, as far as Brazil, California, India and Africa. Sub-races formed from the strains of Turanians, Semites, and Akkadians migrating towards Greenland and Scandinavia, including Brittany and Picardy, now France—then connected to a Scandinavian island. The Lapplanders populated northern Norway, Sweden, Finland and the Kola Peninsula of Russia and the border between southern to middle Sweden and Norway where millions of years earlier, the last of the gigantic Lemurians had existed. The Mongolians commenced settling in eastern Siberia, no longer on the main island of Atlantis. Each of the 7 Deluges left survivors at Atlantis, who henceforward immigrated throughout the world. However, many individuals were hopeful to find a destination before the final turbulent deadly waters of destruction.[43]

We Are the Gods!

This Fourth Race had forgotten that they were the children of God.

"Then the Fourth became tall with pride. We are the Kings it was said; we are the Gods."

"They built temples for the human body. Male and female they worshipped. Then the Third Eye acted no longer."

"They built great images nine yatis high, (27 feet) the size of their bodies. Inner fires had destroyed the land of their fathers. The water threatened the Fourth."

"The first great waters came. They swallowed the seven great islands."[44, 45]

"The time came for Atlantis to be destroyed. "All Holy saved, the Unholy destroyed," say the *Stanzas of Dzyan*. The destruction and sinking of the various islands and peninsulas proceeded gradually, slowly, and bit by bit over thousands of years, eventually resulting in the final great cataclysm – the flooding and submersion of the last island of Atlantis, referred to as Poseidonis – in 9,564 B.C. (11,579 years ago as of this year). That's the date given by the Master Kuthumi in "*The Mahatma Letters*." The last of the huge monstrous animals, now confined to myth and legend in the form of dragons and even stranger things, perished in these disasters."[46, 47]

It is this final ending that Plato refers to in the *Odyssey*.

Atlantis Air Ships

In both the Yugas and Theosophy, the end of a 'Great Year' and the 7th Root Race signifies the continent possessing the majority of its population is destroyed, alternately by fire and water and submerged beneath the ocean.

The early Fifth Root Race required transport to other locations. H.P.B. explains that it was from the Atlanteans that the early Indians "learned aeronautics—Viwan Vidyathe—the knowledge of flying in air-vehicles, and therefore, their great arts of meteorography and meteorology." It is from them, again, that the Aryans inherited their most valuable science of the hidden virtues of precious and other stones, of chemistry, or rather alchemy, of mineralogy, geology, physics and astronomy. It is a proven but much ignored fact that the knowledge and actual utilization of "air vehicles" was a well-known and integral part of ancient Indian civilization, a culture which far surpassed in its greatness anything our Western civilization has ever achieved. There are clear references to such things in numerous Hindu scriptures, including the great Indian epic of "The Ramayana," which later formed the basis and ideological framework for Homer's "*Iliad*."[48, 49]

Pixabay

Atlantean Adepts Transport the Ancient Mysteries

The Atlantean adepts brought the Ancient Mysteries from Atlantis to both Egypt and Sumer, in a similar fashion as the Lemurian-Mayan adepts had journeyed throughout Oceania and the Americas.[50]

Toltec and Theosophy

Tula is a Mesoamerican archeological site, and an important regional center, which reached its height as the capital of the Toltec Empire. It is thought that our Mesoamerican indigenous peoples are related to the Olmec, Maya and thus, the Toltec, with Blavatsky coincidentally writing that Atlantis was ruled by the sub-race—the Toltec. Theosophist W. Scott Elliot describes the Toltec sub-race history in Theosophy as majestic and vital; they ruled the continent of Atlantis for thousands of years in great power and glory. He adds that the Atlantean-Toltec civilization sustained a sophisticated agricultural society with expansion persisting for thousands of years.

Blavatsky says the Toltec were ancestors of the Israelites, "And to begin with, Nunez de la Vega might have pointed out to the *Chronicles of Fuentes*, the kingdom of Guatemala, and to the Manuscript of *Don Juan Torres*, the grandson of the last king of the Quiches (K'iches). This document, which is said to have been in the possession of the Lieutenant-General appointed by Pedro de Alvaro, states that the Toltecas, themselves, descended from the house of Israel, who were released by Moses, and who, after crossing the Red Sea, fell into idolatry. After that, having separated themselves from their companions, and from one continent to another, they came to a place named the Seven Caverns, in the Kingdom of Mexico, where they founded the famous town of Tula (Tollan)."[51, 52]

Teotihuacan

"The place where gods were born" is the Nahuatl translation for 'Teotihuacan.' Conventional archeology places the high time of Teotihuacan between 100 B.C. and A.D. 650. Teotihuacan is equal in magnificence to the pyramids and temple of the Giza Plateau of Egypt. One of the first cities in the West, the origins of the massive Pyramid of the Sun and its Temple in Teotihuacan are a mystery.

Caves are significant of the symbolic underworld imagery of the of Mesoamerican culture, and one lies beneath this pyramid. The location and orientation of this cave may have been the impetus for the Pyramid of the Sun's alignment and construction. Built more than a thousand years ago, the Nahuatl-speaking Aztec discovered this abandoned structure after descending on this central Mexican site, no doubt awestruck.[53, 54]

Aj Toltecat of the City Tula

"The Quiché-K'iche- title *Aj Toltecat* is given to anyone who is highly skilled in art, science, religion, and creative endeavors in general. *Toltecat* refers specifically to the ancient Toltecs, who, under the legendary priest-ruler Topiltzin Quetzalcoatl, founded the city of Tula in Central Mexico in the tenth century A.D. Although the city fell some two centuries later, the fame of its people was passed from generation to generation, undoubtedly embellished significantly the tale with each retelling. At the time of the Spanish conquest, the ancient Toltecs had achieved an almost mythic reputation as masters in all arts. The Aztecs gave the following description in folio 172 of the *Codex Matritensis*:

"The Toltec's were a skillful people; all of their works were good,
All were exact, all well-made and admirable.
Their houses were beautiful, with turquoise mosaics,
The walls finished with plaster, clean and marvelous houses,
Which is to say Toltec houses, beautifully made, beautiful in everything...
Painters, sculptors, carvers of precious stones, feather artists,
Potters, spinners, weavers, skillful in all they made...

The Toltecs were truly wise; they conversed with their own
hearts

They played their drums and rattles;

They were singers, they composed songs and sang them among
the people.

They guarded the songs in their memories, they deified them
in their hearts." (Leon-Portilla, 1980, 207) [55]

Toltec Are Here, Then Gone

The Toltec sub-race became fundamental in peopling the expanse of
South, Central, and North America through constructing of the first
villages in these locations. One only has to comprehend the brilliance
in their pyramids and sacred principles, deeply-rooted within their
culture, to gain a keen understanding of the Toltecs. Toltec design and
construction is best observed at Chichen-Itza, which combines a blend
of the design elements of the Toltec and Mayan cultures. Toltec theology
centered on the deity, Quetzalcoatl, 'the Feathered-Serpent,' which later
became the central figure of the Aztec pantheon. The Toltec were quite
mysterious and their culture disappeared without record, much like their
ancestors, the Olmec.[56]

Aztec Legend of the Fifth Sun

"At the beginning of the world there was only darkness, void. Creation
began when the dual Ometecuhtli—Lord of Duality and Omecihuatl—
Lady of Duality, created itself. This first god was good and bad, male
and female, and gave birth to four other gods: Huizilopochtli, Quetzalcoatl,
Tezcatlipoca and Xipe Totec. These gods created the world. The first
things created by Quetzalcoatl and Huitzilopochtli were fire and a half
sun. They then undertook the creation of humanity by sacrificing a god
whose blood drops on a mass of ground-up bones produced the first
man and woman, named Oxomoco and Cipactonal respectively. The
birth of each took 4 days. After the creation of man, the gods continued
creating the lords of the underworld, the heavens and waters, a crocodile-
like water creature named Cipactli, and the rain god Tlaloc and his wife
Chalchiuhtlicue. When the initial creation was completed, a cycle of 5

Suns followed, which corresponded to 5 World Ages, each one ending in destruction. According to the Aztecs, we are currently on the 5th sun of the creation.

Pacofender, Artist

First Sun: The element of this first age is earth. Tezcatlipoca was chosen to be sacrificed to create an energy source for the planet, though he only managed to become a half sun. During this age, a fight transpired between Quetzalcoatl and Tezcatlipoca. Quetzalcoatl was the victor, but Tezcatlipoca takes revenge by sending jaguars on Earth to destroy the giants. Thus came an end to the first sun.

Second Sun: The element of this second age is air. Quetzalcoatl is in control in this era. Humans were created according to our current likeness but became corrupt. As a result, Tezcatlipoca transformed them into monkeys, and Quetzalcoatl sent hurricanes to wipe the monkeys out.

163

There were survivors who, according to the legend, are current day monkeys.

Third Sun: The element of this age is fire and the god responsible for this era is Tlaloc, the god of rain and water. A fight ensued between Tezcatlipoca and Tlaloc when Tezcatlipoca stole Tlaloc's wife. Out of revenge, Tlaloc transformed all of humanity into turkeys, dogs and butterflies. Quetzalcoatl rained fire and ash down on the atrocities, causing the destruction of humanity for the third time.

Fourth Sun: The element related to this world age is water, and god chosen to reign is Tlaloc's sister, Calchiuhtlicue. During this sun, Quetzalcoatl and Tezcatlipoca were filled with jealousy and brought the sun down. The population was turned into fish, and this age was ultimately terminated by a great flood.

Fifth Sun: This is said to be the age that we are currently in, and the god Nanahuatzin is responsible for it. The legend foretells that this era will end with earthquakes."[57]

The Root 'Virach' in Primordial Humanity, Maya, India and Assyria

In reviewing the cultures of early India and the Maya of Mesoamerica, there is a connection through the root word "vira" in their two respective deities, Virochana and Viracocha. The names are almost identical. When we delve into the actual meanings of the names we see great similarities.

"In the Valmiki Ramayana of India, Virochana was the first great Asura king with supernatural powers. Asuras were power-seeking class of beings. The Upanishads say that Virochana and Lord Indra, together, were taught at the feet of Prajapati. However, contrary to what he was taught, Virochana preached that the Asuras should worship the 'sharira' (body) instead of the 'atman' (absolute consciousness). In the ancient texts of South America, the Vedic 'Viro-Chana' emerges as 'Viracocha.' Scholars regard God Viracocha as the equivalent of Lord Indra. The myths and stories about the two are close. Viracocha is the 'King of Gods' just as Lord Indra. Viracocha also wields the 'Thunderbolt,' like Indra. What would the name Viracocha of South America tradition mean in Sanskrit? The word 'Vira' means 'brave, heroic, powerful, strong.' 'Kocha' means a 'man of mixed ancestry. Scholars say today, the megaliths of South America, such as the Temple of 'Kalasasaya' (which houses an idol of Viracocha) in Bolivia, could not have been made without alien help. Investigations in Assyrian mythology prove the existence of a tradition in Assyrian history of such a king called Berosus – a distortion of Virochana and Viracocha – as it has often been reiterated 'b' and 'v' are commutable."[58, 59]

According to Swami Vivekananda "the western nations are the children of the great hero Virochana."

Inca Creation Myth

"Con, the Creator; was in the form of a man without bones. He filled the earth with good things to supply the needs of the first humans. The people, however, forgot Con's goodness to them and rebelled. So he punished them by stopping the rainfall. The miserable people were forced to work hard, drawing what little water they could find from stinking, drying riverbeds. Then a new god, Pachachamac, came and drove Con out, changing his people into monkeys. Pachachamac then took earth and made the ancestors of human beings."[60]

Creator God Viracocha Comes

"Legends of the Aymara Indians say that the Creator God Viracocha rose from Lake Titicaca during the time of darkness to bring forth light. Viracocha was a storm god and a sun god who was represented as wearing the sun for a crown, with thunderbolts in his hands, and tears descending from his eyes as rain. He wandered the earth disguised as a beggar and wept when he saw the plight of the creatures he had created, but knew that he must sustain them. Viracocha made the earth, the stars, the sky and mankind, but his first creation displeased him, so he destroyed it with a flood and made a new, better one, taking to his wanderings as a beggar, teaching his new creations the rudiments of civilisation, as well as working numerous miracles. Viracocha eventually disappeared across the Pacific Ocean (by walking on the water), setting off near Manta, Ecuador, and never returned. It was thought that Viracocha would re-appear in times of trouble. References are also found of a group of men named the Suncasapa or bearded ones–they were the mythic soldiers of Viracocha, aka the 'angelic warriors of Viracocha.'[61]

The Sacred Valley of the Andes

"The legend of Viracocha and how he "walked" the sacred valley brings us face to face with the enigmas of the Incan civilisation: Tiahuanaco, Cuzco and Sacsayhuaman, Ollantaytambo and Macchu Picchu. The ancient pyramids of Caral predate the Inca civilization by 4000 years, but were flourishing a century before the pyramids of Giza. No surprise therefore that they have been identified as the most important archaeological discoveries since the discovery of Machu Picchu in 1911. The stone face of Viracocha towering over Ollantaytambo is part of the Inca legend; his presence shows that the creator god was still present, "looking," "watching over" his people."[62]

"Sacsayhuaman is a walled complex near the old city of Cuzco, Peru; the imperial city Cuzco, meaning 'navel of the earth,' was laid out in the form of a puma, the animal that symbolized the Inca dynasty. The belly of the puma was the main plaza, the river Tullumayo formed its spine, and the hill of Sacsayhuaman its head." Contained within this ancient city of 3,094 hectares (7,645 acres) are numerous archeological spots with many of the sites echoing a sophistication in culture that only comes with deep spiritual consciousness, correlated with sacred astronomy.[63]

"One of those stones (at Sacsayhuaman) is 29 feet high and weighs more than 360 tons; the equivalent of 500 passenger automobiles. That stone is not even at the base of the wall. The quarry from which the granite blocks were cut was more than 10 miles away."[64]

The Kalasasaya Temple

In ancient times, the indigenous peoples living near Tiwanaka (Tiahuanaco) and Lake Titicaca used sacred geometry and archaeoastronomy to build their magnificent temples, and organize their social and physical landscapes. The great temple complex of Kalasasaya Temple is constructed with tall stone columns and smaller rectangular blocks, ranging from 26 feet to hundreds of tons in weight. The Inca culture describe the site as being constructed by the gods at the first creation, with the first inhabitants possessing mystical powers, enabling them to move stones from the ground and carry them through the air using sound. This is a concept that we have heard before with the ancient Egyptians who were said to move the blocks for their monuments by sound waves. One may suggest that due to their size, the blocks may have been constructed during pre-antediluvian eras, when human height was at its maximum. The temple also incorporates angelic figures, carved with human and animal faces, some now extinct and human images quite difficult to place in humanity's hall of races.

Entry is gained through the remarkable 'Gateway of the Sun.' Incan lore connects this gateway to another doorway under the monument, and a tunnel stretching across South America.[65]

Machu Picchu

Pixabay

"Built as a refuge for the elite of the Incas aristocracy, the fortress was located on the eastern slopes of the Vilcanota mountain range, about 80 miles from Cuzco, the capital of the empire. Its strategic location was chosen with admirable success. Surrounded by steep cliffs and away from the sight of strangers in a tangled forest, the citadel of Machu Picchu had the quality of having only one narrow entrance, allowing it,

167

in case of a surprise attack, to be defended by very few warriors. Occupied by at least three generations of Incas, Machu Picchu was abandoned in a sudden and mysterious decision. The strongest hypothesis explaining this disappearance from the historical memory suggests that Machu Picchu was unknown to the lower castes, its routes possibily being prohibited to anyone who was not part of the small, elite circle of the Inca ruling class."[66]

Puma Punku

Part of the archeological site of Tiwanaka, Puma Punku, means "The Door of the Cougar" in Aymara. "It is considered to be one of the most important sites of Andean history. "The most intriguing thing about Puma Punku is the stonework. The red sandstone and andesite stones were cut in such a precise way that it's as if they were cut using a diamond tool, and they can fit perfectly into and lock with each other. Another phenomenon of engineering is that each stone weighs up to 800 tons. Interviews with modern day stone masons have revealed that even with today's advanced technology, it would be almost impossible to replicate the precision observed in the stones found at Puma Punku."[67]

"Puma Punku is part of a large temple complex or monument group of Tiwanaku, Bolivia. Few people know about the royal Puma Punku grave yard that we discovered about a year ago, featuring elongated skulls." – Brien Foerster[68]

"According to the book, *Tiahuanaco, The Cradle of American Man* by University of La Paz Professor Arthur Posnansky, Tiwanaku is closer to 17,000 years old, perhaps one of the oldest surviving human habitations on Earth. Posnansky based his estimate on the alignment of the Kalasasaya temple stones. Kalasasaya means standing stones and refers to the large stone pylons apparently aligned deliberately around a central courtyard. The current temple is a reconstruction and does not reflect the original architecture that the pre-Incan inhabitants intended. There was no wall between the standing stones as there is today."[69]

Adjacent rock cliffs and man-made piers indicate evidence of limestone deposits with fossilized ocean life and sea shells, visible throughout this portion of the monument. Posnansky theorized that Puma Punku was an ancient seaport to Lake Titicaca, now 12-15 miles away, depending upon its water level, which validates Blavatsky's report that Peru was home to post-deluge humanity.[70]

Aryavarta Flee From Atlantis

"Some of the relatively small number of people who escaped and survived, fled for refuge from the terrible turbulent deadly waters of destruction—some of them with the help of the good Atlantean adepts—to the highest and driest points of land that they could find, the peaks and mountains of the Himalayas of Central Asia, and it was there that the very beginnings of the 5th Root Race occurred. It first flourished in ancient India, once called Aryavarta, which became the mother of our present civilisation and so we generally refer to this Root Race as the Aryan Root Race, although it's also called the Indo-Caucasian and Indo-European." The Masters now keep their sacred space deep within the Himalayas.[71]

Ancient Migration to India

In keeping with the Theosophical baseline of philosophy, we continue to describe *Anthrogenesis* within the continent of India, encompassing a vastly ancient and spiritually-based citizenry. Originally, this Iranian plateau and the predominantly tropical South Asian peninsula commenced from two landmasses which were divided by massive ocean volume. Later, about 35 million years ago, the peninsula broke away from southern Gondwana crashing into Laurasia-Asia, with the vestige or slippage from both continents creating the Himalayan Mountains, thereafter enabling a massive migration of the indigenous people.[72]

Notes

1. Lionel Burnett, *A Dictionary of Some Theosophical Terms*, compiled by Powis Hoult, 1910, London, England.
2. http://www.sacred-texts.com/atl/soa/soa25.htm
3. http://www.grahamhancock.com/fingerprints
4. http://www.sacred-texts.com/atl/ssm/ssm06.htm
5. http://sacred-texts.com/atl/ssm/ssm06.htm
6. http://sacred-texts.com/atl/ssm/ssm05.htm
7. http://sacred-texts.com/atl/ssm/ssm06.htm
8. http://blog.world-mysteries.com/science/2012-and-old-equator/
9. http://philipcoppens.com/mu.html
10. http://maya.nmai.si.edu/the-maya/creation-story-maya
11. http://www.mesoweb.com/publications/christenson/popolvuh.pdf
12. Blavatsky, H. P., *The Secret Doctrine*, Vol. II, 1977., Stanzas of Dzyan
13. *2007 Popol Vuh: Sacred Book of the Quiché Maya People.* Electronic version of original 2003 publication: http://www.mesoweb.com/publications/Christenson/PopolVuh.pdf
14. Blavatsky, H. P., *The Secret Doctrine*, Vol. II, 1977
15. http://www.sacred-texts.com/the/sd/sd2-1-01.htm
16. http://www.mesoweb.com/publications/Christenson/PopolVuh.pdf
17. http://www.mesoweb.com/publications/Christenson/PopolVuh.pdf
18. Blavatsky, H. P., *The Secret Doctrine*, Vol. II, 1977, Stanza VIII, 31.
19. http://www.mesoweb.com/publications/christenson/popolvuh.pdf
20. Blavatsky, H. P., 1977. *The Secret Doctrine*, Vol. II, Stanza IX, pp.33-37
21. http://www.lowchensaustralia.com/names/mayan-goddesses.htm
22. http://www.sacred-texts.com/nam/mmp/mmp08.htm
23. Blavatsky, H. P., *The Secret Doctrine*, Vol. II, 1977
24. Blavatsky, H. P., *The Secret Doctrine*, Vol. II, 1977
25. Blavatsky, H. P., *The Secret Doctrine*, Vol. II, 1977
26. Childress, David Hatcher, *The Free-energy Device Handbook: A Compilation of Patents & Reports*, Adventures Unlimited Press, 1994.

27. http://classics.mit.edu/Plato/critias.html *Critias* by Plato, 360 BCE

28. http://classics.mit.edu/Plato/timaeus.html *Timaeus* by Plato, 360 BCE

29. Blavatsky, H. P., *The Secret Doctrine,* Vol. II, 1977

30. http://classics.mit.edu/Plato/timaeus.html *Timaeus* by Plato, 360 BCE

31. http://classics.mit.edu/Plato/critias.html *Critias* by Plato, 360 BCE

32. http://classics.mit.edu/Plato/critias.html *Critias* by Plato, 360 BCE

33. http://classics.mit.edu/Plato/critias.html *Critias* by Plato, 360 BCE

34. http://classics.mit.edu/Plato/timaeus.html *Timaeus* by Plato, 360 BCE

35. de Purucker, Gottfried, *Studies in Occult Philosophy,* 1973, Theosophical University press, Pasadena, CA.

36. http://www.sacred-texts.com/atl/ataw/ataw502.htm;

37. http://www.sacred-texts.com/atl/ataw/ataw307.htm

38. Scott-Elliot, W., *The Story of Atlantis and the Lost Lemuria,* Theosophical Publishing House, Fletcher & Son, LTD., Great Britain. 1972.

39. http://www.theosociety.org/pasadena/man-evol/mie-ap2.htm

40. www.sacred-texts.com/the/sd/sd2-3-07.htm

41. http://www.lucistrust.org/world_goodwill/key_concepts/education_in_the_new_age1

42 Blavatsky, H. P., *The Secret Doctrine,* Vol. II, 1977, pp. 423-27.

43. Blavatsky, H. P., *The Secret Doctrine,* Vol. II, 1977

44. Blavatsky, H. P., *The Secret Doctrine,* Vol. II, 1977, *Book of Dzyan, Stanza X., 40, 42, 44-45.*

45. http://www.theosophy-nw.org/

46. http://blavatskytheosophy.com/human-evolution-in-the-secret-doctrine/

47. http://classics.mit.edu/Plato/timaeus.html

48. http://blavatskytheosophy.com/the-destruction-of-atlantis/_

49. https://stephenknapp.wordpress.com/2009/07/17/ufos-and-vimanas/

50. de Purucker, Gottfried, *Studies in Occult Philosophy*, Theosophical University Press, NY, 1973.

51. Blavatsky, H.P., *Isis Unveiled, I, Travels in Central America*, Theosophical University Press, 1998, Pasadena, CA.

52. *Holy Bible*, Exodus 32:1-33:4.

53. http://www.aztec-history.com/teotihuacan.html

54. Le Plongeon, Augustus, *Maya/Atlantis; Queen Moo and the Egyptian Sphinx*, Rudolf Steiner Publications, 1973.

55. The Codex Matritensis, from the Aztec folio, 172V – 2007 *Popol Vuh: Sacred of the Quiché Maya People*. Electronic version of original 2003 publication. Mesoweb: http://www.mesoweb.com/publications/Christenson/PopolVuh.pdf

56. http://www.sacred-texts.com/nam/mmp/mmp04.htm

57. http://www.ancient-origins.net/human-origins-folklore/aztec-creation-myths-0071

58. http://www.vediccafe.blogspot.com/2012/07/in-valmiki-ramayan-of-india-virochana.html

59. *Talks with Vivekananda*, Advaita Ashram, Mayavati, Himalayas, January 1939.

60. http://www.bigorrin.org/archive-creation3.htm

61. http://frontiers-of-anthropology.blogspot.com/2014/03/the-mystery-of-tiahuanaco.html

62. http://philipcoppens.com/caral.html

63. http://www.world-mysteries.com/mpl_9.htm

64. http://www.grahamhancock.com

65. http://www.labyrinthina.com/puma-punku-tiwanaku-tiahuo-tiahuanacu.html

66. http://www.machupicchu.org/machu_picchu_history.htm

67. http://www.ancient-origins.net/ancient-places-americas/puma-punku-002

68. http://hiddenhumanhistory.com/puma-punku-further-investigations-of-the-enigma-in-bolivia/

69. http://www.redicecreations.com/article.php?id=24770

70. http://www.ancient-origins.net/ancient-places-americas/puma-punku-002

71. http://blavatskytheosophy.com/human-evolution-in-the-secret-doctrine/

72. McIntosh, Jane, 2008. *The Ancient Indus Valley: New Perspectives*, Illustrated Edition, published by ABC-CLIO.

Anthrogenesis

Nagalinga Sculpture Protects Shiva, courtesy of Pixabay

Chapter Nine
Vedanta and Asiatic Foundations

"Why should we forget that, ages before the prow of the adventurous Genoese clove the Western waters, the Phoenician vessels had circumnavigated the globe, and spread civilization in regions now silent and deserted? What archaeologist will dare assert that the same hand which planned the Pyramids of Egypt, Karnak, and the thousand ruins now crumbling to oblivion on the sandy banks of the Nile, did not erect the monumental Nagkon, Angkor Wat of Cambodia? Or trace the hieroglyphics on the obelisks and doors of the deserted Indian village, newly discovered in British Columbia by Lord Dufferin? Or those on the ruins of Palenque and Uxmal, of Central America? Do not the relics we treasure in our museums, last mementos of the long 'lost arts,' speak loudly in favour of ancient civilization? And do they not prove, over and over again, that nations and continents that have passed away have buried along with them arts and sciences, which neither the first crucible ever heated in a mediaeval cloister, nor the last cracked by a modern chemist, have revived, nor will—at least, in the present century." —H.P. Blavatsky[1]

Lords of Flame Brought Sanskrit

C.W. Leadbeater states in *Man: Whence, How and Whither* (1947) that "In neo-theosophical cosmology, the Lords of Flame were beings from Venus who arrived on Earth in order to form the Occult Hierarchy that has governed our planet since then. They initiated the process of spiritual evolution that gave those creatures evolving from animals to humanoid the spark of consciousness. Also called the light or flame of the soul (*Monadic Spark*), it was embodied within the human, who then became a spiritual being. The Lords of the Flame brought the Sanskrit language from Venus as a part of the spiritual awakening of humanity on Earth. Theosophical works articulate that India was the cradle of humanity, the true source of mankind has been veiled."[2]

Author's Note: The 'monadic spark' is defined as the ray or spiritual spark that gathers together throughout evolution of the soul, from the smallest life-wave to the human spiritual plane and physical body; the immortal spirit reincarnates in the lower kingdoms, and gradually progresses through them to humanity, onward to the final goal of Nirvana.[3]

Krishna's Brother Baladeva/Hercules

Blavatsky states in her *Collected Writings*, "The Occult Doctrine explains that Hercules was the last incarnation of one of the seven "Lords of the Flame." As Krishna's brother, Baladeva's incarnations occurred during the Third, Fourth, and Fifth Root-Races, his worship was brought into Egypt from Sri-Lanka and India by the later immigrants." Continuing on this thought, Heracles (Greek) and Hercules (Roman) and Baal—Phoenician—were one-in-the-same person. Hercules was also Baladeva, the brother of Vishnu, in the Mahabharata; 'Hercules is of Indian origin and he was Baladeva." Mythology has been successful over the ages in making story out of truth and also, cloaking the Mysteries, for what it's worth!

A late sub-race of Atlantean immigrants founded the empire in India and Central Asia, among other locations, sending emissaries to Egypt. The last Mongolians—the 7th sub-race of Atlantis, were settling their colonies in Asia, China, Siberia, and Mongolia and concurrently, the Aryans first sub-race—the Hindus, were arriving into northern, then later to southern India. Referring to themselves as 'Aryans,' or the 'high caste,' they later separated into the four castes that we currently associate with Hinduism: Brahmanas, Kshattriyas, Vaisyas and Sudras.[4]

Lord Krishna by Nicholas Roerich (1874 to 1947)

Lord Krishna in the Himalayas

Vedic Material World

"With its cyclical notion of time, Hinduism teaches that the material world is created not once but repeatedly, time and time again, much like the Mayan story of three successive worlds that prevailed before the current world. Additionally, this universe is considered to be one of many, all enclosed "like innumerable bubbles floating in space." In the life of Brahma, the Universe is born and destroyed, only to be born again – operational within the Yuga system or Precession. Within this Universe there are three main regions: the heavenly planets, the earthly realm and the lower worlds, with relevant scripture recounting some detail as to

177

the nature of these regions and their respective inhabitants. Hinduism is therefore *not* predominantly earth-centered and puts much emphasis on other planes of existence and the realm of spiritual consciousness itself. This is reflected in Hindu stories and specifically through the concept of Lila, the divine pastime. These Lilas take place in the spiritual world and are replicated at sacred locations on Earth. There is no one simple account of the creation, and there are many detailed and interrelated stories. Central is the narration of the sacrifice of the primal being, called Purusha, who is named in the *Rig Veda*. On the metaphysical level, the Universe is created from sound or vak. Sound corresponds to ether, the subtlest of the five material elements. According to such Sankhya philosophy, the elements develop progressively from subtle to gross. The *Atman* is subtler than any matter, and generates his own successive material bodies. This world and its creatures are here to facilitate the soul's self-centered desires, and ultimately to enable its return to the spiritual world."[5]

Author's Note: Atman is defined as Atmâ (Sanskrit) or Atmân; The Universal Spirit, the divine Monad, the 7th Principle in the septenary (seventh) constitution of man. The Supreme Soul.

Philadelphia Museum of Art

Ancient Kumari Kandam

During battle between Ravana and Lord Rama, a request was made to Nala of the Vanara—the monkey army, to fashion a great bridge to Lanka, to rescue Rama's wife, Sita, captured by King Ravana. The bridge reportedly took 5 days to build across many miles, traversing the Indian Ocean. Made of floating stones, the bridge can still be seen today, between India and Sri Lanka from Rameshwaram.[6,7]

The Tamil of India speak of this ancient land bridge built by the monkey army of Lord Rama, connecting the island of Sri Lanka to mainland India, called Kumari Kandam, a land ruled by the Pandiyan kings, allegedly the continent of Lemuria, which was home to sages and a large population that was eventually swallowed by the sea. Kumari Kandam, also named Mu, was located in the subcontinent of India, in the region where Sri Lanka now lies. The oldest culture of people on Earth, the Tamil people long ago began using the turn of phrase, 'Kumari Kandam,' which first came out in *Kanda Puranam*, a 15th century Tamil version of the *Skanda Purana*, written by Kachiappa Sivacharyara (1350-1420). Based upon the ancient flood stories of the Deluge, in part, the first Tamil literature had a legend of an island being flooded in the Indian Ocean. Lemuria's story arrived in colonial India when the country was going through a time when myth began to pervade history. Fortunately, we see in *Anthrogenesis* that many ancient beliefs and philosophies describe similar flood stories across the world! It is noted here that researcher, G. de Purucker, in his book, *Fundamentals of the Esoteric Philosophy*, also located Lemuria in the Pacific Ocean.[8]

Gulf of Cambay in 33,000 BCE

The discovery of megalithic structures and water-aged river pebbles were observed in India's Gulf of Cambay in 2002, establishing a human presence at 33,000 BCE, with an established culture from ~15,000 BCE to ~5000 BCE, from the lab studies which carbon-dated the wood artifacts. Researchers observed a temple with a pool along symmetrical structures and an ancient underwater river.[9,10]

Migrating to New Lands

The continent of India has ancient origins stemming from a variety of voyaging groups over the thousands of years since the post-Oceanic deluge. While there are no exact records, it is thought that India, like Egypt, had mass migrating populaces coming from Sri Lanka, South America, Oceania, later populated by migration from northern peoples following other nomadic wanderers from Sumer, the Phoenician sailors and Southern Egypt. The writer, Valmiki in the *Ramayana* cites the Maya as navigating from the western to eastern oceans and from southern to northern seas so remote that 'the sun had not yet risen above the horizon' when these Maya conquered the southern areas of India. Timing corresponds to millions of years ago. Purucker describes the early Aryan race developing 7-8 million years ago; a migrating assemblage of humans from Atlantis to Central Asia and to what is now the Gobi Desert, at a time of magnificent beauty in its landscape and fauna. Over time, Laurasia evolved into the continent of today. At the onset of Krita Yuga, some 3 million years ago, humanity, under spiritual guidance from the Masters, began migration within the sub-races, including the Assyrians, Hindus, the Iranians-Persians, and the Celtic tribes, the Teutons, the Scandinavians and finally, the Mongolians, being the last sub-race of Atlantis, who went to this new land.[11, 12]

The Ageless Vedas

Blavatsky discusses the origin and description of the Vedas, defined in Sanskrit as 'to know.':

"The scriptures of the Hindus come from the root vid, "to know," or "divine knowledge." They are the most ancient as well as the most sacred of the Sanskrit works. The *Vedas,* on the date and antiquity of which no two Orientalists can agree, are claimed by the Hindus themselves, whose Brahmans and Pundits ought to know best about their own religious works. They were first taught orally for thousands of years and then compiled on the shores of Lake Mânasa-Sarovara, beyond the Himalayas, in Tibet.

"When was this done? While their religious teachers, such as Swami Dayanand Saraswati, claim for them to be of great antiquity, our modern

Orientalists will grant them no greater antiquity in their present form than about 1,000 to 2,000 BCE As compiled in their final form by Veda-Vâysa, however, the Brahmans themselves unanimously assign 3,100 years before the Christian era, the date when Vyâsa flourished. Therefore, the *Vedas* must be as old as this date. But their antiquity is sufficiently proven by the fact that they are written in an ancient form of Sanskrit, so different from the Sanskrit now used, and there is no other work like them in the literature of this eldest sister of all the known languages. Only the most learned of the Brahman Pundits can read the Vedas in their original Sanskrit.

"Colebrooke dated the Vedas at around 1400 B.C. and asserted that this date is corroborated by a passage which he discovered, and which is based on astronomical data. But if, as shown by many Orientalists and Hindu Pundits that (a) the Vedas are not a single work, but that each *Veda*, and almost every hymn and division of the latter, is the production of various authors; and that (b) these have been written (whether as sruti, "revelation," or not) at various periods of the ethnological evolution of the Indo-Aryan race, then what does Mr. Colebrooke's discovery prove? Simply that the *Vedas* were finally arranged and compiled fourteen centuries before our era and this in no way challenges their antiquity. Quite the reverse. Also, there is a learned article, written on purely astronomical data by Krishna Shâstri Godbole (of Bombay), which puts forth the concept that the Vedas must have been taught at least 25,000 years ago."[13, 14, 15]

The Vedic Triad, the Trimurti

The Triad appears again in *Anthrogenesis*. Brahma, not to be confused with the over-arching Bramh, is that reality in its role as Creator of the Universe; in Vishnu we see the preserver and the upholder of the universe; and Shiva is that same reality viewed as the principle of transcendence which will one day destroy the universe. These are the Trimurti, the three forms of God.[16]

The Path of an Initiate

An Initiate is defined as an individual who is spiritually ready to take Initiation into a higher level of the Ancient Mysteries, learning the secrets of Mystical Occultism. This allows the person to better serve humanity in different capacities, based upon their dharma, ray group or ashramic affiliation of a certain type. In our modern days those who 'knock at the door' of Initiation are instructed by the Masters of the Ancient Wisdom, receiving knowledge to enhance service to humanity, spiritual advancement, with increased responsibility.

In times of antiquity, those who were ready for Initiation received similar teaching of arcane knowledge about the Universe, the difference being that in olden days, the Initiate was taught by the Hierophants of the Mysteries.[17, 18]

Spiritual Initiation is a complex system, designed to illuminate individuals to the mysteries of existence and which greatly cross time and cultures. The masterful Carl Gustav Jung (1875-1961), was the

Swiss psychiatrist who founded Transpersonal psychology, a unique approach with an emphasis on understanding the psyche through dreams, art, mythology, world religion and philosophy. Jung's interpersonal life and work with his patients predisposed his belief that spirituality goes far beyond material goals, stating that the main task for humanity is to discover and fulfill our deep, innate potential. Jung believed that we embark on a journey of transformation, to meet the Self and at the same time to meet the Divine. He called this 'individuation' the mystical heart of all religions, based upon his extensive study of Christianity, Hinduism, Buddhism, Gnosticism, Taoism, and other traditions. He felt that the Self and the Ego were intrinsically in alignment. So, as we explore the path of enlightenment, one must attend to all needs, as Jung said, but focus on the reason for life, to begin with![19]

Poem of the Soul by Louis Janmot (1814–1892), courtesy of Rama

The first step on the path includes the need to 'show proof' that she or he is capable in mastery of the physical vehicle, thus taking the 1st Initiation. This step was much more profound for our progenitors, in the first three Root-races. Symbolically, the 1st Initiation signifies Birth, both physical and spiritual. Second, is the astral-emotional; the 2nd Initiation, containing the Initiate's proficiency over the astral-emotional body. The Root-Races exemplified their group capacity, to proceed forward in evolution, having attained a stronger physical sheath versus the previous astral-etheric sheath; thus completing mastery over the astral nature many millennia ago. Today, in the 5th Root Race, we have the astral--emotional body, which we must lovingly incorporate.

The 3rd Initiation requires a readiness of 'Heart'—full of compassion to guide and mitigate the astral-emotional, the Higher Mind or mental body and the personality, comprised of the physical, emotional and mental aspects of the Initiate. The 3rd Initiation takes time, a slow process, as the Initiate both struggles and succeeds along the Path of Return back from whence we came.

The story of *The Wizard of Oz* underscores a necessary perspective. Dorothy treads the 'yellow brick road," laid out for her to follow, but along the way, she is confronted by a number of challenges. They appear as various creatures, or Dorothy herself, becoming lost or carried away from her original destination in route to 'the Wizard of Oz.' Dorothy's outlook transforms throughout her journey, while she gains confidence, and thus, has less fear about responsibilities, both hers and those around her. And she knows that she will finally meet the Wizard.

Thus, the Initiate observes that the "Heart has become my Master," both guiding and directing the Initiate along the 'Path of No Return,' the Path which ultimately leads to the Godhead. The Initiate observes that, in fact, it is Love and Compassion that guides one's personal life, not the small travesties of human affairs or insignificant details of one's personal life. The integrated Mind and Personality act as a guidepost for the Initiate, with the Heart leading.

So, the Soul is readied, perhaps after countless lives, focused specifically on the above tasks. Time draws nigh for the 3rd Initiation to be completed, thus preparing the way for advancement. This disposes the Initiate for advanced knowledge of the esoteric nature of the Ancient Mysteries and of our Universe.

The original code of initiation honored the Spiritual Creator, respecting and following the Golden Rule and using a form of the Lord's Prayer as a mantra in daily life. The practice of initiation into the sacred Mysteries, taught by the Hierophants and learned priests of the Temples was one of the most ancient customs. This was practiced in every old national religion. In Europe it was abolished with the fall of the last pagan temple.

Blavatsky discusses how the Egyptians and Indians began to change the Truths, create castes and separate humanity such that priests and mahatmas could maintain more control over the steps of Initiation. She pondered on why it was that humans needed to control this great spiritual step but then retorted that the post-antediluvian times may have necessitated more caution. When humanity has passed through the materialism of the Fifth Root Race, well into the 6th Root Race, humanity will be much more loving and giving; the need for having control will melt away![20, 21]

In discussing the foundations of Buddhahood in humanity, the Master Morya gives in the *Mahatma Letters* (p. 243) a list of the Bodhisattvas:

- First Root Race: Vairachana, Samanta Bhadra, Kraku-Chandu
- Second Root Race: Akshobyas, Vajrapani, Kanaki Muni
- Third Root Race: Ratna, Ratnapani, Kasyapi
- Fourth Root Race: Amitabha, Avalokitesvara, Gautama
- Fifth Root Race: Amogasiddha , Visvapani, Maiytreya,
- Sixth Root Race: (not given)
- Seventh Root Race: (not given)[22]

Goddess Venerations

Venus of Hohle Fels (Germany) is the most ancient of the female goddess finds (1908), dated at 40,000 BCE. Junoesque in design, she figures to be the epitome of our life-bearing goddess, so similar to other Mother–goddesses, numbering about 13, and excavated around the world.[21]

In *The Book of the Goddess, Past and Present* by Carl Olsen (1983), Anne L. Barstow examines both goddess and female roles in prehistoric cultures by using the archaeological discoveries from Çatal Höyük, the ancient city of Anatolia. She notes that agriculture replaced hunting as the preeminent source of food and wealth in that culture, controlled by women. Like Nicholas Conard (*Nature,* 2009) Barstow attributed a matrilocal (matriarchal) society with a priestly class containing women; the goddess cult predominated over the male gods. Barstow observed one goddess had many roles in that prehistoric period. Although she was associated with many things, the goddess was primarily a symbol of spiritual power, fertility, and a source of materiality. The prehistoric goddess was depicted as faceless, without feet, unclothed, often large-breasted with observable genitalia, nursing a child and sometimes pregnant.[23, 24]

Museum of Anatolian Civilizations, Ankara, Turkey, Nevit Dilmen

The Mother Goddess at Çatal Höyük

Dr. Shahina Farid, the Project Coordinator and Field Director of the Neolithic site of Çatal Höyük, from 1995-2012, was responsible for the site excavations and study. She has discovered that the ancient site consists of solid mud brick houses, laden with goddess figures; 'linked to women's roles in a 'goddess cult' along with bull heads and skin decor, woven baskets and mural painting of people and animals on the walls of the dwellings. Also, she has a theory about these ancient people, it is thought that town folk buried their dead under the bed, in preparation for rebirth!'[25]

Sacred Geometry at Angkor Wat

A number of Asian ancient sites incorporate the sacred geometry of the *Vedas*. However, Angkor Wat is the ultimate masterpiece of Khmer art. While spiritual perspectives vary, based upon the Cambodian station of life and locale, Angkor Wat and India have collective beliefs in Vedic Hinduism. In the Indian traditions of architecture, called "*Sthapatya Veda*," incorporation of sacred geometry in temple construction aims to "mirror the cosmos." One observes a unique blend of feminine and masculine elegance, having its origins in sources from earlier Yuga Sutras. The interior vestiges speak of the battle of Kurukshetra, emulating the depictions of heavens and hells, and battles of Vishnu and the sparring of devas with Asuras. The solar and lunar numbers that show up in the design of the Angkor Wat temple are the number of months in the year, the days in the lunar month and the days of the solar month, with circumferences of the ecliptic, the moon and lunar periodicity, the constellations, the planets, and the celestial year all occurring during the history of King Suryavarman.

Tacluda

"A grid plan, as recommended in the Vedic manuals" advises a "square shape, representing the heavens, with the four directions representing the cardinal directions as well as the two solstices and the equinoxes of the sun's orbit." At Angkor Wat, Cambodia, we witness a masterpiece permutation of customs, aligned with the Vedic tenets of astronomy and cosmology, from a noteworthy culture flourishing well before and during the Khmer Empire: 800 to 1300 BCE, according to a most spellbinding, exquisitely designed architecture.[26]

Mamoon Mengal

Indus Priest-King Statue, National Museum of Pakistan

Like Egypt and Sumer, the Indus River Valley was home to the Harappa culture, which migrated throughout the site of Mohenjo-Daro, c. 3000 BCE. A central structure on the Indian continent, within the Indus River Valley, Mohenjo-Daro contained "thousands of clay tablets," indicating that a script system was in place, perhaps "even older than the Sumerian" cuneiform.[27, 28]

Indus River Valley Roots

The cultivation of the Indus River Valley brought the growth of greater population, and traditions. Being one of six great areas of ancient civilization. Ancient Greek philosophers, such as Pliny the Elder, date India's conception at c. 7000 BCE.

Dwelling Place of Lord Krishna

The ancient city of Dwarka is thought to be located off the western coast of Gujarat, India. The city derives its name from the word "dvar" meaning 'door' or 'gate' in the Sanskrit language. It is located close to where the Gomti River merges into the Gulf of Kutch. However, this river Gomti is not the same Gomti River which is a tributary of the Ganges River. The city lies in the westernmost part of India. The legendary city of Dwarka was the dwelling place of Lord Krishna. It is believed that due to damage and destruction by the sea, Dwarka has been submerged six times. Modern day Dwarka is the seventh such city to be built in the area.[29]

Hindu Theogony

The ten principal texts of Hinduism come from the ancient rishis and sages who assembled them into two constructs: *Shruti* or 'that which has been heard,' and includes the four *Vedas: Rig, Sama, Yajur* and *Atharva*, of which there are over 100,000 verses. *Shruti* is the undeniable canon of Hinduism, including the eternal revelation and ancient truths of which the *Vedas* speak. Also part of *Shruti* is the *Upanishads* (a total of 108 verses) the *Vedanta Sutra*, which are the most ancient religious texts available in written form, and the *Puranas*, the post-Vedic texts of which 18 are recognized *Puranas* related to Brahma, Vishnu and Shiva.

The *Smriti* or 'that which has been remembered,' is an associated text that can change over time and is authoritative to the extent that it conforms to the bedrock of *Shruti*.

The four main *Smriti* texts, which include the *Itihasas-* or histories and epics like the *Ramayana, the Mahabharata, and the Bhagavad-Gita* are the stories of ancient India, which contain much of the Hindu philosophy. The *Dharma Shastra*, the books of Law are also included in this class and form the basis for societal norms and mores. Other related works of Hinduism included in *Smriti* are *108 Upanishads.*[30]

Krishna and Arjuna at Kurukshetra

Sridhar1000, drawing c. 1500

In the travels of Arjuna with Krishna, there were times when the hero was misunderstood. There was a war between two clans, between armies led by two groups of kings and princes who were brothers at Kurukshetra. In the Hindu epic, the *Mahabharata*, why would the Kaurava army wait patiently while Krishna delivered the stories of the *Bhagavad Gita* to Arjuna in the battlefield? The two clans had the ability to capitalize on Arjuna's lack of motivation to fight to their advantage.

Arjuna is in the middle of battlefield, and is confused as to whether he should do his duty and fight, or be morally correct and not slay his relatives. With this confusion, he throws away his weapons and sits down. It is quite possible that before war began, Arjuna developed cold feet when he realized that he was going to fight his relatives and brothers and hesitated to fight.

Krishna comes in to rescue and give practical advice. Arjuna's apprehension is countered by the collective efforts of the Pandavas and the great Krishna, who make Arjuna remember the immense amount of injustice meted out by the Kauravas onto Arjuna. Arjuna then realizes his blunder and decides to fight. Conflict is always present in the mind of a person going into war; conflict over performing his or her duties is understandable to anyone in some part of his or her life.

This is the scenario when Krishna comes as a savior and gives us the practical solutions.

"Do your duties, and leave the rest to the God! Do not expect anything in return; if you deserve it, you will get it! Do not procrastinate!"

"It is the body that dies, not the soul! Soul merely changes bodies, like a man changes his clothes!"

Perhaps Lord Krishna stopped time to explain all 700 shlokas (verses) of the *Bhagavad Gita* to Arjuna![31]

The Philosophy of Hinduism

"The Hindu worldview is grounded in the doctrines of *samsara* or the Cycle of Rebirth and *karma*, the universal Law of Cause and Effect, and basically holds that one's actions and thoughts directly determine one's life, both one's current life and one's future lives. Hinduism is an amalgamation of various philosophical and religious traditions of India with its collection of sacred texts known as *Sanatana Dharma*, or the eternal spiritual path, a complex tradition that encompasses numerous interrelated religious doctrines, philosophies, beliefs and practices in early India.

"It is the world's oldest religion of ancients, known as the Aryans or noble people, whose philosophy, religion, and customs are recorded in their sacred Vedic texts. Hinduism, a mystical religion, has no moment of origin, it precedes recorded history, thus, timeless, having always existed with no specific founder, leading the devotee to personally experience the Truth 'within' and reaching the pinnacle of consciousness where man and God are one. Hindus hold that the cosmos is populated by numerous deities and spiritual beings, gods and goddesses, or devas, who actively influence the world, and who interact with humans embracing sects and sub-sects with local or regional variations of sects seen as distinct religious traditions, specific theologies and ritual traditions. These include the Shaiva, devotees of the god *Shiva*, the *Vaishnava*, devotees of the god Vishnu, the *Shakta*, devotees of the goddess, and the *Smarta*, those who understand the ultimate form of the divine to be abstract and all-encompassing Brahman."[32]

The Buddha Came from Nepal

The Buddha, first called Siddhartha, began his life as a royal prince about 600 BCE in ancient Lumbini, now located in Nepal and preached his first sermon, "The Sutra of Setting the Wheel of Dharma in Motion" (*the Dhamma-cakka-pavattana*) at Sarnath, near Varanasi, India to his five companions, with whom he had practiced serious asceticism, before his enlightenment at Bodh Gaya, India.

Buddha's teaching of the 'Middle Way' (*majjhima patipada*) and 'The Four Noble Truths' (*cattari ariya saccani*) and the 'Noble Eightfold Path' (*ariya atthangika magga*) contain the fundamental principles of Buddhism. It has come down in several slightly different versions, with the most famous one belonging to the Samyuttanikaya, Verse 420 of the Pali Canon of Sri Lanka. In the Dalai Lama's words, "The beauty of the Buddha's wisdom and compassion reached into the very depths of mundane life, providing ordinary people with guidelines for proper conduct and right understanding. Far from being a creed for a monastic elite, ancient Buddhism involved the close collaboration of householders and monastics in the twin tasks of maintaining the Buddha's teachings and assisting one another in their efforts to walk the path to the extinction of suffering." Siddhartha devoted the rest of his life to the teaching of compassion for all life and his dogma spread throughout Asia, especially to China and Tibet.[33]

Boudhanath Stupa, Kathmandu, Nepal, photo courtesy of Gong Jie.

Jainism, an Indian Religion of Salvation

"A nontheistic religion, Jainism, was founded in India in 500 CE by the Jina Vardhamana Mahavira as a reaction against the teachings of orthodox Brahmanism, and is still practiced there. The Jain religion teaches salvation by perfection through successive lives, and non-injury to living creatures, and is noted for its ascetics."

"The Jain faith has a large population of believers, and is quite ancient. In Jainism, one must consider that religion is eternal and imperishable. It is without beginning and it will never cease to exist. The darkness of error enveloping the *truth*, in certain periodically occurring eons, then clears up, again and again, so that the brightness of the Jain faith can sparkle again anew."[34]

The Hurrians or "Khurrites, were a people that entered northern Mesopotamia around 2300 BCE to 1000 BCE. Ancestors spoke the first 'Old Tamil,' which was the language of the Indus River Valley Civilization. They are intrinsically connected to populations spread throughout Central Asia, and later, the Balkans and Anatolia.[35, 36, 37]

Zhengan

Nemrut Dağ

"The mausoleum of Antiochus I (69–34 B.C.), who reigned over Commagene, a kingdom founded north of Syria and the Euphrates after the breakup of Alexander's empire, is one of the most ambitious constructions of the Hellenistic period. The syncretism of its pantheon, and the lineage of its kings, which can be traced back through two sets of legends, Greek and Persian, is evidence of the dual origin of this kingdom's culture."[38]

Mount Nemrut; 'Nemrut Dağ' in Turkish, was a minor Armenian kingdom founded c. 162 BCE. Crowning one of Turkey's elevated peaks, within the Eastern Taurus Mountain range, the phenomenal Nemrut Dağ site dominates these ancient lands.

The 'House of the Gods,' a tomb-sanctuary built by the 'god king' King Antiochus, "consists of a pyramid-shaped mound of stone chips" topped with large ornate statues, illustrating a blend of "Persian and Greek gods." King Antiochus' understanding of sacred astronomy was based on "the Sothic-Anahit (Star of Sirius) and Hayk (Star of Orion) cycle used by the Egyptians," revealing the king's Hermetic philosophy.[39]

Notes

1. Blavatsky, H. P., *The Secret Doctrine*, Vol. II, 1977, p. 430.
2. http://www.archive.org/stream/manwhencehowandw031919mbp/manwhencehowandw031919mbp_djvu.txt
3. http://www.theosophywales.com/seven_bodies_of_man__a_brie.htm
4. http://www.katinkahesselink.net/blavatsky/articles/v14/ph_060.htm
5. http://hinduism.iskcon.org/concepts/112.htm
6. http://www.rense.com/general30/nasa.htm
7. Valmiki Ramayana, Yuddha Kanda, Chapter 22.
8. https://www.quora.com/What-are-some-myths-and-facts-about-kumarikandam
9. https://grahamhancock.com/badrinaryanb1/
10. http://archaeologyonline.net/artifacts/cambay
11. Le Plongeon, Augustus, 1973. *Queen Moo and the Egyptian Sphinx*, Rudolf Steiner Publications, Blauvelt, NY.
12. *Valmiki in Ramayana*, Hippolyte, Fauche's translation, Vol I, page 353.
13. See Theosophist, Vol. II., p. 238 et seq., Aug., 1881).
14. http://www.cyonic-nemeton.com/theosophy/Vpage.html:
15. Blavatsky, H. P., *The Theosophical Glossary*, Theosophical Publishing Society, NY, 1892.
16. http://www.hinduwebsite.com/hinduism/hindutrinity.asp
17. http://www.theosophy.org/Blavatsky/
18. http://www.moryafederation.com/jpc/
19. Jung, Carl Gustav, *Man and His Symbols*, 1964, Bantam Doubleday Dell Publishing Group, N.Y.
20. http://www.theosophy.org/Blavatsky/ SD, Vol. I and II.
21. http://www.moryafederation.com/jpc/
22. http://www.moryafederation.com/jpc/
21. Conard, Nicholas, "A female figurine from the basal Aurignacian of Hohle Fels Cave in southwestern Germany," Vol 459|14 May 2009| doI – 10.1038/nature07995, 248-252.
23. Olsen, Carl, 1983. *The Book of The Goddess, Past and Present*, Crossroad Publishers, NY.

24. Antl-Weiser, Walpurga. "The Anthropomorphic Figurines from Willendorf." Lower Austrian Landes Museum, St. Pölten, Austria 19.477 (2008): 19-30. The Province of Lower Austria. Lower Austrian Provincial Museum. Web. 1 Jan. 2016. http://www.nhm-wien.ac.at/en Natural History Museum Vienna, Department for Prehistory, Burgring 7, 1014 Vienna, Austria.
25. http://www.ucl.ac.uk/archaeology/research/directory/catalhoyuk
26. *Space and Cosmology in the Hindu Temple by Subhash Kak*, presented at Vaastu Kaushal: International Symposium on Science and Technology in Ancient Indian Monuments, New Delhi, November 16-17, 2002, pdf.
27. http://www.harappa.com/har/indus-saraswati.html
28. http://www.mrdowling.com/612-mohenjodaro.html
29. http://www.ancient-origins.net/ancient-places-asia/dwarka-home-krishna-gateway-heaven-and-underwater-city-004227
30. http://www.sacred-texts.com/hin/
31. http://www.ulc.org/wp-content/uploads/2012/10/Bhagavad-Gita.pdf
32. http://www.sacred-texts.com/hin/
33. Bodhi, Bhikku, *In the Buddha's Words*, 2005, Wisdom Publications, Somerville, MA.
34. http://www.oxforddictionaries.com/us/definition/american_english/Jainism
35. http://cw.routledge.com/textbooks/9780415485432/8.asp: Pliny's account of "A Passage to India."
36. http://www.liquisearch.com/hurrian_language
37. http://www.ancientscripts.com/indus.html
38. http://www.whc.unesco.org/en/list/448
39. http://www.ancient-origins.net/ancient-places-asia/mount-nemrut-and-god-king-commagene-001900

Anthrogenesis

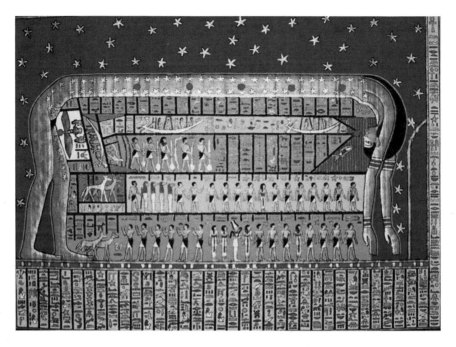

Nut, the Goddess of the Sky. Dendera Temple relief on papyrus.

Chapter Ten

Dreams Of Egypt

Mysteries of Egypt

In exploring the origins and mysteries of Egypt, we observe the pageantry of a people who were unequivocally in sync with the Universe. This ambience is felt through their art and cultural style to reveal a time of beauty, harmony and oneness with their gods, goddesses, and the heavens. One can almost feel the lush tropical climate brushing over the skin with fragrant scents in the air while magnificent art forms occupy the view, encased in a mesmerizing complexity of mindfulness. It was a magnificent time of grace and splendor during a spellbinding chapter of humanity.[1]

The Egyptian Creation Myth

"The Egyptian Creation Myth tells us that, at first, there was only Ocean. This ocean was breadth-less and depth-less and silent until, upon its surface, there rose a hill of earth (known as the ben-ben, the primordial mound, which, it is thought, the pyramids symbolize) and the great god Ra (the sun) stood upon the ben-ben and spoke, giving birth to the god Shu (of the air) the goddess Tefnut (of moisture) the god Geb (of earth) and the goddess Nut (of sky). Ra had intended Nut as his bride but she fell in love with Geb. Angry with the lovers, Ra separated them by stretching Nut across the sky high away from Geb on the earth. Although the lovers were separated during the day, they came together at night and Nut bore three sons, Osiris, Set and Horus, and two daughters, Isis and Nephthys. Osiris, as eldest, was announced as 'Lord of all the Earth' when he was born and was given his sister Isis as a wife. Set, consumed by jealousy, hated his brother and killed him to assume the throne. Isis then embalmed her husband's body and, with powerful charms, resurrected Osiris who returned from the dead to bring life to the people of Egypt. Osiris later served as the Supreme Judge of the souls of the dead in the Hall of Truth and, by weighing the heart of the soul in the balances, decided who was granted eternal life."[2]

Egyptian Pantheon of Gods

Egyptian deity worship shows evidence in written form during the Early Dynastic Period (c. 3100–2686 BCE) however, beliefs were undoubtedly present in prior times. Egyptologist Günter Dreyer has reported on findings dated at c. 3300- 2700 BCE. It becomes clear that Egypt's religion had percolated across centuries. As we have previously discussed in *Anthrogenesis*, pertinent dating techniques of human finds and history are sorely in need of up-to-date, realistic methods. Nevertheless, the Egyptians had several creation myths, emerging out of several temple locations with their various priesthoods and indigenous gods.[3]

Public Domain

Isis and Osiris

The Ogdoad Deities

"Hermopolis means "the city of Hermes" in Greek. The Greeks gave it that name because it was a major cult centre of the god Thoth who they associated with their god Hermes, but the Egyptians knew it as Khmunu ("the City of the Eight"). The Ogdoad was a system of eight deities, four gods and their consorts (the number four was considered to represent completeness). Each pair represented the male and female aspects of the four creative powers or sources. Nun and Naunet represented the primeval waters; Heh and Hauhet represented eternity; Kuk and Kuaket represented darkness; and Amun and Amaunet represented air (or that which is hidden). The gods were all depicted with heads of frogs, while the goddesses had the heads of serpents. Only Amun went on to be considered as more than a primeval force. While Nun was still referred to often, it was only as the representation of the waters of Chaos. These eight elements interacted, causing an explosion (the Big Bang?) and the burst of energy which was released caused the primeval mound (located at Hermopolis, but originally known as the "Isle of Flame") to rise from the water. It was thought the gods and goddesses of the Ogdoad then ruled the earth during the Golden Age. When they died they took up residence in the "Duat" (or "Tuat"—the Underworld). That ensured that the Nile continued to flow, that the inundation would come every year and caused the sun to rise each day."[4]

In *Anthrogenesis*, we have discussed Thoth/Hermes in earlier sections and now we see Thoth later considered as an Egyptian god. He was popular throughout Egypt, but was particularly recognized in Khnum (Hermopolis Magna) where he was revered in the Ogdoad. As the power of Thoth's cult grew, the myth was rewritten to make Thoth the creator god. In this story, Thoth (in the form of an ibis, one of his sacred animals) laid an egg from which Ra (Atum/Nefertum/Khepri) was born. In one creation myth, Thoth/Khnum molded everything on his potter's wheel, including the people and the gods. In Iunyt/Esna, the 3rd Nome of Upper Egypt, it was proposed that he also created the "First Egg" from which the Sun was born.[5]

E. A. Wallis Budge 1857-1937

Ennead of Heliopolis

"The ancient Egyptians had many gods, but some were closely connected to each other in groupings known as "Pesdjets" and associated with a defined location. The *Pyramid Texts* of the Old Kingdom refer to a number of groups of gods, of which the Great Pesdjet is now known to us as "The Ennead." The Ennead (derived from the Greek word for nine) are the nine ancient Egyptian Gods and Goddesses associated with the creation myths of Heliopolis (Iunu) in Lower Egypt."

"In the beginning there was nothing—Nun. A mound of earth rose from Nun and upon it Atum (later Amun or Re) created himself. He did not want to be alone so he masturbated (or spat) producing air—Shu, and moisture—Tefnut. Shu and Tefnut gave birth to the earth—Geb and the sky—Nut. Geb and Nut were separated by Shu, creating our world. The children of Nut and Geb were Osiris, Horus the elder, Set, Isis and Nephthys."

"We do not know when the Ennead were first worshipped, but certainly as early as the Fifth dynasty of the Old Kingdom. However, their prime position was not assured. In Memphis, Ptah was the creator god, while in Thebes, Montu (and later Amun) was the foremost god. By the sixth dynasty Horus (especially when he merged with Ra as Horakhty) was in the ascendancy, although distinct members of the Ennead (especially Osiris, Set, Isis and Nepythys) remained both popular and powerful. The Greek term was coined by Greek scholars in Egypt during the twentieth dynasty towards the end of the New Kingdom."[6]

Sekhmet and the Memphis Triad

In the Memphite Triad, Sekhmet is of the oldest known Egyptian deities, with her name coming from the Egyptian word "Sekhem," implying power or might and translates as "Powerful One" or "She who is Powerful." She is represented as a lion-headed woman, occasionally illustrated with a sun disc on her head. Sekhmet holds the ankh of life while sitting, but when standing, she usually holds the scepter of papyrus, which is the symbol of Lower Egypt. This suggests that she was connected with the north.

In Memphis, Sekhmet was worshipped as "the destroyer" alongside her consort Ptah-the creator god and their son, Nefertum, the healer. The priests of Memphis assimilated all aspects of the Isis and Osiris creation in favor of Sekhmet and Ptah and the new Memphite creation myth. The Memphis version of creation existed alongside the Ennead of Heliopolis, but its followers believed that Ptah created Atum and the ocean from which he rose. Over time Ptah assumed the role of Osiris and he has been credited with inventing the 'opening of the mouth' ceremony (the transition of the soul to the afterlife). The Memphis Triad was perhaps the longest-lasting religion of Egypt until issues of economics, the rise of the waters surrounding Alexandria and finally, Constantine's edict of 380 CE, which forbade any other religion, besides the Nicaean Creed of the Roman Empire brought it to an end.[7]

The Obsequies of an Egyptian Cat – John Weguelin (1849-1927)

Triad of Elephantine

"Elephantine (Abu) was the ancient capital of the first nome of Upper Egypt. It is a small island just north of the First Cataract of the Nile. Khnemu was a ram-headed creator-god whose cult center was at the city of Elephantine". Khnemu was said to have created all men and their ka from clay and straw molding their bodies on a giant potter's wheel."

At the Great Temple of Luxor, Khnemu is depicted sculpting the body and ka of the pharaoh. The ka is a symbol of each human receiving the life powers from the gods, the source of these powers, and is the spiritual double that resides with every human living on after death within the body. The ka is therefore needed by the physical body after death as long as it has a place to live. This is why the Egyptians mummified their dead.

"In the Pyramid Texts of the Old Kingdom, the pharaoh was called the "son of Khnemu." Inscriptions at Elephantine detail the visit to the shrine of Khnemu at Elephantine by Pharaoh Djoser. He was there to request the god's help in ending a seven-year long famine which had plagued Egypt. The queen had conceived the king following intercourse with Amon and Hathor brought the sculptures to life by giving them the ankh. Rounding out the triad of Elephantine was Khnemu's consort, Satet and their daughter, Anqet. Satet, as the "Mistress of Elephantine", was associated with the annual flooding of the Nile. Anqet was the divine child of Satet and Khnemu and was seen as the guardian of Egypt's southern frontier and the Nile cataracts."[8]

Egypt Expands their Creation Stories

"Over time, the rival groups gradually merged, Ra and Atum were identified as the same god, making Atum's mysterious creation actually due to the Ogdoad, and Ra having the children Shu and Tefnut, etc. In consequence, Anubis was identified as a son of Osiris, as was Horus. Amun's role was later thought much greater, and for a time, he became chief god, although he eventually became considered a manifestation of Ra.

For a time, Ra and Horus were identified with one another, and when the Aten monotheism was unsuccessfully introduced, it was Ra-Horus who was thought of as the Aten. Later, Osiris' cult became more popular, and he became the main god, being identified as a form of Ptah. Eventually, all the gods were thought of as aspects of Osiris, Isis, Horus, or Set (who was by then a villain), indeed, Horus and Osiris had started to become thought of as the same god. Ptah eventually was identified as Osiris."[9]

Manetho's Legacy of the Dynastic Kings

Manetho, born in the Delta at Sebennytos, was an Egyptian priest in the Temple of Heliopolis, serving as a scribe for his emperor, Antiochus I, whose reign lasted from 285 to 261 BCE. The 'Ptolemaic Era,' was the time for Manetho's legacy, *Aegyptiaca* — 'the history of Egypt,' to be written. This account of the dynastic kings, who preceded the official record of 'dynastic' Egypt, reportedly spanned about 24,927 years. The Royal Papyrus of Turin reported the period as 36,620 years. Babylonian astronomers stated that their own observational records went back 470,000 years.[10]

The Sacred Pyramids

Since the Earth has enough acreage to provide 3 billion possible building sites for the Pyramids, the odds of them having been built on the Giza Plateau are 1 in 3 billion. Only a solid stone mountain could endure their immense weight. And indeed, a flat solid granite mountain happens to be located just beneath the surface of the ground, directly under the Great Pyramid, which is built to face true North. The Great Pyramid is located at the exact center of the Earth's landmass. That is, its East-West axis corresponds to the longest land parallel across the Earth, passing through Africa, Asia, and America. Similarly, the longest land meridian on Earth, through Asia, Africa, Europe, and Antarctica, also passes right through the Great Pyramid.

Other regal sites on the World Grid (synchronous alignment of sacred, prehistoric sites on our globe; geodesy) are the Carnac stones in France, the ancient Chinese capital of An-Yang, the road Darius I (550–486 BCE) built in 5th century BCE, from Sardis to Susa. "Machu Picchu, the Nazca lines and Easter Island (are) along a straight line around the center of the Earth, within a margin of error of less than one tenth of one degree of latitude. Other sites of ancient construction that are also within one tenth of one degree of this line include: Persepolis, the capital city of ancient Persia; Mohenjo Daro, the ancient capital city of the Indus Valley; and the lost city of Petra. The ancient Sumerian city of Ur and the temples at Angkor Wat are within one degree of latitude of this line. The alignment of these sites is easily observable on a globe of the Earth with a horizon ring."-Graham Hancock.[13, 14, 15]

The Emerald Tablets

Long ago, the ancient Master Thoth, thought to be Atlantean Adept of the Ancient Wisdom, produced the Emerald Tablets, which were translated by Dr. M. Doreal. This exquisite tome of wisdom describes the Way of Initiation through sacred alchemy and uncovering the Temple of God, both within and without, above and below, to become one with God, in His many forms. The Emerald Tablets are mentioned in *The Secret Doctrine* and the Alice Bailey manuscripts, along with many other Hermetic apocryphal writings, as well as in Freemasonry and various schools of Eastern wisdom. So began the Mystery School of eons' past, shedding its guiding light far into the future.[11]

Egyptian-Chaldean Lore Circulates Among Cultures

The teachings of the Chaldeans were passed on to the Egyptians, according to the record of the scholar Berosus who lived during the time of Alexander the Great. Manetho was a contemporary of Berosus, and both scribes contributed to the historical record of Egypt. Many Greek stories of the gods were adapted from the older Egyptian ones, but are similar enough to be recognized as variations on a theme. For example, Typhon (Set) doesn't kill Zeus, instead he just injures him. Zeus recovers then he kills Typhon. Hercules is not needed to kill Typhon, but kills one of his children instead.[12]

Masterpiece of the Gods

The earliest Egyptians believed that Sothis, also called Sirius, was the home of souls that had crossed over after death. This belief is also shared by the Dogon culture of Africa. Blavatsky states that the Pyramids were built during the time of late Atlantis before the Adepts came to Egypt, to serve as a repository for the sacred spiritual records of the Ancient Wisdom. And the Pyramids survived the great flood (quite possibly connected with the story of Atlantis found in Plato's *Timaeus and Critias*, written c. 400 BCE). Thought to be painted specific colors: Menkaure, the smallest pyramid was painted black, Khafre, next to Menkaure was painted red and the Great Pyramid of Khufu was bright white.

Public Domain

The Sphinx, nonetheless, has a fabulous history across time, with tales regarding the archaic 'lost records' of mankind, believed to be buried under its paws or beneath its base. The mystery schools of the Freemasons, the Theosophical Society, the Rosicrucians and the Knights Templar attach similar importance to the existence, relevance, and location thereof, regarding these sacred records of humanity to be buried under the Sphinx.

The Great Pyramid of Giza, also known as the Pyramid of Khufu or Cheops, is the oldest and largest of the three pyramids of Giza Necropolis and the only remaining monument of the *Seven Wonders of the Ancient World*. It stands alongside the smaller Pyramid of Khafre or Chephren a few hundred meters to the south-west, and the smaller sized Pyramid Menkaure, just a few hundred meters further south-west.[16, 17]

Mystery of Sacred Structure and Line

Studies began in 1957, as reported in *The Ancient Orient*, by Ralph Abraham, Ph.D., (Mathematics Department, University of California, Santa Cruz, CA, USA, 95064, rha@ucsc.edu) Dr. Abraham describes the 'New Archaeological Movement,' comprised of archaeoastronomy and geology, as the Symbolist Movement, which originated with the work of "R. A. Schwaller de Lubicz, philosopher and egyptologist, whose multi-volume work, *Le Temple de l'Homme*, was published in 1957." Egyptologist John Anthony West picked up his work and expanded the theory with data in his book, *Serpents of the Sky; The High Wisdom of Ancient Egypt*, 1993. Shortly thereafter, researchers such as Robert Bauval and Graham Hancock, and Robert Schoch added groundbreaking information in archaeoastronomy, geology, and anthropology as it pertains to the Giza Plateau. Robert Bauval discovered that the three 'Belt Stars' of the constellation Orion align perfectly below on Earth with the three pyramids of the Giza Plateau. His theory originally developed with co-author with Adrian Gilbert, presented in their seminal 1994 book, *The Orion Mystery*. Bauval and Gilbert suggested that the pyramidal structures and even the Sphinx were designed by celestial arrangement.

Robert Bauval also reports that the trajectory of the shafts from the Great Pyramid are also aligned with the constellation Orion and the two adjacent pyramids reflect sacred geometry in positioning and design of their structures and dimensions. *The Mystery of the Sphinx*, a documentary by John Anthony West, with Robert Schoch, presents evidence that the Sphinx has undergone water damage over the millennia.

Such weathering is indicative of an earlier date for construction of the Sphinx, now estimated to be at least 7,000 years old.[18, 19, 20]

The Great Sphinx

The Great Sphinx of Giza, adjacent to the Great Pyramid, a limestone figure of a mythical creature that is a mixture of Man, Lion, Eagle and Bull, sits in a depression to the south of the pyramid of the Pharaoh Khafre, on the west bank of the Nile River. The Sphinx Temple is believed to be connected by way of an underground tunnel to the Great Pyramid.[21]

The Great Sphinx is looking at the constellation of Leo in a time frame that is quite ancient. It was reportedly painted red at one time. The Sphinx has been dated as old as 12,000 years, correlating with the last time the constellation of Leo was aligned at Giza, with an undiscovered, but much anticipated underground tunnel thought to connect to the Great Pyramid. This tunnel and space within the Great Pyramid may have been used in very ancient times for Mystery School initiatory ceremonies by the Egyptians.[22]

Deciphering The Sphinx

Dr. Robert Schoch, one of a number of eminent researchers, studied the Sphinx in great detail. He began his scientific investigation of ancient civilizations several decades earlier as an Associate Professor of Geology at Boston University. He had previously been involved with Thomas Dobecki's low energy seismic study in 1992. By 1993, Schoch's study entailed examining the Sphinx through multiple modalities and this became one of the last projects allowed by the Egyptian Antiquities Department and Zahi Hawess, its Director. New data emerged on water damage as significant in the Sphinx's progresive aging, which would absolutely date the Sphinx far older than the authorities had previously estimated.[23, 24]

John Anthony West authored an incredibly innovative and exploratory book entitled, *Serpent in the Sky: The High Wisdom of Ancient Egypt*, 1993, which reviewed history, culture and the beauty of the monuments within the Giza Plateau, He also completed an informative documentary called the *Mystery of the Sphinx*, 1993, which featured himself and Dr. Schoch, presented by Charlton Heston, which was later written off by Dr. Hawass and his institution.

Robert Schoch and his colleagues Robert Bauval, Graham Hancock and John Anthony West continue to be spokesmen for the Sphinx and Giza Plateau research. They have produced an enlightening array of literature, with various theories about the physical structure of the Great Pyramid and Sphinx, when and why they were built, and correlations to other ancient civilizations around the world. New data regarding Schoch's current research at Göbekli Tepe in Turkey, corroborates his hypothesis that ancient civilization goes back many thousands of years earlier than predicted by mainstream archeology. Both Schoch and Hancock see antediluvian cataclysms initiating prehistoric migrations and transoceanic contact in pre-Columbian times. Along with other proponents of revisionist history like David Hatcher Childress, Andrew Collins and Hugh Newman, Robert Bauval, Graham Hancock and Robert Schoch continue to operate off the thesis that we have a very antiquated humanity, chockfull with hidden structures and data to discover, which will shed light on the origins of civilization.[25, 26, 27, 28, 29, 30, 31]

Precession and the Pyramid Code

In her documentary, *The Pyramid Code* (Kudos Films, 2010), Dr. Carmen Boulter examines the sacred technology of the Giza Plateau, with an emphasis on 'precession' and the dating of the pyramids with archeoastronomy. John Anthony West corroborates with details of ages, zodiac, and mistakes in dating of Egyptian ages of culture and onset of the beginning of Earth life. He reports that we are currently in this Kali Yuga with humanity moving away from spirituality, towards materialism. Blavatsky says that the ages of humanity and culture number in the millennia, a belief that Dr. Boulter reflects in her documentary. So, here it is again, we have another source who thinks ancient humanity was more advanced, with a keen sophistication in astronomy and science. Boulter also suggests that the Sphinx was built to look East at rising sun possibly 12,000 years ago when Leo was a constellation rising on the eastern horizon at the Spring Equinox.

Egyptians believed that Isis was connected to the bright star Sirius and that Osiris was connected to the constellation of Orion. Temples and edifices were aligned, heaven to earth, to these two stellar influences, and thus revered Isis and Osiris and their beneficence to the Egyptian people. Reflecting precision alignment is a large, open pyramid with a precision smooth tooling of granite, north of Giza Plateau at Abu Rawash. This kind of skilled craftsmanship could have been diamond-machined to attain such perfection. Various monuments and structures at Saqqara, Dahshour, Luxor Temple, Karnak Temple, Abu Simbel, Nazlet El Semman, Aswan, and Abu Ghraib show amazing ancient artistry in stone. Also to be marveled at are the thousands of ornate carved pillars with symbols reminiscent of the Sumerian cuneiform but clearly more elaborate. There are cut stones, channels and holes, some of which seem to have been made in current times.

Nile River Change in Topography

In her research, Dr. Carmen Boulter explored the entire country of Egypt. She had a hunch that the Nile River had migrated from its earlier position because why would the pyramids be built so far from the conveyance offered by the Nile? It served as an excellent transportation source. Boulter reviewed sequential LIDAR (Light Detection and Ranging- a remote sensing system, like radar, used to examine the surface of the Earth, using laser technology) reports on the Nile region and discovered that, in fact, the river had moved away from the original river bed, farther in distance from the pyramids and the ancient temples. Her conclusion? Egypt is perhaps much more ancient than humanity knows! [32, 33, 34]

The Lost Libraries of Alexandria

"Prior to the Christian Era seven hundred thousand of the most valuable books, written upon parchment, papyrus, vellum, and wax, and also tablets of stone, terra cotta, and wood, were gathered from all parts of the ancient world and housed in Alexandria, in buildings specially prepared for the purpose. This magnificent repository of knowledge was destroyed by a series of three fires. The parts that escaped the conflagration, lighted by Cæsar, in the harbor were destroyed about A.D. 389 by the Christians in obedience to the edict of Theodosius, who had ordered the destruction of the Serapeum, a building sacred to Serapis in which the volumes were kept. This conflagration is supposed to have destroyed the library that Marcus Antonius had presented to Cleopatra to compensate in part for all that had burned in the fire of the year 51."
– Manly P. Hall, *The Secret Teachings of All Ages*, Philosophical Research Society, 1928.

Concerning this, H. P. Blavatsky, in *Isis Unveiled*, has written, "They [the Rabbis of Palestine and the wise men] say that not all the rolls and manuscripts, reported in history to have been burned by Cæsar, by the Christian mob, in 389, and by the Arab General Amru, perished as it is commonly believed; and the story they tell is the following: At the time of a contest for the throne, in 51 B. C., between Cleopatra and her brother Dionysius Ptolemy, the Bruckion, which contained over seven-hundred-thousand rolls all bound in wood and fire-proof parchment, was undergoing repairs and a great portion of the original manuscripts, considered among the most precious, and which were not duplicated, were stored away in the house of one of the librarians. Several hours passed between the burning of the fleet, set on fire by Caesar's order, and the moment when the first buildings situated near the harbor caught fire in their turn; and the librarians, aided by several hundred slaves attached to the museum, succeeded in saving the most precious of the rolls." In all probability, the books which were saved lie buried either in Egypt or in India, and until they are discovered the modern world must remain in ignorance concerning many great philosophical and mystical truths. The ancient world more clearly understood these missing links--the continuity of the pagan Mysteries in Christianity."[35]

Pyramid Powers

Pyramids have been contemplated since the beginning of time. In the 1960s, 'Pyramid Power" was the study theorizing that the shape and mathematics of the pyramid lent an increased awareness or consciousness to the human inside a pyramid, or even with a pyramid shape on their head. In ancient times, the pyramid was thought to be a sacred initiation space for 'disciples' or 'sages' training in the Ancient Mysteries of Egypt.[36]

The former Soviet Union constructed 20 pyramids and Alexander Golod, PhD., began conducting experiments in 1990, in the pursuit of the potential positive outcomes or healing properties of the pyramid. The studies involved medicine, ecology, agriculture, physics, and health sciences. The results included improvement in tissue regeneration, immune systems, and decreases in seismic activity and violent weather, among other outcomes. One result, the "spontaneous charging of capacitors" correlates with Christopher Dunn's work on pyramids as sources of energy. David Wilcock also discussed the Russian studies, "based on the available factual information," in a video about the Russian Pyramid Research Program, recorded in September, 2009 at 'Project Camelot's Awake and Aware' in the LA Conference.[37, 38, 39]

Christopher Dunn conducted research on the pyramids, (*The Giza Power Plant: Technologies of Ancient Egypt*, 1998), observing power being sustained by quartz. He puts forth that 'Tesla technology' from inventor savant, Nikola Tesla, might theorize that the pyramids are sources of power, or ancient power plants.[40, 41]

John Major Jenkins is an original, independent researcher with studies on understanding the Giza pyramids. He currently has shifted his focus to the Maya, and is considered an expert in the Mayan calendar and associated data. Jenkins is a visiting instructor at such institutions as the Institute of Maya Studies in Miami and Esalen Institute, Big Sur, CA.[42]

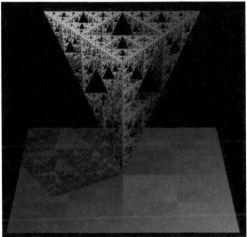

Sierpinskitetraed

The Culture of Nabta Playa

"But why mingle the symbolism and rituals of a cattle cult with the stars of the Big Dipper and Sirius? For nomadic pastoralists in the open Sahara, which was then a savannah with a seasonal monsoon, the dominant preoccupation would have been the survival of their cattle, which totally depended on the rains that came in early summer— "water from the sky" that was a matter of life and death for both people and cattle. Not only did these cattle herders have somehow to ensure that the rains did come, but also—and perhaps more important—they needed to be able to predict the time of their coming. In other words, they needed magical rituals for the former and practical astronomical knowledge for the latter."— Robert Bauval and Thomas Brophy, *Imhotep the African, Architect of the Cosmos.* [43]

Egyptologist and engineer Robert Bauval reports that "Nabta Playa is 130,000 to 70,000 years old and was watery and sea-like, in the Saharan Egyptian desert. Nabta Playa is the oldest monument in Egypt." Nabta Playa appears to be a simple stone circle in the remote western desert of Egypt. But this ancient megalithic site holds far more significance that a gathering of stones.

215

Likened to Stonehenge, Bauval describes Nabta as a calendar used to calculate the summer solstice with a sculpted quartz base stone carved out of the bedrock and reportedly an extended topographic astronomical gage. The Nabta Playa geography of southwestern Egypt has a rich historical heritage dating from c. 11,000 to c. 4,800 years ago. It catered to intermittent travel from nomadic tribes. The area was transformed originally by climate change which caused monsoon rains to move north from central Africa into southern Egypt, well to the west of the Nile River, causing the basin of Nabta Playa. Bedouin workers there provided the name, translating it in Arabic, meaning water basin, and 'little bushes' for the scarce dried plants found in the six-mile long by four-mile wide basin in the desert of southern Egypt.

Raymbetz

Fred Wendorf, a professor of Prehistory at Henderson-Morrison, Southern Methodist University in Dallas, Texas, was the original explorer of Nabta Playa in 1973 and in 1998, but others have followed him; most recently it has been explored by Robert Bauval, who has written extensively on Nabta Playa.[44, 45, 46]

Nabta Playa Beaconed Life

The people of ancient Nabta Playa depended on the weather for their survival so the exact timing of the summer solstice was an important predictive part of their lives. When the Sun reached its northernmost point annually monsoons brought rainfall, no more than four to eight inches a year. During that time water filled shallow desert voids and grass grew around the banks which fed the cattle and gave water to sustain small nomadic tribes for the entire year.[47]

Carlos E. Soliverez

Nomads Appear 9000 BCE

Climatic change was the primary factor in the decline of the Nabta Playa culture. After an initial period, with erratic rain at c. 9000 BCE, the nomadic peoples deserted it when the water dried up. Studies indicate that the nomads returned at c. 7,200 years ago to live continuously in this territory by constructing houses, making pottery, collecting wild foods and excavating for well water.

A multitude of hearths have also been discovered but the timing of when these were built and used is unknown. Many piles of stones were found around the ancient water site, concealing a chamber with an intact young cow skeleton. A large statue like a cow was discovered on engraved bedrock. Climatic changes were influential, but about 7,200 years ago, the rains returned, ushering in a lengthy period of stability and prosperity for Nabta Playa.[48, 49]

Archeoastronomy Examines Nabta Playa

It wasn't until 1991 that an archeoastronomer was consulted to examine the glyphs at this site since some of the stone designs appeared to be calendars. During the exploration satellite equipment such as GPS was used to verify the precision of the cardinal directions, which were shown to be exact degrees of true cardinal directions, thus the astronomical nature of this site was determined to be highly accurate. Quick calculations confirmed that the rising Sun would have appeared between two sets of stones in the calendar circle on the date of the June solstice c. 6,000 years ago with the other pair aligning within just two degrees from a true north-south axis.[50]

The Nabta Megaliths Were Ritual Markers

The Nabta people built an observatory which spread across a square mile. This calendar circle included dark stone megaliths, up to 10 feet above the landscape, a 12-foot circle of flat stones, and four pairs of taller stones aligned opposite to each other. Two pair of megaliths provided a window to the solstice sunrise while the other two aligned to an almost-perfect north-south axis. There were both solstice and cardinal alignments with the cardinal alignments used for observing the stars.

In Nabta Playa, the standing megaliths were used to determine the Sun's zenith near the onset of the rainy season and the megaliths would have been partly submerged in the rising waters of the summer monsoon. Almost a score of other megaliths appear to form four other sight lines. Determining this exact date of the summer solstice meant that summer rains would begin soon thereafter.

For about three weeks before and three weeks after the solstice, the noontime Sun would have appeared at the zenith, which is the point directly overhead. The vertical megaliths or the sighting stones in the calendar circle, would cast no shadows as the Sun passed through the zenith and this moment undoubtedly held great symbolic importance to the culture of Nabta Playa.

Based upon engineering measurements throughout the year, it is believed by current researchers that these alignments within the calendar at Nabta Playa point to important stars or constellations, such as Orion or Sirius. The calendar circle served a ceremonial purpose due the northern position of the solstice Sun so close to the Tropic of Cancer. Nabta's calendar circle and the megalithic standing stones illustrate the interconnectedness of astronomy, daily life, and ritual that was common in most ancient cultures.[51, 52, 53, 54]

Nile River Valley Peoples

In Egypt, pre-dynastic cattle cults existed and were linked to the Nile. Bulls were indicative of the constellation Taurus, seen painted in the Temple at Dendera in Egypt. Blavatsky adds, "But Isis-Osiris reigned in Egypt before the Dendera Zodiac was painted on the ceiling of that temple, and that is over 75,000 years ago!" So, we know that astrology was foremost for the Nile peoples and their successors, the Egyptians.[55]

The cow was considered the Mother of the Sun. Hathor, the great goddess, was depicted as a cow with long horns and benevolent countenance and became a central figure in the Egyptian pantheon. The cattle were deified in ancient Egypt (much like in India) long before development of agriculture on the Giza Plain. In the Sahara Desert at c. 8,000 BCE, many people worshiped their cattle, and their rock drawings remind us of this relationship between humans and cattle. The Nabtans and Egyptians both revered the cow and had similar rituals surrounding the monsoon rains, agriculture and their cattle culture.

It is theorized that the first humans with their domesticated cattle moved into Nabta between 10,000 to 10,500 BCE., after the summer rains to later move away when the water evaporated, about 5,500 BCE. It is theorized that the nomadic populations that gathered here once a year at Nabta Playa were precursors to Egyptian culture that evolved in a more elaborate form. After careful study, no similar archeological sites have been discovered containing this type of megalithic calendar circle and unique cow burials in the area of Nabta Playa-but the desert is a vast place.[56, 57, 58]

Thor NL

Map Locating Nabta Playa

Notes

1. Frankfort, Henri, (1948) *Kingship and the Gods, A Study of Ancient Near Eastern Religion as the Integration of Society and Nature*, with a new Preface by Samuel Noah Kramer, The University of Chicago Press, Chicago and London.
2. http://www.ancient.eu/religion/
3. http://isaw.nyu.edu/people/alumni/2010-2011/gunter-dreyer
4. http://www.ancientegyptonline.co.uk/ogdoad.html
5. http://www.henadology.wordpress.com/theology/netjeru
6. http://www.ancientegyptonline.co.uk/ennead.html: Jenny Hill, 2015
7. http://www.ancientegyptonline.co.uk
8. http://www.egyptianmyths.net/elephant.htm
9. http://www.crystalinks.com/egyptcreation.html
10. http://sacred-texts.com/jud/josephus/apion-1.htm: Against Apion by Josephus, notes on Manetho.
11. https://brotherhoodofthewhitetemple.com/the-emerald-tablets/
12. Asher, R. E. National Myths in Renaissance France, Francus, Samothes and the Druids. 1993, Edinburgh University Press.
13. http://www. grahamhancock.com/geographic-geometric-relationships-alisonj)
14. http://www.robertbauval.co.uk/
15. Herodotus (c.484–425 BCE)
16. http://www.robertbauval.co.uk/
17. http://www.archaeoastronomy.com/pyramids.html
18. Bauval Robert and Gilbert, Adrian, 1994. *The Orion Mystery,* Three Rivers Press, NY
19. Hancock, Graham and Bauval Robert, 1996. *Message of the Sphinx*, Three Rivers Press, NY.
20. West, John Anthony, 1993, *The Mystery of the Sphinx*, a documentary film.
21. West, John Anthony, *Serpent in the Sky: The High Wisdom of Ancient Egypt,* 1993, Theosophical Publishing House, Wheaton, IL.
22. http://www.bibliotecapleyades.net/ciencia/historia_humanidad02. htm

23. Dobecki, T. L. and Schoch, R. M. (1992), *Seismic investigations in the vicinity of the great Sphinx of Giza, Egypt.* Geoarchaeology, 7: 527–544. doI – 10.1002/gea.3340070603 (www.robertschoch.net/).
24. Schoch, Robert M. 2012. *Forgotten Civilization: The Role of Solar Outbursts in Our Past and Future,* Inner Traditions-Bear & Co, Rochester, VT.
25. Bauval, Robert and Gilbert, Adrian, 1994. *The Orion Mystery: Unlocking the Secrets of the Pyramids,* Three Rivers Press, NY.
26. Childress, David Hatcher, 2000. *Technology of the Gods, The Incredible Sciences of the Ancients,* Adventures Unlimited Press, Kempton, IL.
27. Hancock, Graham and Bauval, Robert, 1996. *The Message of the Sphinx: A Quest for the Hidden Legacy of Mankind,* Three Rivers Press, NY.
28. NBC Special Documentary, 1993. *The Mystery of the Sphinx,* hosted by Charlton Heston with John Anthony West. (www.world-mysteries.com/pex_12.htm.) News & Documentary Emmy Award for Best Research and a nomination for Best Documentary to John Anthony West for The Mystery of the Sphinx, 1993. The News & Documentary Emmy Awards are presented by the National Academy of Television Arts & Sciences (NATAS) in recognition of excellence in American national news and documentary programming.
29. West, John Anthony, 1993. *Serpent in the Sky: The High Wisdom of Ancient Egypt,* Theosophical Publishing House, Wheaton, IL.
30. http://www.jawest.net/
31. Hancock, Graham, *The Magicians of the Gods,* 2015, Thomas Dunne Books, St. Martin Press, N.Y.
32. http://www.pyramidcode.com/
33. Abraham, Ralph. "The Ancient Orient." (2013), pdf.
34. West, John Anthony, *Serpent of the Sky; The High Wisdom of Ancient Egypt,* 1993, Theosophical Publishing House, Wheaton, Il. 1993.
35. Refer to http://www.sacred-texts.com/eso/sta/index.htm and, http://www.ibiblio.org/ccer/1928a8.htm for public domain information.
36. http://www.powerpyramids.com/PyramidLegends.html
37. https://www.youtube.com/watch?v=scym0WH3Jww).

38. http://www.ten1000things.org/russian-pyramid-power
39. http://projectcamelot.org/los_angeles_19-20_september_2009. html
40. http://www.ancient-world-mysteries.com/tesla.html
41. Dunn, Christopher, 1998. *The Giza Power Plant: Technologies of Ancient Egypt*, Bear & Company Publishers, Santa Fe, NM.
42. http://www.alignment2012.com/about_jmj.html
43. Robert Buaval and Thomas Brophy, *Imhotep the African, Architect of the Cosmos*, 2013, page 173.
44. Bauval, Robert and Brophy, Thomas, 2011. *Black Genesis: The Prehistoric Origins of Ancient Egypt*, Bear & Company Publishers, Rochester, VT.
45. Brophy, Thomas G. *The Origin Map: Discovery of a Prehistoric, Megalithic, Astrophysical Map and Sculpture of the Universe*, 2002, Writers Club Press (iUniverse), NY.
46. Gaffney, Mark H, *The Astronomers of Nabta Playa: New Discoveries Reveal Astonishing Pre-Historic Knowledge, Atlantis Rising*, No. 56, pp. 42-43, 68-70 (March/April 2006).
47. Bauval, Robert, Brophy, Thomas, Ph.D., *Black Genesis: The Prehistoric Origins of Ancient Egypt*, Bear and Co, Rochester, VT, 2011.
48. Bauval, Robert and Brophy, Thomas, 2011, *Black Genesis, The Prehistoric Origins of Ancient Egypt*, Bear and Company, Rochester, VT.
49. http://www.stardate.org/egypt/nabta01.html
50. http://www.redicecreations.com/radio/2010/11nov/RIR-101114. php: Thomas Brophy, Ph.D. interview with Red Ice Radio, November 14, 2010.
51. http://thesourceinthesahara.com/bagnolds-stone-circle.php
52. Bauval, Robert and Brophy, Thomas, 2013. *Imhotep the African: Architect of the Cosmos*, Disinformation Books, NY.
53. http://www.ancient-origins.net/ancient-places-africa/nabta-playa-and-ancient-astronomers-nubian-desert-002954
54. http://www.ancient-wisdom.co.uk/egyptnabta.htm
55. H.P.B., SD, II.
56. Bauval, Robert, *The Egypt Code,* 2008, Disinformation Books, NY.

57. Bauval, Robert, Brophy, Thomas, Ph.D., *Black Genesis: The Prehistoric Origins of Ancient Egypt,* Bear and Co, Rochester, VT, 2011.
58. http://www.ralph-abraham.org/articles/MS%23137.Orient/ms137.pdf

Sadie from Austria, Pixabay

Chapter Eleven

Our Ancient Africa

"Stephen Hawking says there are more than 200 particles...a Dogon priest says there are 266."

-Laird Scranton, 2014, CPAK Conference

The Dogon, Cosmology from Sirius

The cosmology of the Dogon people is enormously complex, comprised of veiled, sacred and oral accounts, using symbols which are reversible and correspond with a system of signs and images, interwoven with categories and whether they be the same or opposed, they are related.

Deeply seated is ancestor worship embraced by their spirit devotion, which they cultivated during slow migration across the ancestral homelands in Egypt, to their most current tribal homeland of the

Bandiagara region. According to Oumar Cissé, a member of a Dogon family, "Once the residence of the Tellem people, the Dogon moved into the Bandiagara escarpment around the 14th or 15th century. At first sharing the escarpment with the Dogon for a few centuries, the Tellem were pushed out and migrated to Burkina Faso. Until the end of the colonial era, the Dogon were one of the few African groups that had successfully retained their culture and traditional ways of life. Even now, despite the presence of Islam and Christianity, the Dogon people have largely held onto their animist beliefs." [1]

The French anthropology team of Marcel Griaule and Germaine Dieterlen studied the Dogon, between 1931 and 1956, with a report that they had spent extended time with Dogon priests. Much more of the experience is unknown. The French team did come to believe that many, if not all, of the main Dogon sacred sites were related to experiences of the deity, Nommo in their creation stories. The Dogon culture is now located primarily in Mali, West Africa and their tribal homeland encompasses the districts of Bandiagara and Douentza.

"Dogon art is primarily sculpture. Dogon art revolves around religious values, ideals, and freedoms. Dogon sculptures are not made to be seen publicly and are commonly hidden from the public eye within the houses of families, sanctuaries, or kept with the Hogon. The importance of secrecy is due to the symbolic meaning behind the pieces and the process by which they are made."[2]

The tribe asserts they migrated from ancient Egypt to Libya, and later to other areas including Mauritania and Guinea. Sharing certain beliefs with the Sumerians, the Dogon accept as true that their culture descended from sacred gods of the Sirius constellation, an antediluvian experience sustaining knowledge that space ships transporting the Creators will come back again one day.[3, 4, 5]

Dogon Knowledge of Sirius

Sirius is the brightest star in our night sky. The Dogon share a belief with the earliest Egyptians who believed Sirius, also called Sothis, was the home of souls who had crossed over. They observe a DNA helix within the orbital rotation pattern of Sirius A around Sirius B, said to be the crux wherein the Universe constructs matter along with our souls.

A third star, Emme Ya, meaning Sorghum Female, is said to exist in the Sirius system. Being lighter than Sirius B, Emme Ya also revolves around Sirius A, although not yet been proven to exist in mainstream astronomy, some people call it Sirius C.

Nommo, the amphibious beings, were sent to Earth from the star system Sirius to aid humankind. Resembling Mermaids and Mermen, also metaphors for amphibians, these images bridge the collective unconscious, the source of creation, connecting with it analysis of related symbols found in religion, mythology, and mystic systems across cultures and time. These periods within the human collective unconscious contain the memory of all history, beginning in the primordial and ancient past. Carl Jung, psychiatrist and founding father of both Analytical and Transpersonal Psychology expounded on the archetypes that reside in humanity's collective unconscious.[6, 7, 8]

The Colors Black, White, and Red

Black, white, and red are important colors that correlate with the cosmology of many world peoples. This color schema of the black, white, and red is seen in the Dogon culture in much of their masks and ritual

clothing. The Kananga black, red and white masks represent the first human beings. These three colors are found together in ancient tribal art, pottery, landscape painting, in architecture and general tribal themes. Important in other world cultures, black, white, and red are seen in the cultures of the Inca, the Maya, the Hopi and the Zuni, and found in ancient China, Egypt, Minoa and Mesopotamia. These colors have been correlated originally to the sacred creation myths of Lemuria by the Adepts, the Naacal and the Incas.[9, 10, 11]

Dogon dancers, courtesy of Pixabay

Dogon Ancient Wisdom

Laird Scranton has completed extensive research on the Dogon cosmology and Ancient Wisdom. He likens their knowledge to a cosmic encyclopedia as it were, based upon mythological themes, cultural storytelling and the 'parallels between Dogon myth and science run deep'. The Dogon elders reportedly understand and define their own symbols, using keywords such as water, fire, wind, and earth, which are related to common symbols of Egyptian glyphs used to write the words, and whose shapes match related Dogon cosmological drawings.

The Dogon tradition relies on teachings that their civilization was originally founded by amphibious beings known as "Nommos," "Oannes" or "Monitors." The history of the ancestors' chronicles the story in which they came from the white dwarf planet, Sirius B, which is 8.6 light years from the Earth, to found civilization on Earth. The Nome have a male upper torso and the lower torso is a snake or a ram's head with a serpent body, the serpent representing the DNA. The Dogon god, Nommo, with his cone-shaped head, resembles Akhenaten, also with a female body and ritual ceremonies glorifying Nommo by worshipping the ancient sacred rites with men dressed as females on stilts with breasts and the sacred masks, in honor of the ancestors.

The House of Words, the A Togo Na, stands in every Dogon village and marks the male social center. The symbolic meaning of fertility and procreation are attached to these structures, which incorporate carved pillars or sculptured posts, many which are of women's breasts, for as a Dogon proverb says, "The breast is second only to God." The village diviner performs a ritual ceremony by interpreting lines and symbols in the sand with the help of the sacred fox, which the Dogon believe holds supernatural powers. At dusk, the diviner draws a question in the sand for the Sacred Fox to answer. The questions include queries about possible romantic pairing or agricultural blessings coupled with offerings of millet, milk and peanuts.[12]

Dance and Cosmology

"The dancers execute difficult steps while teetering high above the crowd…" (description of the Kanga dancers performing their ritual dance). As a student of African dance and drumming, I understand that the music, movements and dance are cyphers of the Dogon people and the symbol of their life. Dance is meditation and archetypal in origin, sacred to the arrangement of the individual's roles and reverence to the gods, simultaneously.

For example, the star constellations factor into the timing and length of Dogon ceremonial song and dance, while their counterparts the llamas of Tibet, will create an elaborate, multi-faceted sand mandala, only to wipe it away and start again. The meaning of sunrise and sunset is similar for the Dogon, the symbolic world dies at sunset only to rise to life again with sunrise, each act methodically practiced in a daily form of dance.

Rejoicing (2010), acrylic on paper by Martin K. Bulinya.

Woven into this complexity is the demonstration of the social institutions, founded on Dogon myth and the daily activities of human life; tasks, locations and timing provide a system of reference to their myths; the two go hand in hand. So, reverence for the ancestors' wisdom, blessings of family, and gratefulness for food from the land, while explained in a ritual, is the foundation of Dogon myth.

Another example of the interrelated culture of symbols is how the spirit realm is connected by the Awa cult—the Dogon performing the Dama dance, which allows the dead to cross over into peace, since their fundamental law is the worship of ancestors with their death dances representing family and their deep spirituality. Although the Dogon recognize the creator god Amma as the Supreme Being and address prayers and sacrifices to him, the core set of beliefs and practices focuses on ancestor worship, within which is primary for the Binu cult. The third and final cult is Lebe, symbolized by the Earth God, whose priest is named Hogan.[13]

Marcel Griaule and Germaine Dieterlen said that what may appear to be "superficial knowledge" of the general population transcends into a belief with cosmic revelations. In this way, the Dogon have a logical understanding of universal physics, being essentially Adepts, privy to the steps of enlightenment.[14]

The Dogon Knew of Sirius B

The Dogon priests had asserted for over 300 years that Sirius A had a companion star long before proven by science. The Dogon call Sirius B the 'smallest thing there is' and 'the heaviest star', white in color, labelling Sirius B's smallness with the name Po Tolo which means 'star seed' in Dogon translation. The Dogon also attribute Sirius B with its three principal properties; a white dwarf, small yet heavy and white. Researcher Walter Cruttenden maintains in his 'Binary Star Theory' that states Earth has a complimentary star, perhaps in another constellation, serving as our Earth's binary companion, as confirmed by the 'Precession of the Equinox' explanation.[15, 16, 17]

On January 31, 1862 in Cambridgeport, Massachusetts, the 'dark star' we know as Sirius B was inadvertently discovered by Alvan Graham

Clark and his father Alvan Clark, a family of telescope-makers. Verified later by Harvard's College Observatory, Sirius B became official.[18]

Additional explanation in the 1920's, revealed that Sirius B is a dim, small, white dwarf star yet quite dense. To date, Sirius B and C are invisible to the human eye with Sirius being the only visible star. Nearly the diameter of Earth, Sirius has a mass equaling 98% of the Sun. [19, 20, 21]

Dogon ancient Rock Art, courtesy of Pixabay

Dogon Creation Story

As we develop the path of Dogon cosmology, I can only wonder if their likeness of a 'fox' to the Egyptian jackal is merely incidental, given the Dogon tradition of honoring their ancestors in the Pyramids. As the belief system explains, the Dogon left Egypt, bringing with them their sacred knowledge in oral tradition, handed down by the ancient priests of Egypt. The Dogon creation story brings Nommo, the first living being created by Amma, the sky god and creator of the Universe. He soon multiplied to become six pairs of twins or 12, a sacred number. One of the twins rebelled against Amma's wishes thereby destabilizing the Universe. In order to purify the cosmos and restore order, Amma sacrificed another Nommo, whose body was cut up and scattered throughout the Universe. This distribution of the parts of the Nommo's body is seen as the source for the proliferation of Binu shrines throughout the Dogon region, which reminds us of Osiris.[22, 23]

Dogon Connected to Egypt

The Dogon assert that their oral tradition of astronomical knowledge dates back thousands of years when their culture was connected to ancient Egyptian culture and is derived from the star system, Sirius, the Dog Star and is linked with the Egyptian goddess Isis. The oral traditions of the Dogon say it was given to them by the Nommo. The source of their information dates back to the time of the ancient Egyptian priests. This is the story of Isis, Osiris and Horus also reminiscent of ancient Sumer and other cultures of the Americas. Sirius C translates from Dogon vernacular to English as 'Sun of Women' and the Dogon ascribe "the seat of the female souls of living or future beings" to these women. Its symbol contains two pair of lines that are relevant features of a Dogon legend. The Dogon believe that Sirius C sends out two pairs of beams and the beams represent a feminine figure. Some of the ancient Egyptian temples, such as the Temple of Hathor at Dendera, were created so that the light of the helical rising of Sirius would travel down the main corridor to place its red glow upon the altar in the inner sanctum of the temple. When that light reached the altar, the beam of light from Sirius was transformed into Sothis, the Star Goddess, and Isis.[24, 25, 26]

Greek Beliefs Similar to the Dogon

Next to the Dogon, almost identical by design were the Greek beliefs. The Parthenon, a Greek temple, was oriented to receive the beams of light from the Pleiades into the inner sanctum, and the beams were then transformed into seven women. As these beams from the Pleiades entered the Egyptian temple of Hathor, it became the seven Hathors, female judges of mankind. The Hathors, in pairs of feminine figures beamed down from the Star, Sun and Planet of Women to their original home near the Hoggar Mountains, bringing many aspects of their civilization to the ancestors of their tribes. Dogon oral traditions state that for thousands of years they have known that the Earth revolves around the Sun, and that Jupiter has moons and Saturn has rings. Their calendar is quite non-traditional in that its fifty-year cycle is based neither on the Earth's rotation around the Sun, like our Julian calendar, nor the cycles of the Moon's lunar calendar. Instead, the Dogon culture centers on the rotation cycle of Sirius B which encircles the primary star 'Sirius A' every 49.9 to 50 years.

Sans, An African Indigenous People

The San are one of fourteen known extant 'ancestral population clusters' from which all known modern humans have descended. Studies indicate that the San people also have most diverse DNA on the planet, as revealed by a 2009 broad study of African genetic diversity. The results found that the San people were among the top five populations with the highest measured levels of genetic diversity among the 121 samples of distinct African populations. With that thought in mind, the National Geographic Society sponsored the Genographic Project, which was publicly launched in 2005. The composite study measured the DNA of the Earth's populations to determine how dissimilar or alike the human species had become. Simply put, groups of people were divided into clusters, categorized by the origin of the DNA received by participants. Humanity reportedly began with a female African San woman some 200,000 years ago in Ethiopia.

Our anthropologists had a penchant for Africa after excavations produced results in the early 20th century, because Africa is the most prolific site for the study of its numerous hominid remains over the last 91 years, beginning with Raymond Dart, Ph.D., from the University of Witwatersrand, Johannesburg, South Africa in 1924. He discovered *Australopithecus africanus*; the 'Taung child' thus commencing searches throughout Africa by notable scientists, such as Robert Broom, M.D. and Louis and Mary Leakey, to site a few.[27, 28]

Notes

1. http://www.farafina-tigne.com/info/dogon.html
2. http://www.farafina-tigne.com/info/dogon.html
3. http://www.farafina-tigne.com/info/dogon.html
4. Darll Forde, Ed., 1999. African Worlds, Studies in the Cosmological Ideas and Social Values of African Peoples Dist. by Transaction Publishers, Rutgers University, Piscataway, NJ., James Curry Publishers, Oxford, UK. ISBN 3-8258-3086-1.
5. Griaule, Marcel 1965, 1st edition, Conversations With OgotemmelI – An Introduction To Dogon Religious Ideas, ISBN 0-19-519821-2
6. Scranton, Laird, The Science of the Dogon: Decoding the African Mystery Tradition, 2006, Inner Traditions, Rochester, VT.
7. Jung, Carl G., Man and His Symbols, 1974, Dell Publishing Company, NY, pp. 31-32, 41, 58,
8. http://www.muskingum.edu/~psych/psycweb/history/jung.htm
9. http://www.nps.gov/museum/exhibits/chcu/ceramics.html
10. http://www.shannondorey.com/dogongeneticsymbolism.html
11. http://www.bibliotecapleyades.net/esp_dogon03.htm
12. Scranton, Laird, The Cosmological Origins of Myth and Symbol: From the Dogon and Ancient Egypt to India, Tibet, and China, 2010, Inner Traditions, Rochester, VT.
13. http://www.encyclopedia.com/topic/Dogon.aspx
14. Darll Forde, Ed., 1999. African Worlds, Studies in the Cosmological Ideas and Social Values of African Peoples Dist. by Transaction Publishers, Rutgers University, Piscataway, NJ., James Curry Publishers, Oxford, UK. ISBN 3-8258-3086-1.
15. https://grahamhancock.com/scrantonl2/
16. Walter, Cruttenden, 2005. Lost Star of Myth and Time, St. Lynn's Press, Pittsburg, PA.
17. http://www.doyletics.com/arj/loststar.htm
18. http://vega.lpl.arizona.edu/sirius/A5.html
19. http://www.farafina-tigne.com/dogon.html
20. Walter, Cruttenden, 2005. Lost Star of Myth and Time, St. Lynn's Press, Pittsburg, PA.
21. http://www.doyletics.com/arj/loststar.htm

22. http://www.raceandhistory.com/dogon/
23. http://www.africaspeaks.com/reasoning/index.php?topic=5612.0;wap2
24. Bauval, Robert and Brophy, Thomas, 2013. Imhotep the African: Architect of the Cosmos, Disinformation Books, NY.
25. Bauval, Robert and Brophy, Thomas, 2011. Black Genesis: The Prehistoric Origins of Ancient Egypt, Bear & Company Publishers, Rochester, VT.
26. http://www.bibliotecapleyades.net/esp_dogon03.htm
27. https://www.familytreedna.com/genographic-project.aspx
28. http://www.sahistory.org.za/people-south-africa/san

Anthrogenesis

Bear hat Pastel (1926) by W. Langdon Kihn (1898-1957), Wellcome Library
and Trust, London, UK. Photo courtesy of Oxyman, London, UK.

Chapter Twelve

Indigenous North American Peoples

The Ancient One
by Bearwalker

Ancient One sat in the shade of his tree in front of his cave. Red People came to him and he said to Red People, "Tell me your vision."

And Red People answered, "The elders have told us to pray in this manner, and that manner, and it is important that only we pray as we have been taught for this has been handed down to us by the elders."

"Hmmmm," said the Ancient One.

Then Black People came to him and he said to Black People, "Tell me your vision."

And Black People answered, "Our mothers have said to go to this building and that building and pray in this manner and that manner. And our fathers have said to bow in this manner and that manner when we pray. And it is important that we do only this when we pray."

"Hmmmm," said the Ancient One.

Then Yellow People came to him and he said to Yellow People, "Tell me your vision."

And Yellow People answered, "Our teachers have told us to sit in this manner and that manner and to say this thing and that thing when we pray. And it is important that we do only this when we pray."

"Hmmmm," said the Ancient One.

Then White People came to him and he said to White People, "Tell me your vision."

And White People answered, "Our Book has told us to pray in this way and that way and to do this thing and that thing, and it is very important that we do this when we pray."

"Hmmmm," said the Ancient One.

Then Ancient One spoke to the Earth and said, "Have you given the people a vision?" And the Earth said, "Yes, a special gift for each one, but the people were so busy speaking and arguing about which way is right they could not see the gift I gave each one of them." And the Ancient One asked same question of Water and Fire and Air and got the same answer. Then Ancient One asked Animal, and Bird, and Insect, and Tree, and Flower, and Sky, and Moon, and Sun, and Stars, and all of the other Spirits and each told him the same.

Ancient One thought this was very sad. He called Red People, Black People, Yellow People, and White People to him and said to them. "The ways taught to you by your Elders, and your Mothers and Fathers, and Teachers, and Books are sacred. It is good that you respect those ways, for they are the ways of your ancestors. But the ancestors no longer walk on the Face of the Earth Mother. You have forgotten your own Vision. Your Vision is right for you but no one else. Now each of you must pray for your own Visions, and be still enough to see them, so you can follow the way of the heart. It is a hard way. It is a good way.

- Used with permission from Hopi Heritage of Wisdom, 2015.

Above: The Boturini Codex, page one, c. 1530 by an unknown Aztec author. The Codex is the story of the legendary Aztec journey from Aztlán to the Valley of Mexico. Museo Nacional de Antropología, Mexico City, Mexico, courtesy of Pirru.

Departure from Aztlán

Aztalán in Wisconsin

In 1912, Lake Delavan, Wisconsin, 18 skeletons were excavated, exhibiting several unique features including heights ranging between 7.6ft and 10 feet, and skulls which were much larger than current races of today and a double row of teeth, 6 fingers, 6 toes. The teeth in the front of the jaw were regular molars but the skulls were elongated, believed to be a result of living a longer than normal life span. In 1835, pioneers settling in south-central Wisconsin discovered the remains of three flat-topped, truncated earthen pyramidal mounds with artifacts scattered throughout the surrounding area, termed the 'Ancient City,' but soon an interested Milwaukee judge named the site 'Aztalan' from a resemblance to the Aztec legend since Aztec refer to their ancestral lands as Aztalan.[1, 2]

Aztlán, Home of the Aztecs

In the book, *Mexicano and Latino Politics and the Quest for Self-Determination: What Needs to Be Done,* by Armando Navarro, 2015, Navarro describes the Southwest, Utah, Wyoming and Montana as the physical locale of Aztlán, the fabled, ancient Nahua land of their forefathers, where "according to Nahuatl legend and the codices, Aztlán began in the seven caves where the seven tribes lived as Chicmastoc". The other tribes who speak "the Uto-Aztecan branch of Aztec-Tanoan language also include the Utes, Paiutes, Shoshone, Comanche, Hopi and Yaqui", with "Azteca" denoting the "Nahuatl reference to people from Aztlán, specifically, where the Mexica came from."[3]

In *Anthrogenesis*, we ask the question, is it possible that the Indigenous peoples, the mounds, pyramids and remains are remnants from Atlantean ancestors? We know that our ancestors had much larger bodies, which would work well both in building and maneuvering these massive, archaic structures.

The Seven Caves of Chicomostoc

Inuit Indigenous Culture

Vast areas of North America, including Northern Canada, Yukon land sections, the Northwest Territory, Nunavut, Quebec and Labrador were home to the Inuit, the "First Peoples of the Canadian Arctic". Today, there are 227 federally recognized Alaskan Indigenous Peoples tribes. Similar to Indigenous peoples in the 'Lower Fifty' (states in America), the Inuit have healers who use charms, gifts, dances and masks of animals to better speak to and control Spirit. All living and non-living things have Spirit- the animals, forces of nature and objects. When Spirit dies, it moves to living in the Spirit world.[4, 5]

From Historia Tolteca Chicimeca, a post-cortesian codex from 1550, written by the people of Cuauhtinchan (of Chichimeca ancestry) to sustain their right to their lands, under the Spanish Colonial authorities. Photo courtesy of Michel Wal.

Inuit Story of Day and Night

"Sedna, the Spirit Goddess of the sea, lived at the bottom of the ocean and controlled the seal, whales and other sea animals. She was good to the Inuit people if they made her happy and she would continue to provide them with food. A shape shifter, the trickster Raven created the world. When the waters forced the ground up from the deep, Raven poked holes then secured the rising Earth, being lifted by underground waters. The first home was large enough for Raven, the son, his mother and his father. Father had the sacred animal bladder with Spirit, Father

241

had an animal bladder with Spirit inside, suspended over the bed and Raven always asked to play with it, but Father always said no until one day after much begging by Raven, Father agreed to let Raven hold, then play with the special bladder but Raven broke the bladder and Light suddenly appeared in their home. Father didn't want to have Light constantly shining out so Father seized the bladder with Spirit from Raven so it would not release anymore. Thus, the beginning of the day and of the night were created."[6]

See: Appendix XXXVIII – Bat Creek Stone from Jerusalem

Indigenous Native Americans

In the United States, the Indigenous American People's cultural areas span from Alaska, the Northeast Woodlands, Southeast and the Great Plains, the Great Basin and Plateau, the Northwest, and California, along with the Southwest, and the Southern locations.[7]

Indigenous Native Americans Rituals

Rituals include customarily playing sacred drums for ceremonies, with sacred stories passed throughout, accompanied by music and dance, will inspire unity among indigenous peoples.

Feather and Spinning dances use the energy of the Sacred Eagle to achieve a connection with the Great Spirit. The Ghost Dance and Circle Dances reunite the living with spirits of the dead, and may implore these spirits to fight, on the behalf of the living. Other set practices during the year bless events like harvests or hunting, or may announce a vision-journey to the land of the dead or to signal attention to imminent or major changes for the tribe and its peoples.

Native american shared beliefs, mythology, creation myths and supreme beings, deities, medicine women, kivas, herbalism, kachinas, smudging, power animals, prayer sticks, totems, sweat lodges, astronomy, vision quests, cosmology and archaeoastronomy

Indigenous peoples, as well as our ancient ancestors, were hunter-gatherers, animistic and they worshipped nature. They believed that underlying spiritual forces inhabited all living things of the natural world, and that these forces of were a part of all objects within the Universe.

Tribal legends, religion, history, and ritual were woven together, giving order and meaning to life, through repeating themes and imprinting the cultural identity of each tribe. Cosmology and how creator gods made the Universe and then humans, the Earth, the animals, food, death and the afterlife, were incorporated into oral history of each tribe. Mother Earth and Father Sky were creator beings and the Great Spirit, perfect in all ways, the powerful creator/ruler of the Universe, was a Supreme Being in the creation stories of the tribe, also named the Great Mystery, which is a conception of a universal, spiritual force or Supreme Being.

The principal immortals, such as Spider Woman, are found in many tribes-the Hopi, Blackfoot, Pawnee and the Sioux. The Sun God is the supreme creator of the Zuni, with less powerful gods and goddesses of natural forces operating the daily routine and rhythm of everything within the tribal life.

Shamanism has its ancient origins in humanity and is translated from the Sanskrit word 'sraman' or 'worker.' Each indigenous people has a medicine woman or shaman—a tribal spiritual leader who enters dreams states or other supernatural dimensions, with perceived or conveyed influence through animals or material objects by the spirits, speaks with the spirits, addresses problems of the tribe, ancestors, illness, death and afterlife rituals stemming from the creed that the physical feature might be brought under control by the humans. A medicine bag was carried by the medicine woman/man, and like the power animal, it held sacred amulets, carvings, items of healing, power objects and symbols of luck, strength and protection.

The shamanic healing conducted by the medicine woman/man or tribal healer encompassed herbal medicine, using herbs, plants and plant extracts for the mind, body and spirit. The spirit guide is the protector for life, mentor, advisor and guide for each indigenous person.

Sweat Lodge ceremonies, at first, were only for men, but today, women do the 'lodge,' seen as a purification ceremony for ritual healing and rites of passage such as marriage. Smudging, the burning of dried sage, is used in traditional rituals of healing, purification and prayer ceremonies. The Pueblo Indigenous American's 'kiva'—a sacred circular structure, usually underground, is used for spiritual ceremonies and rituals. Playing a central religious role in the Pueblo tribes are the *kachinas*—powerful spirits, perhaps ancestors or nature spirits of great antiquity. In ritual dances set at certain times of the year, young men are honored to wear kachina masks and do special prescribed dances to activate and enlist the support of kachinas, for the tribe's wellbeing. The indigenous people, like all world-wide ancient peoples of age-old heritage, have dancers. Southwest indigenous tribes used prayer sticks for offerings to petition the spirits in ritual and ceremonies.

Historically, meteors, falling stars, changes in the Sun or Moon, eclipses or other observations made in the heavens were thought to be bad luck. Many indigenous American tribes of the Great Plains such as the Pawnee, Shoshone, Arikara, and Wichita had multifaceted celestial charts. Solar and lunar beliefs related to every aspect of tribal life—agriculture, seasons, trade, marriage, birth and death. The Cherokee understood that all of life on Earth is a reflection of the stars, while the Pawnee thought stars were deities that had once lived on Earth and at death, were transformed into stars. Many indigenous people have studied and relied on the stars and constellations for millennia, to predict events, gain spiritual understanding or become attuned to the Great Spirit. Vision quests were aided through fasting, meditation or medicinal potions, to ascertain the future from spirits, the direction or knowledge from supernatural forces and predilection aimed at tribal harmony or events requiring understanding. Northwest peoples believed that a totem—a natural item or bird, would be the protector spirit for the tribe.[8, 9, 10, 11]

The Navajo Gods

Origins of Indigenous North Americans

Most archaeologists were schooled that Native Americans first arrived from northeast Asia, migrating across the Bering Strait some 12,000 years ago, then traveling throughout North and South America, citing the "Ice-Free Corridor" of the Bering Strait. We consider these people members of the North American Indian tribes and the Clovis tribe, thought to have migrated from Asia, and characterize a New World cultural stage, c. 22,000–6000 BCE, distinguished by fluted-point tools and cooperative hunting methods, especially of large animals.[12]

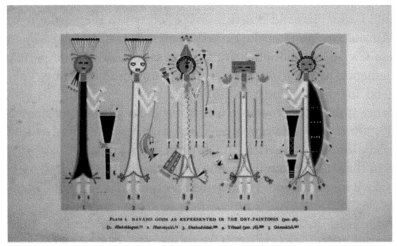

Numerous studies are now showing that various portions of the 'corridor' were blocked by ice from between some 30,000 to about 13,000 years ago and Pleistocene geology, archaeology, physical anthropology and DNA analysis have produced new information about the migration. Scholars supporting these research-based studies now cite age-dating between 15,000 to over 75,000 years ago. Evidence of a south arrival (not north) by humans from Oceania, beginning at least by 13,500 years ago was cemented with the studies at Monte Verde, Chile. These studies single-handedly postdate arrival of the Clovis people, who were reportedly established in North America by 12,000 years ago.

As we continue to explore *Anthrogenesis*, we postulate that other passages existed to North America.

Is it possible that this migration was synced with a post-destruction migration from Lemuria, with later peoples migrating in from Atlantis?

The Chilean study revealed that the South American skulls were small, slender faced, more closely resembling the people of Oceania, different from the northeast Asian Indigenous American lineages. This information has led to speculation that the First Americans and Native Americans came from different homelands or migrated from Asia at different times and stages in their evolution. DNA studies have shown that some of indigenous peoples came from the 'Oceania' area as long ago as 60,000 years.[13, 14]

Old Crow Flats and Bluefish Caves, located in the northern Yukon of Canada, are some of the earliest known sites of human habitation. These Canadian Aboriginal Indigenous cultures illustrate permanent settlements, agriculture, civic and ceremonial architecture, complex societal hierarchies and trading networks. The excavations revealed evidence from Old Crow basin which suggests a human presence as early as 35,000 to 40,000 years ago. These findings indicate that humans migrated into the Americas much earlier; up to 40,000 years ago, as seen in these Old Crow Basin studies. So, with this evidence, we could say Clovis migration into North America occurred after 35,000 to 40,000 years ago.

Additional documentation from the Baja California study indicates that initial settlement of North America was driven by Southeast Asians—Oceania, who occupied Australia 60,000 years ago, then spread out into the Americas about 13,500 years ago, before the Mongoloid Indigenous peoples arrived from northeast Asia. [15, 16, 17, 18, 19, 20]

Origin Patterns of Indigenous Peoples

The indigenous peoples within modern Canada are comprised of the First Nations, Inuit and Métis peoples. The Métis are Aboriginal Canadians of mixed blood which originated in the mid-17th century when First Nation and Inuit people married Europeans and Africans and are recognized as an Aboriginal people, with formal recognition equivalent to that given to the Inuit and First Nations peoples. The Métis are linked to the Mi'kmaq, Algonquin, Saulteaux, Cree, Ojibwe, Menominee, and Maliseet peoples with the Métis homeland including areas scattered across Canada, as well as portions of the northern United States; northwest Minnesota, North Dakota, and Montana. Native American source populations have additional DNA groupings from Asian, Mongolian, Amur, Japanese, Korean, and Ainu populations, with these populations emanating from the east of the Yenisei Valley, adjacent to the Altai Mountains by Russia, China, Mongolia and Kazakhstan and Lake Baikal, south of the Russian region of Siberia. [21]

Zuni Indigenous Americans

"The Zuni people have lived in the American Southwest for thousands of years. Their cultural and religious traditions are rooted, in large part, in the people's deep and close ties to the mountains, forests, and deserts of this ancient Zuni homeland. Primarily being farmers, the Zuni raise maize and wheat and engage in jewelry making. It has become an important additional source of income for the people. Traditional Zuni life is oriented around a matrilineal clan system and a complex ceremonial system based on a belief in the ancestors (ancient ones). There are six specialized esoteric groups, each with restricted membership and its own priesthood, devoted to the worship of a particular group of supernaturals. During the well-known Shalako Festival, held in early winter, dancers representing the couriers of the rain deities come to bless new homes. One way the Zuni people express these cultural traditions is through their art: in painting, pottery, jewelry, and fetish carving, for example. These things have significant meaning, and, to the Zuni, serve to help unite the past with the present. So, on the one hand, Zuni art is a material record of the past."[22]

The Hopi Creation Story

"Taiowa created Sotuknang first, followed by Spider Woman, then the Twins. These first people created by the creator were in tune with the creator in a way which modern day people are not. The first Hopi people were committed to their creator and only wished to do as the creator commanded them.

The Hopi believe that the human race has passed through three different worlds and lifeways since the beginning. At the end of each prior world, human life has been purified or punished by the Great Spirit due mainly to corruption, greed and turning away from the Great Spirit's teachings. The last great destruction was the flood which destroyed all but a few faithful ones who asked and received a permission from the Great Spirit to live with Him in this new land. The Great Spirit said, "It is up to you, if you are willing to live my poor, humble and simple life way. It is hard but if you agree to live according to my teachings and instructions, if you never lose faith in the life I shall give you, you may come and live with me." The Hopi and all who were saved from the great flood made a sacred covenant with the Great Spirit at that time. "We Hopi made an oath that we will never turn away from Him. For us the Creators laws never change or break down."

The first of these three worlds gave the Hopi people a simple life with the animals. The second world produced further developments such as crafts, homes and villages. The third world proved to be a great world with mass multiplication, advances in society such as big cities, countries and a higher form of civilization. This proved to be too difficult a barrier to carry on the wishes and plan of the creator. The more advanced a society became, the more the people became preoccupied with their own earthly plans. Those who remained close to the creator and his plan recognized that the more advanced society became and the longer people remained on earth, the harder it was to keep the wishes of the creator.

In this third world, the creator allowed for the world to be destroyed by flood. The Hopi who believed were guided by Spider Woman to safety, and then the earth was flooded. After a long period of time in safe keeping, the Hopi people were instructed as how to journey to the Fourth World, known as *Tuwaqachi*, or World Complete. Once the journey was complete the people were instructed that although this new world is not as beautiful and easy as the previous worlds, it has everything the people need and allows them great choice. The manner in which the people choose will determine whether or not this world must be destroyed as the previous three, or whether the Creator's plan will be carried out by the people.

A gift given to the Hopi by the Creator was the ability to communicate with each other even though they did not speak the same language. They could do this through a closeness of spirit which allowed them to see and talk to each other through the center on the top of their head. They had this ability because of the continuance of singing praises to the creator.

The Hopi believed there is a consequence to every action. There is also a distinct difference between the balance of nature on earth and human nature on earth. Human nature has some characteristic flaws such as greed, hatred, and violence. The Hopi believe that human nature has destroyed three previous worlds due to a lack of respect for nature by humans as well as a lack of respect for one another, as well as a lack of respect and reverence toward the Creator.

The people once dwelled in the Third World inside the earth and lived there in good ways for many years, but eventually materialism prevailed and the people forgot the laws of the Great Spirit. Corruption ensued and a great division of the people resulted for some wanted to continue to follow the good laws and live simply, while self-importance took over the hearts of many. Immorality flourished so the high priests and the leader gathered together to smoke and pray for guidance. This is when the idea came to them to move. Because they had been hearing

249

footsteps in the sky above them, they sent a red racer snake and birds to investigate, neither of which was successful. Finally, an ootsa, or small sparrow hawk, found the *sipapuni*, or hole in the sky, and emerged into this, the Fourth World. There it found a well-dressed and handsome young man sitting next to a fire. Around his neck were four strands of turquoise and from his ears hung large pendants of this same precious stone. Streaks of black hematite ran from the bridge of his nose downward to each cheek. He identified himself as Maasaw, Caretaker of the Earth. He knew of the situation below and because of the trouble the people had brought upon themselves, he refused to grant them permission to enter the Fourth World.

When the sparrow hawk returned to the leader and priests with this disheartening news, they tried again. This time they sent along *paho*, or prayer feathers, and instructed the bird to present this to Maasaw for an offering. The leader pledged that only good people would enter the Fourth World if permission to enter were granted. The young man was impressed by the prayer feathers and granted permission, but only if the people agreed to practice his way of life. But the evil ones must stay behind.

The leader and priests were overjoyed with the news and instructed by guidance, planted a spruce tree and pine trees. As they sang creation songs and prayed, the trees shot up into the air but the branches were too soft to support the people all the way into the upper world. So, a bamboo reed was planted.

Because all of this was kept secret from the corrupt people, only the good-hearted people knew of the plans to leave. They climbed the bamboo reed, which did not have sections in the beginning, and as they grew tired, rested between the joints as they worked their way up. Thus sections were created in the bamboo reed where the people rested. Finally, the pointed end of the bamboo pierced the sky and the people climbed through the emergence hole into this, the Fourth World, where Maasaw gave them his rules for living a proper way of life, along with the *navoti*, or prophetic statements. He then instructed the Hopi to migrate to the four corners of the earth, assuring them that after their wanderings they would eventually meet at a common site. It was there they were to found a village, name it Oraibi and settle permanently. Here they would gather eternal benefits from the land for the area was the "backbone of the earth."

Old Spiderwoman, who emerged with the people, was given a stone tablet on which she magically inscribed Maasaw's instructions on life. Then, breaking it in two, Maasaw gave one half of the tablet to the Hopi and one half to the Pahana, the Elder White Brother, who had also emerged with them."

Quote above used with permission from Barbara Hayes Waters, wife of Frank Waters, 2015

The Mound Builders

Blavatsky speaks about the dolmens and colossal monuments… "There is no country from which they are absent. Who built them? Why are they all connected with Serpents and Dragons, with Alligators and Crocodiles? Because remains of "Paleolithic man" were, it is thought, found in some of them, and because in the funeral mounds of America bodies of later races were discovered with the usual paraphernalia of bone necklaces, weapons, stone and copper urns, etc., hence they are declared ancient tombs. But surely the two famous mounds -one in the Mississippi valley and the other in Ohio – known respectively as "the

Alligator Mound" and "the Great Serpent Mound," were never meant for tombs* (Vide infra). * We take the following description from a scientific work.

"The first of these animals (the alligator), designed with considerable skill, is no less than 250 ft. long. The interior is formed of a heap of stones, over which the form has been molded in fine stiff clay. The great serpent is represented with open mouth, in the act of swallowing an egg of which the diameter is 100 ft. in the thickest part; the body of the animal is wound in graceful curves and the tail is rolled into a spiral. The entire length of the animal is 1,100 ft. This work is unique . . . and there is nothing on the old continent which offers any analogy to it... Except its symbolism, however, of the Serpent -- the cycle of Time -- swallowing Kosmos, the egg."[23]

The Indigenous American mound builders were the Adena people, known for their legendary site the 'Serpent Mound' in Peebles, Ohio, who began building earth mounds c. 3500 BCE. Many ancient people have built mounds all over the planet, with some having been excavated, revealing the remains of large human bones, such as at the West Virginia Mounds. It appears that the mounds of Europe are of the passage-type, which aligns most commonly with the winter or summer solstice sunrises. England's Silbury Hill in Avebury, County Wiltshire, is the world's largest mound found to date.[24, 25, 26]

Who is Kennewick Man?

"The identity of the first Americans is an emotive issue for American Indians, who believe their ancestors were the first to inhabit the Americas. Controversy erupted after skeletal remains were found in Kennewick, Washington, in 1996. This skeleton, estimated to be 9,000 years old, had a long cranium and narrow face—features typical of people from Europe, the Near East or India—rather than the wide cheekbones and rounder skull of an American Indian. A coalition of Indian tribes, however, said that if Kennewick Man was 9,000 years old, he must be their ancestor, no matter what he looked like. Invoking a U.S. federal law that provides for the return of Native American remains to their living descendants, the tribes demanded a halt to all scientific study and the immediate return of the skeleton for burial in a secret location."[27]

Pixabay

The case for Kennewick Man was examined by archaeologists for his population origins and DNA studies finally occurred, the results being published in the journal, *Nature*, July 23, 2015, Vol. 523, 455-58. The conclusion was that "among the groups for which we have sufficient genomic data, we find that the Colville, one of the Native American groups claiming Kennewick Man as ancestral, show close affinities to that individual or at least to the population to which he belonged, Kennewick Man is directly related to contemporary Native Americans, and thus show genetic continuity within the Americas over at least the past 8,000 years. Although our individual-based craniometric (measurement of the skull) analyses confirm that Kennewick Man tends to be more similar to Polynesian and Ainu peoples than to Native Americans, Kennewick Man's pattern of craniometric affinity falls well within the range of affinity patterns evaluated for individual Native Americans."[28]

Luzia Woman

The Luzia Woman, excavated in Lapa Vermelha, Brazil, in 1975 by archaeologist Annette Laming-Emperaire, is over 11,000 years old. Her evocative facial features include a narrow, oval cranium, projecting face, pronounced chin, dissimilar to most Native Americans and their reported indigenous Siberian forbears. Anthropologists described Luzia's features as resembling those of indigenous Australian Aborigines – dating back 60,000 years ago, or possibly the Oceania peoples– indigenous Australians, Melanesians and Negritos of Southeast Asia. Luzia is also reminiscent of the Olmec, with their many faces.[29, 30, 31]

Blavatsky on Antiquity of Humanity

Blavatsky sums up mainstream science of the day quite well in the section 'A Panoramic View of the Early Races.'

"There is a period of a few millions of years to cover between the first "mindless" race and the highly intelligent and intellectual later Lemurians. There is another between the earliest civilization of the Atlanteans and the historic period. As witnesses to the Lemurians but a few silent records in the shape of half a dozen broken colossi and old cyclopean ruins are left. These are not allowed a hearing, as they are "productions of blind natural forces," we are assured by some; "quite modern," we are told by others. Tradition is left contemptuously unnoticed by sceptic and materialist, and made subservient to the Bible in every case by the too zealous Churchman. Whenever a legend, however, refuses to fit in with the Noachian "deluge theory," it is declared by the Christian clergy "the insanely delirious voice of old superstition. Atlantis is denied, when not confused with Lemuria and other departed continents, because perhaps, Lemuria is half the creation of modern science, and has, therefore, to be believed in; while Plato's Atlantis is regarded by most of the scientists as a dream."- H.P. Blavatsky, 1977, *The Secret Doctrine*, Vol. II. Page 263.

Aryan Root Race Picks Up Speed

The first sub-race of the Aryan Root Race began in Mongolia. This Fifth Root Race began to expand, already well advanced in India from the late sub-races of the Atlanteans, and by 60,000 BCE had developed into Arabia. The Arabs settled into Persia (Iran) by 40,000 BCE with this sub-race expanding outward to establish settlements in Celtic Western Europe by 30,000 BCE. The Celtic peoples proceeded through Mesopotamia towards Western Europe by 20,000 BCE onward to Greece, with the Mycenaeans occupying southeast Europe. The Teutons, the Germanic peoples, went towards Germany through Mesopotamia and later, the Slavic races relocated towards Russia, which brings the migrations to the present time.[32]

Atlantean Initiates Travel East

The Rosicrucians and Gnostics state that a colony of initiates founded Stonehenge about 100,000 years ago, when it belonged to the Scandinavian part of the continent of Europe, bringing initiated priests of the Akkadian sub-race who were tall and fair with lengthier heads than those of this land. Stonehenge stood as a rebellion in simplicity to protest the Atlantean temples who were deeply engrossed in their downward spiral into materialism. Egypt became the first base for the White Lodge of Initiates at that time, 100,000 years ago, and for thousands of years they maintained this location, later moving to the Himalayas. The Great White Lodge founded the 'divine dynasty' of Egypt with colonists from Atlantis receiving the teachings of the Ancient Mysteries many thousands of years ago. The two pyramids of Giza, were reportedly built 10,000 years before the 2nd Atlantean Deluge, as permanent Halls of Initiation and shrines for the 'Jewel of Great Power' (relics of the Ancient Wisdom), so needed on Earth prior to the 3rd Deluge, which the Initiates knew was coming. Egypt remained under water for a considerable period and began to receive more Atlanteans who founded the 2nd Divine Dynasty of Egypt ruled by the Initiated Adepts. The 4th Deluge was considerably less destructive 80,000 years ago with the 3rd Divine Dynasty beginning its rule, and building the great Temple of Karnak and many of the ancient buildings still standing in Egypt. No building in Egypt reportedly predates the cataclysm of c. 80,000 years ago. The spiritual alchemists of that time were said to have made the gold and silver structural decoration.[33, 34, 35]

At the time of Poseidonis, a tidal wave *also* swept over Egypt, and while short-lived, it ended the Divine Dynasties and The White Lodge moved to other lands. One must realize that at the end of the Atlantean period there existed three groups of man-like beings. There were the evolved souls, who were ahead of most people. They taught Divine Wisdom and accomplished divine deeds; the second mass of humanity who were slow thinking beings, with sensory or low psychic abilities which most modern humanity had lost; and finally, a small group of those who were developing the Manu or faculty of thought.[36]

Atlantis Ends

The Mandala Comes Full Circle

The first sub-race branched into the Incas of Peru. The ancient name given to the creative gods in Peruvian theology and their true origins is unknown. Blavatsky says that the Incas, grouped within 'the Seven', re-birthed Earth's humanity after the Deluge of Atlantis and reminiscent of previous races, the Kings of Light came to humanity to assist in the preparation of the next race. They were the Adepts priests of the Ancient Wisdom.[37]

The first sub-races were described as 'moon colored,' and created from spiritually evolved souls from Atlantis, by the Vaivasvatu Manu. The Aryan sub-races include: Hindu, Arabian, Persian, Celts, Teutonic, Austral-American and survivors of the last great cataclysm, bringing wisdom and intuition with psychic vision and astral powers, which were developed in Atlantis. Humanity originated from ancient progenitors of the early Fourth Root Race that migrated throughout the planet.[38]

In the upcoming sub-races, the Aryan Race will have a division much like that of the Lemurians and Atlanteans in c. 20,000 years hence, in which the goal of spirituality will once again be challenged by the power of materialism. The challenge will be balancing of the 'Pair of Opposites'— good and bad, yin and yang, and between these sides, we shall see some balance in humanity's world, with evolution bringing about resolution of the issues. By this time, the Sixth Root Race will have begun and humanity will revert back to the physicality of the earlier Root Races with an increase in wisdom and spirituality.[39]

Kalachakra depiction, painted in Sera Monastery, Tibet. Photo by Kosi Gramatikoff, (Private Collection).

It is called the 'mandala of expression,' the Tibetan has said, that we reincarnate and come full circle around the Great Mandala of Rebirth. At the onset of the Cycle of Rebirth, the human character is quite unevolved and self-driven prior to the First Initiation—the Birth of Water, then to the Second Initiation—the Birth of the Heart, then to the Third Initiation—during which the Soul overshadows the Personality; operating through the vehicle of the Personality. The Aspirant serves the Master within the Ashram, on the higher planes of endeavor. So, this spiritual unfolding manifests with all humans in our Universe.[40]

On the Path of Return during the Third Initiation,
'the Third Eye' endows the Aspirant to Discipleship an
expansion in spiritual vision, among other spiritual attributes.

The human consciousness has always aspired to goodwill and it must
be sought out, exercised by the imagination and developed in thought
and deed, keeping that loving eye at work, in the dynamic of relationships
in our world and practice in life. Love in Action is the mainstay of the
Masters and our legacy on the Path of Service until the completion of
the Third Initiation. The Light of the Mind endows the Aspirant to
Discipleship an expansion in spiritual vision, among other spiritual
attributes. The last two races will bring 'hunches' emanating first from
the senses, and then the intuition. The pineal gland will function again,
in the distant future, as the organ of the seventh and highest sense.[41]

The Aryans Migrate

The Aryan Root Race began to migrate several different directions;
from the South-west to Iran, and towards North Afghanistan, to the
Hindu Kush, towards South Afghanistan and to North Pakistan and
finally, towards North-Western India.[42, 43]

Notes

1. http://www.sott.net/article/256712-A-giant-mystery-18-strange-giant-skeletons-found-in-Wisconsin-Sons-of-god-Men-of-renown

2. http://www.mysteriousworld.com/journal/1998/winter/aztalan/

3. Navarro, Armando, Mexicano and Latino Politics and the Quest for Self-Determination: What Needs to Be Done, 2015, Lexington Books, Lanham, MD, 20706, Page 5.

4. http://www.native-languages.org/alaska.htm

5. http://firstpeoplesofcanada.com/fp_groups/fp_inuit5.html

6. http://www.firstpeoplesofcanada.com/fp_groups/fp_inuit5.html

7. http://www.native-languages.org/culture-areas.htm

8. http://www.native-languages.org/culture-areas.htm

9. Means, Robert. Where White Men Fear to Tread: The Autobiography of Russell Means. Macmillan, 1995. ISBN 0312147619 pg. 241.

10. http://www.warpaths2peacepipes.com/native-american-culture/native-american-mythology.htm

11. http://www.warpaths2peacepipes.com/native-american-culture/native-american-religion.htm

12. http://dictionary.reference.com/

13. http://news.nationalgeographic.com/news/2003/09/0903_030903_bajaskull.html

14. González-José, Rolando, Antonio González-Martín, and Miquel Hernández. "Craniometric Evidence for Palaeoamerican Survival in Baja California." Nature 425.6953 (2003): 62-65.

15. http://pubs.aina.ucalgary.ca/arctic/Arctic64-1-127.pdf

16. Goebel, T., M. R. Waters, and D. H. O'Rourke. "The Late Pleistocene Dispersal of Modern Humans in the Americas." Science 319.5869 (2008): 1497-502. Web.

17. Morlan, R.E. et al. "Accelerator Mass Spectrometry Dates on Bones from Old Crow Basin, Northern Yukon Territory". Canadian Journal of Archaeology / Journal Canadien d'Archéologie 14 (1990): 75–92. Web.

18. http://news.nationalgeographic.com/news/2003/09/0903_030903_bajaskull.html

19. http://csfa.tamu.edu/who.php

20. http://www.smithsonianmag.com/science-nature/dna-12000-year-old-skeleton-helps-answer-question-who-were-first-americans-180951469/#53kV3LimvWJWgxGA.99

21. http://www.nativeweb.org/resources/organizations/aboriginal_indigenous_nations/

22. http://www.ashiwi.org/Culture.aspx

23. Helena Petrovna Blavatsky, *The Secret Doctrine*, Vol. II., pp. 752-753.

24. http://www.greatserpentmound.com

25. http://grahamhancock.com/dewhurstr1/

26. http://www.wvculture.org/history/mounds.html

27. http://news.nationalgeographic.com/news/2003/09/0903_030903_bajaskull_2.html

28. http://www.nature.com/nature/journal/v523/n7561/full/nature14625.html

29. Williams, Frank L'Engle, "Kennewick and Luzia: Lessons from the European Upper Paleolithic "in the American Journal of Physical Anthropology, 2003

30. González-José, Rolando, Maria Cátira Bortolini, Fabrício R. Santos, and Sandro L. Bonatto. "The Peopling of America: Craniofacial Shape Variation on a Continental Scale and Its Interpretation from an Interdisciplinary View." American Journal of Physical Anthropology 137.2 (2008): 175-87

31.http://news.nationalgeographic.com/news/2003/09/0903_030903_bajaskull.html

32. de Purucker, Gottfried, Studies in Occult Philosophy, 1973, Theosophical University Press, Pasadena, CA.

33. Clymer, Reuben Swinburne, The Mystery of Osiris; Egyptian Initiation, 1909, Philosophical Publishing Company, Allentown, PA, (Assisted by F. Oscar Biberstein) Copyright 236576.

34. http://gnosticteachings.org/books-by-samael-aun-weor/the-perfect-matrimony/945-initiation.html

35. http://www.sacred-texts.com/atl/soa/soa26.htm

36. Scott-Elliot, William, The Story of Atlantis and The Lost Lemuria, 1925. Theosophical Publishing Society, NY.

37. Blavatsky, H.P., SD, I, 1977.

38. http://www.mystic-history.angelfire.com/evo-invo.htm

39. Bailey, Alice, 1959. A Treatise on White Magic, Lucis Publishing Company, NY.
40. http://www.lucistrust.org
41. http://www.lucistrust.org
42. H.P.B., SD, II
43. Purucker, G. de, Studies in Occult Philosophy, 1973, Theosophical University Press, Pasadena, CA.

Anthrogenesis

Bonnyb Bendix, Germany, Pixabay

Chapter Thirteen
The Triad Persists To The Present

"There was a time when the whole world, the totality of mankind, had one religion, and when they were of "one lip.""

–H.P. Blavatsky, *The Secret Doctrine, Vol II*, p.760

The Three-Fold Triangle

The Lemurian people received spiritual gifts from the advanced Teachers from Venus who also took on roles as "Manus," founding the first 'Lodge of Initiation' in Lemuria. These Venusian adepts brought wheat, fruit and bees from their home planet.

The spiritual principles of the Golden Rule and for the Lord's Prayer given to the Lemurians were quite plain because their lives were very basic in the beginning, encompassing the virtues of morality and goodness, intrinsic to their spiritual devotion.

The Lemurian adepts would later migrate to Oceania, and the Fifth Root race was off and running to India and Egypt, about 60,000 years ago; later they migrated to Persia. The human race moved forward in growth and development and spiritual concepts spread across the globe. The devotion to the Father; the Golden Rule and the Father's Prayer, at some time, were shared with an initiate, or initiates, from Atlantis, and sacred spiritual gnosis and traditions were brought to Egypt and India, to not only 'keep the fires lit' but to build a base for the future mystery school of initiations to come. The yoga of enlightenment and discipleship became an inherent part of the theology of many races. Thus the origin of the Triangle: threefold, tripled, triplicate, tripartite, triune or triadic, or as a trinity came into being. Spells and hymns in the Greek's magical papyri refer to the goddesses, called Hecate, Persephone, and Selene, among other names, as "triple-sounding, triple-headed, triple-voiced, triple-pointed, triple-faced, triple-necked." In Anthrogenesis we observe that the number 'three' has been used in many sacred ways: the Triad, the Rays 1, 2, 3; and positive, negative, and zero. Thesis, antithesis, and synthesis were developed much later by the philosopher, Georg Wilhelm Friedrich Hegel, using the same concept of THREE.[1]

The Tripartite Of Wisdom

A story is told about how the cosmos is animated into consciousness by an all-powerful intergalactic being, hidden in deep space, with the darkness as her realm. She moves through space and time, conveying her preeminence, while giving life to matter. She is Essence, Spirit and Light- the tripartite wisdom- three-in-one. Her name is Father, Mother and Son incarnate, and known as 'The One About Whom Naught May Be Said.'

Joseph Campbell says that this multi-goddess perspective does not represent "pantheism, a misleading word" but rather that God doesn't inhabit the world. Goddess-God is "trans-theological, an inconceivable mystery, thought of as power, the source and end and supporting ground of all life and being." Brahma, the creator, Vishnu; the preserver and Shiva, the destroyer or transformer; Power, Intelligence and Will in theosophy; Father,

Mother and the Son in Zoroastrianism; Isis, Osiris and Horus in Egypt; and in Phoenicia: Baal, Mot and Yam. She 'speaks' All matter into being, and the world comes into being, crowned with a nest of sky to be the roof, the heavens beyond, she moves slowly with knowledge and entrusts her emissaries with powers to create more life. The son, another powerful emanation, is a powerful, perfect entity unto himself. He dies for his people, and later resurrects for the good of his society, providing an afterlife quite similar to earthly existence.[2]

Zarathustra's Written Teachings

Zarathustra was an ancient Adept of the Ancient Wisdom. Blavatsky says that Zarathustra incarnated many times throughout Atlantis and later, in *The Secret Doctrine*, Vol. II, she states, "…it may be useful to agree upon the names to be given to the Continents on which the four great Races, which preceded our Adamic Race, were born, lived, and died. Their archaic and esoteric names were many, and varied with the language of the nationality which mentioned them in its annals and scriptures." Blavatsky says that "the original Zoroaster was born of the land of the 'Gods' under their chiefs, the 'Spirits of this Planet.' By "original" we mean the 'Amshaspend' called Zarathustra: the lord and ruler of the Vara (sacred Persian sanctuary), made by Yima (a mortal Persian man) in that land…There were several Zarathustra or Zertusts; the Dabistan (a Persian compilation of religious beliefs, observances and customs of the East) alone enumerating thirteen; but these were all the reincarnations of the first one. The last Zoroaster was the founder of the fire temple of Azareksh (historical Zoroastrianism temple) and the writer of the works on the primeval sacred Magian religion (Zoroastrian religion) destroyed by Alexander.[3, 4, 5, 6, 7, 8]

Zarathustra is reported to have touted the basic teachings, originating in Lemuria and Atlantis, which embody the great credos of love and compassion for all humanity. He was successful for some years, especially when the Semites and the Persians spoke the same language. The following work, *The Oracles of Zoroaster* known throughout the ages, is thought to descend from ancient, oral tradition, possibly part of Zarathustra's original teachings which embody the Hermetic principles.

Note: This Oracle does not appear in either of the ancient collections, nor in the group of oracles given by any of the mediaeval occultists. Cory seems to have been the first to discover it in the voluminous writings of Eusebius, who attributes the authorship to the Persian Zoroaster.

The entire text is included in the Appendices.

The Oracles Of Zoroaster; Cause. God. Father. Mind. Fire Monad. Dyad. Triad

1. But God is He having the head of the Hawk. The same is the first, incorruptible, eternal, unbegotten, indivisible, dissimilar: the dispenser of all good; indestructible; the best of the good, the Wisest of the wise; He is the Father of Equity and Justice, self-taught, physical, perfect, and wise—He who inspires the Sacred Philosophy.
– Eusebius. *Præparatio Evangelica,* Liber. I., Chap. X.

2. Theurgists assert that He is a God and celebrate him as both older and younger, as a circulating and eternal God, as understanding the whole number of all things moving in the World, and moreover infinite through his power and energizing a spiral force.
– Proclus on the *Timæus* of Plato, 244. Z. or T.

The Egyptian Pantheon had an Elder and a Younger Horus—a God—son of Osiris and Isis. Taylor suggests that he refers to Kronos, Time, or Chronos as the later Platonists wrote the name. Kronos, or Saturnus, of the Romans, was son of Uranos and Gaia, husband of Rhea, father of Zeus.[9, 10]

See: Appendix XXXIX "The Oracles of Zoroaster."

Persian Woman Plays a Tar

Painting from Hasht Behesht Palace, Isfahan, Iran, 1669. Zeresh.

Theosophy on Zoroastrianism

Vedic Hinduism's translation of the Hermetic writings were contributory to Theosophy's teachings, echoing Zoroaster's *Oracle*. Rudolf Steiner also corroborates Blavatsky's account of Zoroaster's previous embodiments, beginning in late Atlantis, with each reincarnation carrying the essence of the original Trinity: The Monad, the Dyad and The Triad. Theosophist, Arthur Powell said in his book, *The Solar System*, 1930, that in 29,700 BCE, the Mahâguru (the future Gautama Buddha) came to the Third sub-race as the first Zarathustra (Zoroaster) and founded the 'Religion of the Fire,' the Zoroastrian religion.[11]

The Chaldean Oracle narratives were translated by the ancient Sumerian priests, and were a prologue to Biblical stories. In fact, much of Genesis is copied from the Chaldean Oracle with Zoroaster's account of the creation of the Universe.[12]

Zoroaster's Citations about the Soul

96. Since the Soul perpetually runs and passes through many experiences in a certain space of time; which being performed, it is presently compelled to pass back again through all things, and unfold a similar web of generation in the World, according to Zoroaster, who thinketh that as often as the same causes return, the same effects will in like manner be sure to ensue. -Ficin. *De Im. An.*, 129. Z.

97. According to Zoroaster, in us the ethereal vestment of the Soul perpetually revolves (reincarnates).—Ficin. De Im. An., 131. Z.

153. Enlarge not thy Destiny. -Psell, 37; Pletho, 4.

(This is the cosmic Law of Cause and Effect commonly called karma by the masses.)[13]

The Oannes—Half Man, Half Fish

Blavatsky says the original Chaldean Oracles are quite specific about the Monadic tradition, in the Babylonian tradition, with creation stories wherein civilization was originally founded by the Oannes, Musari, or Annedoti, who were amphibious beings. This tradition is in striking agreement with Egyptian and Dogon traditions of the amphibious Nommos, or 'Monitors', who came from the constellation of Sirius, providing a link to their spiritual genesis on Earth.

"Oannes (Assyrian-Babylonian) is a deity, half man, half fish, who rose every day from the Persian Gulf and taught the people wisdom, the arts and sciences, agriculture, etc. Identified with the deity Ea and also called Dogon and Annedotus. A somewhat similar story is related in the Sanskrit Hari-Purana about Vishnu during his Matsya-avatara (fish incarnation).

"There were Annedoti who came after him, five in number (our race being the fifth) -'all like Oannes in form and teaching the same'; but Musarus Oannes was the first to appear, and this he did during the reign of Ammenon, the third or fourth of the ten antediluvian Kings whose dynasty ended with Xisuthrus, the Chaldean Noah. This allegory of Oannes, the Annedotus, reminds us of the 'Dragon' and 'Snake-Kings'; the Nagas who in Buddhist legends instruct people in wisdom on lakes and rivers, and end by becoming converts to the good Law and Arhats. The meaning is evident. The 'fish' is an old and very suggestive symbol

The Semitic fish-god Dagon, by R. Russell[14]

in the Mystery-language, as is also 'water.' Ea or Hea was the god of the sea and Wisdom, and the sea serpent was one of his emblems, his priests being 'serpents' or Initiates. Thus one sees why Occultism places Oannes and the other Annedoti in the group of those ancient 'adepts' who were called 'marine' or 'water dragons' or Nagas. Water typified their human origin (as it is a symbol of earth and matter and also of purification), in distinction to the 'fire Nagas' or the immaterial, Spiritual Beings, whether celestial Bodhisattvas or Planetary Dhyanis, also regarded as the instructors of mankind. The hidden meaning becomes clear to the Occultist, once he is told that "this being (Oannes) was accustomed to pass the day among men, teaching; and when the Sun had set, he retired again into the sea, passing the night in the deep, 'for he was amphibious,' i.e., he belonged to two planes: the spiritual and the physical. The Greek word *amphibios* means simply 'life on two planes.' The word was often applied in antiquity to those men who, though still wearing a human form, had made themselves almost divine through knowledge, and lived as much in the spiritual supersensuous regions as on earth. Oannes is dimly reflected in Jonah, and even in John, the Precursor, both connected with Fish and Water."[15]

Intrinsic Nature of Tripartite

The Hindu writings, originating c. 3000 BCE, are laden with the heroes, gods and goddesses. By c. 2100 BCE, Sumer had the Tammuz story, borrowed from Phoenicia's *Triad of Divinity*—Anu, Bel and Ea. The Persians (Iranians) took their story of the *Descent of Inanna* from the Phoenicians.In Palestine, c. 1440 BCE, the story of Abram was established. In ancient Greece, c. 2600 BCE, the god, Adonis, dies and later revives himself. Rome, in 100 CE, had their gods and goddesses to create the hero to rescue the world.[16]

Esoteric Brahmanical, Buddhistic, and Chaldean Cosmology

"We here give the diagrams of the Hindu and the Chaldeo-Jewish cosmogonies. The antiquity of the diagram of the former may be inferred from the fact that many of the Brahmanical pagodas are designed and built on this figure, called the "Sri-Iantara." And yet we find the highest honors paid to it by the Jewish and mediaeval kabbalists, who call it "Solomon's seal." It will be quite an easy matter to trace it to its origin, once we are reminded of the history of the king-kabbalist and his transaction with King Hiram and Ophir--the country of peacocks, gold, and ivory--for which land we have to search in old India."-Blavatsky[17]

Phoenicians Embody Tripartite

Beginning in mainstream recorded history, c. 2700 BCE, the Phoenicians, developed the tripartite division between Baal, Mot and Yam, the great god Baal who dies and returns to life to battle the chaos of the Yamm. In the *Epic of Gilgamesh*, an evil humanity is destroyed in a flood by the gods. The Akkadian flood history dates back to 2000 BCE, being inherited from the Chaldean Flood Tablets. Utnapishtim, a righteous man, builds the boat with various gods interfering and assisting in the process. The Utnapishtim family survives the flood, become blessed by the gods and flourish, according to Gilgamesh, who then maintains a lifelong quest for eternal life or the equivalent thereof.[18]

Nammu, the Primordial Sea, Births the Gods

"In the beginning there was only the goddess Nammu, the Primordial Sea who lived in total darkness until she gave birth to the Universe, Anki, who was heaven and Earth in one. Anki then made the air god Enlil who split the Universe in two, making An, the god of the sky and Ki, who became the goddess of the Earth. Enlil and Ki would go on to have a child together named Enki, who was the god of water and the lord of the whole universe. He took some water from Nammu and created the rivers Tigris and Euphrates, making the soil fertile and rich so that he could introduce animals to the area. Many other gods and goddesses would soon be born and lived in great cities in the land between the two rivers."[19]

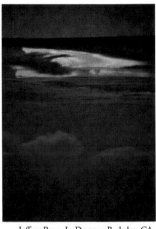

Jeffrey Pang, In Dreams, Berkeley, CA

Sumerian Creation of the Moon

"Enlil lived in the city of Nippur along with other deities including the young goddess Ninlil, whose mother warned her to be wary when bathing in the local canal as Enlil would want to have his way with her if he were to see her naked. This motherly advice turned out to be sound and when the air god saw the young goddess, he immediately tried to seduce her. When Ninlil refused his advances, Enlil was not deterred and after obtaining a boat, he went over to where she was washing herself and raped her, impregnating her in the process with the moon god Nanna."

"The other gods were furious with the forced copulation of Enlil and Ninlil and exiled him for his crime, forcing him to head for the underworld. As she was now pregnant with his child, Ninlil followed him but the pair would soon realise independently of each other that if she continued, her unborn baby would be forever doomed to live in the underworld. Not wanting this, Enlil disguised himself three times; once as a gate keeper, once as the man in charge of the river leading to the underworld and the third time as the ferryman. Each time Enlil and Ninlil encountered each other, he told her that she must sleep with him so that he can impregnate her with a child to reside in the underworld, taking Nanna's place. Each time, the young goddess grudgingly obeyed, realizing that it was the Moon's destiny to go heavenward."[20]

Ageless Sumer History

As discussed in previous sections, the archaic Levantines and their ancestors, the Natufians, once shared language, culture and land, with ancient Mesopotamian. The Sumerian cylinder, tablets and archives give a numerical censuses of population which scholars now estimate that they account for thousands of years in BCE. Keep in mind that people lived longer in the past, as verified in the Vedas, Genesis and *The Secret Doctrine*.[21, 22]

Yarmukian Mother Goddess

Museum of Yarmukian Culture, Kibbutz
Sha'ar Hagolan, Jordan Valley, Israel, c. 8000 BCE

The Eridu Genesis, the Barton Cylinder, the 'Debate Between Sheep and Grain' and the 'Debate Between Winter and Summer', carved in cuneiform on ancient tablets, estimated to be at least c. 5,000 years old, were excavated at Nippur. In the Eridu Genesis, Enki, the Lord of the Earth, and Ninhursag, the Earth goddess, created the world. The great creation myths survived in many forms and are among the first written archives of civilization.

The translation reads as follows:

"Dilmun is described as "the place where primeval cosmic events occurred, Nippur existed before creation when heaven and earth separated. Those days were indeed faraway days. Those nights were indeed faraway nights. Those years were indeed faraway years. The storm roared, the lights flashed. In the sacred area of Nibru-Nippur-the storm roared, the lights flashed. Heaven talked with Earth, Earth talked with Heavens." An, Enlil, Enki and Ninhursag create the "black-headed people" and animals in secure enclosures. Several flood stories follow with a close comparison to the story of the Ark of Genesis. After this time frame, the dynasties began with the kingship descending from heaven and was in Eridug. In Eridug, Alulim became king; he ruled for 28,800 years."[23, 24]

Anu, Enki and Enlil Create Humanity

"While only the gods existed, all the hard work such as digging ditches and farm labour had to be done by the minor deities. They toiled at this work for 3,600 years before finally they decided they had had enough. They went on strike, burned their tools and surrounded the temple of Enlil who was fearful of the angry mob so sought the advice of the other great gods, especially Anu and Enki. Together, Anu, Enki and Enlil came up with a plan and decided to create a new race of beings to act as servants to the gods and do all the hard labour for them. They selected Geshtu-e, a god who was blessed with great intelligence, and sacrificed him. The birth goddess, Ninmah, mixed his flesh and blood with clay after which all the gods spat on the mixture.

Enki, along with the womb goddess, Nintu, then took the mixture into the room of fate where she recited magical incantations over it until finally, she pinched off fourteen pieces of the clay. She then set seven of the pieces to the right, which would become men and the other seven to the left, which would become women. Next the womb goddess impregnated herself with the new creation of the gods and when nine months had passed, she gave birth to them. Ninmah declared that from that day forward when a human child was born, celebrations would last for nine days, after which conjugal relations between the husband and wife could resume."[25]

Enki Challenges Ninmah

After humanity's creation, the gods put on a festival. Becoming rather intoxicated, a dispute ensued between the two gods, Enki and Ninmah. Ninmah decreed that her creation of humans would have poor health conditions, with disapproval from Enki, bringing a glimmer of hope to her actions stating: he would acquire a position for all of these humans. Heeding Enki's words, she selected clay, creating people with illnesses and disabilities, with Enki always finding places for:

"A man with shaking hands who became an attendant to the king,
A blind man who became a story teller,
A man with twisted ankles who found a place with the metal workers,
A barren woman who was given the task to oversee the queen's weavers,
    A person with neither male nor female genitals who became an aid to the king."

Ninmah was infuriated, defeated by Enki's manipulations, and in a cruel game of posturing, the god, Enki formed a disabled infant—unable to walk or eat, or even defecate, clearly unable to tend to the field, since she was crippled, with a shaking palsy of the hands, and feet that were deformed and her insides were utterly broken. An unimaginable dare to Ninmah came from Enki, with this poor child, tormenting her with her own words...'secure a livelihood for this innocent child'. But Ninmah resisted, understanding that humanity would no longer worship her if children were created as such. Enki, wishing to comfort his goddess, reminded Ninmah that while he could perform human creation alone, humanity would be lacking without her creation effort. So, having agreed, Enki and Ninmah moved forward together, making human design with appropriate societal position.[26]

The Sumerian King List

There were numerous dynastic kings for thousands of years in Sumer. The ensuing wars between contiguous cultures, especially the Akkadians, brought the people of the general geography into an expansive metropolis. Sumeria was colonized by the Assyrians, also called 'Ubaidians' in post-deluge times, which is estimated at c. 2000 BCE. The ancient Sumerian city of Assur came under Assyrian control by about 2000 BCE, serving as the capital of the Assyrian Kingdom. During the antediluvian periods of Mesopotamia, Dilmun near present day Bahrain, had massive burial mounds. The Assyrians promoted agriculture, and trade with the basic crafts of weaving, pottery, leathers, metallurgy and masonry. The ziggurats were constructed for specific gods or goddesses. Enmerkar, son of Uta, the Sun god, is credited with developing the cuneiform tablets and built Urak, reigning for 450 to 900 years. The parallels are consistent between historical accounts of Sumer in Genesis and in the Epic of Gilgamesh; Enmerkar and the Lord of Aratta battled over a "conflict of tongues" which correlates with the Biblical story of the Tower of Babel. Comparable too, are the stories of the *Popul Vuh, The Secret Doctrine, Mahabharata, Gilgamesh*, and the Vedic stories of creation.[27, 28]

The Levant-Canaan

In the Levant area, also referred to as Canaan, several historical markers need to be listed. In the area called Ohalo by the Sea of Galilee, the presence of hunter-gatherers was discovered c. 21,400 BCE. In the Mesopotamian area, located in the Zagros Mountains, western Iranian farming was discovered to have begun c. 34,000-20,000 BCE. The Levanto-Aurignacian farmers began agriculture c. 25,000–18,000 BCE, and the Natufian culture commenced farming practices at c. 15,000 BCE.[29]

The Near East and Middle East

The Near East and Middle East areas include the: Arabian Peninsula, Cyprus, Egypt, and Iraq with its Kurdistan region, Iran, Israel, Jordan, Lebanon, Palestinian territories, Syria, and Turkey. Deciphering the chronology of ancient peoples in these areas can be difficult. "Around 10,000 B.C., many hunter-gatherers living along the coastal plains of modern Syria and Israel and in the valleys and hills near the Zagros Mountains between Iran and Iraq began to develop special strategies that led to a transformation in the human community."[30]

Scientists assert that early Neolithic societies in southern Turkey, from c. 11,000 to 9000 BCE, were merely assembled bands of hunter-gatherers.[31] However, Andrew Collins, in his book, *Göbekli Tepe: Genesis of the Gods: The Temple of the Watchers and the Discovery of Eden*, cites that Göbekli Tepe, dated around c. 10,000 BCE, this same hunter-gatherer period, was evidence of a culture quite refined in tools and technology. What other evidence is there that humans had such skills?

"The answer is the Swiderians, whose mining operations in Poland's Swietokrzyskie (Holy Cross) Mountains are among the earliest evidence of organised mining activities anywhere in the world. This advanced society, who thrived in both Central and Eastern Europe around the time of the comet impact event of 10,900 BC, was responsible for the foundation of various important post-Swiderian cultures of the Mesolithic age as far north as Norway, Finland, and Sweden, as far south as the Caucasus Mountains, and as far east as the Upper Volga river of Central Russia. The Swiderians' highly advanced culture, which included a sophisticated stone tool technology, was derived from their distant ancestors, the Eastern Gravettian peoples that thrived between 30,000 and 19,000 BC in what is today the Czech Republic and further east on the Russian Plain." This advanced culture would perhaps correlate with the Indo-Aryan Root Race migrations in Theosophy—Hindu and Arab-Semite sub-races, appearing in northeastern Asia from 60,000 to 40,000 years ago.[32]

Ancient Persian Empire

The Persian (Iranian) Empire had an established culture dating to 7000 BCE. During the times of the Persians, the world's first and largest empire was founded on moral integrity, a solid 'declaration of human rights' and the prohibition of slavery. The world's first gardens were established here—The Gardens of Babylon, which was said to be magnificent and beautiful beyond belief by ancient Babylonian scholars and priests. This culture also developed medicinal alcohol for health practices, cuisine, and the first monotheistic religion, the domestication of European horses, backgammon, and major architectural influences which were much later reflected by the Europeans.[33]

Zarathustra and Pourushaspa

"Nearly 3,500 years ago, at Rae, in Media, there lived a man of the name of Pourushaspa, who led a holy and righteous life with his wife Dogdho. It is related of this holy man, on the authority of the ninth chapter of the Yaçna, that, being desirous of perpetuating his posterity, he prepared a religious ceremony as a thanksgiving to the Almighty, and solemnly prayed for the favour of a child. This worthy man's prayers were duly answered, and a son was born to him, who laboured amongst our primitive forefathers for the amelioration of mankind and their deliverance from the everlasting ruin. His mission was prior to the advent of Buddhism, Christianity, and Islam. He left behind him, written in letters of golden fire, in the History of the World, his illustrious name, Zarathustra, as a permanent landmark and everlasting beacon for the welfare of the body and the guidance of the soul in its passage from the known to the unknown. "O Maker of the material world! To what greatness, goodness, and fairness, can this daêva-destroying teaching Monotheism of Zoroaster be compared?"

The answer came:

"As high as Heaven is above the earth, which it encompasses, so high above all other utterances the law of Mazdeism stands.

"You shall therefore hearken to the Soul of Nature."[34]

Society Alters the Golden Rule in 2500 BCE

The Atlantean-Aryan race had an overwhelming sense of self-importance and arrogance that changed the simplest way of spirituality, which the Lemurians had followed so long ago. We know this as *the Golden Rule*: "Do unto others as you would have them do unto you." Cultures took from the original "basin of knowledge," from Lemurian, Atlantean, Chaldean, Sumerian, Babylonians and later, Egyptian wisdom, infusing their beliefs with vaguely-seminal truths, ever diluting the original essence of the foundational teachings.

The truth of these simple adages became confused. Today, save for few, there is continued, intensifying conflict over religion, race and cultural beliefs, with little accomplishment to show for our human race, given the reign of dominance and control.

Perhaps it is time for humanity to actually embrace what the ancients knew and, were successful at creating—the high civilizations based upon the Golden Rule, love and compassion.[35]

The Code of King Hammurabi

One of the most comprehensive legal codes from antiquity was proclaimed by the powerful figure of Hammurabi, a conqueror and legislator of his time. His reign of forty-three years has been illustrated with a beautiful collection of seals and inscriptions, which describe him as "a youth full of fire and genius; a very whirlwind in battle who crushes all rebels; cuts his enemies into pieces; marches over inaccessible mountain; and never loses an engagement."

The Akkadian king, Hammurabi, "was the sixth king of the Amorite First Dynasty of Babylon, assuming the throne from his father, Sin-Muballit." Hammurabi reigned from 1792 to 1750 BCE, and "according to his own inscriptions, letters and administrative documents from his reign, sought to improve the lives of those who lived under his rule. Credited as the first sovereign to unite his expansive empire under one ruler since Sargon of Akkad in 2300 BCE, Hammurabi also increased the geographical area of the city-state of Babylon, along the Euphrates River, to blend all of southern Mesopotamia. His Code of Hammurabi, combines a collection of 282 laws and standards, specified rules for commercial interactions with an established set of fines and penalties to meet the necessities of justice. Hammurabi's Code was decreed when his reign had ceased, inscribed onto the immense, conical black-stone stela.[36]

Anthrogenesis of Hebrew Culture

Ancient humanity continued to develop polytheistic belief systems, based upon the Sun and Moon cycles, the stars and the seasons, by which they tended their crops, and organized their rituals and belief systems. So, too, with the early Hebrew culture, which began to emerge (by examination of ancient papyri, Sumerian cylinders and fragments of the Chaldean writings), with a history of the known world added from experts in the literary and scientific fields. The prehistoric heritage of the Hebrew peoples apparently connects to ancient Natufian culture, (sedentary hunters and gatherers, and early agriculturalists c. 13,000 years ago) in the Near East; surrounded by the Taurus Mountains of Anatolia in the North, the Mediterranean Sea in the west, and the north Arabian Desert and Mesopotamia in the east, in a region called the 'Levant.'

The hill tribes in proximity to the Jordan River, and the sea people of the Mediterranean comprise the assemblage of migratory tribes constituting the archaic Hebrew nation. Later, indigenous ancestors migrated from the 'Hatti' people, only known from their drawings in excavated cities—drawings of yellow to red-brown skin color, black hair, dark eyes, beardless faces, with receding foreheads and chins or '*long head*' with an angled nose, full lips, high cheek bones and projecting eyebrows, much like the North American Indian tribes. The classical Syriac language of the Northwest Semitic peoples is 'Aramaic', one of the oldest known Semitic languages and the principal dialect being predominant in Canaan, Assyria and the Mesopotamia, and in the Aramean hill kingdoms.

The Merneptah Stele, dated at c. 1200 BCE, is an Egyptian archeological treasure commemorating the victories of Merneptah, son of Ramses the Great. Discovered by Flinders Petrie in 1896 in Thebes, it is the first historical record found to mention the state of Israel. Also, the Elephantine Papyri, a collection of over 175 documents spanning 1,000 of history, indicate that there was a Jewish colony in Elephantine, and temple dedicated to Yahweh and his consort and sacred wife Anat Yahu. Clearly, the older tradition of reverence for the divine feminine was preserved in this little pocket of Jewish life along the upper Nile. This collection dates from around 500 BCE, from the Elephantine area during the period of King Manasseh, Menasheh ben Hizqiyah, known as the first king of Judah, and the earliest known ruler of the Israeli people. In a contradictory act, he returned pagan worship to the Judeans. With opposition mounting from the Hebrews as a possible reaction to King Manasseh's polytheism, they constructed the temple for the use of their constituents.

As we can see, the roots of Judaism extend deeply into the past and are recorded in a collection of works known to Jews by the acronym Tanak, sometimes spelled "Tanakh which represents the Torah, the five books of Moses, the Nevi'im, the prophets, and Kethuvim; these writings, comprise the essential canon of Judaism. The Torah, being a compendium of the Hebrew religion, is the legitimate history of these teachings. The Kabbalah, a masterpiece of philosophy, emerged from pageantry in text, discovered in the Zohar and aptly applies the original occult philosophy in the teachings of the ancient mysteries.[37, 38, 39]

Berosus, the Chaldean Priest

Berosus is credited with literary arrangement of the Chaldeans fragments although the fragments have never been located, with reports that the fragments were possibly altered later, by a Dominican friar, named Annius of Viterbo. Given this information, the fragments appear to be other than mere counterfeits, from events that are now discernible in newly found parchments and other ancient sources recently discovered in the last century. Such as it is, there are no complete histories.

In the 3rd century BCE, Berosus, being a Chaldean priest and astronomer, served in Bel, Babylon. He was keenly familiar with astronomy and the history of the ancient world. He had left Babylon by Alexander the Great's time and established himself in Asia Minor, on the island of Cos near Rhodes, where he set up an observatory and a school of astronomy, and also in Athens. As the Greek language spread through Asia during the Macedonian conquests, public interest peaked in histories that had been preserved by the Babylonians. Berosus, fluent in Greek, was surrounded by an inquisitive public who encouraged him to write his histories. He wrote his three books, c. 290 BCE, and although they are lost, their contents are known, from the aforementioned authentic fragments.[40, 41]

Humanity's Battles with Language

In this and previous sections of *Anthrogenesis*, such as the *Popul Vuh* and *The Secret Doctrine*, the 'mothers and fathers' had communication problems with their children; not hearing them, not understanding their words, children not worshipping them, and essentially, not doing what the mothers and fathers expected of them. This story is truly a lesson for all time!

Here, in 'King Enmerkar and Lord Aratta,' we will discuss one of humanity's tales from ancient Sumeria.

King Enmerkar and Lord Aratta

In one of many tales from ancient Sumer, Uruk's king, Enmerkar, son of Uta, "the Sun god" married the goddess, Inanna of Uruk, who had chosen him. Vexed by this arrangement, Lord Aratta insisted that he was the bridegroom. After Enmerkar had send off a "messenger" to conclude the issue with threats, "Lord Aratta challenged" King Enmerkar to a weighty competition of several tests, the winner would rule both of their kingdoms! Enki's advice proved to be a godsend to King Enmerkar, who won every test, usurping Lord Aratta. A final request was made from Lord Aratta, offering "one last challenge"—a contest between two victors, "one from Aratta and one from Uruk". His single request was that King Enmerkar's candidate should "wear a garment of no known color". Enmerkar's champion was thus supplied with an undyed vestment that had "no color", arranging to dispatch a message to Lord Aratta, insisting submission. The messenger was unable to memorize the very long message from King Enmerkar, so, he used cuneiform in his response to Lord Aratta. But Lord Aratta was unable to read such inscriptions, and while angry, he relented as he realized he had been overpowered by King Enmerkar's clever mind. As luck would have it, "Ishkur, the Storm god sent rain storms to Lord Aratta's land, ending "the famine" as well as the argument between the two royals.[42, 43, 44]

Babylon, a Magnificent City in Paradise

Nebuchadnezzar II (605-563 BCE), was absolutely assured that his Babylon was certain to be the most resplendent city in the Middle East and Mediterranean. And so, this last well known dynasty, during which Babylon achieved its zenith, was witness to the massive beauties of the Ishtar Gate and a well-fortified design of the walled city, resplendent with temples and palaces, including such treasures as the Hanging Gardens of Babylon, one of Seven Wonders of World, who Nebuchadnezzar built for his wife Amytas.

Roaring lion from the Throne Room of Nebuchadnezzar II, Babylon. 605-562 BC, British Museum, London. Photo Joaquim Alves Gaspar, Portugal.

Amongst all this splendor stood the Tower of Babel, with its adjacent ziggurat, serving to highlight humanity's striving towards 'god-dom'. Reportedly destroying humanity's ability to understand one another, confusion and splits arose within the population, dividing humanity into seventy nations and tribes, each having a language of its own.[45, 46]

Ziggurats of Ur

Babylon Destroys Assyria's Nineveh

"After the fall of Assyrian power in Mesopotamia, the last great group of Semitic peoples dominated the area. Suffering mightily under the Assyrians, the city of Babylon finally rose up against its hated enemy, the city of Nineveh, the capital of the Assyrian empire, and burned it to the ground. The chief of the Babylonians was Nabopolassar; the Semites living in the northern part of Mesopotamia would never gain their independence again."

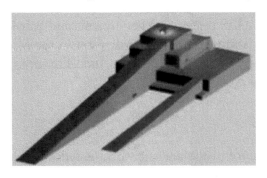

Ziggurat from CAD, courtesy of Sadegh Malek Shahmirzadi

"Son of Nabopolassar, Nebuchadnezzar I (605-562 BCE), was the equal of all the great Mesopotamian conquerors, from Sargon onwards; he not only prevented major powers such as Egypt and Syria from making inroads on his territory, he also conquered the Phoenicians and the state of Judah (586 BCE), the southern Jewish kingdom that remained after the subjugation of Israel, the northern kingdom, by the Assyrians. In order to secure the territory of Judah, Nebuchadnezzar brought Jehoiachin and Zedekiah, the two kings of Judah (in succession) and held them in Babylon. In keeping with Assyrian practice, the "New Babylonians," or

Chaldeans forced a large part of the Jewish population to relocate. Numbering possibly up to 10,000, these Jewish deportees were largely upper class people and craftspeople; this deportation marks the beginning of the Exile in Jewish history." However, other problems continued, due to the loyalty of the Assyrians causing an end to "the Babylonian empire after a dynasty of only five kings."[47]

Nabonidus Replaces Marduk with Sin, the Moon God

"Babylon in 555 BCE came under the control of a king loyal to the Assyrians, Nabonidus (555-539 BCE), who attacked Babylonian culture at its heart: he placed the Assyrian moon-god, Sin, above the Babylonian's principal god, Marduk, who symbolized not only the faith of Babylon but the very city and people itself. Angered and bitter, the priests and those faithful to Babylon would welcome Cyrus the Conqueror of Persia into their city and end forever Semitic domination of Mesopotamia. The center of the Middle Eastern world shifted to Cyrus' capital, Susa, and it would shift again after the Greeks and then the Romans. For almost two and a half centuries, Mesopotamia and Babylon at its center, dominated the landscape of early civilization in the Middle East to be finally eclipsed by the rising sun of the Indo-European cultures to the north and to the west."[48]

Plato's Legacy

Plato's influence in the ancient world is renowned and his bequest was influential, well into the Renaissance, up to modern literary times, as much, if not more than was applauded during his natural lifetime. After all, he founded the Academy, the first learning institution in Hellenistic times. Plato became immortalized by his accounts of Atlantis (Timaeus and Critius), as a city guarded by gates and towers with a wall surrounding each of the city's rings. The walls were constructed of red, white and black rock, and were covered with brass, tin and orichalcum, a brass alloy. "Silenus describes the Meropids, a race of men who grew to twice normal size, and inhabited two cities on the island of "Meropis."

Author's Note: Again, we observe the use of red, black and white colors: spiritually thematic of ancient Lemurians, the Adepts and the Indigenous Incas and Mayans.

Greek geographer and historian Strabo (63BCE-21CE) characterizes Atlantis in the following manner in his work, *Geographia*: "The whole race is fanatically fond of warfare. They are vociferous and act on impulse. When they are upset, they immediately gather together in groups in the open, to urge on to warfare, without the slightest preparation or reflection. They are therefore quite easily deceived and overpowered."[49]

Another scholar, Ammianus, wrote about the Druids of Gaul, reporting that a part of Gaul's inhabitants migrated from distant islands. Ammianus' testimony has been understood by some as a claim that when Atlantis sunk into the sea, its inhabitants fled to Western Europe; Ammianus adds that the Druids remember the indigenous population and those migrating from islands and lands beyond the Rhine.[50]

Plato and the Academy of Marsilio Ficino

Several differing schools diverged after Plato. One pupil, Marsilio Ficino, embraced Platonic sagacity and maintained that all the world's religions could be related to one another because in the heart of every religion was a belief in one God and the variety of religions was not a bad thing, but rather an expression of the complexity and beauty of God worshipped in all his infinite aspects. His philosophy is based on the principle that the human soul is immortal, sits at the center of the universe and is the only thing between the abstract realm of ideas and the physical world; it is the mediator between these two worlds. He developed original and highly influential ideas from Plato and Neoplatonism, becoming the founder of the Academy in Firenze under the patronage of Cosimo de' Medici, a man of great power, who in later life become a champion of Neo-Platonism in the Renaissance. One example of a Neo-Platonism adage is: "There really is no solidly coherent body of philosophy that is Platonic, but rather a series of philosophies openly or implicitly derived from work of the fourth century Athenian philosopher, Plato." In addition, Platonism never really faded out of the Western tradition nor was the Italian Renaissance a rediscovery of Plato; rather, the Italian Renaissance forged new philosophies from Plato and the Platonic tradition in antiquity and the middle Ages. This renewed Platonic philosophy represented one of the essential currents of Renaissance thought and had far reaching consequences for the future development of European thought and science. And for hundreds of years, civilization would be deeply indebted to the great philosophical inquiries of Plato and his students.[51, 52]

Pletho

During the Byzantine Empire, Pletho and other contemporaries respected and preserved the treasure of Plato's beloved *Dialogues*, in the original Greek compilation style. However, even nine hundred years later, European scholars remained generally unaware of Plato's method of thought, perhaps due in part to linguistics, but also due to their extreme reservation to embrace Plato's belief in the reincarnation of souls. This important knowledge- lost due to the intervention of the early Church and the Council of Nicaea—essentially spoke of the soul's travel after physical death in the heavenly ethers for a time and then dipping back into a new body for another human experience on Earth. [53]

My ancient mentor, architect of the logical method of science is Aristotle. This bearer of Socratic philosophy had enhanced popularity in the Middle Ages. His great legacy helped mankind with a comprehensive system of philosophy of ethics, metaphysics, aesthetics, logic, epistemology, politics and science, and establishing the judicious approach to thought and experience. With logic and the deductive method leading thought to a final conclusion, Aristotle is unequivocally the father of the scientific method.

Centuries of European history embraced Aristotelianism. There are numerous misconceptions about the Platonic tradition and their "revival" in the Italian Renaissance as reported by Margaret Williams in her *Antiquity and the Italian Renaissance: Platonic Building Blocks*. She states that "Plato would likely not be the first name to come to mind when contemplating the Italian Renaissance," the importance of Da Vinci, for example, or even Machiavelli should not be underestimated.[54, 55, 56,]

Hermetic Infinity

Plutarch and Reincarnation

An example of early writings include Plutarch (Plutarch of Chaeronea, 46 BCE-122 CE) plead with to his wife not grieve after the death of their two-year-old daughter, later inferring that he sustained a belief in reincarnation in that letter of consolation.

Ouroboros drawing, symbolizes the cyclic renewal of life and infinity, from a late medieval Byzantine Greek alchemical manuscript, attributed to Synesius of Cyrene (c. 373— c. 414), a Greek bishop of Ptolemais, in the Libyan Pentapolis. Recent facsimile drawn by Theodoros Pelecanos, 1478, Corfu in Khandak, Iraklio, Crete. Image uploaded by Carlos Adanero.

"The soul, being eternal, after death is like a caged bird that has been released. If it has been a long time in the body, and has become tame by many affairs and long habit, the soul will immediately take another body and once again become involved in the troubles of the world. The worst thing about old age is that the soul's memory of the other world grows dim, while at the same time its attachment to things of this world becomes so strong that the soul tends to retain the form that it had in the body. But that soul which remains only a short time within a body, until liberated by the higher powers, quickly recovers its fire and goes on to higher things." – Plutarch from *The Consolation, Moralia*
Plutarch of Chaeronea, 46 BCE-122 CE[57]

Delineating Theosophy

Theosophy is NOT a religion, only a philosophy that sees the Divine in All Life. We must remember that Blavatsky *did not* believe in any type of personal or anthropomorphic God. She believed and taught that there is but ONE Infinite Divine Life which *is* everything and *in* everything and that It has no adversary or enemy, since there is nothing but that–the boundless, impersonal, omnipresent Principle of Absolute Existence Itself. She taught that 'evil' is imperfection, which is the automatic and inevitable byproduct of the existence of matter.

Theosophy Describes the Divine Principle

The Masters K.H. and M. used the term 'Parabrahm' or Brahman from Hindu Vedanta terminology when talking about the 'Absolute' (which is not 'God', stated as such) to avoid any inaccurate assumptions. Parabrahm is described as the Supreme Universal Divine principle, an indisputable eternal state like the Adi-Buddhi or Adi-Buddha of esoteric Buddhism. The Master K.H. has added that Parabrahm is 'Absolute Law' or also referred to as the ONE LIFE. The Master K.H. had expectations of humanity's understanding the truth of the Ageless Wisdom and instructed D.K. in the philosophy as given to the Trans-Himalayan Masters.[58]

The Christ

Blavatsky's View on Jesus

Blavatsky did liken 'Apollonius of Tyana' (3CE-100 CE), a 1st-century Greek orator and philosopher, to Jesus, stating that they appeared quite analogous; a possible reincarnation so similar to "a contemporary of Jesus of Nazareth, was, like him, an enthusiastic founder of a new spiritual school. Perhaps less metaphysical and more practical than Jesus, less tender and perfect in his nature, he nevertheless inculcated the same quintessence of spirituality, and the same high moral truths." -Blavatsky[59]

Nevertheless, H.P.B. did say that "For me Jesus Christ, i.e., the Man-God of the Christians, copied from the Avatâras of every country, from the Hindu Krishna as well as the Egyptian Horus, was never a historical person. He is a deified personification of the glorified type of the great Hierophants of the Temples, and his story, as told in the New Testament, is an allegory, assuredly containing profound esoteric truths, but still an allegory". "Every act of the Jesus of the New Testament, every word attributed to him, every event related of him during the three years of the mission he is said to have accomplished, rests on the programme of the Cycle of Initiation, a cycle founded on the Precession of the Equinoxes and the Signs of the Zodiac."—Blavatsky[60, 61, 62, 63]

Buddha and Christ, the Sphere of the Bodhisattvas

Rudolf Steiner, in his lecture, "Buddha and Christ, The Sphere of the Bodhisattvas," Milan, Italy (September 21, 1911), discusses "... when Gautama Buddha was born as the son of King Suddhodana, he rose from the rank of Bodhisattva to that of Buddha, and to become a Buddha means that the Individuality concerned does not incarnate again on Earth in a body of flesh."

"The Bodhisattva-Individuality who became Buddha five or six centuries before the beginning of the Christian era has not since incarnated, nor can he incarnate, in a physical body. But instead he sends down his forces from the higher worlds, from the super-sensible worlds, and inspires all bearers of culture who are not yet permeated by the Christ Impulse."

Steiner states qualitatively different perspective from Blavatsky: "We must therefore clearly understand that in the fourth post-Atlantean epoch, men were only capable of beholding the physical Christ; He therefore came in a physical body. Conditions in that epoch were therefore especially suitable for men to experience the Christ on the physical plane in a physical body."[64]

The Buddha is quoted as stating, "The Maitreya comes when the Dispensation of the perfect Buddha is 5000-years-old."

"Buddha who was sent to India spoke to a Hindu audience in terminology that they could relate to and understand. Considering that Buddha was speaking to followers of Hinduism, He was speaking in terms of the Hindu system of dating."[65]

The Christ and Jesus

Steiner makes a distinction between The Christ and Jesus who he identifies as two separate beings that become one at the baptism in the Jordan by John, The Baptist.

"The Christ's descent on Jesus became necessary because man's consciousness had progressively become too focused on the material realm and had completely lost touch with the spiritual nature behind physical reality. The danger was that this situation could become permanent. To prevent this, the Christ's initial goal was to "incarnate" into a human being (Jesus) so he could accomplish his greater goal of "incarnating" from Jesus into the "etheric earth." Occultists believe an etheric earth exists behind the physical earth. The etheric earth is thought to be made up of a fine energy substance from which is created the mold for every form that is manifested in the physical plane. Every material object on the physical plane has an etheric counterpart. All material forms in the physical universe find their ultimate source in this energy substance of the etheric realm. The Christ desired to enter this etheric earth so he could bring about spiritual changes among people living on the physical earth. But in order to transfer from his spiritual realm to the etheric realm, he needed a human instrument through which to work. This instrument was found in Jesus."

"The Christ "incarnated" into Jesus, and three years later was crucified. At the crucifixion, the Christ left Jesus' body and "incarnated" into the

290

etheric earth." Steiner says that the "Christ impulse will penetrate humanity. He belongs to the whole earth and can enter all human souls, regardless of nation and religion. This, says Steiner, is the true "second coming."[66]

The Great Invocation

From the point of Light within the Mind of God
Let light stream forth into the minds of men.
Let Light descend on Earth.
From the point of Love within the Heart of God
Let love stream forth into the hearts of men.
May Christ* return to Earth.
From the centre where the Will of God is known
Let purpose guide the little wills of men –
The purpose which the Masters know and serve.
From the centre which we call the race of men
Let the Plan of Love and Light work out
And may it seal the door where evil dwells.
Let Light and Love and Power restore the Plan on Earth.

*Many religions believe in a World Teacher, the "Coming One," knowing him under such names as the Lord Maitreya, the Imam Mahdi, the Kalki Avatar and the Bodhisattva. These terms are sometimes used in versions of the Great Invocation for people of specific faiths.[67]

The Christ and the Path of Discipleship

As we explore this aspect of spirituality in Anthrogenesis, it becomes clear that neo-Theosophy has a variety of belief systems. The Christ Consciousness taught by Alice Bailey, illustrated in the Stages of Humanity on the Path of Discipleship, are as follows:

–The 1st Initiation: The Birth (physical) signifies mastery of the physical body.

–The 2nd Initiation: The Baptism (by water) signifies control over the astral-emotional body.

–The 3rd Initiation: The Transfiguration is where the integrated personality and soul guide the life of the disciple to serve humanity through the Higher Will.

–The 4th Initiation: The Crucifixion occurs when the disciple moves to the buddhic-spiritual plane, no longer requiring further incarnations to develop spiritually, no longer in a physical form.[68]

Treasure of the Mountains by Nicholas Roerich, 1933, New York Museum, NYC

"The Divine-Nature of The Christ is said to have ascended to higher plane of endeavor. He is that Great Being Whom the Christian calls the Christ; He is known also in the Orient as the Bodhisattva, and as the Lord Maitreya, and is the One looked for by the devout Mohammedan, under the name of the Imam Mahdi. He is 'Who' has presided over the destinies of life since about 600 B.C. and He it is Who has come out among men before, and Who is again looked for. He is the great Lord of Love and of Compassion, just as his predecessor, the Buddha, was the Lord of Wisdom." "He is the World Teacher, the Master of the Masters, and the Instructor of the Angels, and to Him is committed the guidance of the spiritual destinies of men, and the development of the realisation within each human being that he is a child of God and a son of the Most High." —Alice Bailey, Lucis Trust[69]

Theosophy, while only a philosophy, is helpful to Christian theology, if only to provide understanding for the light, which it throws upon the nature of the Christ. Among the religions of the world, Christianity is unique in the emphasis that it places upon the Incarnation of a transcendent God on Earth, in human form, and of the divine sacrifice, which were dramatically portrayed in the life of Jesus. Joseph Campbell likens Jesus to great heroes such as Buddha, Osiris and Moses. In the Emerald Tablets of Thoth, it appears that the coming of a Great Being is described as someone that "every eye shall see him," meaning that those who have their eyes opened, 'the third eyes,' will see him. It is said that he will come from the sky; meaning the same as heaven, and heaven means Pure Consciousness," and "... he comes as an Avatar-god-man."[70, 71]

Long before the time of Jesus, the Jews were divided into three sects, the Sadducees, the Pharisees, and the Essenes. Jesus is chronicled as admonishing and condemning both the Sadducees and Pharisees, and "he once mentioned the Essenes by name" so it is plausible that Jesus may have been an Essene. The Essenes were the scribes the Dead Sea Scrolls and their powerful sect was an important protector of the true Hebraic mysteries.[72]

The Shifts in Theosophical Personalities

While Blavatsky and her co-founder, William Quan Judge (1851-1896), continued with development of the original Theosophical principles, establishing the Theosophical Society in Adyar, India, (and later in the United States in New York City), others developed philosophies which were offshoots from H.P.B.. An early reformer, Christian and wife of a minister, Annie Besant (1847-1933) became a formidable woman of strength in England. After having read *The Secret Doctrine*, she became passionate about H.P.B.'s work and left behind her secular environment (which caused her marriage to break down), moving to London, which allowed her to expand her independence and reformer activities of the day. A few years later, after obtaining membership into the Theosophical Society, Besant became a great helper to H.P.B., becoming her greatest follower and student. In the early 1890s, Besant traveled to Adyar, in the company of Col. H. S. Olcott, the first President and Founder of the Theosophical Society, devoting herself to his causes in India. Besant later became the next International President of the Theosophical Society. Besant wrote numerous books and articles, and created reform in Theosophical circles, as well as in the cause for freedom in India, during her life.[73]

Rudolf Steiner

Rudolf Steiner (1861-1925) experienced of spiritual second-sight at an early age, which greatly influenced the development of his spiritual school of thought called Anthroposophy. Steiner was an eloquent philosopher, humanist, innovator and spiritual teacher. Besides his experience with Madame Blavatsky, Steiner was involved in a number of pursuits throughout his life, perhaps the most inspirational being the development of 'Waldorf Education,' an inspired understanding of teachings dedicated to the growth and development of child and young adult, incorporating not just the basic 'A, B, C's', but integrating a foundation for the 'whole child'—spirituality, art, and philosophy. He designed agricultural practices, art forms, visual arts, architecture and sculpture.

Steiner was the first to elaborate on the details of the 'Root Races,' while not addressing them as such, he crafted the information of our ancient history and human spirituality in a non-judgmental format. Steiner broke away from Blavatsky and the Theosophic Society to establish the 'Anthroposophical Society,' based upon his expansive knowledge of cosmology, embodying principles laden with occult, Buddhist, and Hermetic creeds. Steiner focused on the cosmic Spiritual Hierarchies and the Akashic Records, along with emphasizing psychic and spiritual interpretations of phenomena for the individual. His thinking was to promote the 'Christ Consciousness." In later life, Steiner was instrumental in inspiring the 'Christian Community,' which spread worldwide in conjunction with Waldorf Education.[74]

Neo-Theosophy

Neo-Theosophy is a recent term which designates the adapted ideologies of the Theosophic groups that post-dated Madame Blavatsky. One example is the work of C. W. Leadbeater (1854-1934), and another is that of Alice Bailey (1880-1949), who placed more emphasis on standards, with a strict code of beliefs. Both Leadbeater and Bailey had a strong background in Christianity, which influenced their philosophies and approaches towards Theosophy.

Alice A. Bailey

Alice Bailey channeled her writings through the Tibetan, D.K. (Djwhal Khul) moving forward with the design and foundation of the Arcane School, and Lucis Trust, a Mystery School with a curriculum of study for the individual. As the disciple of both the Master Kuthumi –K.H., and the Master Morya –M., Djwhal Khul –D.K., a Tibetan Buddhist, as we have seen, telepathically dictated the Ageless Wisdom via Alice Bailey, between 1919 and 1949. Described as "neo-Theosophists, both D.K. and Alice Bailey used the term "Master of the Masters" when referring to the Master Jesus, who is Dhyani-Chohan—and said to be the 6th Ray Master.[75]

Gottfried de Purucker

A significant teacher of Theosophy, advancing Blavatsky's principles, was G. de Purucker (1874-1942). One of his more famous works, *Studies in Occult Philosophy* (1973), provided an in-depth representation of Theosophy, the Vedic Yugas and the specifics of astrology, Root Races and Precession. Purucker wrote about 16 books in his career, serving as President for the Pasadena, California branch of the Theosophical Society, somewhat differentiated from the Theosophical Society of America.[76, 77]

The Gnostic Sophia

The Gnostics had practiced traditions of the Ancient Wisdom long before the time of The Christ. Inclusive in their doctrine was the 'sacred feminine.' Thus, the 'En-Soph' of Hermetic antiquity became their 'Sophia,' which means 'wisdom'—along with reincarnation and purification from materialism. The deity, Abraxas (see below), symbolized as emerging from an egg, bridges both the material and spiritual planes. On December, 1945, an Arab peasant recovered an earthenware jar in Upper Egypt. Thirty years would pass before world publicity revealed that the Gnostic *Nag Hammadi* texts or the Gnostic Gospels, with thirteen papyri bound in leather (resulting in 52 texts), literally came to light in 1975. When the *Nag Hammadi* texts were translated, one writing (among others!) prompted disbelief by Christian theologians. It was titled '*The Sophia of Jesus Christ*' and recounted the story of Jesus'

transcendence of the earthly plane in 'spirit form', while appearing to 12 males and 7 female disciples."[78, 79]

Abraxas Gem

Image above extracted from the work *The Gnostics and Their Remainsancient and Mediaeval. Ed. 2.*[80]

Catharism

Originating in southern Europe, Cathar beliefs were comparable to other Gnostic traditions. Ascetic priests, both men and women were seen as equals and participated in the sacred rituals. They believed in reincarnation, and practiced vegetarianism, contraception and even euthanasia when appropriate. The Cathars strove toward a purity in all things and even preached an avoidance of the material world and all its vices. The Roman Catholic Church was unable to endure the Cathar's popularity in Southern France and envied their lands and wealth, subsequently unleashing the 'Inquisitors' and thereby causing a bloody end to the Cathar sect in the 13th century.[81]

The Burning of Darkness by Nicholas Roerich (1874-1947)

Anthrogenesis Hero Equation

From the beginning of Anthrogenesis we observe the 'Hero" within the framework of cosmogenesis. There will always be heroes and heroines along with the philosophical themes presented in this book. It begins with the creation of all existence. Supernatural beings play a direct role in designing how the world comes into being, using spoken communication. Additional supernatural beings emanate from the first immortals. The greatest among them has a son, who is compelling and perfect, and after an unfortunate death, the immortal son is much lamented by the people. This great son of the divine returns to life for the good of his people. Thereafter his immense sacrifice, he is able to gift an 'afterlife' to humanity. Death and Resurrection is the greatest of all the hero's triumph.

Stages of the Heroes Journey

Joseph Campbell, the master of mythology and one of my personal favorites, described the *12 Stages of the Heroes Journey: The Ordinary World*; Call to Adventure; Refusal of the Call; Meeting with the Mentor; Crossing The First Threshold; Tests, Allies, Enemies; the Approach;

Supreme Ordeal; the Reward; the Road Back; the Resurrection; and the Return with Elixir. Campbell's short description of the hero is: "The hero's journey is a skeletal framework that should be fleshed out with the details and surprises of the individual story. The structure should not call attention to itself, nor should it be followed too precisely. The order of the stages given here is only one of many possible variations. The stages can be deleted, added to, and drastically shuffled without losing any of their power. The Hero's Journey is infinitely flexible, capable of endless variation without sacrificing any of its magic, and it will outlive us all."[83]

Notes

1. The Story of Atlantis and The Lost Lemuria by W. Scott-Elliot, 1972, Theosophical Publishing House, Fletcher & Son, LTD., Norwich, Great Britain.
2. The Power of Myth, Joseph Campbell, with Bill Moyers, Anchor Books, NY, 1991, p. 40
3. Zoroaster, another incarnation of Zarathustra, was the founder of the 'Philosophy of the Parsi Religion, The Wisdom of the East', the Vendidad or (Sacred Books of the East), The Zend-Avesta, Part I, The Vendidad, Trans. by James Darmesteter, Clarendon Press, 1880.
4. http://www.theosociety.org/pasadena/sd/sd2-0-pn.htm
5. The Dabistán or Book of Manners, translated by David Shea and Anthony Troyer, © 1901, by M. Walter
6. Dunne, Publisher, https://books.google.com/books?id=WwYe4FS NCOYC&source=gbs_navlinks_s
7. https://archive.org/stream/zendavestapart1t025014mbp/ zendavestapart1t025014mbp_djvu.txt
8. http://www.sacred-texts.com/zor/toz/toz00.htm
9. Unattributed Contents © 1997 – 1999 The Hermetic Library
10. http://hermetic.com/texts/chaldean.html
11. Powell, Arthur E., 1930, The Solar System, Theosophical Publishing House, UK.
12. Bilmoria, Nasarvanji F., Zoroastrianism In The Light Of Theosophy, Published by Blavatsky Lodge-Theosophical Society, Madras, Adyar, India. Tatva-Vivechaka Press, Bombay. 1896. Preface; Speech by Annie Besant on the sacred nature of Zoroastrianism.
13. W. Wynn Westcott, The Chaldæans Oracles of Zoroaster, 1895. http://www.sacred-texts.com/eso/coz/coz05.htm
14. http://www.bible-history.com/past/dagon.html 15. Theosophical Glossary, by H. P. Blavatsky, 236-7, http://www.theosociety.org/ pasadena/etgloss/oa-oz.htm
16. http://www.ancient.eu/religion
17. H.P.B., Isis Unveiled, Volume II, 1877, Theosophical Society, pages 265-271.
18. Sandars, N.K. The Epic of Gilgamesh, 1972, Penguin Books, NY, pp. 108-13.

19. http://www.world-myth.com/mesopotamian.php

20. http://www.world-myth.com/mesopotamian/sumerian-creation-myth

21. Potts, D. T., A Companion to the Archaeology of the Ancient near East, Volume 1, 2012, John Wiley & Sons, NY.

22. http://www.jstor.org/stable/41492539

23. Barton, George A. Miscellaneous Babylonian Inscriptions, Bryn Mawr College, 1918, Yale University Press, New Haven, CT.

24. https://books.google.com/books?id=nn5hAAAAMAAJ&num=11

25. http://www.world-myth.com/mesopotamian.php

26. http://www.world-myth.com/mesopotamian/sumerian-creation-myth

27. https://oi.uchicago.edu/sites/oi.uchicago.edu/files/uploads/shared/docs/as11.pdf

28. Thorkild, Jacobsen, The Sumerian King List, Assyriological Studies, No. 11, The Oriental Institute Of The University Of Chicago, Assyriological Studies, John Albert Wilson & Thomas George Allen • Editors, The University Of Chicago Press, Chicago 60637. The University of Chicago Press, Ltd., London © 1939 by The University of Chicago. All rights reserved. Published 1939, Fourth Impression 1973. Printed by Cushing-Malloy, Inc., Ann Arbor, Michigan, United States of America.

29. https://aratta.wordpress.com/neolithic-revolution/

30. http://www.historyguide.org/ancient/lecture2b.html

31. https://journals.lib.byu.edu/spc/index.php/CCR/article/download/13053/12914 32. http://www.andrewcollins.com/page/articles/Go_Tep_launch.htm : Collins, Andrew, Göbekli Tepe: Genesis of the Gods: The Temple of the Watchers and the Discovery of Eden, 2014, Bear & Company, Rochester, VT.

33. http://www.thetoptens.com/best-ancient-civilizations

34. Kapadia, S.A., The Teachings of Zoroaster and the Philosophy of the Parsi Religion, John Murray, Albemarle Street, London, 1905, page 21-22: http://www.sacred-texts.com/zor/toz/toz04.htm

35. http://www.blavatskytheosophy.com/2013/09/06/the-golden-rule-was-not-original-with-jesus36. http://www.ancient.eu/hammurabi

37. http://prophetess.lstc.cdu/~rklein/Doc6/Merneptah.htm

38. http://www.theosophy.ph/encyclo/index.php?title=Judaism

39. http://www.ancient.eu/Achaemenid_Empire

40. http://www.billheidrick.com/Orpd/Sacr1917/Sacred_Books_1.pdf

41. http://mini-site.louvre.fr/babylone/EN/html/1.4.9.html

42. An Encyclopedia of Mythology and Folklore, Volume One to Volume Three, 2008, edited by Josepha Sherman, M.E. Sharpe, Inc., Armonk, NY, pages 140-141.

43. An Encyclopedia of Mythology and Folklore, Volume One to Volume Three, 2011, Edited by Josepha Sherman, Routledge Publishers, NY.,

44. https://books.google.com/books/about/Storytelling.html?id=ZQraAAAAMAAJ

45. http://www.jewishvirtuallibrary.org/jsource/History/Chaldeans.html

46. http://www.chabad.org/library/article_cdo/aid/246611/jewish/The-Tower-Of-Babel.htm

47. http://www.jewishvirtuallibrary.org/jsource/History/Chaldeans.html

48. http://www.jewishvirtuallibrary.org/jsource/History/Chaldeans.html

49 http://www.ivargault.com/kelterne/celts.html

50. Bacon, Sir Francis, 1942. Essays and New Atlantis, Published by Walter J. Black, NY. 1942.

51. http://www.britannica.com/EBchecked/topic/372301/Cosimo-de-Medici

52. Hooker, Richard, The Platonic Tradition, 1997, revised.http://hermetic.com/texts/neoplatonism.html

53. http://www.britannica.com/EBchecked/topic/228130/George-Gemistus-Plethon

54. http://www.philosophybasics.com/movements_aristotelianism.html

55. Antiquity and the Italian Renaissance: Platonic Building Blocks by Margaret Williams: https://www.lvc.edu/vhr/articles/williams.pdf

57. Incognito, Magus, *The Secret Doctrine of the Rosicrucians*, 1918, Advanced Thought Publishing Co., Chicago, Ill: http://www.sacred-texts.com/sro/sdr/sdr11.htm

58. http://penelope.uchicago.edu/Thayer/E/Roman/Texts/Plutarch/Moralia/Consolatio_ad_uxorem*.html

59. http://www.katinkahesselink.net/blavatsky/articles/v9/y1888_033.htm

60. Blavatsky, H. P. Isis Unveiled, Vol. II, 1999, NY.

61. H.P. Blavatsky Collected Writings, Volume 9, Page 225.

62. http://www.adolphus.nl/xcrpts/xcmead.html

63. https://www.theosophical.org/

64. http://wn.rsarchive.org/Lectures/19110921p01.html

65. http://www.maitreya.org/english/PBuddhism.htm

66. http://home.earthlink.net/~ronrhodes/ChristNAM.html

67. https://www.lucistrust.org/the_great_invocation

68. https://www.lucistrust.org/arcane_school/twelve_spiritual_festivals/gemini/christ_festival_talk1

69. https://www.lucistrust.org/resources/the_christ

70. Campbell, Joseph. *The Hero with a Thousand Faces*, 1949. 2nd edition, Princeton University Press.

71. Doreal, *The Emerald Tablet of Thoth*, The Atlantean, 2002, Brotherhood of the White Temple, Inc., Sedalia, CO. pg. 20.

72. http://www.sacred-texts.com/chr/jae/jae03.htm

73. http://www.ts-adyar.org/content/annie-besant-1847-1933

74. http://www.kheper.net/topics/Theosophy/schools.htm

75. https://www.lucistrust.org/resources/the_christ

76. Blavatsky, Helena Petrovna, *The Secret Doctrine, Vol. I & II*, 1973, Theosophical Publishers, Adyar, India.

77. Purucker, G. de, *Studies in Occult Philosophy*, 1973, Theosophical University Press, Pasadena, CA.

78. http://gnosis.org/library.html

79. http://gnosis.org/naghamm/nhl.html

80. The Gnostics And Their Remainsancient And Mediaeval. Ed. 2. by Charles W. King, MA, David Nutt Publishers, London, England. 1887.

81. http://www.cathar.info/

82. http://www.maitreya.org/english/PBuddhism.htm

Anthrogenesis

83. http://www.thewritersjourney.com/hero's_journey.htm

Chapter Fourteen

Aryan Root Race Migrates to Europe and Asia

Creation Story of China

Chaos was all that existed in the Universe except for the large black egg, containing heaven and earth. Pan Gu, who was born inside the egg, slept and grew for 18,000 years while Yin and Yang became balanced. Upon awakening, Pan Gu understood his confinement within the egg and successfully divided it, parting Yin from Yang, with the upper shell-half becoming the sky above and the bottom shell-half changing into the earth. As Pan Gu sustained the breach, both he and the two halves grew larger—10 feet per day. After 18,000 years had passed, both the Sky and the Earth had grown immensely, but Pan Gu stood at about 4,925 li (or 2,693,024 yards) in height, so great that Yin and Yang could never join again. Once more, another 18,000 years passed and Pan Gu died, but his body transformed into nature, "His breath was the wind

305

and clouds and his voice became the rolling thunder." One eye "became the Sun" and the other, "the Moon," with his torso and limbs becoming five big mountains and his blood made the water. His veins stretched far and wide into roads with his muscles directed to productive lands. Countless stars arose from his hair and beard, flowers and trees from his skin and fine body hair with marrow converting to jade and pearls. Sweat streamed like rain with fragrant dew that cherishes all the Earth, tears surging into rivers and glowing eyes became thunder and lighting.[1]

Heroine Nü Wa Creates, then Saves Humanity

The first ancestor was the Goddess Nü Wa who parted the firmament from Earth, forming the Divine Land of China. Nü Wa, also called Feng, was a righteous divine being, with a snake body and human head. Nü Wa revered in harmony, delighting in creating objects; thus, she wished for humanity to create their own families. She fashioned figures from yellow clay, with the gifts of life and fertility. Later, during a terrible battle, the monsters destroyed the four columns supporting the heavens, and it opened the sky, releasing great waters, while the creatures devoured the infirmed and weak. Nü Wa knew

lazyseal8/Manga & Anime/Digital Media/
Drawings ©2012-2015

she must save humanity, so she melted down five colored stones to patch the fissure, and "cut off" Great Turtle's feet "to support the four pillars," slaying the monsters and blocking the flood waters until the task was completed. So fatigued from her labors, Nü Wa rested on the Earth, then metamorphosed into an immense mountain range and in so-doing, Nü Wa cultivated China by bestowing a bountiful and fertile land to her people.[2]

Qin Shi Huangdi Burial Mound

The Qin tomb, named for Qin Shi Huangdi (3rd century BCE), was first emperor of the Qin dynasty. Located near the city of Xi'an in Shaanxi, China, the site is a vast mortuary compound, with a centered burial mound, one of many mounds found in East Asia. In 1974, thousands of life-sized terra-cotta figures representing the emperor's army were unearthed within the compound, about three-fourths of a mile from the tomb proper. The area was designated a UNESCO World Heritage site in 1987. It is believed that China's first emperor, Qin Shi Huangdi, lies in the main burial chamber, which is housed within a large pyramidal earth mound thought to contain an inner city for his afterlife. The size of this mound of earth approximates a 'football stadium' and currently remains sealed. An alluring detail is that mercury was used to fashion the hundred rivers, the Yellow River and the Yangtze River, and the seas in such a way that they flowed. Chinese scientists have measured high levels of mercury on top of the burial mound.[3]

Tibetan Cosmology and the Teachings of Impermanence

The concept of impermanence is central to Tibetan teachings. The individual is born, dies, and is reborn, in universal transmigration. This cyclical Universe is considered to be natural and not supernatural or transcendent. In Tibetan cosmology the mandala is a symbolic illustration of the cosmos, and conceptualizes the palace of a spiritual deity in a three-dimensional structure. A mandala can be a two-dimensional painting on fabric, or created from sand. When the sand mandala is complete, the monks run their hands through the design in an act that symbolizes the teaching of impermanence. And, just like the sand mandala will be redone, so will the cosmological system return into being, existing for a Kalpa, then dissipating, before returning into existence again. The Buddha employed various texts and meditational systems because there are countless ways on the road to enlightenment, and believed that mandalas and meditational deities serve different purposes.

Our world is only one planet in an incalculable number (more than a billion) of world systems, called a trichilicosm. Our world scheme is supported by a layered base which floats within the cosmic-etheric plane like the representation in the mandala. It is a spiritual view that observes the planet, and includes a view of Mount Meru, the orbits of the planets, the sun and the moon. The sacred Mount Meru is the axis of the cosmos, positioned within the center of the physical, metaphysical and spiritual Universes, the transcendent birthplace of Buddhism, Hinduism and Jainism.[5, 6]

Mount Meru ~ a Buddhist Mantra

The fundamental ground is scented with incense and strewn with flowers, adorned with Mount Meru, the four continents, the sun and the moon. I imagine this as a buddhaland and offer it. May all sentient beings enjoy this pure realm.[4]

Legends and Lore

The Mighty Titans, Mongols, Persians, Gaels, Scythians, Druids, Celts, Norse, Vikings, Slavs, Teutons, Greeks, Romans, Visigoths

Central Asian Cradle of Ancestors

In *Anthrogenesis*, we have observed human origins, DNA studies, and information extracted from historians and specialists on mythology, geography, anthropology, linguistics and Theosophy. The migrations of the Atlantean sub-races form the basis of human history, as we know it. In his book, *Studies in Occult Philosophy*, theosophist Gottfried de Purucker describes the legacy that we received from Atlantis. The Fifth Root Race began mid-cycle in Atlantis. Purucker then reports that approximately 3,800,000-years ago in Krita Yuga the first migrations left from Atlantis, and the Fifth Root race began.

This dispersion of humanity in the late sub-races of Atlantis trickled into Asia over eras, penetrating Northwest China, Mongolia, the Gobi Desert (which had been the Gobi Sea in past millennia), Tibet and the Himalayas. The Persians (Iranians), Babylonians, Assyrians established primal civilizations renowned for beauty, grace and sophistication and an appetite for expansion, establishing settlements in the beautiful green, fertile lands in Persia (now Iran and Afghanistan), Bukhara, (now Uzbekistan), Turkey; the Aral and Caspian Seas; the Pamir Range at the confluence of the Himalayas and the Hindu Kush Ranges, and Tien

Shen, (Kyrgyzstan); Kazakhstan, China and Uzbekistan, with later nomadic inroads into Scandinavia.'

Establishment of the Sub-races

As Atlantis dwindled into extinction, one important people from Atlantis migrated to Central Asia, later developing into a potent prototype race. From the north, this Hindu sub-race migrated to the Indian subcontinent using the name 'Aryan'- derived from the Sanskrit word ārya, the self-designation used by Vedic Indic people migrating into India. They became the 'high caste,' which subsequently divided into the *four castes*: brahmanas, kshattriyas, vaisyas and sudras.

These nomadic tribes expanded into the ancient lands of Greece and Italy, following their predecessors who began the magnificent creation of Grecian culture. In *The Secret Doctrine*, Blavatsky explains the phenomenon of 'cyclops' and 'titans' of the Hesiod, as well as others strange creatures in Homer's works; also too, the Hindu giants in the Puranas. (Blavatsky describes the Titans as giants, the Sons of Kronos.) These mythic creatures from an earlier age are at the epicenter of the tales of super human heroes with the strength of a hundred men, commanding and subduing the 'monsters' from the Age of Reptiles. So often is the observation true that the origin of myth and legend may be drawn from facts in nature. The early city-states hold the geological, ancestral memories of our past and that is why so much archeological work is currently being done to uncover the secrets that may be unlocked for understanding our human journey. Myth and fiction become 'reality,' based on the new findings discovered everywhere on the planet.[8]

Mythic Giants and Monsters

Viking Deities from Asgard

Ancient humanity had tales and legend of giant monsters, cyclops and terrible creatures who hunted man and animal alike. Professor Adrienne Mayor is a scholar at Stanford University and academician of a rather novel science: geomythology—or the study of pertinent geological data that corresponds to the origin of myths and legends. She has excavated worldwide to show the correlation between myth and geological remains. In Samos, it was Mayor's initial find of large bones that lent credence to many of the giants, and other bizarre creatures that are found in archaic mythology.

Blavatsky credits the Fourth Race of giant humans with building these colossal antediluvian structures and tombs, some of which are multimillion-ton megaliths, which are found on every continent. It is interesting to note that human height began to dwindle in size from 15 ft. to 10 ft. by the third Aryan sub-race.[9]

Author's note: Geomythology is the study of etiological oral traditions created by pre-scientific cultures to explain, in poetic metaphor and mythological imagery geological phenomena such as volcanoes, earthquakes, floods, fossils, and other natural features of the landscape.

Peter Nicolai

Akkadians and Mongolians to East Asia

The Sixth sub-race of Atlantis, the Akkadians, were masters of the sea and descendants from their Fifth sub-race predecessor, the Semites, which included the Phoenician stem of the sub-race. These sea peoples had originated in the mountains of northeastern Atlantis to later seed

311

the enigmatic, white people of North Africa—the Berbers of Morocco, Algeria and Tunisia. Born explorers, the Akkadians found their way into the Mediterranean as far as Italy. Blavatsky indicates in *The Secret Doctrine* that the Seventh or last Atlantean sub-race, christened the Mongolians (apparently with Mongolian human features), founded the first race outside of Atlantis, in East Asia. Far and away, the indigenous peoples recite myths of a 'land of the ancestors" that sank beneath the waves of the ocean, with voyages to a 'Land of Sun.'[10]

Saharan City of the Sun

To further explain, a sub-group left the main group of migrant Atlanteans who were traveling to the Gobi. They headed south to another inland sea, a fertile and lush section of the Sahara. They are thought to have established the 'City of the Sun' there c. 70,000 BCE. This, we believe, is located in Illizi Province, southeast Algeria. If this was the 'fertile Sahara Sea' described by Herodotus, it might also be 'Lake Tritonis,' traveled by Jason and the Argonauts. Later on, the Greek city states expanded into this area, establishing a successful a trade center in the city of Emporia. This 'inland sea' appears to have contained ancient waters, formed during the Pliocene (leaving remnants of sporadic waters in oases) during antiquated times—situated by the Aurès Mountains, and contiguous to the larger Atlas chain (considered proximal to the city of ancient Byzantium).

Within the Saharan Atlas in northeastern Algeria and northern Africa, there is a fertile and lush section of the Sahara where the Aurès Mountains present a segmented contour—the northern part abuts rocky cliffs which run southward to two luxuriant valleys. At Abiod the slopes run down into the dry climate vegetation of the Sahara. "Long inhabited by seminomadic Berber tribes, the mountains gradually became settled by a majority of Arab nomads from the Sahara," with the inhabitants practicing "seasonal migration based on villages regulated by collective granaries."[11, 12, 13, 14]

Out of the Gobi Sea

With the earlier migrations of the Atlanteans to India, Egypt and Africa taking root, the Aryan Root Race had a firm foundation for expansion into Europe and Asia, around 60,000 BCE. The Hindus were the first Fifth Root sub-race who arrived at the then inland sea of the Gobi Desert, now no longer in existence. As is usually the case with a mass exodus, this group mixed with the local tribes on their journey. The Sarasvati River Valley, now extinct too, was the sacred land of the Rig Veda, and close to many archaic shrines and temples. It rivaled Mohenjo-Daro and the Harappan culture in the Indus Valley. The Hindus populated southward towards the southern peninsula, bringing the sacred teachings of the Adepts with them.

Atlantean Tribes Migrate

The earlier Atlantean tribes of central Asia developed elaborate kingdoms whose ruins may still exist in Tibet, hidden within the Himalayas, or in the vast expanse of central Asia. However, time moved forward and with it the Second sub-race, the Arabians, at c. 40,000 BCE, journeyed from the 'City of the Bridge' (the ancient Gobi Sea, which most of the Fifth sub-races used as a base of deployment), and traveled outward through the Hindu Kush, Pakistan, and Persia (Iran) in route to Arabia.

From the ancient Gobi Sea streams of people moved west again. Forerunners of the ancient Persians (Iranians) c. 30,000 BCE, traveled the routes used by their predecessors, pushing on past the Hindu Kush and into Persia (Iran); and thereafter, developing perhaps one of the most superb and eloquent societies of the ancient ages. The Celts arrived at c. 20,000 BCE, heading into southwestern Europe with an offshoot forming the Mycenaean Greeks. The Fifth and current sub-race, the Teutonic peoples, migrated towards Germany c. 20,000 BCE, also populating the lands that they passed through with their cultures. An offshoot of the Teutons was the Slavs, who populated Russia and the surrounding areas c. 20,000 BCE.[15, 16, 17]

The Gods of Olympus 'Take' from Theosophy

"Prometheus is something more than the archetype of humanity; he is its generator. In the same way that we saw Hephaestus molding the first woman (Pandora) and endowing her with life, so Prometheus kneads the moist clay, of which he fashions the body of the first man whom he will endow with the soul-spark." The Monad is the source of the Soul in mankind.[18]

In *The Secret Doctrine*, Blavatsky discusses the 'Titans' of Atlantis; the 'Giants' of Genesis, some of whom were the Hierophants, and the highest adepts of the Ancient Mysteries— children of those born from the sacred Sea of Gobi. Some of these descendants misused their spiritual gifts. In quoting a colleague, she gives us her opinion of the giant, "We see in him a dark Atlantean or perhaps even an earlier Lemurian, who had survived till the birth of the British Islands-giants in every and any case."

In describing the story of the Gods of Olympus, it seems to be another veiled way to share our ancient history of Atlantis, the 'enormous' beings who succumbed to materialism; Gaia warned Rhea about Kronos and his proclivity for a power so intense that he disallowed any offspring from gaining their own life-form. The Titans of Olympus were egotistical, dispensing wrath to others, i.e., lesser gods or humans that became their targets. Diodorus Siculus, a Greek philosopher reports in one of his works that in the days of Isis, all men were of a titanic stature, dominated by the Hellenes' Giants.[19]

Author's Note: The term hierophant literally means, "one who explains sacred things, and the discloser of sacred learning. This title belongs to the highest Adepts in the temples of antiquity, who were the teachers and expounders of the Mysteries and the Initiators into the final great Mysteries. The Hierophant represented the Demiurge, and explained to the postulants for Initiation the various phenomena of Creation that were produced for their tuition. He was the sole expounder of the esoteric secrets and doctrines. It was forbidden even to pronounce his name before an uninitiated person. He sat in the East, and wore as a symbol of authority a golden globe suspended from the neck. He was also called "Mystagogus" (Kenneth R. H. Mackenzie, ix. F.T.S., in The Royal Masonic Encyclopædia). In Hebrew and Chaldaic, the term was Peter, the opener, discloser; hence the Pope as the successor of the Hierophant of the ancient Mysteries, sits in the Pagan chair of St. Peter."[20]

Goddess Eurynome Bears her Universe

In the beginning was Chaos, an amorphous, gaping void encompassing the entire Universe. It was the domain of a goddess named Eurynome, which means "far-ruling" and "wide-wandering." She was surrounded by an unending stream of water ruled by the god Oceanus. She was the Goddess of All Things, and desired to make order out of the Chaos. By coupling with a huge and powerful snake, Ophion, or as some legends say, coupling with the North Wind, she gave birth to Eros, god of Love, also known as Protagonus, the *firstborn*.

Eurynome separated the sky from the sea by dancing on the waves of Oceanus; she created great lands upon which she might wander, a veritable Universe, populating it with exotic creatures such as Nymphs, Furies, and Charites and countless beasts and monsters. Three other gods that were born from Chaos were Gaia, called Mother Earth; Ouranos, the embodiment of the Sky and the Heavens; and Tartarus, the god of the sunless and abysmal expanse beneath Gaia, the Earth. Gaia and Ouranos married and gave birth to the Titans, a race of formidable Giants, which included a particularly devious Giant named Kronos. Gaia and Ouranos warned Kronos that a son of his would one day overpower him. Kronos, therefore, swallowed his numerous children by his wife Rhea, to keep that forecast from taking place. This angered Gaia greatly, so when the youngest son, Zeus, was born, Gaia took a stone, wrapped it in swaddling clothes and offered it to Kronos to swallow. This satisfied Kronos and Gaia was able to spirit the baby Zeus away to be raised in Crete, far from his covetous father.[21, 22]

Wikimedia

Ancient Grecian History

It is said that Pythagoras narrated a story about the sinking of Atlantis. The sacred priestesses and priests had been warned about the upcoming flood and set sail to various places to preserve their "sacred flame" which was kept in the Temple of Initiation. One vessel commanded by the priest, Hilarion, was protected by the goddess named Pallas Athena on its journey to Crete with the 'Flame of Truth.'

Kybele

Kybele, the great Phrygian mother of the gods was a primal nature goddess, goddess of fertility and motherhood and worshipped with orgiastic rites in the mountains of her birth in her Anatolia—central and northwestern Asia Minor. Her cult was later brought into Greece by Samothrace and into Thebes. Kybele was connected with several Greek goddesses; Rhea, the Greek mother of the gods (Meter Theon), but sometimes also Demeter (particularly in the Samothracian cult), Aphrodite (on Mount Ida) and Artemis (in Karia). Depicted in classical sculpture as a crowned, mature woman, Kybele was royally consecrated and surrounded by lions.

The earliest evidence of Greek burials is found in the Franchthi Cave, Argolid, Greece, dated c. 7250 BCE. Simple food production, hut construction, and seafaring took place along the Greek coastal waters and the Aegean Sea. Mainstream research states that Grecian culture became established during the Neolithic Era, c. 6800 BCE with Anatolia, Turkey, Cyprus, Ionia on the Aegean coast of Turkey, Sicily and southern Italy—all part of *Magna Graecia*. Evidence of the diffusion of Greek culture is also found in

René Antoine Houasse (1645 to 1710)

Albania, Bulgaria, Egypt, southern France, Libya, Romania, Catalonia, and the Ukraine.[23, 24, 25]

Zeus and the Gods of Mount Olympus

Zeus battled against his his own father, Kronos. Zeus needed his brothers' and sisters' help in slaying the tyrant and Metis, Zeus's first wife, found a way of administering an emetic to Kronos, who threw up his five previous children. They were Hestia, Demeter, Hera, Hades, and Poseidon. Together they battled against their father and all of his children, led by Zeus, forever vanquished Kronos into Tartarus' domain, and the Dark World under the Earth. Zeus prevailed over his father and his father's family of Giants, along with his brothers and sisters. Then he made the choice of dividing the Universe. Now that the Universe had order, Zeus appointed himself Supreme God over all, creating a great and beautiful place for his favored gods to live on Mount Olympus, in Thessaly. All the others were left to fend for themselves in lands below

Mount Olympus. Zeus made himself God of the Sky with all its phenomena, including clouds and thunderbolts.

Hestia became goddess of the Hearth. To his brother Poseidon, he gave the rule of the Sea. Demeter became a goddess of Fertility; Hera was goddess of Marriage and Childbirth, prior to her marriage to Zeus.Hades, one of his other brothers, was made god of the Underworld. Zeus did bring order out of Chaos, but one of his failings was that he did not look kindly upon the people, those creatures that populated the lands over which he reigned. Many were not beautiful, and Zeus had contempt for anyone who was not beautiful. And, of course, they were not immortal, as the Olympian gods were, and they complained about the lack of good food and the everlasting cold nights. Zeus ignored their complaints, while he and the other gods feasted endlessly on steaming hot game from the surrounding forests, and had great crackling fires in every room of their palaces where they lived in the cold winter.[26, 27]

The Epic of Prometheus and Pandora

Prometheus, the last of the Titans, molded a race of people from clay. Blended together from crumbs of every living creature, the new race was called the Common Man. And Prometheus was now the common man's champion, in confrontation with Zeus. Fire for home and hearth had always been for the gods alone until Prometheus stole sparks of glowing fire from Mount Olympus, sharing it with the mortals for cooking and warmth. Zeus became incensed at this insult to his supreme power, and pronounced that Prometheus be bound and chained to a mountain, attacked daily by an eagle. Zeus then asked the goddess Hephaestus and the Olympians to create a wicked but beautiful creature, to torment naïve Epimetheus, the brother of Prometheus. Her name was Pandora, meaning "all gifts" and thus, having being endowed as instructed by Zeus, he also provided her with a wedding present with instructions _not_ to open the gift. After being received into Epimetheus' home, Pandora became curious and opened the gift, which contained a swarm of evil spirits trapped inside…then released. These ills would forever plague mankind. Only 'Hope' remained behind, a single blessing to comfort mankind in their suffering. Pandora had a daughter named

Pyrrha—meaning Fire—and she was the first mortal child born. Pyrrha and her husband, Deucalion, survived the Great Deluge.[28, 29]

The Birds of Joy and Sorrow by Victor Vasnetsov (1848-1926)

Eleusinian-Mysteries

"The Eleusinian Mysteries, held each year at Eleusis, Greece, fourteen miles northwest of Athens, were of vital importance to the Greeks. The Sacred Way or the road from Athens to Eleusis, was the *only* road in all of central Greece. The Eleusinian Mysteries celebrated the stories of Demeter and Persephone, but details of the rituals are unknown because the initiates were sworn to secrecy on pain of death. We do know, though, that those who participated in the Mysteries were forever changed for the better and that they no longer feared death.[30]

Sparta

Made famous through Plato's writings, the city state of Sparta had the greatest military power of Greece and played a catalytic role in the history of the Peloponnese Island chain. Sparta's people have been historically admired for their valor and for keeping alive the noble Greek values. Sparta, the dominant power in Greece, was in decline by the year 362 BCE.[31]

Samothracc

The Greeks took the teachings of the 'ancient wisdom' and incorporated them into many of their legends and folklore. The fame of Samothrace and its mystery school (8 BCE – 1 BCE) centered on the cult of the Megaloi Theoi, or the Great Gods. Their rites of initiation were well known to the mystery students of their day. Famous pre-Hellenic and Hellenic personalities who visited their shrine to be initiated into the island cult were: Lysander of Sparta, Philip II of Macedonia and Lucius Calpurnius Piso Caesoninus, father-in-law of Julius Caesar. The Temple of Palaiopoli has a distinctive aura of a sacred ground; it was set in a cleft facing the sea at the base of Mt. Phengari. This haven of the 'great gods' physically integrated the divine forces of earth, sky, and sea that played a fundamental role in the Greek mysteries. Within its sacred landscape, events occurred that shaped both the myth and history of the ancient world, including a legendary family that sired the Trojan race and also embodiment to the goddess, Harmonia. The daughter of Aphrodite and Ares, Harmonia bequeathed love, unity and harmony to the human race. Harmonia is said to have established the dynasty of Thebes, as the ancestress of the illustrious Dionysian women; Semele, Agave, Autonoe, and Ino. At Harmonia's wedding, the Olympians presented her with the well-known magical necklace from Aphrodite, imbued with undying beauty or feminine allure, depending on the wearer.[32]

Were the Griffins Protoceratops?

"Folklorist and historian of science Adrienne Mayor of Stanford University has suggested that the exquisitely preserved fossil skeletons of *Protoceratops* and other beaked dinosaurs, found by ancient Scythian nomads who mined gold in the Tian Shan and Altai Mountains of Central Asia, may have been at the root of the image of the mythical creature known as the griffin. Griffins were described as lion-sized quadrupeds with large claws and a raptor bird-like beak; they laid their eggs in nests on the ground.

Greek writers began describing the griffin around 675 BCE., at the same time the Greeks first made contact with Scythian nomads. Griffins were described as guarding the gold deposits in the arid hills and red

320

sandstone formations of the wilderness. The region of Mongolia and China where many *Protoceratops* fossils are found is rich in gold runoff from the neighboring mountains, lending some credence to the theory that these fossils were the basis of griffin myths."[33]

Southern Netherlands, c. 1350, National Library of the Netherlands

Thrace

"Thrace had a heritage which matched that of its southwesterly neighbors, the Mycenaeans. Thracians were allied to Troy during the Trojan War. Homeric Thrace was known as a center for music. During this period, it encompassed a wide swath of territory to the north of Greece proper, stretching from the River Axios in the west, to the Hellespont and the Black Sea in the east, and the Balkan Mountains in the north. Sometimes Thrace could be used to define all the territory to the north of Thessaly, incorporating Scythia and even Macedonia. In addition to the tribe that Homer called Thracians (in reality several very warlike tribes), ancient Thrace was home to numerous other Indo-European tribes, all non-Greek speakers."[34]

Anthrogenesis

Strabo of Greece

One of the major Grecian icons was Strabo (63 BCE – BCE 24), the Greek geographer, philosopher, and historian. He spent his life traveling to neighboring cultures and localities gathering history, societal practices and other data, which he shared with Greece. A noteworthy tour was his trip to Egypt where he gathered information about their pre-deluge culture and Atlantis, plus spent time with the Egyptian temple priests, prior to returning to Greece. It would not be until several hundred years had passed that the stories would be told about these ancient times.[35, 36]

Birth of the Roman Gods

The Romans knowledge of the 'divine nature' of all things in the natural world was evidenced in their pantheon of gods and goddesses and abundant nature spirits. Also, their heartfelt inclinations toward family and state were everywhere apparent. The Romans adopted many of the Greek gods, c. 200 BCE, and gradually deified them with names and attributes appropriate to the growing Roman Empire, retaining their basic recognizable essences.

"From the deep, silent and endless depth of darkness is Chaos, from which all things were created and thus came *Terra,* the Earth. *Terra* brought forth Ouranos, the Heavens, and Terra and Ouranos produced the Titans with the first cohort containing six male and six female children." (Kragh, 2010)

"The second generation of Titans consisted of Hyperion's progeny- from the first generation, including Eos, the Dawn, Helios, the Sun, and Selene, the Moon, and the children of Iapetus- from the first origination, which included Atlas, Prometheus, and Epimetheus. These Titans coupled and created a collection of gods and goddesses. Cronus, the youngest Titan, and his sister Rhea became parents of six of the twelve Olympians, but Cronus became fearful of sedition by his brood so he devoured his five first infants upon birth. Rhea pleaded for help from her parents to spare her next infant so they took her to Crete, where Rhea bore Jupiter, which she hid in a cave, later returning to Cronus. Cronus consumed the bundled infant, but Rhea had deceived him, switching baby Jupiter for a stone, thus successful in saving

322

him. Jupiter stayed in Crete, growing into manhood and journeyed to Mount Olympus, anticipating a battle with Cronus. Compelling Cronus to reject his relations, Jupiter and his family fought Cronus and his allies, the other Titans. The Titans were conquered, then exiled, with Jupiter taking reign of the Olympians and ruler as god of the sky."[37]

The Sack of Rome

The Roman Empire, per their 'mission statement,' conquered the vast lands far away from the homeland. Born of a tragic beauty inherited from Greece, Rome had a rather short lifecycle, in truth, considering its colossal yet staggering achievements and conquests. The Visigoths brought to an end a monumental period of grace and beauty and conquest.

Évariste Vital Luminais (1822-1896), Sherpherd
Gallery, NY, by Romaino

In Norse Creation, Odin Surveys His Warriors.

Nicholas Roerich, New York City Gallery

"The Germanic Root Race included the people of Denmark, Sweden, Norway, Iceland and Finland and they created their Norse myth and cosmology. The Norse cosmology is akin to Brahma, in which a life cycle is born and then destroyed at the end of the Universe, to be created again. Ragnar, which means "the Doom of the Gods" is the end of their world cycle, in which the cosmos, the gods and goddesses are destroyed. The beloved god Baldur was killed by Loki and sent to the underworld – the gods had to prepare to face their tragic destiny with Odin carefully choosing the ablest human warriors to join him in the final battle against the world-devouring giants. But, although their desperate actions were in vain, there would be another world cycle."[38]

Muspell, the Viking First World

Muspell, the first world, was a place of light and heat whose flames were too hot unless one was an indigenous of the land and could tolerate the temperature. Beyond Muspell was a massive and bottomless cavern named Ginnungagap, and past Ginnungagap was the gloomy, wintry land of Niflheim, from which came the chilling, icy frost, wind, and rain, converging in Ginnungagap, between the flowing air, heat and light from Muspell. Melting drops soon appeared where heat and cold met, and this liquid grew into a giant frost ogre named Ymir. Ymir fell asleep and became surrounded in sweat. Beneath his arm grew a man and then a woman, with a son emerging from his one of his legs.

This melting of the frost then became a cow called Audhumla, with four rivers of milk trickling from her breast and she fed Ymir. Audhumla loved the salty ice blocks and a day of licking released the hair of a man from within ice. The next day his head come out and by the third day, the whole body had materialized in the image of a towering, robust, and good-looking man named Buri. Buri produced a son named Bor and he wed Bestla, the daughter of a giant. Bor and Bestla give birth to three sons, starting with Odin, then Vili, and finally Vé, the third son. The sons of Bor killed the giant, Ymir. So much blood was shed from his wounds, as the great giant fell, that it drowned all the frost ogres, except for one giant, who fled with his wife by climbing onto a huge carved-out tree trunk—called a 'lur,' almost resembling a casket. Bergelmir, the giant, and his wife then began to bring forth the families of the frost ogres.[39]

The Sons of Bor Create the World and Humanity

"The sons of Bor carried Ymir into the middle of Ginnungagap, making a world from him and, using his blood, they made the sea and lakes, and from his flesh came the earth, and with his hair, the trees were created, and from his bones came the mountains. Bor's sons made rocks and pebbles from Ymir's teeth and broken bones and when the maggots hatched from Ymir's flesh, they looked like humans but lived in the earth after the gods gave them human understanding. Ymir's skull became the sky and Bor's sons set it over the earth and under each of the four sides they put a dwarf; whose names are East, West, North, and South. The sons of Bor flung Ymir's brains into the sky, and they became the clouds. Then they gathered the ashes and embers from the air, from the explosion at Muspell, and placed them in Ginnungagap, to give light to heaven above and earth beneath and placed the stars in special places and paths; then the earth was surrounded by a deep sea. The sons of Bor gave the sea lands to the families of giants for their settlements and the sons of Bor built an inland fortress for themselves for protection from the hostile giants, using Ymir's eyebrows and naming this fortress Midgard. While walking along the sea shore, the sons of Bor found two trees, and from them they created a man and a woman. Odin gave both the man and woman spirit and life while Vili gave them understanding and the power of movement, with Vé giving them clothing and names. The man was named Ask-'Ash' and the woman Embla-'Elm' and from them came the races of men who lived in Midgard and in the middle world."[40]

Brunehilde Discovers Sieglinde and Siegmund, Gaston Bussiere (1862 to 1928)

The Sons of Bor Build Asgard

The sons of Bor built a fortress for themselves named Asgard. The gods and their kindred lived in Asgard, with wonderful times and memories to last an eternity. Odin was the supreme patriarch of the Universe, the legendary creator of the gods, humanity, and all the creations of the Earth. Together with his brothers, Odin ruled the heavens and the Earth, spending his time in the great hall named Hlidskjalf, and carefully observed his people all over the world, and he was said to have understood them.

The Frog Princess, Viktor Vasnetsov, 1918

When Odin married Frigg, from the family Fjorgvin, he joined the ancient family—the kingdom of Asgard—the Aesir, the divine rulers, subsequently retaining the moniker, 'All-Father,' due to their status. Odin's wife and daughter were 'one-in-the-same'—the 'Earth'; they bore the first son to Odin—the strong and mighty Thor, who controlled all living creatures on Earth. The gods then built a mighty bridge named Bifrost, using knowledge and craftsmanship, which was a three colored rainbow, going from Earth to Heaven. No one could be held accountable when the sons of Muspell went on the warpath, riding over and breaking the bridge each day. High court was held daily by the gods at the first haven, Yggdrasil, the most magnificent of all ash trees, with its boughs dispersed across the Earth, reaching beyond the heavens.[41]

Source Unknown

Druid Astrology and Sacred Tree of Life

The Story of the Hero and the Maid

There existed the 'otherworld, often called 'the sea islands,' dubbed the 'land of the living,' where time was relative. In Celtic folklore, the hero appears to take a magical voyage after the beautiful girl who listened to his bard (or song) of his most happy land. They sail away in a boat of glass never to be seen again. As there were offshoots of this story, the hero might return after a time, finding all his companions dead, but in actuality, hundreds of years have passed.

In this second tale, the hero is surrounded by a magic mist upon him, only if his quest be noble in deed, and he stumbles upon a palace, bearing forthright in his mind, to make a suitable entrance, only to come across a warrior and a beautiful maiden who provide him welcome! It is only upon a careful gaze that the hero sees truth; the warrior stands as High King Lugh himself and the maiden his wife, Bui'! The hero enjoys many more extraordinary escapades to be once again in his home, that of the Celts.[42]

Public Domain

Druid Celtic Priesthood and Gods

The Druids were the ancient Celtic priesthood thought to have originated from the Atlantean priesthood with both women and men in ecclesiastic duties. Their ritual practices in sacred oak groves played a vital role in the passing on of the Druidic knowledge. Mystery teachings included the soul's transmigration, nature, and power of the gods, healing and the creative or alchemical processes for life.[43]

A Myriad of Migration

Besides coming from sub-races of late Atlantis, the Celtic people's roots reach from a diversity of locations in our world, starting with Southern Poland, Austria, Germany and Czechoslovakia, we move to other Celtic origins from Portugal, parts of Spain, Galicia and Aragon and the Lepontic area of Northern Italy. The Nordic regions and Austria, west of Vienna provide another locale; the Galicia area Celtic people; north central Asia Minor or Turkey. Celtic languages are not nowadays widely spoken and are limited to selected places in Western Europe such as Ireland, Isle of Man, Wales, Cornwall, Scotland, Brittany, Patagonia, and Cape Breton Island.[44]

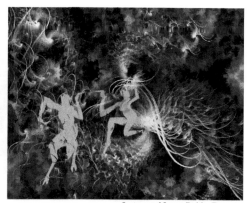

Sprites and Imps, **Public Domain**

The Prophetic Bird, Viktor M Vasnetsov
(1848-1926), Daghestan Museum of Fine Art,
Makhachkala Russia

Faerie Folk Creation Lore

The *Lebor Gabala* records the Celtic people's movement into Ireland:
"In this way they came, in dark clouds from northern islands of the
world. They landed on the mountains of Conmaicne Rein in Connachta,
and they brought a darkness over the sun for three days and three
nights. Gods were their men of arts, and non-gods their husbandmen."
According to the mythic tales, the Tuatha de Danann arrived in western
Ireland, close to modern Connacht, before the Milesians arrived. The
population divided into two social classes: the teachers of medicine,
smithing, communication or druidry... and the farmers or shepherds.
Although no one knows for certain what the Tuatha de Danann looked
like, descriptions of their female war leader, Eriu, indicate a tall,
attractive people with pale skin, high foreheads, long red hair and large
blue eyes. It is told that the Tuatha de Danann and the Milesians had
battles, and later, some of the kinfolk began to live below the hills,
closer to the earth, and it is they who transformed into the legendary
faerie folk of Ireland.[45, 46]

Faeries and the Kingdom of Devas

Theosophy describes the diverse Kingdom of Devas (Daevas), which includes the faeries, because *elementals* exist in and among each other in every substance. The Elementals appear in the myths, fables, traditions, or poetry of all nations, ancient and modern, and comprise the devas, genii, satyrs, fauns, elves, dwarfs, trolls, brownies, neck (nykk in Norwegian), sprites, goblins, banshees, and the pixies, to say the least.[47]

Origins of the Gaelic Peoples

The Gaelic peoples, a branch of the Celtic races, were believed to have originated from the Hallstatt culture in central Europe. They would include the Austrians, the Czechs, Southern Poles, and Southern Germans, c. 1500-1000 BCE. After the fall of Rome, the Celts in both Scotland and Ireland became free of Roman intrusion into their lands. Many Gaels traveled from Ireland to Scotland; and over time, Gaelic clans could look to multiple lands for their ancestry, not just the Scottish Highlands. During the Middle Ages, to be a Gael was to be a speaker of Gaelic.[48, 49]

Slavic Creation Myth

"In the beginning there was nothing and then there was an old, dark, dark sea and sky. The only existing thing created by Rod was World Egg, in which rested Svarog, the Divine creator. Under the influence of life forces, the egg cracked open and created a light that shone, Svarog, and created its shadow, from which originated Crnobog. Voden, god of the sea and the water came from the glare of Svarogos old-sea. Svarog launched the forces that created the world. From the top of the egg shell dust-creating the world tree, ash tree, which was rising, separated the heavens from the earth and sea. His crown was created Nav, the world of the gods. Svarog and Crnobog or Drognjuš were the force without form, so they created their counterparts, avatars, in which they acted as the counterparts to the world. The Savior used gold powder from the bottom of the world; fire that created all life and the world, and created the sun and moon. Lower half of debris from an egg created humans and all other creatures on earth. People eventually became masters of this world; wise, cunning, and began to cultivate the land, livestock breeding, building their cities and towns, as most other creatures, mythological, and so, gradually suppressed in the rugged and wild lands and people were less encountered."[50, 51]

Michael Hansford ©

Megaliths, Ley-Lines and The World Grid

Or, what you ought to know about sacred monuments, earth chakras and pole alignment…

The megaliths are usually surrounded by many sacred sites. Found across our planet, they number in the millions if we count the stones or materials hewn and raised within circles or alignments. As pointed out in the chapter on Egypt, the Great Pyramid of Giza lies at the exact center of all land mass on Earth and is aligned with Easter Island, the Nazca Lines, Machu Picchu, Sacsayhuaman, the Oracle of Amun, Giza Plateau, Petra, Persepolis and Mohenjo-Daro. Preben Hansson first discovered a direct line of flight from Trelleborg to three other Viking fortresses, which are also the same in design. Gobekli Tepe in Turkey, is estimated to be 11,000 to 12,500 years old. In 13 years, only 5% or less of it has been excavated with the structure representing abstract human and animal forms. Dederiyeh Cave in Syria revealed the first human habitation at 700,000 years ago. Carahunge, Armenia has a 7,500-year old stone circle with a solstice alignment for the Cygnus constellation.[52, 53, 54]

Göbekli Tepe, Evidence of Advanced Societies

Göbekli Tepe, at c. 10,500 BCE, is the oldest monument discovered to date. Robert Schoch, Ph.D., describes the find: "At Göbekli Tepe immense, finely carved and decorated T-shaped limestone pillars, many in the range of two to five and a half meters tall and weighing up to an estimated 10 to 15 tons, stand in Stonehenge-like circles. Various pillars at Göbekli Tepe are decorated with bas-reliefs of animals, including foxes, boars, snakes, aurochs (wild cattle), Asiatic wild asses, wild sheep, birds (cranes, a vulture), a gazelle, and arthropods (scorpion, ants)."[56]

Teomancimit

Graham Hancock describes Göbekli Tepe as an "intricacy of the stonework, the size of the megalithic pillars, and the sheer magnitude of man-made hill it was carefully covered with. The original construction was built on solid bedrock, then mounds were constructed on top of these, and further structures built on top over a period of around two thousand years, with the final enclosures containing smaller stones stones and less sophistication than the earlier levels."

The Carnac Stones

The Carnac Stones are counted as one of the most magnificent of the megalithic sites in the world. Numbering more than 3,000 stones, Carnac is a pattern of line and height in stone.[55]

Somadjinn

Ley-Lines

Our Universe is governed by systematic principles with spiritual antecedents. Throughout the book, we have discussed in *Anthrogenesis*, the observations in human life, and on our planet, that often times appears to be mysterious. Plato stated that our Earth, viewed from above, resembles a 'ball sewn from twelve pieces of skin' using Pythagorean geometry as his foundation. This patchwork of energy is thought to be magnetic in origin or perhaps 'prana,' from the universal etheric source of Light. These 'ley-lines' are described as straight fault lines, which connect to Earth's tectonic plates. Defined as alignments affecting numerous geographical locations such as ancient monuments and megaliths, ley-line existence was first suggested in 1921 by the amateur archaeologist, Alfred Watkins, whose book *The Old Straight Track* brought alignments to the attention of the wider public.

Humanity's funerary rituals and traditions include using a footpath for funerary parties associated with ley-lines and are called 'death roads.' The use of 'spirit paths,' which are the walkways of the spirits or devas, are unmarked but known paths that have been historically straight and quite often mimic ley lines. This practice has an ancient foundation with Feng Shui (the art of wind and water), which is another example of using life-energy in ritual. Indigenous peoples, worldwide, utilized the spirit-energy connected to ley markers to heal, talk to the gods and conduct sacred rites at sacred and ritual places. Spirit paths assisted humans in locating other ley markers for planting crops, building temples and villages.[57]

Hopi Ley-Markers Denote Orion and Chakras

Researchers Gary A. David and Bethe Hagens, Ph.D. have extensively researched the world grid, and report that the Hopi Three Mesas align with the three stars in Orion's Belt. Additionally, David states that the constellation of Orion is mirrored among their sacred ley-markers. The Base Chakra is located at Mesa Verde, the Sun (Orion) Temple in southwestern Colorado. The Sacral Chakra is pinpointed at Burnt Corn Ruins near the village of Pinon, Arizona (corresponding to the Orion Nebula). The Solar Plexus (Navel) Chakra is at the Second Mesa and the Hopi village of Shongopovi. The Heart Chakra is at Kachina Point, a mesa southwest of Oraibi (also called Monument Point). The Throat Chakra is at Grand Falls on the Little Colorado River. The sixth or third Eye (Pineal) Chakra is at Walnut Canyon Ruins in the foothills of the San Francisco Peaks, and the Crown Chakra is located at Tuzigoot Ruins and the red rock country of Sedona in Verde Valley.[58, 59]

Geodesy and the World Grid

Pioneers in these new sciences of geodesy and the world grid are Graham Hancock, Robert Bauval, Robert Schoch, Gary A. David Hugh Newman, Freddie Silva and others. The practice defined as geodesy is the basic conception in the study of the world grid. Measurement combined with uniformly spaced latitude (horizontal lines) and longitude (vertical lines) are used to locate points by synchronizing distances between locations on the straight line. The worldwide pattern of ley-lines, called the world grid, is a subject being investigated in the new sciences of sacred site research and archaeoastronomy. The fascination of this science is how the ancients had a deep understanding of the movements of the sun, moon, planets and constellations of our Milky Way galaxy and relied upon their priests and shamans to guide them in aligning their temples and edifices, to tap into both the telluric and stellar energies available in their regions on Earth. Rituals and ceremonies were coordinated corresponding to the time of year and stellar alignments which enhanced the power and potency of their sacred practices.[60]

Earth Chakras and Vortices

"Ancient civilizations and modern esoteric traditions believe that the body of our physical blue planet materialized from a universal energy matrix and has a subtle structure, similar to the human energy field. This energetic structure peaks in seven major "chakra sites" located on each continent, where the strongest Energy Vortexes are situated. Hundreds of minor earth chakras are also spread all over the planet. They are believed to be spherical in shape, expanding in all three dimensional directions in a spiral motion, with a radius extending for hundreds of kilometers. They may either spin clockwise or anti-clockwise. Their location varies according to different traditions, but most accept the 7 Main Chakras as being:

1. The Root Chakra is at Mt. Shasta, California, United States.

2. Sacral Chakra: Lake Titicaca, on the border of Bolivia and Peru.

3. Solar Plexus Chakra: Uluru-Kata Tjuta, Australia.

4. Heart Chakra: Glastonbury and Shaftsbury, England.

5. Throat Chakra: Great Pyramid of Giza and Mt. Sinai, Egypt; Mt. Olives, Jerusalem.

6. Third Eye Chakra: Kuh-e Malek Siah, Triple border of Iran, Afghanistan and Pakistan.

7. Crown Chakra: Mt. Kailash, Tibet."[61]

Flower and Tree of Life

The Flower of Life is thought to be the multi-dimensional polyhedron that creates the World Grid.

Public Domain

Researchers such as Graham Hancock, Robert Schoch and Robert Bauval report that various monuments such as the Great Pyramid of Giza, the Hopi's Three Mesas, in northern Arizona and Teotihuacan in Mexico, are all aligned with the ley-markers connecting them to the Sirius constellation. Found in all major religions of the world, the Flower of Life contains the archetypes of creation which emanated from the Great Void. It is the basis for all life in our Universe.[62]

Kabbalistic Merkaba

This design is found in the six-fold symmetry of a hexagon with the center of each circle on the circumference of six surrounding circles of the same diameter, forming the Kabbalistic Merkaba. From this form, other designs in sacred geometry are the Egg of Life, illustrated in the third embryonic division after human conception equaling eight cells.

The Star Tetrahedron is a three-dimensional polyhedron composed of four triangular faces, three of which meet at each corner or vertex and the total of six edges with four vertices and two interlocking tetrahedrons resemble the Star of David. This completes the Star Tetrahedron, which is found surrounding all life and is considered to be multi-dimensional.[63, 64]

Public domain

Teotihuacan Aligns to the Pleiades

Teotihuacan is oriented 15 to 25 degrees east of true north with the Pyramid of the Sun's front barricade precisely perpendicular to the horizontal locus of equinox sunsets. The ceremonial structures of the monument are aligned at right angles to the Pyramid of the Sun with the Avenue of the Dead aimed at the setting of the Pleiades in the Orion constellation.[65]

Pole Alignment Changes

Blavatsky says that at each time a new Root Race is born, there is always a shift in the Earth Poles. So, in addressing the planetary pole alignment and arrangement of the vectors of our Earth, Blavatsky stated, "The occult sciences show that the founders (the respective groups of the seven Prajapatis) of the Root Races have all been connected with the Pole Star."

In her commentary we find: "He who understands the age of Dhruva* who measures 9090 mortal years, will understand the times of the pralayas, the final destiny of nations, O Lanoo." The equivalent of this name is given in the original—Alpha Polaris—the same as Dhruva, the pole-star of 31,105 years ago.

Moreover, there must have been a good reason why an Asiatic nation should locate its great progenitors and saints in the Ursa Major, a northern constellation. It is 70,000 years, however, since the pole of the Earth pointed to the further end of Ursa Minor's tail; and many more thousand years since the Seven Rishis would have been identified with the constellation of Ursa Major. The Aryan race was born and developed in the far north, though after the sinking of the continent of Atlantis its tribes 'immigrated' further south into Asia. Hence Prometheus is son of Asia, and Deucalion, his son, the Greek Noah—he who created men out of the stones of Mother Earth—is called a northern Scythe, by Lucian, and Prometheus is made the brother of Atlas and is tied down to Mount Caucasus amid the Snows."

Deucalion is said to have brought the worship of Adonis and Osiris into Phoenicia. Now the worship is that of the Sun, lost and found again in its astronomical significance. It is only at the Pole where the Sun dies out for such a length of time as six months, for in latitude 68 [degrees] it remains dead only for forty days, as in the festival of Osiris. The two worships were born in the north of Lemuria, or on that continent of which Asia was a kind of broken prolongation, and which stretched up to the Polar 'Regions'. This is well shown by de Gebelin's *"Allegories d'Orient,"* p. 246, and by Bailly; though neither Hercules nor Osiris are solar myths, save in one of their seven aspects."[66]

Earliest astronomy holds that repetitive pole shift has occurred across scores of millennia, not only influencing the pole star   witnessed and recorded by the ancients—but revealing an underlying foundation of human consciousness. In an interview with world-mysteries.com, Walter Cruttenden, (*Lost Star of Myth and Time,* 2005), maintains that "it is really about what happens to the Earth and consciousness as our Solar System moves through space in the mysterious motion known as the "Precession of The Equinox." This astronomical phenomenon has, since Newton, been attributed to local gravitational forces wobbling the Earth's axis. Lost Star now shows us, in no uncertain terms, that the Earth's axis does not change orientation relative to objects inside the Solar System, at the same rate that it changes orientation to objects outside the Solar System, meaning precession must be due to our Sun's binary motion around another star."[67, 68, 69, 70]

Divergence of Anthrogenesis

Phenomenal sites such as Cappadocia, Çatal Höyük and the complex at Gobekli Tepe exist in Turkey. In Bosnia-Herzegovina, the Bosnia Pyramids, megaliths and Stone Spheres resonate with the other sites worldwide, especially the Giza's pyramids and the pyramids in the Amazon jungle, the colossal Olmec heads, and the Stone Spheres of Costa Rica, just to mention a few. We are all connected through the great sacred planetary grid and our ancestors knew this. Now we are discovering more and more of our exquisite past, and the mysteries are being explained. The study of Anthrogenesis brings alive the most divergent of fields and shows their inherent common characteristics—a living thread that passes through all branches of the sciences and the humanities. Anthrogenesis gives us, modern-day students of the Ancient Wisdom, a synthesis of information and a growing understanding of life.[71, 72]

Dolman at Viseau Portugal, João Carvalho

Notes

1. http://www.olc.edu/~khecrow/webfolder/Creation%20Stories%20 from%20around%20the%20World.rtf

2. http://chineseculture.about.com/library/weekly/aa_nuwa02a.htm

3. http://www.rsc.org/chemistryworld/2015/01/flowing-rivers-mercury

4. http://web.ccsu.edu/astronomy/cosmic_mandalas.htm

5. http://web.ccsu.edu/astronomy/tibetan_cosmological_models.htm

6. http://www.gomang.org/mandala.html

7. de Purucker, G. Studies in Occult Philosophy, 1973, Theosophical University Press, Pasadena, CA.

8. http://www.www.sacred-texts.com/the/sd/sd2-1-07.htm

9. Mayor, Adrienne, *The First Fossil Hunters: Paleontology in Greek and Roman Times*, Princeton University Press. 2000. Geomythology © Adrienne Mayor in Encyclopedia of Geology, editor, Richard Selley, Robin Cocks, and Ian Palmer. Forthcoming, Elsevier, 2004.

10. H.P.B., *The Secret Doctrine*, vol. II.

11. Champlin, Jr., John D. "The Proposed Inland Sea in Algeria", Popular Science Monthly, Volume 8, April 1876, p. 665-670.

12. http://www.algeria.com/north-east/batna/

13. http://www.algeria.com/blog/the-aures-mountains-of-algeria

14. http://www.thefreedictionary.com/wadies

15. Cerve, Wishar S. 1984, *Lemuria- The Lost Continent of the Pacific: The Mystery People of Mt. Shasta*, Rosicrucian Library, Volume XII, Supreme Grand Lodge of AMORC, San Jose, CA.

16. http://www.sacred-texts.com/atl/soa/soa21.htm

17. http://www.campbellmgold.com/archive_esoteric/root_races.pdf

18. http://www.sacred-texts.com/the/sd/sd2-2-07.htm

19. http://www.theoi.com/Pontios/DaimonesProseoous.html

20. http://www.phx-ult-lodge.org/Thegloss.htm#h , p. 141

21. http://www.pantheon.org

22. http://www.theoi.com/

23. Hall, Manly P., *The Secret Teachings of All Ages* (1928), The Myth of the Dying God, p.36.

24. http://www.theoi.com/Cult/KybeleCult.html

25. http://www.nndb.com/people/156/000097862/

26. http://www.pantheon.org/

27. http://www.webgreece.gr/greekmythology/myths

28. http://www.theoi.com/greek-mythology/

29. http://www.greekmythology.com/Myths

30. http://www.ancient.eu/article/32

31. https://www.jstor.org/stable/pdf/20097762.pdf

32. http://www.samothrace.emory.edu/project-overview

33. Mayor, A., *The First Fossil Hunters: Paleontology in Greek and Roman Times*. (2000). Princeton University Press, Princeton, New Jersey.

34. http://www.historyfiles.co.uk/KingListsEurope/GreeceThrace.htm

35. http://www.maryjones.us/ctexts/index_classical.html

36. http://www.ancient-greece.org/resources/timeline.html

37. Kragh, Helge, Ph.D., *Ancient Greek-Roman Cosmology: Infinite, Eternal, Finite, Cyclic, and Multiple Universes*. Journal of Cosmology. Vol. 9. July (2010): 2172-178.

38. http://www.norse-mythology.org/tales/ragnarok

39. http://www.pitt.edu/~dash/creation.html

40. http://www.pitt.edu/~dash/creation.html

41. http://www.pitt.edu/~dash/creation.html

42. http://www.mythicalireland.com/mythology/tuathade/lugus.php

43. MacKillop, James, *Dictionary of Celtic Mythology*, 1998, Oxford University Press.

44. http://www.ancient-origins.net/human-origins-folklore/celtic-myths-creation-0072

45. http://www.druidcircle.org/library/index.php?title=Celtic_Creation

46. http://www.irishtribes.com/articles/2012-11-lost-celtic-creation-myth-in-english.html

47. http://www.blavatsky.net/index.php/17-H.P.B.lavatsky/H.P.B.-articles/256-elementals

48. Besant, Annie and Leadbeater, C.W., *Man: How, Whence, and Whither*, 1913, Theosophical Publishing House, Adyar, India,

49. http://www.cranntara.org.uk/gaelic.htm

50. http://www.slavorum.org/slavic-creation-myth/

51. http://www.chlive.org/pbeck/eastlibrary/mythology.htm

52. http://www.andrewcollins.com/page/articles/carahunge.htm
53. http://www.ancient-code.com/
54. http://www.robertschoch.com/turkey.html
55. http://www.megalithia.com/brittany/carnac/
56. Schoch, Robert, *Forgotten Civilization, The Role of Solar Outbursts in Our Past and Future,* 2012, Inner Traditions, VT.
57. http://www.ancient-wisdom.co.uk
58. http://www.theorionzone.com/maps.htm
59. http://www.missionignition.net/bethe
60. http://www.sacredgeometryinternational.com
61. http://www.in5d.com/earth-chakras-and-vortices/
62. https://grahamhancock.com/interview-jaw/
63. Melchizedek, Drunvalo, *The Ancient Secret of the Flower of Life,* Volumes 1 & 2, 1999, 2012, Light Technology Publishing, Flagstaff, AZ.
64. https://archive.org/details/Ascension_97
65. https://grahamhancock.com/alignment-2012-jenkins/
66. H.P. Blavatsky, *The Secret Doctrine*, Vol. II, page 768.
67. Walter Cruttenden, CPAK, 2007.
68. http://www.world-mysteries.com/Walter_Cruttenden_1.htm
69. Cruttenden, Walter, *Lost Star of Myth and Time*, 2005, St. Lynn's Press, Pittsburgh, PA
70. http://sacredgeometryinternational.com/category/esoteric-history/earth-energy-ley-lines
71. http://www.archive.archaeology.org/0811/abstracts/turkey.html
72. http://www.bosnianpyramids.org/

Anthrogenesis

Chapter Fifteen

Humanity's Road Forward

Lao-Tze Tung, the Father of Taoism

Lao-Tze Tung lived sometime between the 4th and the 6th century BCE. Lao-Tze became famous as a sage, or wise man, during China's *Age of Philosophers*. He is the reputed author of the *Tao Te Ching* and founder of the Taoist religion in China. His name means "Old Master" and "Tao" means the "Way." The *Tao Te Ching* teaches a nonaggressive approach to life and a stoic indifference to the powers of the world. It called for a return to a simple way of the past and for a style of life in harmony with the Universe. It says that man must imitate the Universe, which endures because it does not live for itself. Lao-Tze worked as a librarian at the court of Zhou. When the kingdom showed signs of decay Lao-Tze left and was never heard of again. Legend has it that Lao-Tze, saddened by the evil of men, set off into the desert on a water buffalo

345

leaving civilization behind. When he arrived at the final gate at the great wall protecting the kingdom, the gatekeeper persuaded him to record the principles of his philosophy for posterity. The result was the eighty-one sayings of the *Tao Te Ching*."[1]

The Life of Confucius

Confucius was an influential Chinese philosopher, teacher and political figure known for his popular aphorisms and for his models of social interaction. Confucius was born in 551 BCE in the Lu state of China, near present-day Qufu. His teachings focused on creating ethical models of family and public interaction, and setting educational standards. Confucius recognized an opportunity, and an obligation, to reinforce the societal values of compassion and tradition. His social philosophy was based primarily on the principle of "ren" or "loving others" while exercising self-discipline. He believed that *ren* could be put into action using the Golden Rule: "What you do not wish for yourself, do not do to others." He attempted to realign humanity as his ancestors of the Third Root Race had done, which was to bring the Golden Rule into society. Confucius strove to resurrect the traditional values of benevolence, propriety and ritual in Chinese society. Convinced that his teachings had not made a significant impact on Chinese culture, Confucius died on November 21, 479 BCE in Qufu, China, a year after losing his son, Tzu-lu, in battle. He died in 479 BCE. Confucianism later became the official imperial philosophy of China, and was extremely influential during the Han, Tang and Song dynasties. Confucius is credited with writing and editing some of the most influential traditional Chinese classics. Today, he is widely considered one of the most influential teachers in Chinese history.[2]

The Four Noble Truths and Eightfold Path of Buddha

For most Tibetan Buddhists, Padmasambhava is regarded as a second Buddha. When he was eight years old, he appeared on a lotus flower in the middle of Lake Dhanakosha in Oddiyana, a place probably in the border of Afghanistan and Pakistan. Courtesy of Nicholas Roerich Gallery, NYC.

The Buddha has taught us that every living being has the same basic wish to be happy and to avoid suffering. Even newborn babies, animals, and insects have this wish. Since the beginning of time each of us have this desire for happiness, even during our sleep. Buddha said that humans spend their whole life working hard to fulfill this wish and throughout the course of evolution, humans continue to assign great energy towards improving their external conditions in search for happiness, seen as a solution to their many problems. Buddha says, "What has been the result?" Instead of wishes being fulfilled, human suffering has continued to increase while the experience of happiness and peace is decreasing.

Wisdom and Compassion

When difficult situations occur and things go wrong in life, humans have a tendency is to *regard the situation itself* as the problem, but in reality Buddha says, whatever problems we experience come from the

347

mind. If we were to respond to difficult situations with a positive or peaceful mind, they would not be problems for us— indeed we may even come to regard them as challenges or opportunities for growth and development.

Problems arise when we respond to difficulties with a negative state of mind. Therefore, if we want to be free from problems we must learn to control our mind.[3]

Buddha's Four Noble Truths

1. Noble Truth of Suffering

Chasing after the delights of the world, expecting them to bring lasting pleasure, always leads to disappointment. These things are all subject to the miseries of birth, old age, sickness and death. Even when you do find something pleasant how soon do you grow tired of it? None of these 'things' offer any real satisfaction or peace.

2. Noble Truth of the Cause of Suffering

Not being able to be content with what we have or who we are, our mind is filled with a greed or desire and suffering of all types automatically follows. This attitude of selfishness and greediness is the cause of our dissatisfaction, robbing us of our peace of mind.

3. Noble Truth of the End of Suffering

Seeing the suffering that comes from these attitudes we are liberated from our heart and all our suffering and dissatisfaction will come to an end. We shall experience a happiness that is far greater than our ordinary pleasures and a peace that is beyond words.

4. Noble Truth of the Middle Path or the Nobel Eightfold Path

This path leads to the end of all suffering. If we avoid harming all other living beings, if we sharpen and focus our mind, and if we gain wisdom, each of us can reach perfect happiness, the end of all misery.

The way to end suffering is to follow the Noble Eightfold Path, namely:

Right Understanding

Right Thought

Right Speech

Right Action

Right Livelihood

Right Effort

Right Mindfulness

Right Concentration.[4]

Islam Is Born

Islam, a monotheistic religion, is articulated by the Qur'an, and considered by its believers, who are called Muslims, to be the precise 'word of God' as demonstrated in the teachings, and the humble and normative example of Muhammad (Mohammed). Regarded as the last prophet of God, Mohammed founded Islam c. 622 CE, with the migration from Mecca to Medina, considered the beginning of the Islamic calendar.

Muslims believe that God is one and incomparable and that the purpose of existence is to worship God. Muslims also believe that Islam is the complete and universal version of a primordial faith that was revealed many times before through prophets including Adam, Noah, Abraham, Moses, and Jesus. They maintain that the previous messages and revelations have been partially misinterpreted or altered over time. They consider the Arabic Qur'an to be the unaltered and final revelation of God, whom they call Allah.[5]

Nicholas Roerich (1874-1947) Nicholas Roerich Gallery, NYC.

Mohammed

Conference of Nicaea

The death of Jesus Christ and the subsequent sprouting of many dogmas associated with Christ was enigmatic in these early times. In 325 CE, the early Orthodox Church conducted the Conference of Nicaea, convened by the Roman Emperor Constantine I, in May of that year. This Council was the first ecumenical dispute held by the youthful Christian church. Many conclusions were subsequently written in stone, such as the establishment of the doctrine of the Holy Trinity, which we have discussed previously in the examination of Anthrogenesis, as the 'Three in One' or the 'Trinity' developed from the ancient 'love of humanity,' 'compassion for one another as asked by the Father,' the 'Golden Rule' and "the Lord's Prayer.' These axioms were the foundational principles that Zarathustra shared to the Sumerians, to Hebrews, and throughout the ancient world. This ancient Zoroastrian theme was solid, with subsequent Mosaic attributes and derivation, which satisfied the foundation that was deficient in the Roman Catholic Church canon.

The question now arises, did the Church realize the antiquity of the concept of the Trinity… and that it had been shared with humanity by our ancestors, the Lemurian and Atlantean Adepts and the Masters?

The 'Arian' credo of Jesus Christ occurred when 'Arius,' the Alexandrian priest, questioned the divinity of Jesus Christ. Arius pointed out that Jesus Christ had a mortal birth and beginning, unlike God, and yet he was called the 'Son of God' who was not co-eternal with the Father, nor of the same substance. Jesus Christ was created by the Father, from nothing, as an instrument for the creation of the world, and thus, inferior to God. The council deemed this Arian belief as sacrilege, thus resolving the early eruption in the Church and most probably when completed, the results were a decidedly smaller Biblical foundation for Christian churchgoers. Arius, who had been a Libyan priest and scholar, educated by the eminent Greek scholar, Presbyter, was also in agreement with his fellow Egyptian theologians, Lucian and Meletius, who were then considered heretics and removed from their ecumenical positions. Arius was later ordained as a Deacon by Peter I, the Patriarch of Alexandria from 300 to 311 CE.

Ultimately, the esoteric groups, such as the Essenes, Gnostics, Therapeutae and other secret circles went underground, protecting the treasure of the Ancient Wisdom, and guarding for posterity the true Biblical, Hebrew and Christian mystery wisdom in their sacred texts.[6, 7]

The Spiritual Hierarchy and World Goodwill

"In approaching the problems of humanity, it became clear that the World War, and by that I refer to both World Wars, that a greater issue was presented to the world, that required spiritual intervention. A rent was made in the astral plane, such that energies would be released to assist humanity in its dire response to the evil that had been accumulating within the planet's etheric-physical vehicle. The events that began in 1914 that carried over to the next war was a burden humanity could not resolve on its own. The Spiritual Hierarchy has been attuned to the needs and status of humanity since this time, perhaps even more so than ever, because this energy, while allowing for humanity to become more spiritually stimulated, it can increase the intensity of the astral-emotional plane, causing humanity to be over stimulated with the sudden inflow of a new form of astral energy."

Nicholas Roerich (1874-1947),

Saint Francis of Assisi

"This is the time of opportunity for aspirants to the spiritual path to take charge and move forward along with this energy that is now available. Master D.K. has said that promotion of World Goodwill is so important, because in so doing, every nation may have its group of men and women dedicated to the establishing of right human relations. Humanity has so many problems which require the help of able aspirants and devotees, who will work for peace, education for all the children on the planet, support for the mothers and children of the world, right relations with finance and business, advancement in the social sciences and psychology, the development of right relations between the countries of the world, establishing the schools of science, the solution of world poverty and starvation and the development of the new world religion."[8]

Spiritual Effects of the World Wars

"The World War marked a climax in the history of mankind, and its subjective effect was far more potent than has hitherto been grasped. Through the power of prolonged sound, carried forward as a great experiment on the battlefields all over the world during a period of four years (1914-1918), and through the intense emotional strain of the entire planetary populace, the web of etheric matter, called the "Veil of the Temple," which separates the physical and astral planes was rent or torn asunder, and the amazing process of unifying the two worlds of physical plane living and of astral plane experience was begun and is now slowly going on. It will be obvious, therefore, that this must bring about vast changes and alterations in the human consciousness. Whilst it will usher in the age of understanding, of brotherhood and of illumination, it will also bring about states of reaction and the letting loose of psychic forces which today menace the uncontrolled and ignorant, and warrant the sounding of a note of warning and of caution."[9]

Approach by the Masters of Wisdom

"It has been known for a long time by mystics of all the world religions and by esoteric students everywhere, that certain members of the planetary Hierarchy are approaching closer to the earth at this time. The thought, or the mental attention, of the Christ and of certain of His great disciples, the Masters of the Wisdom, is directed or focused at this time on human affairs, and that some of Them are also preparing to break Their long silence and may appear later among men. This necessarily has a potent effect, first of all upon Their disciples and on those who are attuned to and synchronized with Their Minds, and secondly, it should be remembered that the energy which flows through these focal points of the Divine Will, will have a dual effect and be destructive as well as constructive, according to the quality of the bodies which react to it. Different types of people respond distinctively to any inflow of energy, and a tremendous psychic stimulation is at this time going on, with results both divinely beneficent and sadly destructive. It might be added that certain astrological relationships between the constellations are releasing new types of force which are playing through our Solar System and on to our planet, and thereby, making possible developments hitherto frustrated in expression, and bringing about the demonstration of latent powers and the manifestation of new knowledge."[10]

Master Morya by unknown artist

Creation of the United Nations

"World Peace is a task for all the nations of our planet. The United Nations is an international organization founded in 1945. After the World War, the Charter of the United Nations was signed on June 26, 1945, in San Francisco, at the conclusion of the United Nations Conference on International Organization, and came into force on October 24, 1945. The Statute of the International Court of Justice is an integral part of the Charter. It is currently made up of 193 Member States. The mission and work of the United Nations are guided by the purposes and principles contained in its founding Charter.

The Preamble incorporates many of the lessons humanity embodied through the World War and is as follows:

> To save succeeding generations from the scourge of war, which twice in our lifetime has brought untold sorrow to mankind, and

> To reaffirm faith in fundamental human rights, in the dignity and worth of the human person, in the equal rights of men and women and of nations large and small, and

> To establish conditions under which justice and respect for the obligations arising from treaties and other sources of international law can be maintained, and

> To promote social progress and better standards of life in larger freedom,

> To practice tolerance and live together in peace with one another as good neighbours, and

> To unite our strength to maintain international peace and security, and

> To ensure, by the acceptance of principles and the institution of methods, that armed force shall not be used, save in the common interest, and

> To employ international machinery for the promotion of the economic and social advancement of all peoples.

Accordingly, our respective Governments, through representatives assembled in the city of San Francisco, who have exhibited their full powers found to be in good and due form, have agreed to the present Charter of the United Nations and do hereby establish an international organization to be known as the United Nations."[11, 12]

Dwapara Yuga Transmutation

It is the Great Circle of Rebirth, D. K., the Tibetan, has said, that we reincarnate and come full circle around the great mandala of Rebirth.

At the onset, the human character is quite unevolved and self-driven prior to the First Initiation, the Birth of Water, then to the Second Initiation, the Birth of the Heart, then to the Third Initiation; within which the Soul envelops the Personality and the aspirant serves the Ashram and Master on the Higher planes of endeavor. So, this spiritual unfolding process goes on with all beings in the Universe.[13]

Humanity commenced from the ancient Fourth Root Race prototypes and have continued to migrate throughout the planet. The first sub race of the Aryans was the Peruvian Incas and the ancient name given to the creative gods in Peruvian theology and their true origins are unknown; "The Incas, seven in number have re-peopled the Earth after the Deluge," and as in Egypt, India and Chaldea, the Kings came to prepare humanity for the next race; they were Adepts or priests of the Ancient Wisdom. The origins of the first sub race were described as 'moon colored' and created from spiritually evolved souls from Atlantis, by the Vaivasvatu Manu.

The seeds of the Fifth root race materialized about 7 to 8 million years ago, with the Satya Yuga of the Fifth race, commencing around 4.5 million years ago, as Atlantis was concluding its Kali Yuga. The Aryan sub races include Hindu, Arabian, Persian, Celts, Teutonic, Austral-American and the 7th- the *New Great Cataclysm Survivors*,' bringing with them wisdom and intuition with psychic vision and astral powers, from the advancements made in Atlantis. The Aryan Root Race humans became a distinct root race about one million years ago, in Central Asia and was followed by the European sub race, originating about 9,000 years ago, with vast expansion and evolution in physical ingenuity. This Kali Yuga of our fifth race began in 500 CE.

As planetary consciousness continues to evolve, people will become more aware of the power of consciousness. They will understand that consciousness precedes energy and that through 'right use' of the mental body, and aspiring to the Soul, they can direct energy to accomplish lofty, noble acts for humanity. This understanding will be the hallmark of the next Treta Yuga, or 'The Age of Mental Power,' which will begin in 4100 CE, with the current Dwapara Yuga continuing for another c. 2,080 years.[14, 15]

The Balance of Mind and Intuition

Ultimately, the Aryan Root Race will have a separation analogous to the Lemurians and Atlanteans in the next 20,000 years, when the goal of spirituality will once again be challenged by the power of materialism. As this Fifth Race evolves in the final thousands of years, the aspirant must remember to maintain the balance of Mind and Intuition, as there will be a propensity towards the psychic side only. Humanity must acknowledge the expanse of the senses and use the mind fully, the integration of the Soul with the personality vehicle. The 'Pair of Opposites' between these sides will see some balance in humanity's world, with evolution bringing about resolution of the issues. As is the paradigm of each final root race, the Adepts move in one path and the 'Sons of Darkness' in the other direction, with a probable termination by earthly fires, possibly volcanoes and flooding.[16]

On the Path of Return, during the Third Initiation, the 'Third Eye' endows the Aspirant with an expansion in spiritual vision, among other spiritual attributes. The human consciousness has always aspired to goodwill and it must be sought out, exercised by the imagination and developed in thought and deed, keeping that loving eye at work, in the dynamic of relationships in our world and practice in life. 'Love in Action' is the mainstay of the Masters and our legacy on the Path of Service through the completion of the Third Initiation and beyond. The Light of the Mind endows the Aspirant to Discipleship an expansion in spiritual vision, among other spiritual attributes.[17]

Since the commencement of the Aryan race, the European races have been steadily rising following the downfall of the Roman Empire, and will continue in this way, with several smaller physical body types across the next 6,000 to 8,000 years. A European natural catastrophe follows a swift decline in about 16,000 years, at which time the British Isles, most of France, Holland, part of Spain, and much of Italy will sustain a submersion, preceded by premonitory signs, such as slow collapsing of the coast with major earthquakes.[18, 19, 20, 21]

Pixabay

The Indigo Children, the Star Children

The consciousness of the upcoming Race, in conjunction with Treta Yuga, will be the aspiration of the Soul combined with spiritual energy through the mental body already appearing as seedlings of amazement in intuition and concentration. In her book, *Children of the New Millennium*, Dr. P. M. H. Atwater reports that these child wizards have reportedly been observed with qualities measured as increases in nonverbal intelligence quotient (IQ) scoring, between '24 to 26 points,' with descriptions including assertion, positive self-esteem, a tendency towards logic and an expansive mental body, and these children are observed worldwide.

So, the mind works together with the Soul to accomplish lofty, noble acts for humanity from these first-players of the forthcoming marvelous Root race called the 'Star Children.' By that I mean individuals with higher mental gifts observed in childhood and possibly misunderstood in those early years. These children and young adults have an innate blend of intuition and intellect, a sense of wanting to assist humanity in various settings and themes, including healing, education, arts and sciences. These individuals may establish the new education and the new religion, which seems to be on the brink of creation, in the years to come.

Future Race Qualities

In the Americas, the Sixth Root Race is now evolving and souls are being attracted for incarnation to this developing race, which ought to be established by the end of this Yuga. So it is, with the Four Yugas, interwoven within the philosophy of Theosophy, Hinduism and Buddhism, for starters—the upcoming Root Race has its seeds in the previous race—beginning mid-cycle at about 4.5 million years into the Race, then blooming into development by the last few sub-races. The lands of the current Root Race will be destroyed by fire—volcanoes, earthquakes, and subduction or flooding. It is thought that the Indo-American or Aryan Root race lands will end in flooding, but, of course, the Masters of the Spiritual Hierarchy, those Trans-Himalayan Adepts, along with the Logos and Sanat Kumara—the Lord of the World, will ultimately cause an appropriate climax to the race.

At the close of the Treta Yuga, the Sixth Root Race inception is activated and humanity slowly reverts back to the attribute of physicality, noted in the first three early Root Races, but with the additional increase in wisdom, etheric vision and clairvoyance, extrasensory perceptions, and other extraordinary qualities such as telekinesis, telepathy, and far-sighted, visionary, perceptive and prognostic qualities. It has been theorized that the Atlanteans had 360 senses—like the 360° of the circle. The future holds some amazing possibilities.

Hermaphroditism will again return, becoming more cultured with children being produced by Kriya Shakti—using the power of thought to manifest things in the physical plane—by use of the imagination and will, during the Sixth Race, and with active comprehension in the Seventh Race. Humans recapitulate back to the fleshy, delicately pliable composition, and by Seventh Root Race, the physical sheath will once more become transparent. The human physical height and size reduces dramatically but meanwhile intelligence, spirituality and heightened cognitive functions advance, with remarkable expansion. These last two races, the Sixth and the Seventh, will generate our human intuition beyond our current understanding, emanating first from the senses, and later from the advanced brain and cognitive principles. The pineal gland will function again in the distant future, as the organ of the seventh and highest sense.[22, 23]

The Pushkara

The Pushkara is the term used for the Seventh Root Race, named for an island that is to emerge in the Pacific Ocean as a result of subduction, flooding and general geophysical changes. The Aryan—Indo American race—will continue to develop extraordinary sensory powers, within the cognitive structures, as well as a considerable range of extra-sensory mechanisms, along with pure refinement of the ethereal body, as described in the previous section of 'Future Race Qualities.' Humanity returns to its beginnings, as is the case, spelled out in precession and the Four Yugas, synonymous with the physical underpinnings which initially appeared in the First Root Race. All kingdoms of life on our planet will continue in kind, throughout the end of the Seventh Round.[24, 25]

Monadic Consciousness

Some additional clarity is important in order to understand Theosophical principles, even if we have mentioned this before. It's important to fully comprehend the system. The impulses of monadic consciousness will evolve to higher planes of endeavor in the seven-fold nature of the chain of planets, with Seven Incarnations of each Root Race, on each planet and Seven Monadic chapters through Earth; each are a Round, each with a new Root Race, moving through the ethers, commencing in the astral-ethereal and finishing in a physical state with a sense of 'compassionate brotherhood'—a lovely intrinsic component we inherited from the Lemurians. In the beginning of the Moon Chain, our ancestral Monads evolved the previous (Third Round) embodiment of Earth and our present human- spiritual Monads were animal monads. The ape souls were the last group to be brought in before the entrance process for incoming beings was halted, and the ape's destiny incorporates the abilities of low functioning human beings, coming to fruition before the end of this round, and repeated again in the Fifth Round. This does not mean that ape bodies will evolve into human bodies, but that the

Monads now in ape bodies will incarnate into bodies available in the ape-human realm.[26, 27]

Advancement of the Human Monads

By the end of the Seventh Round of the Earth Chain, Theosophical Masters and their authors predict that our lower human monads will have become higher Human or Manasaputric Monads and will be the lowest in the Dhyani-Chohanic kingdoms on the next Earth Chain embodiment. In the future Manvantaras, these Monads will be spiritual, then finally divine Monads. They will have concluded the journey of evolution from unselfconscious 'Spark of the Monad' to self-consciousness. The Monad evolves spiritually through Planetary Rounds, both physically and psychically. To review, a Planetary Round comprises one chain of the Divine Monad, concluding Seven Globes, with each round evolving proliferating materialism; similar to the evolution of humanity through the Races. Monads accomplish seven mystical elements; including Fire, Air, Water, Earth, with the next higher stage repeating and expanding the enlightenment of the Monad. The Divine Monads of the distant future will continue the parallel evolutionary pilgrimages on other planetary chains, in other Solar Systems and in other galaxies.[28, 29]

The Ancient of Days, courtesy of William Blake (1757-1827)
Whitworth Art Gallery, The University of Manchester,
The Bridgeman Art Library, UK

Enduring Guidance by the Great White Lodge on Sirius

Our world is governed by the Spiritual Hierarchy of Masters, the Great Masters of the White Lodge, whose physical location is thought to be in the constellation of Sirius. They have guided and directed humanity from the beginning of time as we know it. Isis and Osiris were connected to this star system, and guided Egypt more than 75,000 years ago, before the zodiac and stars were painted on the ceiling in the Temple at Dendera. These Great Beings will continue, as always, to guide humanity through the ages to come.[30, 31]

Janet Hizar Hansford

Anthrogenesis

Author's Final Thoughts...

The illumination of knowledge is the mission of Anthrogenesis. The proposition to examine humanity's ancient beginnings through origins, spirituality and mythology was conceptualized through the spirit and vision of our ancestors.

Needless to say, I have been profoundly affected in the compiling of the Earth's history and peoples in the story of Anthrogenesis. Collecting as I have through the years, I never suspected that the many scraps of paper, notes, folders and thousands of books would coalesce to form such an expansive vision of our collective past.

Connected to every single atom and particle from this Big Bang onward, man is destined to emerge as a brilliant, loving and compassionate species, as foretold by the great prophets and seers of the past. We, as a human race, have a great destiny. Although the journey's long and at times traumatic, defying the odds of survival; we have bravely persevered and triumphed in creating civilizations of great magnificence, spreading out, embracing life, and yes, contracting in when cataclysms ground us to dust and erased almost all trace of our earthly presence. Only to birth anew, the seed of human life grows ever again in many soils and blooms with unfailing tenacity evolving the Great Plan and the impossibly amazing design of the Great Architect of Life.

Humanity's journey was laced together by inclusion of geological records from mainstream science, drawing evidence from fossils, rocks and archeological remnants of earlier times to build a bedrock of the book. Amazement was incited by the dawn of the Denisovans in remote locations, correlating a conceivable antiquity with the ancient Truth. Heavy reliance upon the bright beacon of Light supplied by Theosophy provided the spiritual record, revealing the Ancient Wisdom of spiritual teachers, avatars, wise guardians and heroes. Inclusion of the Big Bang theory seemed rudimentary, especially in view of underwritten aspects of expansion and condensation of the universe found in Vedic principles.

Myth, lore, and legend let us see through the eyes of past cultures and help us piece together history from the perspective of the mythopoeic mind; lost now in pace and pedantry of materialism, technology and fumes of fossil fuels and pollution. The notion that our past is not what we were told in education is an interesting contradiction. Brave new explorers and researchers have brought forward a different view for our planet. Bucking the entrenched bastions of academia, and geo-political elite that create stories to fit their global agenda, the Truth always finds its way past the corridors of discredited breakthroughs and pundits.

Our exploration of humanity has led us through many cultures as we travelled to retrieve humanity's voyage.

In Anthrogenesis, we have observed that human physical structure has changed and evolved over multi-millions of years, and most dramatically during the last three root races, especially inclusive of the current Aryan Root race. The sacred Vedas and the the Four Yugas elucidate a time when we began with massive, ovoid bodies, initially cloaked in etheric matter, and slowly over millennia we developed into hermaphrodydes. By mid to late Lemuria, in the Third Root Race, high spirituality was aided by the use of the pineal gland and a belief system based on Love, the Golden Rule and the Lord's Prayer. The Lemurians were both massive stature and in their abundance of love and goodwill.

Briefly reviewing the Olmec history, we observe an advanced people with sophisticated ceremony and ritual pointing to ancient roots, and too, possible migration from the Oceania. Did they migrate from the volcanic cataclysms that beset the great civilization of Mu? Hawaii, Tonga or even Polynesia may have been part of ancient Lemuria's extensive chain of islands. Survivors would have easily achieved passage to a remnant island such as Easter Island, thought to be substantially larger in that epoch; perhaps building their likenesses in massive stone statues!

In Anthrogenesis the inclusion of thought-provoking materials surrounding manuscripts, culture and social history offer a stalwart foundation for knowledge. Relying on the ancient works of Plato, Aristotle, Pythagoras, and many others, we have also added the principles of Hermetic philosophy, mathematics and physics, so strongly incorporated by ancients into both physical and spiritual architecture over the millennia.

Continents came and went; yet the spark of human life always remained lit. Are we now ready to continue forward with this knowledge? The rhythmic spiraling to the embodiment of our true spiritual potential naturally bequests a high sacredness to this very human odyssey-Anthrogenesis.

Appendices

Appendix I – Earth Age Estimation

So far scientists have not found the perfect method of dating Earth because Earth's oldest rocks have been recycled and destroyed by the process of plate tectonics. If there are any of Earth's primordial rocks left in their original state, they have not yet been found. Nevertheless, scientists have been able to determine the probable age of the Solar System and to calculate an age for the Earth by assuming that the Earth and the rest of the solid bodies in the Solar System formed at the same time, and therefore are of the same age.

http://pubs.usgs.gov/gip/geotime/age.html

Estimating Earth's age can be undertaken by using Earth and meteorites as part of the same evolving system, in which the composition of lead is measured against radioactive components. These RD techniques are firmly grounded in physics and are used to measure the most recent time that the rock being dated was either melted or disturbed enough to re-homogenize its radioactive elements.

http://www.arxiv.org/abs/1210.8255

Appendix II – Radiometric Dating Methods

Researchers use various methods to date the Solar System, age of rocks on the Earth and time-frames of the Earth. The general term for this is Radiometric Dating (RD).

A.1 Stratigraphy

Along with RD dating methods, scientists use stratigraphy; which is the study of rock, its layers, types of rock, especially sedimentary and volcanic rocks and fossil evidence in the rocks.

http://archaeology.about.com/od/sterms/g/stratigraphy.htm

A.2 Half-Lives in Radioactivity and Chemical Elements

RD was originally discovered by Bertram Boltwood in 1907, with his integration of Ernest Rutherford's findings of half-lives in radioactivity, proving that chemicals change and separate into smaller particles. Rutherford won the 1908 Nobel Prize in Chemistry for this exact process, maintaining ongoing studies of the atom, and later being credited as the first to 'split the atom' while a professor at Cambridge University.

http://hyperphysics.phy-astr.gsu.edu/hbase/nuclear/halfli2.html

A.3 Uranium and Lead Isotope Dating

In 1956, a geochemist named Clair Cameron Patterson and his colleague, George Tilton, developed the RD method of uranium-lead into the lead-lead dating method. Additionally, he used lead isotopes (elements) from the Diablo Canyon meteorite to date Earth's age (called geochronology) at 4.55 billon years, still the current time recognized today. Lead-isotope dating is quite effective in determining ages of planetoids, or smaller objects in our Solar System. Uranium-lead dating, (U–Pb) however, is the oldest and most reliable form of RD.

http://www.berkeley.edu/news/media/releases/2004/09/16_uranium. shtml

A.4 Radio Carbon Dating

Conceived by Willard Libby in 1949, who received the 1960 Nobel Prize in Chemistry for this creation, Carbon 14 dating (14C) deciphers the age of organic materials using radioactive elements of carbon. Essentially, the older the sample is, the less Carbon 14 will be observed, due to the half-life of the 14C, when half of the sample is decayed, which can vary to almost 6,000 years or even more.

http://www.c14dating.com/int.html

A.5 Potassium-argon Dating

Potassium-argon dating or K–Ar dating is another RD method used to date mineral elements in ancient pottery, clay, volcanic elements, crystals and earth or soil findings with iron, or other metal components.

http://physics.info/half-life/

Appendix III – Geologic Time Scale

UCB has an excellent link. California University at Berkeley has an online tour of the GTS, sponsored by the National Science Foundation. For a pleasant visual tour, check it out at:

www.ucmp.berkeley.edu/education/explorations/tours/geotime/index.html

Appendix IV – Global Boundary Stratotype Section

In 1977, the Global Boundary Stratotype Section and Point (GSSP), an international institution that establishes agreement on the reference point of stratigraphic sections, (which define lower boundary stages on the GTS), began a stage to complete the defining effort. In 2012, 64 out of the 101 stages requiring GSSP were completed.

Author's Note: This change in dating the Earth posed an interesting position for me, since I had been accumulating geological and other related scientific data for some years. I am hopeful to now have the proper times which have been rigorously reviewed by my editor and myself!

http://www.stratigraphy.org/index.php/ics-gssps

Appendix V – Acasta Gneiss Rock Formation

Acasta Gneiss took shape from ~4 to ~2.5 Ga and is the oldest intact rock formation on the planet. It was formed in what is now the Northwest Territories in Northern Canada, bordered by the Arctic Ocean and the Beaufort Sea, Nunavut to the east, the Yukon Territory to the west, and British Columbia, Alberta, and Saskatchewan to the north.

http://geology.com/canada/northwest-territories.shtml

Appendix VI – Isua Greenstone Belt

The Isua Greenstone Belt is in Greenland. It's a regional rock with an overall age range of ~3.82–~3.85 Ga and is representative of the global terrestrial processes at ~3.8 Ga, the most ancient rock on Earth.

http://home.earthlink.net/~douglaspage/id87.html

Appendix VII – Continent: Vaalbara

Vaalbara, as ancient as ~3.6 Ga, is identified from the evidence of the Yilgarn Craton, Western Australia and the worldwide Archean greenstone belts that were subsequently spread out across Gondwana and Laurasia.

Note: A craton is described as the stable portion of the continental crust from regions that are more geologically active that acts as a shield.

http://basementgeographer.com/ur-the-oldest-continent/

Appendix VIII – Continent: Ur

Ur formed at ~3 Ga ago, a vast, solitary Supercontinent, yet still smaller than Australia.

http://endeavors.unc.edu/spr97/ur.html

http://www.ucmp.berkeley.edu/precambrian/archean_hadean.php

Appendix IX – Continent: Kenorland

Kenorland is now roughly situated in the Arctic around the current North Pole, forming at ~2.7 Ga, with archaic continental shields and a new continental crust, which evolved with protracted tectonic magma plume rifting a massive extrusion of the mantle that caused pluming, caused by a hotspot within igneous areas, and from ~2.48 to ~2.45 Ga, contributed to the Proterozoic glacial events, from ~2.45 to ~2.22 Ga. The final breakup occurred ~2.1 Ga.

http://www.sciencedirect.com/science/article/pii/S1674987114000620

http://www.newgeology.us/presentation23.html

Appendix X – Continent: Arctica

Arctica formed at ~2.5 Ga, beginning in the early Proterozoic Era and consisting of both Canadian and Siberian shields. At ~2.45 Ga, Arctica was part of the major Supercontinent, Kenorland. At ~2.1 Ga, Kenorland shattered the Arctican craton; part of the continent Columbia-

Nena along with Baltica and Eastern Antarctica. Arctica is now roughly situated in the Arctic around the current North Pole.

http://www.jstor.org/stable/30068065

Rogers, John J. W. "A History of Continents in the past Three Billion Years." The Journal of Geology J GEOL 104.1 (1996): 91-107. Web.

Appendix XI – Stromatolites

Stromatolites, created from piles of plant-like (photosynthetic) bacteria emerged as Earth's first form of life, during the Archean Eon, from ~4.0 to ~2.5 Ga, when Earth's atmosphere was composed of toxic gases, which would be unbreathable by current living organisms. The beauty of the stromatolites is that because they were photosynthetic, their massive colonies released oxygen into our atmosphere, preparing the atmosphere for oxygen-breathing life in Earth's future. They survive today in small quantities at Shark Bay, Australia.

http://www.ucmp.berkeley.edu/precambrian/archean_hadean.php

Appendix XII – The Proterozoic Eon

During the Proterozoic Era (from ~2.5 Ga to ~542 Mya), oxygen began amassing with the earliest multi-cellular life evolving on Earth. They left their fingerprint on rocks deposited during the Proterozoic. The stromatolites continued to diversify and colonize in shallow waters of the Proterozoic Eon oceans and single-celled microorganisms, referred to as extremophiles, lived in severe habitats where water was very hot and extremely salty.

http://www.ucmp.berkeley.edu/precambrian/proterozoic.php

Appendix XIII – Continent: Columbia-Nena

Columbia-Nena was a major Supercontinent, ~2.1–~1.8 Ga, completed by global impact events, consisted of the rock remnants of Laurentia, Baltica, Ukrainian Shield, Amazonian Shield, Australia; perhaps Siberia, North China, and Kalaharia. Columbia-Nena contained Laurentia from ~1.8 to ~1.5 Ga.

http://js.ing.uni.wroc.pl/teksty/seminar/3.pdf

Rogers, John J.w., and M. Santosh. "Configuration of Columbia, a Mesoproterozoic Supercontinent." Gondwana Research 5.1 (2002): 5-22. Web.

Appendix XIV – Continent: Atlantica

Atlantica is an ancient continent that formed at ~2 Ga, from the stable portion of the continental crust, located in what is now West Africa and Eastern South America. Atlantica formed simultaneously with Columbia-Nena at ~1.9 Ga from Archaean cratons, including Amazonia, in present day South America, and the Congo, West Africa and North Africa Cratons in Africa.

Rogers, John J. W. "A History of Continents in the past Three Billion Years." The Journal of Geology J GEOL 104.1 (1996): 91-107. Web

Appendix XV – End of the Proterozoic Eon

By the end of the Proterozoic Eon, cells with a nucleus developed, being progenitors of all modern life. One of the first extinctions occurred when oxygen amassed in the atmosphere, causing bacteria to die, required for life in the Archean. The Proterozoic experienced two Ice Ages from ~ 2.4 to ~ 2.1 Ga, when atmospheric constituents changed and during 'Snowball Earth'; from 850 to 600 Mya, when polar ice became a kilometer deep, covered areas extending to the equator. The Vendian Period, from ~650 to ~544 Mya, produced sponges and multi-celled animals during Supercontinent Rodinia.

http://www.eoearth.org/view/article/155427/

Appendix XVI – Continent: Rodinia

Supercontinent Rodinia existed from ~1.1 Ga to ~750 Mya, comprising the independent continent, Laurentia, at ~1.5 Ga. Rodinia, at ~2.5 to ~1.6 Ga, was formed from Arctica joining with continents Atlantica and Columbia-Nena at ~1 Ga. Rodinia rifted apart into three continents at ~750 Mya; Proto-Laurasia, the continental Congo cratons, and Proto-Gondwana.

http://paleobiology.si.edu/geotime/main/htmlversion/proterozoic1.html

Appendix XVII – Continent: Pannotia-Vendian

The continent of Pannotia-Vendian occurred from ~650 to ~500 Mya. At ~600 Mya, Laurentia was part of the major Supercontinent Pannotia-Vendian.
http://io9.com/5744636/a-geological-history-of-supercontinents-on-planet-earth

Appendix XVIII – Continent: Laurasia

Laurasia occurred from ~510 to ~200 Mya, a large Supercontinent in the northern hemisphere and also an independent continent north of Gondwana during the Cambrian, from ~542 to ~488.3 Mya. Laurasia began to break up ~200 Mya, consisting of the modern day continents of North America, Europe and Asia.
https://www.uwgb.edu/dutchs/EarthSC102Notes/102PTEarthHist.htm

Appendix XIX – Continent: Laurentia

Laurentia was salvaged, ultimately moving north of Gondwana to include land in today's continents of the Northern Hemisphere, i.e. the North American continent, Baltica, Siberia, Kazakhstania, and the North China and East China cratons. Laurentia was part of the minor Supercontinent Proto-Laurasia at ~750 Mya. Proto-Laurasia rotated southward toward the South Pole while Proto-Gondwana rotated counterclockwise and the Congo craton came between Proto-Gondwana and Proto-Laurasia at ~600 Mya, forming Pannotia-Vendian.

Laurentia began shrinking in the Ordovician, from ~488 to ~443 Mya, and Baltica got bigger with Laurentia and Baltica colliding during the Devonian, from ~416 to ~359 Mya, forming the minor Supercontinent Euramerica.
http://palaeos.com/earth/paleogeography/laurentia.htm

Appendix XX – The Paleozoic Era

The Paleozoic Era lasted from ~544 to ~245 Mya including the Periods: the Cambrian, from ~542 to ~488 Mya, the Ordovician, from ~488 to ~443 Mya, the Silurian, from ~443 to ~416 Mya, the Devonian from ~416 to ~359 Mya and the Carboniferous, from ~359 to ~299 Mya. The Cambrian Period produced an explosion of life forms, coinciding with the first appearance of animals with external skeletons, including the first shellfish, primitive fish, trilobites, corals and mollusks, later ending in a mass extinction.

http://www.ucmp.berkeley.edu/exhibit/histgeoscale.html

Appendix XXI – The Ordovician Period

The Ordovician period, from ~488 to ~443 Mya, generated the first insects and first water bearing plants with a stem, which are the oldest known plants. Next, the Silurian Period ensued from ~443 to ~416 Mya, yielding the first amphibians, sharks, bony fish, squid-like creatures, spiders and many different species of fish. The Devonian, from ~416 to ~359 Mya, introduced the first trees and forests and the first tetrapod, the land-living vertebrate.

http://www.ucmp.berkeley.edu/ordovician/ordovician.php

Appendix XXII – The Carboniferous Period

The Carboniferous Period followed the Devonian Period from ~359 to ~299 Mya and amassed widespread coal swamps, the first reptiles and winged insects.

http://www.geocraft.com/WVFossils/Carboniferous_climate.html

Appendix XXIII – The Permian Period

The rocks deposited during the Phanerozoic Eon, from ~542 Mya to the present, contain evidence of fossilized hard body parts of that current life. A few addition periods occurred here, including the Permian Period, from ~299 to ~251 Mya; with sail-back reptiles and abundant amphibians, forming the continent of Pangea.

http://www.ucmp.berkeley.edu/permian/permian.php

Appendix XXIV – Continent: Pangaea

Supercontinent Pangaea existed from ~300 to ~210 Mya, between the close of the Paleozoic and start of the Mesozoic. Early in the Permian Period (~300 Mya), Pangaea became the first transformed Supercontinent, surrounded by Super Ocean, Panthalassa. Pangea later began to break apart at ~100 Mya, forming with supercontinents Laurasia and Gondwana, with most of the land masses in the Southern Hemisphere, tallying with the 'Great Dying' mass extinction.

http://www.livescience.com/38218-facts-about-pangaea.html

Appendix XXV – Tethys Ocean

The long direction of the Tethys, a trending ocean dating roughly from ~250 to ~50 Mya, separated Gondwana from Laurasia, running east to west like the Atlantic and Pacific Oceans. It allowed currents to flow around the Earth, causing the Earth's climate to be very different.

http://palacos.com/earth/paleogeography/tethys.htm

Appendix XXVI – Continent: Gondwana

Gondwana (Gondwanaland) occurred from ~510 to ~180 Mya, beginning in the Late Proterozoic Period, from ~1 Ga to ~542 Mya. Supercontinent Gondwana observed the 'Cambrian Explosion' of life. Gondwana began to break up at ~200 Mya and the 'K-T Mass Extinction', later occurred ~65 Mya, obliterated all life, along with the majority of dinosaurs and land mammals. Comprising today's Southern Hemisphere, Gondwana reunited, gathering near the Antarctic Circle with continents Antarctica, South America, Africa, Madagascar, and Australia. The remnants of Gondwana also encompass the Arabian Peninsula and the Indian Subcontinent, now moved entirely into the Northern Hemisphere

http://www.parks.tas.gov.au/file.aspx?id=6555

Appendix XXVII – The Mesozoic Era

The Mesozoic Era from ~251 to ~65 Mya, includes several periods, the Triassic, from ~251 to ~199 Mya, with the first mammals, dinosaurs, frogs, turtles, and crocodyloformes- crocodilians and the Jurassic, between ~199 to ~145 Mya, eliciting abundant dinosaurs and the first birds.
http://www.ucmp.berkeley.edu/mesozoic/mesozoic.php

Appendix XXVIII – The Cretaceous Period

The Cretaceous Period, from ~145 to ~65 Mya produced the first flowering plants and snakes ending with the K-T mass extinction, which killed the dinosaurs and most species of life.
http://www.ucmp.berkeley.edu/mesozoic/cretaceous/cretaceous.php

Appendix XXIX – The Cenozoic Era

The Cenozoic Era was comprised of three periods; the Paleogene; ~65 to ~23 Mya, the Neogene; ~23 to ~2.5 Mya and the Quaternary, from ~2.5 Mya to present day. During the Paleogene at Kara-Kul, eastern Tajikistan, close to the Afghan border, a lake was formed from a meteorite impact ~25 million years ago, leaving a crater with a 28 mile rim diameter.
http://www.ucmp.berkeley.edu/cenozoic/cenozoic.php
Generally, the Cenozoic saw *hominin Australopithecus* appear on the scene along with the first sheep, cattle, modern whales, bears, apes, monkeys, dogs, rats and modern birds. Also in this category are Homo sapiens, mammoths, mastodons and saber-toothed cats.
http://anthro.palomar.edu/hominid/australo_1.htm

Appendix XXX – The Paleogene Period

The Paleogene Period, from ~65 to ~23 Mya, produced the first deer, cats, pigs, tapirs, and rhinos. Also appearing were the elephants, horses, owls, shrews, hedgehogs, and rabbits. The Eocene, from ~55 to ~33 Mya, produced the oldest known fossils, containing the modern orders of mammals, during a brief period in the early Eocene and the Oligocene, at ~33 to ~23 Mya, with rock beds defining this period. The Grande Coupure (great break) intersperses this period with a notable extinction event, featuring replacement of European fauna with Asian fauna, except for endemic rodent and marsupial families.

http://www.fossils-facts-and-finds.com/paleogene_period.html

Appendix XXXI – The Pliocene Epoch

The Pliocene Epoch covers a period of time from ~5.3 to ~2.5 Mya, when the Earth was cooling after the warmer Miocene on our planet. As the grasslands expanded throughout the major continents, ice was accumulating at the poles, which would ultimately cause extinction of most species living there.

http://www.ucmp.berkeley.edu/tertiary/pliocene.php

Appendix XXXII – Ancient Biology

Archaic life constitutes the birth of eukaryotic cellular organisms, due to their importance in the evolution of life and inclusion of these lives in ancient oceanic realms. When primordial cellular life began, the relationships of early life on Earth were chemical cell processes that broke down molecules, releasing energy and include:

1) The chromalveolates are photosynthetic, single celled, with "hairy" flagellum and diatoms-present in marine plankton and golden algae,

2) The cryptomonas are fresh or marine water algae with high levels of chlorophyll and two unequal flagella and,

3) The alveolates supply cellular energy, have micro tubes and flagella with ancestors having been photosynthetic. The timetable of the origin of ocean life is difficult to determine with estimates at ~1.6 to ~2.1 billion years ago (Ga). Some ancient life forms are at ~1.65 Ga and the algae, Grypania, has been found as far back as ~2.2 Ga. Fossils that are clearly related to modern groups start appearing in water, around ~1.2 Ga, in the form of a red alga.

http://www.ucmp.berkeley.edu/plants/plantae.html

http://www.ucmp.berkeley.edu/phyla/phyla.html

http://autocww.colorado.edu/~blackmon/E64ContentFiles/AlgaeAndFungi/Algae.html

Appendix XXXIII – New World Hominids

In referencing New World hominids, it is important to note that teeth grouping, types of claws or nails, human body shape and a prehensile tail comprise the traits of *catarrhines*, considered to be more evolved than their *platyrrhini* cousins. A major split in the human lineage occurred between the infraorders *platyrrhini* and *catarrhini*. The *platyrrhine* monkeys are also known as New World monkeys since their geographical distribution is exclusively in Central and South America where they are the only primates found. The *catarrhines* include the Old World monkeys; monkeys found in Africa and Asia, Apes and Humans.

Morphologically and behaviorally the New World monkeys are quite variable. They have a general dental formula (incisors-I, are indicated first, canines-C, second, premolars- P, third, and finally molars- M, giving I – C:P:M. For example, the formula 2.1.2.3 for upper teeth indicates 2 incisors, 1 canine, 2 premolars, and 3 molars on one side of the upper mouth or '2.1.2.3') 2.1.2.3 or 2.1.3.3 but about half of them have lost a molar.

They (monkeys) also include the only clawed primates [(primate generally have flattened nails like humans)], the only nocturnal anthropoid [(having characteristics of a human being, usually in terms of shape or appearance or having characteristics of an ape)] and the only primates with prehensile tails (an animal that has adapted to be able to grasp or hold objects with the tail has a prehensile tail).

Dr. Hawks adds that evolutionary trends are happening in humanity with his recent comment that a "7% change in human DNA has occurred in the last 5,000 years."

John Hawks, Ph.D., 2009, email communicationhttp://anthro.palomar.edu/primate/prim_4.htm

http://johnhawks.net/weblog/fossils/afarensis/early_hominid_dental_change.html

Appendix XXXIV – The Monkeys, Apes and Hominins

Ancient hominins, as seen in fossils, lived alongside evolved *hominins* with societies of their own, but disappeared in the great Earth changes. Apes continue to maintain complex skeletal and muscular structures.

Humans continue with simplicity in design and a highly developed cerebrospinal system. Human most notable common ancestors are the macaques which are primitive *catarrhines* from the latest Eocene and Oligocene.

Cremo, Michael A. and Thompson, Richard L., 1993, *Forbidden Archeology: The Hidden History of the Human Race*, Bhaktivedanta Book Publishing

John Hawks, Ph.D., email communication, 2009. *Aegyptopithecus* fossils have been found primarily in modern-day Egypt. *Aegyptopithecus* is a crucial link between Eocene fossil and Miocene *hominoids*. *Aegyptopithecus* had an unusually small brain for a primate. As it is considered a common ancestor of old and new-world monkeys, or at least a close relative of one, it is considered by some to be evidence that large brained primates evolved separately in the Old and New World primates.

http://archaeologyinfo.com/aegyptopithecus/

Appendix XXXV – Splits in Old World Monkeys

Primate and *hominin* evolution, with its' many splits in Old World monkeys, says evolution wants to place primates and *tarsiidae* which are small nocturnal, arboreal primates, large round-eyed, a long tail, long fingers and toes tipped with soft disk-like pads, with anthropoids being the higher primates and apes. Currently these primates and *tarsiidae* are classified as prosimians, a primitive primate of a group of lemurs, lorises, bush babies, and tarsiers. The range of living prosimians is massive and while often described as primitive due to smaller brains that have cranial features common with early mammals, they have very specialized locomotor anatomy, dentitions and digestive systems. The nocturnal varieties are widespread in the Old World monkeys although diurnal prosimians are restricted to the island of Madagascar.

Tarsiidae can be related to anthropoids-in a class of their own position with no known bridge to New Age monkeys including *catarrhini* to *platyrrhine* to *aegyptopithecus* to macaques to *hominidea*. It has been theorized that humans and macaques share a common ancestry with *Aegyptopithecus*. Dr. John Hawks suggests the common ancestor of human and macaques are primitive *catarrhines* from Late Eocene and

Oligocene Periods and suggests that *Aegyptopithecus* is a relevant genera to study for possible similar genealogy.

Djebelemur, which lived around 50 million years ago, is a new and contentious find of a fossil similar to *tarsiidae* primates and due to its antiquity, the genetic models may need to be updated.

John Hawks, Ph.D., 2009, email communication

http://johnhawks.net/explainer/primates/primate-classification-phylogeny/

http://phys.org/news/2013-12-fossil-primate-history-strepsirrhines.html

Appendix XXXVI – Orangutans and Gibbons

In her book, *The First Human*, (2007) Ann Gibbons points out that after Darwin, Ernst Haeckel developed his theory wherein man evolved from the orangutans and gibbons and not the African apes, propagated in 1868. His theory, while brief in paleontology, started other researchers on the search for the oldest *hominin*. Haeckel was on the right track because we know that the other apes — chimp, bonobo, gorilla, orangutan, and gibbon- would not form a natural group that includes all the descendants of a common ancestor if humans were excluded. Humans share many traits with apes.

Gibbons, Ann, *The First Human*, First Anchor Books, 2007, www.anchorbooks.com, pg. 28-29.

http://evolution.berkeley.edu/evolibrary/article/evograms_07

Appendix XXXVII – Hominin Fossil Record

Supported by the field of evolutionary paleo-anthropology, the *hominin* fossil record of human evolution was expanded by paleo-anthropologists during exploration and excavations with a 2010 find by Lee Berger from the University of the Witwatersrand, and of a 1.98-million-year-old *hominin*, *Australopithecus sediba*, in a cave site, Malapa, South Africa. Many paleoanthropologists seem to see a connection between *A. africanus, genus Homo; H. erectus, Neanderthal*, and humans.

http://phys.org/news/2013-04-australopithecus-sediba-hominid-reveals-human.html

http://news.nationalgeographic.com/news/2013/11/131106-lee-berger-human-ancestor-fossil-excavation/

Appendix XXXVIII – Bat Creek Stone from Jerusalem

In 1889, the Bat Creek Stone was excavated from an undisturbed burial mound by the Smithsonian's Mound Survey project in Eastern Tennessee. The first impression by the lead researcher was the curious stone inscriptions were "beyond question, letters of the Cherokee alphabet. "Later, in the 1960s, Henriette Mertz and Corey Ayoob observed the inverted inscription, stating that it gave the impression of ancient Semitic script. Cyrus Gordon, a Semitic language scholar confirmed that it was "Paleo-Hebrew as old as 100 CE, due to the angles and type of commas used to divide the words. He reports that it said "for Judea, or for the Judeans." Later scholars continued examination of the scripting, most indicating a common Judean translation. In 1988, wood fragments found with the inscription were Carbon-14 dated to between 32 CE and 769 CE, which is consistent with Gordon's dating of the letters. At that time, it was thought that a few of the letters could be Cherokee in either orientation, and while the letters are not perfect as Paleo-Hebrew, the inscription matched Hebrew much better than Cherokee. In 2010, a Petrographic Analysis was conducted with the following results: "A new petrographic analysis of the stone by Scott Wolter and Richard Stehly of American Petrographic Services concludes:

1. Our geological findings are consistent with the Smithsonian Institute's field report written by John W. Emmert.

2. The complete lack of the orange-colored silty-clay residue in any of the characters of the inscription is consistent with many hundreds of years of weathering in a wet earth mound comprised of soil and "hard red clay."

3. The inscribed stone and all the other artifacts and remains found in the mound with it, can be no younger than when the bodies of the deceased were buried inside the mound. (Wolter and Stehly 2010) Archaeologists have yet to react to this new study."

Thomas (1890, Fig. 7). Image out of copyright, in public domain. Director of the Project, Cyrus Thomas, Thomas 1894: 391:4.

http://economics.sbs.ohio-state.edu/jhm/arch/batcrk.html

McCulloch, J. Huston, "John Emmert, Demon Rum, and Bat Creek: Excavations in the Smithsonian Archives," July 1987.

McCulloch, J. Huston, "The Bat Creek Inscription-Cherokee or Hebrew?" Tennessee Anthropologist 1988 (2), pp. 79-123. See also comment by Robert C. Mainfort, Jr. and Mary L. Kwas, TA 1991(1), pp. 1-19, reply by JHM TA Spring 1993, pp. 1-16, rejoinder by M&K, TA Fall 1993, and pp. 87-93.

McCulloch, J. Huston, "The Bat Creek Inscription: Did Judean Refugees Escape to Tennessee?" Biblical Archaeology Review July/August 1993, pp. 46-53 ff. See also comment by P. Kyle McCarter, BAR July/August 1993, pp. 54-55 ff., reply by JHM BAR Nov. /Dec. 1993, pp. 14-16, and numerous letters, esp. those by Robert R. Stieglitz and Marshall McKusick, in the Nov. /Dec. 1993 and Jan./Feb. 1994 BAR.

McCulloch, J. Huston, "The Bat Creek Stone Revisited: A Reply to Mainfort and Kwas in American Antiquity," Feb. 2005. Forthcoming in Pre-Columbiana.

Authors Note: The image is reversed so as to better read the Paleo-Hebrew.

FIG. 7.

Appendix XXXIX – The Oracles Of Zoroaster

Cause. God. Father. Mind. Fire Monad. Dyad. Triad

1. But God is He having the head of the Hawk. The same is the first, incorruptible, eternal, unbegotten, indivisible, dissimilar: the dispenser of all good; indestructible; the best of the good, the Wisest of the wise; He is the Father of Equity and Justice, self-taught, physical, perfect, and wise—He who inspires the Sacred Philosophy.
– Eusebius. *Præparatio Evangelica*, Liber. I., Chap. X,
*This Oracle does not appear in either of the ancient collections, nor in the group of oracles given by any of the mediaeval occultists. Cory seems to have been the first to discover it in the voluminous writings of Eusebius, who attributes the authorship to the Persian Zoroaster.

2. Theurgists assert that He is a God and celebrate him as both older and younger, as a circulating and eternal God, as understanding the whole number of all things moving in the World, and moreover infinite through his power and energizing a spiral force.
– Proclus on the *Timæus* of Plato, 244. Z. or T.
The Egyptian Pantheon had an Elder and a Younger Horus—a God—son of Osiris and Isis. Taylor suggests that He refers to Kronos, Time, or Chronos as the later Platonists wrote the name. Kronos, or Saturnus, of the Romans, was son of Uranos and Gaia, husband of Rhea, father of Zeus.

3. The God of the Universe, eternal, limitless, both young and old, having a spiral force.
Cory includes this Oracle in his collection, but he gives no authority for it. Lobek doubted its authenticity.

4. For the Eternal æon* —according to the Oracle— is the cause of never failing life, of unwearied power and unsluggish energy.
– Taylor.—T.
* "For the First æon, the Eternal one," or as Taylor gives, "Eternity."

5. Hence the inscrutable God is called silent by the divine ones, and is said to consent with Mind, and to be known to human souls through the power of the Mind alone.

– Proclus in *Theologiam Platonis*, 321. T.
Inscrutable. Taylor gives "stable;" perhaps "incomprehensible" is better.

6. The Chaldæans call the God Dionysos (or Bacchus), Iao in the Phoenician tongue (instead of the Intelligible Light), and he is also called Sabaoth,* signifying that he is above the Seven poles, that is the Demiurgos.
– Lydus, *De Mensibus*, 83. T.
* *This word is Chaldee, TzBAUT, meaning hosts; but there is also a word SHBOH, meaning "The Seven."*

7. Containing all things in the one summit of his own Hyparxis, He Himself subsists wholly beyond.
– Proclus in *Theologiam Platonis*, 212. T.
Hyparxis, is generally deemed to mean "Subsistence." Hupar is Reality as distinct from appearance; Huparche is a Beginning.

8. Measuring and bounding all things.
– Proclus in *Theologiam Platonis*, 386. T.
"Thus he speaks the words," is omitted by Taylor and Cory, but present in the Greek.

9. For nothing imperfect emanates from the Paternal Principle,
– Psellus, 38; Pletho. Z.
This implies—but only from a succedent emanation.

10. The Father effused not Fear, but He infused persuasion.
– Pletho. Z,

11. The Father hath apprehended Himself and hath not restricted his Fire to his own intellectual power.
– Psellus, 30; Pletho, 33. Z:
Taylor gives: "The Father hath hastily withdrawn Himself, but hath not shut up his own Fire in his intellectual power."
The Greek text has no word "hastily," and as to "withdrawn—Arpazo means, grasp of snatch, but also "apprehend with the mind."

12. Such is the Mind which is energized before energy, while yet it had not gone forth, but abode in the Paternal Depth, and in the Adytum of God nourished silence.
– Proc. in *Tim.*, 167. T.

13. All things have issued from that one Fire. The Father perfected all things, and delivered them over to the Second Mind, whom all Nations of Men call the First.
– *Psellus*, 24; *Pletho*, 30. Z.

14. The Second Mind conducts the Empyrean. World.
– Damascius, *De Principiis*. T.

15. What the Intelligible saith, it saith by understanding.
– *Psellus*, 35. Z.

16. Power is with them, but Mind is from Him.
– Proclus in *Platonis Theologiam*, 365. T.

17. The Mind of the Father riding on the subtle Guiders, which glitter with the tracings of inflexible and relentless Fire.
– Proclus on the *Cratylus of Plato*.

18. ...After the Paternal Conception I the Soul reside, a heat animating all things. ...For he placed the Intelligible in the Soul, and the Soul in dull body, Even so the Father of Gods and Men placed them in us.
– Proclus in *Tim.*, *Plat.*, 124. Z. or T.

19. Natural works co-exist with the intellectual light of the Father. For it is the Soul which adorned the vast Heaven, and which adorneth it after the Father, but her dominion is established on high.
– Proclus in *Tim.*, 106. Z. or T.
Dominion, krata: some copies give kerata, horus.

20. The Soul, being a brilliant Fire, by the power of the Father remaineth immortal, and is Mistress of Life, and filleth up the many **recesses of the bosom of the World.**
– *Psellus*, 28; *Pletho*, 11. Z.

21. The channels being intermixed therein she performeth the works of incorruptible Fire.
– Proclus in *Politica*, p. 399. Z. or T.

22. For not in Matter did the Fire which is in the first beyond enclose His active Power, but in Mind; for the framer of the Fiery World is the Mind of Mind.
– Proclus in *Theologiam*, 333, and *Tim.*, 157. T.

23. Who first sprang from Mind, clothing the one Fire with the other Fire, binding them together, that he might mingle the fountainous craters, while preserving unsullied the brilliance of His own Fire.
– Proclus in *Parm. Platonis*. T.

24. And thence a Fiery Whirlwind drawing down the brilliance of the flashing flame, penetrating the abysses of the Universe; for from thence downwards do all extend their wondrous rays.
– Proclus in *Theologiam Platonis*, 171 and 172. T.

25. The Monad first existed, and the Paternal Monad still subsists.
– Proclus in *Euclidem*, 27. T.

26. When the Monad is extended, the Dyad is generated.
– Proclus in *Euclidem*, 27. T.
Note that "What the Pythagoreans signify by Monad, Duad and Triad, or Plato by Bound, Infinite and Mixed; that the Oracles of the Gods intend by Hyparxis, Power and Energy."
– Damascius *De Principiis*. Taylor.

27. And beside Him is seated the Dyad which glitters with intellectual sections, to govern all things, and to order everything not ordered.

– Proclus in *Platonis Theologiam*, 376. T.

28. The Mind of the Father said that all things should be cut into Three, whose Will assented, and immediately all things were so divided.

– Proclus in *Parmen.* T.

29. The Mind of the Eternal Father said into Three, governing all things by Mind.

– Proclus, *Timaeus of Plato.* T.

30. The Father mingled every Spirit from this Triad.

– Lydus, *De Mensibus*, 20. Taylor.

31. All things are supplied from the bosom of this Triad.

– Lydus, *De Mensibus,* 20. Taylor.

32. All things are governed and subsist in this Triad.

– Proclus in *I. Alcibiades.* T.

33. For thou most know that all things bow before the Three Supernals.

– Damascius, *De Principiis.* T.

34. From thence floweth forth the Form of the Triad, being preexistent; not the first Essence, but that whereby all things are measured.

– Anon. Z. or T.

35. And there appeared in it Virtue and Wisdom, and multi-scieno Truth.

– Anon. Z. or T.

36. For in each World shineth the Triad, over which the Monad ruleth.
– Damascius in *Parmenidem*. T.

37. The First Course is Sacred, in the middle place courses the Sun,* in the third the Earth is heated by the internal fire.
– Anon. Z. or T.
*Jones gives Sun from Hellos, but some Greek versions give Herios, which Cory translates, air.

38. Exalted upon High and animating Light, Fire, Ether and Worlds.
– Simplicius in his *Physica*, 143. Z. or T.

http://hermetic.com/texts/chaldean.html

Index

Anthrogenesis

Anthrogenesis

O

P

Anthrogenesis

Bibliography

2007 Popol Vuh: Sacred Book of the Quiché Maya People. Electronic version of original 2003 publication: http://www.mesoweb.com/publications/Christenson/PopolVuh.pdf

Against Apion by Josephus, notes on Manetho.

An Encyclopedia of Mythology and Folklore, Volume One to Volume Three, 2008, edited by Josepha Sherman, M.E. Sharpe, Inc., Armonk, NY.

Antiquity and the Italian Renaissance: Platonic Building Blocks by Margaret Williams:

Asher, R. E., 1993. National Myths in Renaissance, France, Francus, Samothes and the Druids ISBN 0748604073.

Asher, R. E., 1993. National Myths in Renaissance, France, Francus, Samothes and the Druids, Edinburgh University Press, UK.

Bacon, Francis, 1942. Essays and New Atlantis, Walter J. Black Publishers, NY.

Baigent, Michael, Leigh, Richard and Lincoln, Henry, 1983. Holy Blood, Holy Grail, Dell Publishing Company, Inc., NY.

Bailey, Alice A. Esoteric Psychology I, 1984, Lucis Publishing Company, NYC., 10017.

Bailey, Alice. A Treatise on Cosmic Fire, Fort Orange Press, Inc., Albany, NY, 1962.

Bailey, Alice. Esoteric Psychology I, Lucis Publishing Company, New York, N.Y., 10017, 1984.

Bailey, Alice. Esoteric Psychology II, Lucis Publishing Company, New York, N.Y, 10017, 1984

Bailey, Alice. The Light of the Soul. Lucis Publishing Company, New York, N.Y, 1955.

Bailey, Foster, 1974. Things to Come, Lucis Trust Publications, NY.

Barton, George A. Miscellaneous Babylonian Inscriptions, Bryn Mawr College, 1918, Yale University Press, New Haven, CT.

Bauval, Robert and Brophy, Thomas, 2013. Imhotep the African: Architect of the Cosmos, Disinformation Books, NY.

Bauval, Robert and Gilbert, Adrian, 1994, The Orion Mystery: Unlocking the Secrets of the Pyramids, Three Rivers Press, NY.

Bauval, Robert and Gilbert, Adrian, 1994.The Orion Mystery: Unlocking the Secrets of the Pyramids, Three Rivers Press, NY.

Bauval, Robert, and Brophy, Thomas, Black Genesis: The Prehistoric Origins of Ancient Egypt by Inner Traditions/Bear & Co, Mar 2011.

Bauval, Robert, Brophy, Thomas, The Egypt Code, Disinformation Books, NY, 2008.

Besant, Annie, 1977. The Ancient Wisdom, Theosophical Publishing House, Adyar, India.

Besant, Annie, Leadbeater, C.W., 1913, Man: How, Whence, and Whither, Theosophical Publishing House, Adyar, India.

Bilmoria, Nasarvanji F., Zoroastrianism in The Light of Theosophy, Published by Blavatsky Lodge-Theosophical Society, Madras, Adyar, India. Tatva-Vivechaka Press, Bombay. 1896. Preface; Speech by Annie Besant on the sacred nature of Zoroastrianism.

Blavatsky, H.P. and Chodkiewicz, K. The Stanzas of Dzyan, Part III, Descent of the Monads, Kessinger Publishers.

Blavatsky, H.P. The Secret Doctrine, I and II, Theosophical Publications, Pasadena, CA, 1977.

Blavatsky, H.P. The Secret Doctrine, III Occultism, 1977. Theosophical Publications, Pasadena, CA.

Blavatsky, H.P., 1972. The Key to Theosophy, Theosophical Press, Pasadena, CA

Bleeck, Arthur H. Avesta, 1864. The Religious Books of the Parsees, Republished by Elibron Classics, Middletown, DE, 2015.

Bodhi, Bhikkhu, 2005. In the Buddha's Words; the Pali Canon, Wisdom Publications, Somerville, MA.

Bodhi, Bhikku, In the Buddha's Words, 2005, Wisdom Publications, Somerville, MA.

Brophy, Thomas G. The Origin Map: Discovery of a Prehistoric, Megalithic, Astrophysical Map and Sculpture of the Universe, 2002, Writers Club Press (iUniverse), NY.

Budge, E. A. Wallis, 2007. The Kabra Nagast: The Queen of Sheba and Her Only Son Menyelek, Forgotten Books, FB & c Ltd, Dalton House, 60 Windsor Avenue, London, UK.

Calleman, Ph.D., Carl Johan, The Purposeful Universe: How Quantum Theory and Mayan Cosmology Explain the Origin and Evolution of Life, Inner Traditions & Bear & Co, 2009.

Campbell, Joseph, 1949. The Hero with a Thousand Faces, New World Library, Novato, CA.

Campbell, Joseph, 1951. Flight of the Wild Gander, New World Library, Novato, CA

Campbell, Joseph, 1991. The Power of Myth with Bill Moyers, Ed: by Betty Sue Flowers, Published by Apostrophe S Productions and Alfred Van der Marck Editions and First Anchor Books, NY.

Campbell, Joseph, The Power of Myth, with Bill Moyers, Anchor Books, NY, 1991.

Capra, Fritjof, 1999. The Tao of Physics, Shambhala Publications, Inc., Horticulture Hall, Boston, MA, 02115.

Castle, Leila, Ed, Earthwalking Sky Dancers: Women's Pilgrimages to Sacred Places, Issue 56, Journey to Mu, by Carol Hadley Nervig, 1996, Frog Books, Berkeley, CA.

Cerve', Wishar S., Lemuria-The Lost Continent of the Pacific, Vol. XII, Rosicrucian Library, Supreme Grand Lodge of AMORC, Inc., Printing and Publishing Dept., San Jose, CA. 1984.

Chang, Garma C.C., Ed, A Treasury of Mahayana Sutras, Penn State University Press, PN, 1983.

Charles, R.H., The Book of Enoch, The Prophet, 2003, Red Wheel Reiser, LLC, Boston, MA. ISBN-I-57863-259-5.

Childress, David Hatcher, 1987. Anti-Gravity and the World Grid, Adventures Unlimited Press, Kempton, IL.

Childress, David Hatcher, 2000. Technology of the Gods, The Incredible Sciences of the Ancients, Adventures Unlimited Press, Kempton, IL.

Childress, David Hatcher, 2000. Technology of the Gods, The Incredible Sciences of the Ancients, Adventures Unlimited Press, Kempton, IL.

Childress, David Hatcher, 2009. Lost Cities & Ancient Mysteries of the Southwest, Adventures Unlimited Press, Kempton, IL.

Childress, David Hatcher, 2011. The Mystery of the Olmec's, SCB Distributors, Gardena, CA.

Childress, David Hatcher, The Free-energy Device Handbook: A Compilation of Patents & Reports, Adventures Unlimited Press, 1994.

Churchward, James, Sacred Symbols of Mu, 1988, CW Daniel Co, LTD, Essex, England and The   Brotherhood of Life, Inc., Albuquerque, NM.

Clymer, Reuben Swinburne, The Mystery of Osiris; Egyptian Initiation, 1909, Philosophical Publishing Company, Allentown, PA, (Assisted by F. Oscar Biberstein), Copyright 236576.

Collins, Andrew, The Cygnus Mystery, Watkin USA, Dist. Penguin Random House Publishers, 2010.

Cremo, Michael A. and Thompson, Richard L., Forbidden Archeology: The Hidden History of the Human Race, 1993, Bhaktivedanta Book Publishing, San Diego, CA.

Crichton, Michael, 2006. Next, HarperCollins Publishers, NY.

Cruttenden, Walter, 2005. Lost Star of Myth and Time, St. Lynn's Press, Pittsburg, PA.

Darll Forde, Ed., 1999. African Worlds, Studies in the Cosmological Ideas and Social Values of African Peoples Dist. by Transaction Publishers, Rutgers University, Piscataway, NJ., James Curry Publishers, Oxford, UK. ISBN 3-8258-3086-1.

Darll Forde, ed., 1999. African Worlds, Studies in the Cosmological Ideas, Transitions Publishers, NJ.

Darwin, Charles, The Descent of Man, 1871, John Murray, London, England.

de Lubicz, R. A. Schwaller 1981.The Temple in Man, Sacred Architecture and the Perfect Man, Inner Traditions Publishers, Rochester, VT.

de Purucker, G., Dialogues of G. de Purucker, 1948, Theosophical University Press, Pasadena, CA.

de Purucker, G., Fountain- Source of Occultism, 1974, Theosophical University Press, Pasadena, CA.

de Purucker, G., Man in Evolution, 1973, Theosophical University Press, Pasadena, CA.

de Purucker, G., Studies in Occult Philosophy, 1973, Theosophical University Press, Pasadena, CA.

de Purucker, G., The Esoteric Tradition, 2013, Theosophical University Press, Pasadena, CA.

Disorders of Sex Differentiation, by Grumbach, M.M., Conte, F.A., 1998, Williams Textbook of Endocrinology, eds. J.D. Wilson, D.W. Foster, H.M. Kronenberg, and P.R. Larsen, Philadelphia, W.B. Saunders:1303-1425.

Donnelly, Ignatius, 1976, Atlantis, the Antediluvian World, Dover Publications, NY.

Dunn, Christopher, 1998. The Giza Power Plant, Technologies of Ancient Egypt, Bear & Company, Rochester, VT.

Dunn, Christopher, 2010. Lost Technologies of Ancient Egypt. Advanced Engineering in the Temples of the Pharaohs, Bear & Company, Rochester, VT.

Evans-Wentz, W.Y., 1960. The Tibetan Book of the Dead, with a Psychological Commentary by C.G. Jung, M.D., Published by Oxford University Press, NY.

Fitzgerald, Robert; Translator, 1990. The Aeneid, Vintage Books, A Division of Random House, NY.

Frankfort, Henri, (1948) Kingship and the Gods, A Study of Ancient Near Eastern Religion as the Integration of Society and Nature, with a new Preface by Samuel Noah Kramer, The University Of Chicago Press, Chicago & London, An Oriental Institute Essay, The University Of Chicago Press, Chicago, 60637. The University Of Chicago Press, Ltd., London © 1948, 1978 by The University Of Chicago. All rights reserved. Published 1948. Phoenix Edition 1978. Printed in the United States of America. International Standard Book Number 0-226-26011-9. Library of Congress Catalog Number: 48-5158. Note: Internet publication of this work was made possible with the generous support of Misty and Lewis Gruber.

Gaffney, Mark H, The Astronomers of Nabta Playa: New Discoveries Reveal Astonishing Pre-Historic Knowledge, Atlantis Rising, March/ April 2006, no. 56.

Godley, A. D., 1920. Herodotus, with an English translation, Cambridge. Harvard University Press.

Griaule, Marcel 1965, 1st edition, Conversations with Ogotemmell – An Introduction To Dogon Religious Ideas, Oxford University Press, London, UK.

H.P. Blavatsky, The Theosophical Glossary, 1892/2006, Theosophical Publishing Society, London, Theosophical Trust.

Haeckel, Ernst, History of Creation, 2nd ed., 1876, Vol. I., Crown Publishers, New York.

Hall, Manly P., 1928, Secret Teachings of All Ages, Philosophical Research Society, Inc., Los Angeles, CA.

Hall, Manly P., 1951. The Mystical Christ, Religion as a Personal Spiritual Experience, Philosophical Research Society, Inc., Los Angeles, CA.

Hall, Manly P., 1976. The Lost Keys of Freemasonry, or, the Secret of Hiram Abiff, Jeremy P. Tarcher, Penguin Publishers, NY.

Hammer, Olav, 2004.Claiming Knowledge: Strategies of Epistemology from Theosophy to the New Age, Koninklijke Brill NV, Leiden, The Netherlands

Hancock, Graham and Bauval Robert, 1996. Message of the Sphinx, Three Rivers Press, NY.

Hancock, Graham, 1992. Sign and the Seal: The Quest for the Lost Ark of the Covenant, Crown Publishers, NY.

Hancock, Graham, The Magicians of the Gods, 2015, Thomas Dunne Books, St. Martin's Press, N.Y.

Hancock, Graham. Fingerprints of the Gods, Three Rivers Press, Division of Crown Publishers, NY. 1995.

Hart, Will, The Genesis Race: Our Extraterrestrial DNA and the True Origins of the Species, Inner Traditions /Bear & Co. 2003.

Hippolyte, Valmiki in Ramayana, Fauche's translation, Vol I.

Holinshed, Raphael, 1587 edition. Chronicles of England, Scotland and Ireland, 6 volumes, Raphael Holinshed and others, Reprinted in 1807 for J. Johnson and others, London. Facsimile reprint 1965 by AMS Press Inc., New York, NY 10003.

438

Homer, The Iliad, 1995. Wordsworth Editions, LTD, Hertfordshire, UK.

Homer, The Odyssey, 1995. Penguin Book Publishers, Ltd, London, UK.

Hoult, Powis, A Dictionary of Some Theosophical Terms, 1910, Theosophical Publishing Society, London, England.

http://sacred-texts.com/jud/josephus/apion-1.htm

https://docs.google.com/file/d/0B17t2HhTjZgFcnMzaW4wanRYc1U/ edit:

https://www.lvc.edu/vhr/articles/williams.pdf

Incognito, Magus, The Secret Doctrine of the Rosicrucians, 1918, Advanced Thought Publishing Co., Chicago, Ill: http://www.sacred-texts.com/sro/sdr/sdr11.htm

Introduction by NK Sandars, 1972. The Epic of Gilgamesh, Penguin Books, printed by Clay's LTD, London, England.

Isis Unveiled, I and II, by HP Blavatsky, 1998, Theosophical University Press, PO Box C, Pasadena, CA 91109-7107

Jaynes, Julian. The Origin of Consciousness in the Breakdown of the Bicameral Mind, Princeton University, Houghton Mifflin Company, Boston, MA, 1st Ed. 1976.

Jogi, Dr. Sunil, Lord Hanuman, 2014, Diamond Pocket Books Pvt., Ltd., Chapter 19, Spiritual and Blessed One.

Jung, Carl Gustav, Man and Hs Symbols, 1964, Bantam Doubleday Dell Publishing Group, N.Y.

Kapadia, S.A., The Teachings of Zoroaster and the Philosophy of the Parsi Religion, John Murray, Albemarle Street, London, 1905. http://www.sacred-texts.com/zor/toz/toz04.htm

Lamsa, Holy Bible, from Ancient Eastern Manuscripts, 1968, A.J. Holman Co., HarperCollins Pub., NY.

Le Plongeon, Augustus, Maya/Atlantis; Queen Moo and the Egyptian Sphinx, Rudolf Steiner Publications, 1973, Herndon, VA.

Leadbeater, Charles Webster, The Devachanic Plane, Theosophical Publishing Society, London, England, 1896.

Leadbeater, Charles Webster, The Masters and The Path, Cornerstone Book Publishers, 2007

Leakey, Louis S. B., By The Evidence: Memoirs, 1932-1951, Harcourt Brace Jovanovich, N.Y. 1974.

Magnusson, Eirikr and Morris, William, translators, 1900. The Story of Grettir the Strong, Published in Lexington, KY, 2014. ISBN: 9781500232863.

Maitreya, Ananda, Translator and Hanh, Thich Nhat; Foreword, 1995. The Dhammapada, Published by Unified Buddhist Church, Inc., Parallax Press, Berkeley, CA.

Major Jenkins, John, Maya Cosmogenesis, 1998, Bear & Company, Inc., Santa Fe, NM.

McIntosh, Jane, 2008. The Ancient Indus Valley: New Perspectives, Illustrated Edition, published by ABC-CLIO, Santa Barbara, CA.

McIntosh, Jane, 2008. The Ancient Indus Valley: New Perspectives; Illustrated Edition, Published by ABC-CLIO, Santa Barbara, CA.

Mead, G.R.S. 2011. The Chaldean Oracles, Lightening Source Publishers, UK

Mead, G.R.S. 2011. The Chaldean Oracles, Lightening Source Publishers, UK., Pgs. 19-25.

Milton, John, 2005. Paradise Lost, Dover Publications, Inc., Mineola, NY.

Navarro, Armando, Mexicano and Latino Politics and the Quest for Self-Determination: What Needs to Be Done, 2015, Lexington Books, Lanham, MD.

Olsen, Carl, 1983. The Book of the Goddess, Past and Present, Crossroad Publishers, NY.

Oppenheimer, Stephen, 1999. Eden in the East: The Drowned Continent of Southeast Asia, Orion Publishers, London, UK. Locating the lost civilization: the biblical flood and the real Atlantis.

Ovid, Metamorphoses, Translated by Rolfe Humphries, 1983. Indiana University Press, Bloomington, IA.

Paramahansa Yogananda, 1975. Autobiography of a Yogi, Bombay: Jaico.

Phelon, M. D., W. P. Our Story of Atlantis, Written down for the Hermetic Brotherhood, San Francisco, CA., Hermetic Book Concern.

Potts, D. T., A Companion to the Archaeology of the Ancient near East, Volume 1, 2012, John Wiley & Sons, NY.

Powell, Arthur E., 1930, The Solar System, Theosophical Publishing House, UK.

Powell, Arthur E., The Causal Body and the Ego, The Theosophical Society, London, UK. Accessed 2015.

Prabhupada, HDG, AC Bhaktivedante Swami, 1979. Srimad Bhagavatam, Sixth Canto, Prescribed Duties for Mankind-Part 1-Chapters 1-5, Published by the Bhaktivedante Book Trust, Los Angeles, CA.

Robinson, James, M, 1988, The Nag Hammadi Library, HarperCollins Publishers, NY.

Roerich, Nicholas, Altai-Himalaya: A Travel Diary, New York: Nicholas Roerich Museum, 1991.

Roerich, Nicholas, Shambhala, New York: Nicholas Roerich Museum, 1991.

Rossi, Ph.D., Earnest Lawrence, 2004. A Discourse with our Genes, The Psychosocial and Cultural Genomics of Therapeutic Hypnosis and Psychotherapy, 1st Edition, Ed: by Salvatore Iannotti, M.D. Printed in Italy, Editris SAS. ISBN: 88-89396-01-6.

Schoch, Robert M., 2012, Forgotten Civilization: The Role of Solar Outbursts in Our Past and Future, Inner Traditions-Bear & Co, Rochester, VT.

Schoch, Robert M., and McNally, Robert A, Voice of the Rocks: A Scientist Looks at Catastrophes and Ancient Civilizations, Harmony Books, NY, 1999.

Scott-Elliot, W. Legends of Atlantis and Lost Lemuria, Quest Books, Theosophical Publishing House, Wheaton, IL, 2015.

Scott-Elliot, W., The Story of Atlantis and the Lost Lemuria, 1972, Theosophical Publishing House, Fletcher and Son, Norwich, UK.

Scranton, Laird, 2006. The Science of the Dogon: Decoding the African Mystery Tradition, Inner Traditions, Rochester, VT.

Scranton, Laird, 2007. Sacred Symbols of the Dogon: The Key to Advanced Science in the Ancient Egyptian Hieroglyphs, Inner Traditions, Rochester, VT.

Scranton, Laird, 2010. The Cosmological Origins of Myth and Symbol: From the Dogon and Ancient Egypt to India, Tibet, and China, Inner Traditions, Rochester, VT.

Sertima, Ivan Van, African presence in Early America, Transaction Publishers, 1992.

Sertima, Ivan Van, They Came before Columbus, New York: Random House, 1976.

Shaw, Ian and Jameson, Robert, ed., A Dictionary of Archaeology, Blackwell Publishers Ltd, OX, UK, 1999.

Sinnett, A.P., The Solar System, 1930, the Theosophical Society, UK.

Spenser, Edmund, 1590. The Faerie Queene, Edited by Thomas P. Roche, Jr. and C. Patrick O'Donnell, Jr., 1987. Penguin Putnam Books, NY.

Steiner, Rudolf, Compiled Lectures, 1969, Health Research Books, Pomeroy, WA.

Steiner, Rudolf, Cosmic Memory, Rudolf Steiner Publications, Inc., Great Barrington, MA, 1959.

Steiner, Rudolf, The Occult Significance of the Bhagavad Gita; Nine lectures, New York: Anthroposophic Press, 1968.

Stephenson, James, 1983, Prophecy on Trial, Trans-Himalaya, Inc., NY.

Swan, James, Ph.D., Sacred Places, 1990, Inner Traditions/Bear & Co, Santa Fe, NM

Swinburne-Clymer, Dr. R., The Mystery of Osiris; Or, Egyptian Initiation., Privately printed by

Talks with Vivekananda: Advaita Ashram, Mayavati, Himalayas, January, 1939:   http://www.vediccafe.blogspot.com/2012/07/in-valmiki-ramayan-of-india-virochana.html

Temple, Robert, 1998. The Sirius Mystery New Scientific Evidence of Alien Contact 5,000 Years Ago, Destiny Books-Inner Traditions Publishers, Rochester, VT.

Temple, Robert, and Temple, Olivia, 2009. The Sphinx Mystery; The Forgotten Origins of the Sanctuary of Anubis, Inner Traditions Publishers, Rochester, VT.

The Book of Enoch, The Prophet, 2003, Red Wheel Reiser, LLC, Boston, MA.

The Origin of Consciousness in the Breakdown of the Bicameral Mind by Julian Jaynes, Ph.D., Professor of Psychology at Princeton University, Houghton Mifflin Company, Boston, MA, 1st Ed. 1976.

The Philosophical Publishing Company, Allentown, PA. Copyright Entry, April 14, 1909.

Translation from 1611, A.D., The Holy Bible, 1962. The Revised Standard Version, World Publishing Company, Cleveland, OH.

West, John Anthony, 1985. The Travelers Key to Ancient Egypt, Knopf Doubleday Publishers, NY.

West, John Anthony, 1993, The Mystery of the Sphinx, a documentary film:

West, John Anthony, 1993. Serpent in the Sky: The High Wisdom of Ancient Egypt, Theosophical Publishing House, Wheaton, Il.

Wilcock, David, Shift of the Ages, Convergence, Volumes I-III, 2002.

Wilkins, Harold T., Mysteries of Ancient South America, Reprinted, September, 1947. Rider & Co., 68 Fleet Street, E.C-4, London, UK, Printed in Great Britain by The Anchor Press, Ltd., Tiptree, Essex, UK.

www.world-mysteries.com/pex_12.htm

Yukteswar, Swami Sri, 2010. The Holy Science, International Publications Council of Self Realization Fellowship, Los Angeles, CA.

Periodicals

American Antiquity
American Journal of Human Genetics
American Journal of Physical Anthropology
American Journal of Physical Anthropology
Annual Review of Anthropology
Arctic
Astrophysics
Current Anthropology
Current Anthropology
Developmental Science
eLife
Enclopedia of Geology
European Journal of Obstetrics and Gynecology and Reproductive Biology
Family Practice
General Psychology
Genetics Society of America
Genomics and Evolutionary Biology
Geology

Geology of Greenland Survey Bulletin
Gondwana Research
Infinite Energy
International Journal of Astrobiology
Journal of Affective Disorders
Journal of Ancient Mesoamerica
Journal of Archaeological Science
Journal of Astronomy and Astrophysics
Journal of Cosmology
Journal of Emergency Medicine
Journal of Geophysical Research
Journal of Human Evolution
Journal of Polynesia Science
Mediterranean Archaeology and Archaeometry
Molecular Biology
National Genetics
Nature
Nature Communications
Nature Neuroscience
Petrology: Igneous, Sedimentary and Metamorphic
Physics of the Earth and Planetary Interiors
Proceedings of the National Academy of Sciences of USA
Proceedings of the Royal Society
Psychological Bulletin
Science
ScienceNOW
South African Journal of Science
Stratigraphy
The American Institute of Medical Climatology
The Geographical Journal
The Journal of Heredity
The Journal of Psychiatry
The Royal Society
Theosophical Society
Transcultural Psychiatry
Yearbook of Physical Anthropology

Internet Sites

http://www.adolphus.nl/
http://www.africaspeaks.com/
http://www.ancientegyptonline.co.uk/
http://www.archaeoastronomy.com/
http://www.ashiwi.org/
http://www.billheidrick.com/
http://www.cathar.info/
http://www.csfa.tamu.edu/
http://www.doyletics.com/
http://www.egyptianmyths.net/
http://www.farafina-tigne.com/
http://www.firstpeoplesofcanada.com/
http://www.gnosis.org/
http://www.gnosticteachings.org/
http://www.greatserpentmound.com
http://www.henadology.wordpress.com/
http://www.hermetic.com/
http://www.historyguide.org/
http://www.isaw.nyu.edu/
http://www.ivargault.com/
http://www.mini-site.louvre.fr/babylone/EN/
http://www.mrdowling.com/
http://www.muskingum.edu/
http://www.mysteriousworld.com/
http://www.mystic-history.angelfire.com/
http://www.native-languages.org/
http://www.nativeweb.org/
http://www.oxforddictionaries.com/
http://www.powerpyramids.com/
http://www.projectcamelot.org/
http://www.prophetess.lstc.edu/
http://www.pubs.aina.ucalgary.ca/
http://www.raceandhistory.com/
http://www.ralph-abraham.org/
http://www.redicecreations.com/ Thomas Brophy, Ph.D.

http://www.sahistory.org.za/
http://www.smithsonianmag.com/
http://www.stardate.org/
http://www.thesourceinthesahara.com/
http://www.thetoptens.com/
http://www.thewritersjourney.com/
http://www.ucl.ac.uk/
http://www.ulc.org/
http://www.warpaths2peacepipes.com/
http://www.whc.unesco.org/en/
http://www.wvculture.org/
https://www.aratta.wordpress.com/
https://www.brotherhoodofthewhitetemple.com/
https://www.familytreedna.com/
https://www.journals.lib.byu.edu/
https://www.nps.gov/
https://www.oi.uchicago.edu/
https://www.sott.net/

GLOSSARY

ABBREVIATIONS USED:
TT:
A Dictionary of Theosophical Terms, complied by Powis Hoult, 1910, London, England (out of print).
TG:
The Theosophical Glossary, by H.P. Blavatsky, 1885-2006, Theosophical Publishing Society, Theosophical Trust, United Lodge of Theosophists, Los Angeles, CA 90007.
TS and GD:
Studies on Occult Philosophy, by G. de Purucker, 1973, The Theosophical Press, Pasadena, CA.
Reference to pages of *The Secret Doctrine* (**S.D.**) is to the 1977 edition.
Unless otherwise noted, all definitions come from the above noted sources.

A
Abel – **Female aspect of Cain** – **see Cain.** TT
Abraxas or Abrasax – See TAO. TT
Acharya – Sanskrit—1.One who knows the ACHARA; a religious teacher. 2. An Initiate. TT
Adamic Race – The First Root – race. TT
Adam-Kadmon – Hebrew—the symbol for the Archetypal Man; the "Heavenly Man." TT
Adept – A fully initiated BEING who watches over and guides the progress of humanity. (See ARHAT.) Some are of this, others have come over from an earlier MANVANTARA. See MAHATMA.
Adhi Buddha – the Buddha beyond (or within) the Buddha. TT
Adhi Buddhi – the Existence beyond Buddhi; the Logos. See *Bhagavad Gita,* viii. 4. TT
Aditya – Sanskrit—1. The Sons of Aditi; a class of RUDRAS or super-physical beings. 2. One of the twelve classes of Vedic Deities (JAYAS), created by BRAHMA to assist Him in the work of creation. 3. The sun. TT
Adonai – Hebrew: my lord Jehovah. TT

Aeon or Eon – Greek. In Gnosticism, an emanation from Deity, and the medium of Its expression. 2. A KALPA or age. The AEONs are "identical with the DHYAN CHOHANS of the Esoteric Doctrine." – S.D., III. 160. Current spelling in English language is eon. TT

Agni – Sanskrit 1. Fire and its personified principle. In the Hindu pantheon, it is one of the three great fire deities – AGNI, VAVU, and SURVA – manifesting respectively on the earth as fire, in the air as lightning, and in the sky as the sun. 2. The manifestation of the Third Logos on the mental plane; TAIJAS. 3. The form, or objective, side of the mental world. TT

Agnishvattas – Sanskrit – AGNI-SATTVAS – The Kumaras; also known as the " Lords of the Flame," the " Sons of Fire," the "Fire Dhyanis," the "Pitris of the Devas," the "Triangles, Trimurti, the "Heart of the Body." Annie Besant includes the AGNISHVATTAS among the sixth of the great Hierarchies of Spiritual Beings who guide the solar system.1. They are those who were in the forefront of the evolution of the Second Planetary Chain (Brahma's "Body of Light") and now, like the other "Creative Hierarchies," help on the evolution of the human races, giving to them the " middle principles," that is, those principles of mind by means of which the physical is brought into touch with the spiritual. The AGNISHVATTAS, thus belong to the great class of celestial Beings referred to as MANASAPUTRAS, Sons of Mind. TT

Ahankara – Sanskrit – 1. Egotism; individualization. 2. "The I-making principle necessary in order that self – consciousness may be evolved, but transcended when its work is over." (See quotation under ADHIBHUTA.) "The mind furnishes [consciousness] with the protecting wall of Ahamkara." —*Theosophical Review*. The Ahankara acts both in the mental and the astral worlds. "The Vedantic, as well as, possibly, the inmost Buddhist teaching, was that this human or microcosmic AHAMKARA was nothing, in reality, but the Universal Self or LOGOS; in other words, the Ahamkara is simply the reflection of the One Self."—Theosophical Review. 3. He who, not unifying himself with the Divine, remains self – centred within the causal body. TT

Ain Soph – Hebrew – in the Kabballah, the Ancient of all the Ancients; the First Cause; the Eternal. TT

Aja – Sanskrit – unborn – Existing from eternity: an epithet applied to several Hindu deities, e.g. to BRAHMA, SHIVA, or VISHNU. TT

Ajna – Sanskrit – with the Yogis, the sixth lotus or ganglionic centre. TT

Akasha – Sanskrit – light, ether—1. AKASA is described by Mme. Blavatsky as "primordial substance." More technically it is that TATTVA which is the manifestation of the THIRD LOGOS on the ATMIC PLANE. From this all the lower (or more outward) manifestations – VAYU, TAIJAS, APAS, and PRITHIVI— proceed. "The Akasa is not that ether of science—not even the ether of the occultist, who defines the latter as one of the principles of Akasa only: it is as certainly the cause of sound, only a psychical and spiritual, not a material, cause."— S.D. I.2. The elements, Air, Fire, Water, and Earth, these all being but lower manifestations of the "primordial substance." 1 According to the cuneiform inscriptions. TT

Alaya – Sanskrit – that manifestation of Brahma known as "The Soul of the World "; ATMA-BUDDHI, "the Divine Essence which pervades, permeates, animates, and informs all things." 1 "In the Yogacharya system of the contemplative Mahayana School, Alaya is both the Universal Soul, ANIMA MUNDI, and the Self of a progressed Adept."—S. D, I. 80. TT

Alkahest – Arabic – With the alchemists, the universal solvent; esoterically, the Higher Mind. TT

Amenti – Egyptian – The KAMA-LOKA of the Egyptians. It had fourteen divisions, each representing some special condition of the departed soul. TT

Anahata – Sanskrit – the fourth ganglionic or heart centre or chakra, opposite the throat. TT

Ancient of Days – Ain-Soph, the Eternal. "And is not Old Time of the Greeks, with its scythe and sand – glass, identical with the Ancient of Days of the Kabbalists; the latter . . . being one with the Hindu…BRAHMA"—S.D, 1. 496. TT

Anagamin – Pali Canon – not liable to return 1. In Buddhism, the third initiation, having passed through which there is no further need for the incarnation of the soul. 2. One of the four paths to Nirvana. TT

Ananda – Sanskrit – joy—Buddhi, the bliss aspect of the One Existence. "Ananda is the wisdom that realizes the unity of all things, and that accomplishes union, thus finding the joy that lies at the very heart of life."—Evolution of Life and Form.1 See *Bhagavad Gita*, x. 27, xiv. 20; *Voice of the Silence*, II. 46; S.D., I. 97, II. 398.

Apas – Logos on the Astral Plane. TT

Ark of the Covenant – Every ark shrine, whether with the Egyptians, Hindus, Chaldeans or Mexicans, was a phallic shrine, the symbol of the yoni or womb of nature. The Ark of Osiris and the Hebrew Ark that King David of Israel worshipped, were both carried by priests through rings, in a sacred procession. The Mexican gods, Diana, Ceres and other goddesses and gods had their arks. The ark was a vehicle in every case and Egypt's 'winged Isis' was the cherub or Arieh, commemorating Re and Thmei, the "Two Truths." The chosen people appropriated the idea and sadly forgot to acknowledge its source to the ancestors. TG.

Archetype – Greek – the ideal, abstract, or essential type. The term is generally used for manifestations in the ARUPA spheres of the mental world: the subjective of which form manifestations are the objective. TT

Archetypal Globe – the first globe of a planetary chain, generally referred to as "Globe A." TT

Archetypal Man – the earliest semblance or type of man; PURUSHA; Adam Kadmon. TT

Arhat – Pali Canon – the worthy – 1. With the Buddhists, this word is used in a general sense for "the spiritual Intelligence that has conquered, subdued, and trained matter until his body is but the materialised expression of himself"; 1 but technically it signifies the fourth and final initiation: one who passes through this becomes an Adept. 2. One of the four paths to Nirvana. The Sanskrit equivalent is PARAMAHAMSA. TT

Armait – in Zoroastrianism: 1. Mind. 2. The Third Logos. "Armaiti was at first Wisdom and the Goddess of Wisdom. Later, as the Creator, she became identified with the earth, and was worshipped as the Goddess of Earth."—*The Ancient Wisdom. TT*

Arjuna – Sanskrit – the character in the Mahabharata, who is warring with many factions and VISHNU drives his chariot. LT

Antakarana – Sanskrit – the internal cause – 1. "The name of that imaginary bridge between the divine and the human egos."—H.P.B. 2. The centre through which the lower mind may reach up to the higher; MANAS as the controlling power of the senses and the reflection of ATMA; SATTVA. TT

Anu – Sanskrit – 1. As a prefix, after, near to, of like kind, 2. An atom. 3. The primordial atom; Brahma. "Anu is one of the names of Brahma, as distinct from Brahman, and it means 'Atom,' ANIYAMSAM, ANIYASAM, the most atomic of the atomic."—S.D., I.592 – 3. 4. Man. 5. In the Chaldean Trinity, Sin, the moon. TT

Anuloma – Pali Canon – in regular order or succession—In Buddhism, the fourth and last stage of the Probationary Path. TT

Anunaki – In the Chaldean theogony: I. "Angels of Earth." 2. Terrestrial elementals. TT

Anupadaka – Sanskrit—1. Parentless; existing eternally, having never been born. 2. The second field of LOGOIC manifestation. TT

Anupadaka Plane—the second plane of our system coming downwards (or outwards); the plane of the MONAD; the PARANIRVANIC PLANE. 1. See *A Study in Consciousness*, p. 4. 2. See *The Gita*, xv. 14, and S.D., II. 598 – 600. TT

Astaphai, Astaphoi – Gnostic – from the Greek 'astaphaios.' With the Egyptian Gnostics, the genius of the planet Mercury, corresponding to the Egyptian Thoth and the Greek Hermes. TS

Atma or Atman – Sanskrit – the breath of life – Spirit; the universal Super – consciousness. With the VEDANTISTS, ATMA is the seventh, the highest principle in man; hence it is often used as synonymous with the SELF, and sometimes with the Higher Self. This last term is, however, technically used for the Individuality of the man (q.v.), or for the ATMA-BUDDHI-MANAS. See also under SELF. "Atman is Breath, the breath of God, who is almighty in His breathings on all planes; for not only is Atman the Self of things in the sense of self as something different from the things themselves, but it is also the essence of them on all planes."—G. R. S. Mead. 1. See *The Pedigree of Man*, and S.D. II. 525, 62. 2. See *The Story of*

Atlantis, Scott – Elliot. 3. See – *The Secret Doctrine, The Story of Atlantis, and The Pedigree of Man.* See KSHETRAJNA. TT

Atmu – the Egyptian equivalent of ATMA. TT

Atom, The Permanent—See PERMANENT ATOM. TT

Atomic Sub – plane—the name given to the highest (or innermost) of the seven subdivisions of each plane or world. It denotes matter in the most intense state of vibration, or substance in the finest form, of which it is capable on that plane. See SUB-PLANE. TT

AUM—the name or symbol of Brahman, the Supreme. "The Aum of the Hindus, the sacred syllable, had become the *Aiwv* with the Greeks, and the *Aevum* with the Romans."—*S.D., III. 92.*

Auphanim – Hebrew – In the Kabballah, the Angels of the Spheres. TT

Aura – Greek and Latin – 1. That manifestation of the higher substance that extends beyond the physical body. In the human subject, the trained clairvoyant can distinguish five auras interpenetrating, of which the health-aura appears to be the lowest or most dense. 2. The higher vehicles of a man as perceived by others. TT

Avatar or Avatara – Sanskrit – descent – in its highest manifestation, an Avatara is an incarnation of the Second Aspect of the Trinity. This is known among the Hindus as a PURNA, or perfect, AVATARA. "What is an AVATARA? ... It is a descent of the manifested Deity—whether under the specific name of SHIVA, VISHNU, or ADI-BUDDHA—into an elusive form of individuality, an appearance which to men, on this illusive plane, is objective, but is not so in sober fact."—*S.D., III. 364.* But the term is also applied to the lesser manifestations of the Divine Nature in the human. See ANSA AVATARA; AVESHA AVATARA; KALKI AVATARA; and SHAKHYA AVATARA. There are said to have been nine of the AVATARAS OF VISHNU, the tenth (KALKI) having yet to come. See VISHNU. TT

Avitchi or Avichi – Sanskrit – the Eighth Sphere". A state of misery: hell as a state, not as a place, whether on earth or not."—ANNIE BESANT. TT

B

Baal – See Bel. TT

Bala – Sanskrit – power—certain powers acquired by yogic practices. They are given by Mme. Blavatsky as faith, energy, memory, meditation, and wisdom. TT

Banyan Tree – The Tree of Knowledge of good and evil; the Tree of Life. See ASHVATTA; YGG-DRASIL. TT

Barhishad Pitris – Sanskrit – a class of PITRIS OR DEVAS (PITRI – DEVATAS) belonging to the Seventh of the great Spiritual Hierarchies of the SOLAR SYSTEM. They are those who progressed furthest during the lunar MANVANTARA. Their work now is said to be that of physical evolution on our globe. "Possessing the fourfold matter, and also the creative fire, they were able to give to man his ETHERIC DOUBLE, PRANA, ANIMAL KAMA, and animal germ of mind. Beyond this they could not go."—*The Pedigree of Man.* There are four classes of the BARHISHADS, presiding severally over the building of the physical forms for the four successive ROUNDS of the TERRENE CHAIN. Each of these classes is further divided into seven sub-classes.1 The BARHISHADS are spoken of in the S.D. as "Lunar Gods," and "Lords of the Moon, of the Airy Bodies." TT

Batm – In Islamism, the un-manifested Logos. TT

Bel or Baal – the Third Person of the Chaldean Trinity—Anu, Hea, and Bel; the Creator. TT

Boat of the Dead – This sacred solar boat was called SEKTI, and it was steered by the dead. The highest exaltation of the Sun in Egypt was in Aries and the depression in Libra. The Egyptians taught that the real color of the Sun was blue, and our sun is a blue star. In reality, the Egyptian priests discovered this fact without known scientific instruments many thousands of years ago. TG.

Bhadra Kalpa – Sanskrit – the "good KALPA" of the Buddhists; the present age; the present ROUND. TT

Bhakti – Sanskrit – Devotion; faith; love. Bhakti is "the devotion that surrenders itself wholly and unreservedly to God and to the Divine Man through whom God is manifest in the flesh."—ANNIE BESANT.

Bhakti – Yoga—the Yoga of Devotion and faith; the realization of the Self through devotion. TT

Bhuta – Sanskrit – existing – 1. The ghosts or shells of departed spirits; manes. 2. An elemental or nature – spirit of the goblin type. 3. " Fierce beings . . . and eaters of flesh," brought forth in anger by their Creator, BRAHMA. VISHNU PURANA. 4. Amorphous – shaped protean masses of ethereal matter. "Their Progeny were BHUTA, with neither form nor mind."—*Stanzas of Dzyan*. 5. An element. 6. Physical matter. 7. See BHUTA CREATION. TT

Bhuta Creation or Bhuta Sarga – Sanskrit – the second of the Seven Creations of the PURANAS, the creation of the Elements (q.v.), "the first differentiation of universal indiscrete substance." "The Second Creation, BHUTA, was of the Rudimental Principles or TANMITRAS; thence termed the Elemental Creation or BHUTASARGA."—*S.D.*, I. 488. TT

Binah – Hebrew — I. The Light of Reason; the Third Person of the Trinity. 2. Intelligence; MANAS. 3. With the Kabalists, a feminine aspect of the Jewish God, Jehovah. "Binah, whose divine names are Jehovah, Yah, and Elohim, is . . . the female power who presides over the Chaos, and was made out later, by Christian Theology, to be the Serpent and the Devil." —*S.D.*, I. 423. TT

Black Age – an epithet applied to the present age, the KALI – YUGA. See YUGA. TT

Bodha – Sanskrit – Understanding. "The innate possession of divine intellect or understanding." *S.D.*, Introduction. TT

Bodhi—Sanskrit – perfect wisdom, wisdom – knowledge – SAMADHI. TT, TG.

Bodhisattva – 1. With the Buddhists, one who has BODHI, or self – consciousness in the mental world, but is not yet a full Buddha. 2. The manifestation of a Buddha on the lower mental plane. "In the Northern Buddhist system it is taught that every Buddha . . . manifests himself simultaneously in three worlds: —in the formless world as a DHYANI-BUDDHA, in the world of forms as a Bodhisattva, and in the world of desire ... as a man." —*S.D.*, I. 625. 3. A Buddhist who has attained PRAJNA, or Enlightenment, but who postpones Nirvana in order to help others to attain Enlightenment. A term from Sanskrit – BODHISATTVA, one whose

essence is enlightenment: BODHIH – perfect knowledge; see
BHEUDH – in Indo – European roots + SATTVAM, essence, being
(from sat – , existing; see es – in Indo – European roots). TT, TG.
http://www.thefreedictionary.com/bodhisattva

Bodhi Tree – the ASHVATTA. TT

Bodhyanga – Sanskrit—A condition of Bodhi. TT

Body of Darkness – Brahma in his manifestation as the First
Planetary Chain. TT

Body of Dawn – Brahma in his manifestation as the Fourth
Planetary Chain, that to which the Earth belongs; JYOTSNA. TT

Body of Day – Brahma in his manifestation as the Second
Planetary Chain. It is also known as the *' Body of Light." TT

Body of Light – See Body of Day. TT

Body of Night – Brahma in his manifestation as the First
Planetary Chain; RATRI. TT

Body of Twilight – Brahma in his manifestation as the Third (the
Lunar) Planetary Chain; SANDHYA. TT

Brahma – Sanskrit. 1. The First Person of the Hindu
TRIMTURTI (q.v.), the Creator. See SAT CHIT ANANDA. 2. The
name should be distinguished from Brahman (neuter), the Source of
all Existence; but this has by no means always been done, either in
the Hindu Scriptures or in modern writings. 3. The neuter is the
impersonal, supreme and unrecognizable Principle of the Universe
from the essence of which all emanates, and into which all returns,
which is incorporeal, immaterial, unborn, eternal, beginning – less
and endless. It is all – pervading, animating the highest god as well as
the smallest mineral atom. TG, TT

Brahman – Sanskrit – worship, 1. The Absolute; the
UNMANIFESTED; That. BRAHMAN generally referred to the root
BRIH, to grow, to increase; and so has come to mean the expansive
Energy pervading nature. 2. The Supreme Logos of the Hindus. 3.
BRAHM, 4. The male creator of the Indian Pantheon, is male and
the alleged Creator, existing periodically in his manifestation only,
and then again goes into PRALAYA, i.e., disappears and is
annihilated. TG, TT

Brahma's Day. A period of 2,160,000,000 years during which
Brahma having emerged out of his golden egg (Hiranyagarbha),

creates and fashions the material world (being simply the fertilizing and creative force in Nature). After this period, the worlds' being destroyed in turn, by fire and water, he vanishes with objective nature, and then comes Brahama's Night. TG.

Brahma's Night – A period of equal duration, during which Brahma is said to be asleep. Upon awakening he recommences the process, and this goes on for and AGE OF BRAHMA, composed of alternative 'DAYS and "NIGHTS', and lasting 100 years of Brahma (or 2,160,000,000 years each). It requires fifteen figures to express the duration of each AGE; after the expiration of which the MAHAPRALAYA, or the Great Dissolution sets in, and lasts in turn for the same space of fifteen figures. TG.

Breath, The Great – A symbolization of the Divine Activity. TT

Buddha – Sanskrit – enlightened – 1. A wise or enlightened one; specifically, Gautama Buddha. 2. The attainment of divine understanding or enlightenment as a Buddha. 3. Buddhi. TT

Buddha – Kalpa – Sanskrit – the age of Buddha—the present era. TT

Buddhi – Sanskrit – 1. The bliss aspect of the Trinity. 2. Subjectively, BUDDHI is the MONAD or SELF in its activity as spiritual discernment or cognition. "BUDDHI is the faculty above the ratiocinating mind, and is the Pure Reason exercising the discriminative faculty of intuition, of spiritual discernment."— ANNIE BESANT. 3. Objectively considered, BUDDHI is the first manifestation of ATMAN, that is, as the Fourth, or BUDDHIC PLANE. TT

Buddhic Plane – the Fourth World of consciousness: that wherein human evolution reaches the Divine; for while there is still duality here, there is, withal, no separation. TT

Buddhi-Taijasi – Sanskrit – the radiant Buddhi—"The human soul illuminated by the radiance of the Divine Soul; the human reason lit by the light of the Spirit or Divine Self – consciousness." H. P. Blavatsky. See *Bhagavad Gita*, VI. 25. TT

Buddhi-Yoga – the Yoga of Discrimination or Enlightenment. TT

Bythos, Bythus – Greek 1. The depth; chaos, the primeval deep, frequently used by the Gnostics. For example, with Valentinus it was the cosmic source whence emanated two by two the series of aeons.

Sometimes it was considered as one member of a primordial cosmic mystic square – sige (silence), bythos (depth), nous (intellect), and aletheia (truth); sometimes bythos was paired by Gnostics with sige as composing a primordial cosmic binary. 2. An aspect of the Second Logos. TS

C

Cain – Hebrew – *Qayin* – In the Bible, the son of Adam and Eve, and a tiller of the ground. Becoming jealous of the offering which his brother Abel presents to the Lord, Cain, according to the legend, slays him (Genesis 4). This allegory signifies that "Jehovah – Cain, the male part of Adam the *dualman, having separated himself from Eve, creates in her 'Abel,' he first natural woman, and sheds the Virgin blood*" (SD 2:388). Cain and Abel represent the third root – race or the "*Separating* Hermaphrodite" (SD 2:134). Again "beginning with Cain, the first murderer, every *fifth* man in his line of descent is a murderer. . . In the *Talmud* this genealogy is given complete, and thirteen murderers range themselves in line below the name of Cain. This is *no* coincidence. Siva is the Destroyer, but he is also the *Regenerator*. Cain is a murderer, but he is also the creator of nations, and an inventor" (Isis Unveiled 2:447 – 8). In Biblical genealogy, the line of Cain is Enoch, Irad, Mehujael, Methuselah, and Lemech, whose sons were Jubal, Jabal, and Tubal – Cain; the line of Seth, the third son of Adam and Eve, is Enos (Enoch), Cainan, Mehalaleel, Jarad (or Irad), Enoch, Methuselah, Lamech, and Noah (Genesis 4 – 5). Blavatsky calls it "fruitless [to] attempt to disconnect the genealogies of Cain and of Seth, or to conceal the identity of names under a different spelling…all these are Kabbalistic symbols of solar and lunar years, of astronomical periods, and of physiological (phallic) functions, just as in any other pagan symbolical creed." (SD 2:391n).

Caduceus – Latin – A herald's staff; specially, the wand of Mercury or Hermes, god of wisdom, corresponding to Thoth. It consists of a rod or tree with two serpents wound in opposite directions round it, their tails meeting below, and their heads approaching each other above. At the top of the rod in the Greek version is a knob, in the earlier Egyptian form a serpent's head, from which spring a pair of wings. From the central head between the wings grew the heads of the entwined serpents (Spirit and Matter), which descended along the Tree of Life, crossing the neutral laya – centers between the different planes of being, to manifest where the two tails joined on Earth (SD 1:549 – 50). The analogy is found in every known cosmogony, all of which begin with a circle, head, or egg surrounded by darkness. From this circle of infinity – the unknown All – comes forth the manifestations of spirit and matter. The emblem of the evolution of gods and atoms is shown by the two forces, positive and negative, ascending and descending and meeting. Its symbology is directly connected with the globes of the planetary chain and the circulations of the beings or life – waves on these globes, as well as with the human constitution and the after death states. Significantly, in ancient Greek mythology, Hermes is the 'psychopomp,' 'psychagog'; the conductor of souls after death to the various inner spheres of the universe, such as the Elysian Plains or the Meads of Asphodel. The Caduceus also signifies the dual aspect of wisdom by its twin serpents, Agathodaimon and Kakodaimon, good and evil in a relative sense. TS

Causal Body – the immediate body of the Reincarnating Ego or Thinker vibrating to the ARUPA levels of the mental plane. It has been so named because it "gathers up within it the results of all experiences, and these act as causes, moulding future lives. It is the only permanent one among the bodies used during incarnation." 1. "As body after body disintegrates ... the colouring matters are handed on to the Auric Egg, where they remain in a latent state as karmic seeds from which will spring forth at the re – awakening of the Ego its lower principles and bodies; and hence it is that the Auric Egg is also called the Causal Body."—"THE DREAMER." *The Ancient Wisdom.* TT

Centre – this word is used by Theosophists with its ordinary English meaning. It may be defined as a focus of life, or consciousness, on any plane. Thus, on the physical plane, it would be applied to the nervous ganglia; and on the astral, to the astral counterpart of those ganglia that receives sensations and translates them into terms of feeling. "No form can exist in the universe save as there is a centre within it round which that form is drawn."—ANNIE BESANT. "What then are the centres in man? They are the reflections in the respective nuclei of the UPADHI of the one Self."—"The Dreamer." The six centres known to the Yogi are the MULADHARA, the SVADHISTHANA, the MANIPURA, the ANAHATA, the VISHUDDHA, and the SAHASRA, each in turn to be energised by the awakened KUNDALINI. TT

Chakra – Sanskrit – a circle, wheel, or quoit – 1. A higher self – conscious centre of the astral body. The chakras are so called from the whirling motion they present, "like wheels of living fire." They must not be confounded with those astral sense-centres that represent the sense-organs of the physical body. (SEE CENTRE.) "These astral chakras are the organs of the astral body as such, and are used for clear vision, etc., on the astral plane, as the physical eye is used for clear vision on the physical plane."— Theosophy and the New Psychology. 2. A symbol of Vishnu. TT

Chat – In ancient Egypt, the physical body. TT

Chaya – Sanskrit – a shade—the astral image or "shadow"; the type of the etheric double; the LINGA-SHARIRA. "During the third, the boneless animals grew...their CHHAYAS became solid."— Stanzas of Dzyan. "The BARHISHAD PITRIS . . . separate off from their own ethereal bodies a chhaya, a shadow, a seed of life, which contains within it the potentialities of developing into the human form."—The Pedigree of Man. TT

Chela – Sanskrit—A disciple or pupil; one who has entered on the Probationary Path—the "Outer Court"—as the pupil of a GURU or master. TT

Chhay – and its compounds—SEE CHAYA and its compounds. TT

Chohan – Tibetan – "Lord or Master". 1. A chief thus DHYAN – CHOHAN would answer to "Chief of the DHYANIS," 2. Celestial lights – which in English would be translated as "ARCHANGELS", 3. A high spiritual entity not generally embodied in the matter of our objective universe. There are many grades of these entities."— Theosophical Glossary. TG, TT

Christos – Greek—in its essence, Atman. "—that principle of our inner nature which develops in us into the Spiritual Ego . . . formed of the indissoluble union of BUDDHI, the sixth, and the spiritual efflorescence of MANAS, the fifth principle."—S.D. II. 241. TT

Clairaudience – Hearing in the inner worlds, the higher planes. TT

Clairvoyance – Sensing, after the manner of sight, the vibrations of worlds higher (or more inward) than the three lower stages of the physical. Thus there is etheric clairvoyance, astral clairvoyance and mental clairvoyance, according to the plane on which the faculty is exercised. C. W. Leadbeater: *Clairvoyance* further divides the subject into: 1. *Simple clairvoyance*—a mere opening of sight, enabling its possessor to see whatever astral or etheric entities happen to be present. 2. *Clairvoyance in space*—the capacity to see scenes or events too far away for ordinary observation, or concealed by intermediate objects. 3. *Clairvoyance in time*—the capacity to look either into the past or into the future. TT

Cosmic Gods – Inferior gods, those connected with the formation of matter. TG.

Cosmic physical plane – that etheric plane comprised of seven planes and seven sub – planes; total of 49. LT.

Cosmos – Greek—1. An ordered whole; hence, the universe as manifesting the principle of order. 2. The solar system. See KOSMOS. TT.

Cubes – a name given to the BARHISHAD PITRIS because they have conquered matter in its fourfold form. TT

Cycle – "Any defined period, complete in itself, returning to a point higher than, but corresponding to, that of departure, after describing a curve—of evolution, of manifestation, of experience, etc." 1 1 *A Short Glossary of Theosophical Terms,* by Annie Besant and H. Burrows. TT

D

Dabar or Dabarim – Kabalah, the Logos or Word. TT

Dangma – "A purified soul; one who has become a JIVAN – MUKTA." "That All – Presence which is sensed by the Opened Eye of Dangma."—*Stanzas of Dzyan.* TT

Dark-face – Lords of the dark face, Sons of the dark face or The Dark Lords; the ASURAS who incarnated in the Fourth Race and rebelled against the White Emperor of the "City of the Golden Gates, Atlantis." TT

Daiviprakriti – Sanskrit – Primordial, homogenous light, called by some Indian Occultists "the light of the Logos" (reference – *"Notes on the Bhagava Gita"* by T. Subba Row, B.A., L.L.B.); when differentiating this light from FOHAT. TT, TG

Day of Brahma – A MAHA – MANVANTARA. TT

Deva – {Sanskrit, the shining one; same root as DEUS)—In Hindu literature, this word has a very wide signification; it is applied to almost any being functioning on planes higher than the physical, whether concerned with human evolution or no. See **ARUPA DEVA, RUPA DEVA,** and the following compounds. "The Devas who superintend the building of forms, and the fashioning of the tabernacle of man, came out of the Second Life – wave."—" The Dreamer." Devas are "the Spiritual Intelligences who help in reflecting the outward vibrations carried through the senses to the perceiving ego in terms of consciousness."—*Ibid.* A DEVA is lord of each class of ELEMENTALS, such are INDRA, AGNI, PAVARA, VARUNA, AND KSHITI. TT.

Devachan – Tibetan – a happy place—the heaven world—or, rather, state—in which the soul exists when it has transcended the ASTRAL BODY. Devachan corresponds with the MANASIC or mental plane. SEE DEVACHANIC PLANE. "The word Devachan is the theosophical name for heaven, and, literally translated, means the Shining Land, or the Land of the Gods. Devasthan, the place of the Gods, is the Sanskrit equivalent. It is the Svarga of the Hindus; the Sukhavati of the Buddhists; the Heaven of the Zoroastrians and Christians, and of the less materialized among the Mahomedans." – *The Ancient Wisdom.* TT

Dharma – Sanskrit – *Dharma*; from the verbal root *dh*– to bear, support. Equity, justice, conduct, duty; right religion, philosophy, and science; the law per se; the rules of society, caste, and stage of life. Secondarily, an essential or characteristic quality or peculiarity, approaching closely to the meaning of svabhava. See Svabhava. TS

Dhyan-Chohan – Sanskrit—1. An Archangel or high spiritual Being charged with the supervision of the Cosmos. Such are the KUMARAS and the ROOT – MANUS of a race. They are variously spoken of as "Lords of Light," "Sons of Wisdom," etc. 2. One of the

SEVEN "intelligent, conscious, and living Principles of the Logos." 1. TT

Dhyan or Dhyana – Sanskrit – meditation – 1. The concentrated mind engaged in abstract contemplation. It is the seventh stage of yoga. "A state of abstraction which carries the ascetic far above the region of sensuous perception." – *The Key to Theosophy*. 2. Direct knowledge by meditation. It is one of the six PARAMITAS or "perfections" of Buddhism. 3. One of the hierarchy of spiritual beings; a DHYAN CHOHAN. TT

Dhyanis – Sanskrit – a generic name for spiritual Beings ranging from the PLANETARY LOGOS to any of the ARUPA DEVAS. See FIRE DHYANIS, LOWER DHYANIS, SI – xFOLD DHYANIS. 1. Twelve hierarchies of DHYANIS or angels. "*S.D.*, II. 30. TT

Downward Arc – Theosophists by this term symbolize the descent of spirit into matter. TT

Dragon of Wisdom – 1. The One; the Logos; EKA. 2. As used in the plural, the term generally signifies those great Beings from the planet Venus who came to this globe during the Third Race period as the teachers of the nascent humanity. They are often called the "Sons of Fire", though it must be remembered that this is also an appellation of the AGNISHVATTA PITRIS. TT

Durga – Sanskrit – the inaccessible – 1. "The personification of illusion." 2. MAYA, or Mary the Virgin. S.D. I, 426. TT

Dvapara Yuga – See **Yuga.**

Dyad – Greek—With the Gnostics, the dual emanations from the Father, these being conceived of in pairs, positive – negative, male – female, etc. TT

E

Earth Chain – the Fourth Planetary Chain. See Planetary Chain. TT

Egg – born – A name given in *The Secret Doctrine* to the Third Root – race in its life – period before sexual generation.1 TT

Ego – Greek and Latin—the "I"; the focus of the consciousness. Thus the Ego may mean the Thinker or Higher Ego, or the same as it expresses itself through the personality (KAMA – MANAS), when it is known as the LOWER or PERSONAL EGO. TT

Eighth Sphere – Personalities, by continued wrong – doing—that is to say, by a continued and determined turning away from their SURIC or rightful evolution,—may become severed from the Source of their being, and pass to a region known as the "Eighth Sphere," there to be disintegrated and resolved into their cosmic elements. Beyond implying that the Moon is its locale, there is almost complete reserve on the part of theosophical teachers with regard to this subject. "The spheres of the cyclic process of evolution are seven in number, but there is an eighth in connection with our earth, our earth being the turning – point in the cyclic chain; and this eighth sphere is out of circuit, a cul – de – sac, and the borne from which it may be truly said no traveler returns." – Esoteric Buddhism. TT

Eka – Sanskrit – one, The One; Mahat. "The ' One ' and the ' Dragon ' are expressions used by the ancients in connection with their respective Logoi." – (S.D), I. 102.

El – Hebrew – strong – Elohim (q.v.) in its singular form; perhaps the earliest name for the Deity with the Semitic nations. TT

Element – With the Buddhists, and as spoken of in occult books generally, there are four "elements," air, fire, water, and earth. Each round, it is said, develops a fresh ELEMENT, and they may be considered to be types of the different worlds or planes. In Hindu philosophy there are usually five elements, viz. AKASHA or KHA, ANILA or VAYU, TEJAS, JALA, and BHO. These correspond, respectively, to sound, touch, sight, taste and smell. TT

Elemental – a comprehensive term for any semi – conscious or conscious non – human being or natural energy manifesting on the ETHERIC or astral PLANES. A similar entity on the higher planes is more correctly termed a deva, though the word elemental has often also been applied to these higher beings. Elementals may be grouped in two classes: 1. the natural elementals or nature spirits. These include all those entities popularly known as fairies, gnomes, brownies, pixies, nixies, undines, sylphs, salamanders, etc. They belong principally to the astral world, but there are many which manifest on the etheric sub – planes of the physical. 2. The ARTIFICIAL elementals or thought forms. These are forms given to a portion of elemental essence by the thoughts of mankind. Their existence is generally very transitory. TT.

Elemental Essence – The substance of the ELEMENTAL KINGDOMS. 1. Below the first, the atomic or monadic subdivision. "When a portion of the monadic essence of any plane clothes itself in the molecular matter of that plane, in addition to its permanent sheath of the atomic matter, it is then called ' elemental essence ' of such and such kind. – The Vahan." *Elemental Essence* consists of aggregations of matter on each of the six non – atomic sub – planes of the mental and desire planes." – Annie Besant. TT.

Elemental Kingdom – Spirit, descending into matter, reaches and vivifies the region known on the ascending arc as the MANASIC or MENTAL PLANE. The higher, the ARUPA, subdivisions of this plane are called the FIRST ELEMENTAL KINGDOM; the lower, the RUPA, subdivisions are called the SECOND ELEMENTAL KINGDOM. Below this, again, is the THIRD ELEMENTAL KINGDOM, corresponding to the ASTRAL PLANE on the upward arc. The Second Life – wave of the Logos, on its downward course, energizing "in the matter of the higher part of the mental plane, is known as the First Elemental Kingdom. It descends to the lower or RUPA levels of the same plane, and there it ensouls the Second Elemental Kingdom." – C. W. Leadbeater TT

Elohim – Hebrew – the Powers—1. Deity; the LOGOS. 2. A planetary Spirit or Creator, corresponding to the DHYAN CHOHANS of the Hindus. "Universal tradition shows primitive man living for ages together with his Creators and first Instructors— the Elohim—in the world's 'Garden of Eden ' or 'Delight' " – S.D., II. 365. TT

Ennoia or Ennoea – Greek – Among the Gnostics, an aspect of the Divine Mind. See Bythos. "As a unity, Ennoia and Ophis are the Logos: when separated, one is the Tree of Spiritual Life; the other, the Tree of Knowledge of Good and Evil." – Isis Unveiled, II. Page 293. TT

Esoteric – the inner or hidden. 1. Esoteric truth is that which underlies forms and dogmas; that which is veiled to the common people, but is revealed to the initiated. 2. Hidden, secret. 3. From the Greek esotericos, "inner", concealed. TT, TG

Ether – that which forms the four higher or finer sub – planes of the physical world. These different sub-planes are known as the First

466

Etheric or Atomic, the Second Etheric or Sub-atomic, the Third
Etheric or Super-etheric, and the Fourth Etheric or Etheric, and
collectively as the Etheric Plane. TT

Etheric Body – a body formed of the matter of the etheric sub-
planes; the ETHERIC DOUBLE. TT

Etheric Double – the counterpart of the dense physical body,
pervading and sustaining it, formed of the matter of the four etheric
sub – planes. The etheric double (in Sanskrit, the LINGA-
SHARTRA) serves as the vehicle of the life (PRANA), passing on the
same to the denser matter that we perceive with the ordinary physical
senses. TT

Etheric Plane – the four etheric sub-planes of the physical world.
See ETHER. TT

Exlunar Monads—the name introduced by MRS. BESANT 1 to
differentiate the seven lower classes of entities from the Lunar Chain,
often referred to in The Secret Doctrine as the " LUNAR PITRIS,"
from the more progressed beings, viz. the BARHISHADS and the
SOLAR PITRIS. TT

Eye of Dangma – See DANGMA. TT

Eye of Shiva – The Third Eye. TT

Eye, The Third – with the evolution of the Third Race came the
earliest organ of vision, a single eye, situated in the centre of the
forehead, in relation, mainly, with the astral WORLD. Towards the
close of this race – period two further eyes, answering to those we
have at present, were developed for definite perception on the
physical plane, and the "eye of Shiva," retreating inwards, afterwards
became the pineal GLAND. 1 "The third eye . . . disappeared
altogether as a physical organ during the Toltec sub-race, but
remained functionally active for long ages in the succeeding sub-
races."—The Pedigree of Man. * See *The Pedigree of Man.* p. 30. TT

F

Fakir Arabic – A Mussulman or Mahomedan – which is an archaic word for Muslim, an ascetic.
dictionary.reference.com/browse/mussulman, TT

Fifth Dimension – See FOURTH DIMENSION. TT

Fifth Race or Fifth Root Race – the Aryan Race. Its progenitors were taken from the fifth Atlantean sub-race, the Semitic. The type being established, it was led by the Manu Vaivasvata, some 850,000 years ago, to the plains of Northern India, warring against the indigenous peoples, the Titans, the Daityas, and the Rakshasas, as recorded in Hindu sacred books. Five of the seven sub-races of this Root – race have already appeared and partly run their course, viz.:1. the INDO-ARYA; 2. the ARYO-SEMITIC; 3. the IRANIAN; 4, the KELTIC; AND 5, the TEUTONIC. TT

Fire Dhyanis – the AGNISHVATTAS. TT

First Life Wave or First Outpouring – see LIFE WAVE. TT

First Race or First Root Race – see ROOT RACE. TT

Fohat – Tibetan—I. DAIVA – PRAKRITI; the Divine Thought or Energy (Shakti) as manifested on any plane of the Cosmos. 2. The relation between spirit and matter. The relation between matter and consciousness **is magnetic, but of magnetism of the subtlest kind, called FOHAT or DAIVA PRAKRITI, 'The Light of the Logos.' It is of Substance, and in it the essence of consciousness and the essence of matter exist, polarized, but not drawn apart." – *A Study in Consciousness.* 3. The "thread" (SUTRATMA) that unifies the Monad within the Creative Spirit. TT

Fourth Dimension – Besides the three dimensions, length, breadth or width, and thickness, generalizations or abstractions founded on our ordinary sense perceptions, the possibility of a fourth dimension has often been contended for by mathematicians. This fourth dimension, occultists declare, is not only a fact, but is one of the categories of observation on the Astral Plane. On the Mental Plane a further power of perception in five dimensions is said to be evolved. The fourth dimension " is, by a strange limitation of our faculties, inconceivable by most of us, but we know that it is an ordinary mathematical straight line exactly like the three straight lines which form the three independent directions of the space with which we are familiar. Four-dimensional space is filled with an infinite number of three-dimensional spaces running parallel to each other and intersecting each other at all conceivable angles. To a being living in another three-dimensional space, one lying at right angles to the particular three-dimensional space in which we live, one of our three dimensions is the fourth dimension: to us, one of his three dimensions is the fourth." – The Vahan. TT

Fourth Race or Fourth Root – race – The Atlantean Race. TT
Fravarshi or Fravashem – Zend—In Zoroastrianism, ATMA. TT
Fylfot Cross – The SVASTIKA. TT

G

Gaea or Gaia – Greek – In early Grecian mythology, the personification of the Earth or Nature. It may be taken as the equivalent of the Sanskrit ADITI. TT

Globe – a world. See Planetary Chain. TT

Gnosis – Greek – Knowledge, especially esoteric knowledge. The Sanskrit equivalents are JNANA and BRAHMA-VIDYA. Against Agnosticism "Theosophy rises up as the Gnosis; again asserting that the physical is not the only region into which man can penetrate." – Annie Besant. TT

Golden Age – The Krita Yuga is sometimes so called. TT

Golden Gates, City of the—the chief city of Atlantis. Degenerating into "a den of iniquity," it was destroyed in the great catastrophe of some 200,000 years ago. TT

Group – soul—a term used to denote the life or consciousness that lies behind a number or "group" of forms in the mineral, vegetable, or animal kingdoms. "In the vegetable kingdom we have not a soul for one plant, but one group-soul for an enormous number of plants, perhaps, in some cases, for a whole species. In the case of the higher animals, a comparatively small number of physical forms are the expression of one group – soul." – *The Vahan.* "A group-soul is a collection of permanent triads in a triple envelope of monadic essence."—Annie Besant. The form is sometimes perpetuated when the group – soul has passed on." The group-soul drops off the one kind of form manifestation and concerns itself with others." – A. P. Sinnett. "Creatures of very great variety may be found emanating from the same group – soul; indeed, the evolution of the group – soul could not proceed without this provision." – A. P. Sinnett. TT

Guna – Sanskrit – a string, a chord—a quality or fundamental attribute of PRAKRITI; an expression of the universal substance. The SANKHYA philosophy knows three GUNAS, or modes of cosmic manifestation: TAMAS, inertness or darkness; SATTVA, the rhythmical expression—hence purity, truth, or light; and RAJAS, the energy or expression which has not yet been harmonised — hence the perceptible activity. See under these heads: "These three fundamental qualities of matter—answering to three fundamental modifications in the consciousness of ISHVARA,—inertia, activity, and harmony, these are the famous three GUNAS without which PRAKRITI cannot manifest. Fundamental, essential, and unchangeable, they are present in every particle in the manifested universe, and according to their combinations is the nature of each particle."—Annie Besant. "TAMAS is the unconscious unity or PRAKRTI; Rajas is its expression in manifold and diverse forms; SATTVA is the return to unity again, but unity of a higher kind, the unity of knowledge instead of ignorance." *Theosophy in India.* TT

Guru – Sanskrit—1. A religious teacher. "The real Guru is always an adept in the Occult Science."—*The Theosophist.* 2. Brihaspati as the preceptor of the gods. TT

H

Hall of Ignorance – A metaphor of Mme. Blavatsky's for the physical body as manifesting the consciousness of the ego. TT

Hall of Learning – A metaphor of Mme. Blavatsky's for the ASTRAL PLANE"—the plane where sentiency and thirst after rasa (sensation) are the characteristic features. The Dreamer." TT

Hall of Wisdom – a metaphor of Mme. Blavatsky's for the CAUSAL BODY as that in which the wisdom gained from incarnate existence is garnered. TT

Health Aura – the first aura. It appears to the clairvoyant as a series of almost colourless lines radiating from the physical body. In health, these lines are said to radiate straight out from the body, but in sickness they droop, and become entangled with one another;

hence the name "Health Aura": it may be considered to be an emanation of the ETHERIC DOUBLE. TT

Heavenly Man – an appellation in the Kabala and in the Hermetic Schools for the Adam – Kadmon; the Son, the Third Person of the Trinity in the Secret Doctrine. 1 See Man, Visible and Invisible. TT

Hermetic – Pertaining to the founder of a school of initiation; hence, esoteric. TT

Higher Ego – The Thinker, whose expression is the Individuality, or, regarded objectively, the Causal Body. See EGO. TT

Higher Manas – the higher mind; the region of abstract thought whence knowledge comes as direct intuition. See MANAS. TT

Higher Self – See SELF, THE. TT

Holy Ghost – the Third Person of the Christian Trinity, the equivalent of the Hindu BRAHMA, the Hebrew SHEKINAH, or the Gnostic SOPHIA. Usual symbol, a dove. Type, fire. TT

Horus – Egyptian – The last in line of divine Sovereigns in Egypt, said to be the son of Osiris and Isis. He is the great god "loved of Heaven", the "beloved of the Sun, the offspring of the gods, the subjugator of the world". At the time of the Winter Solstice (our Christmas), his image, in the form of a small newly – born infant, was brought out from the sanctuary for the adoration of the worshipping crowds. As he is the type of the vault of heaven, he is said to have come from the *Maem Misi,* the sacred birth – place (the womb of the World), and is, therefore, "the mystic Child of the Ark" or the *argha,* the symbol of the matrix. Cosmically, he is the Winter Sun. A tablet describes him as the 'substance of his father", Osiris, of whom he is an incarnation and also identical with him. Horus is a chaste deity, and "like Apollo has no amours. His part in the lower world is associated with the judgement. He introduces souls to his father, the judge" (Bonwick). An ancient hymn says of him, "By him the world is judged in that which it contains. Heaven and earth are under his immediate presence. He rules all human beings. The sun goes round according to his purpose. He brings forth abundance and dispenses it to all the earth. Everyone adores his beauty. Sweet is his love in us." TG

Hyle – Greek—matter; Primordial substance. "The first principle out of which the objective universe was formed." TT

Hyperborean – the continent inhabited by the Second Race, the Hyperborean. See ROOT RACE. " – the land which stretched out its promontories southward and westward from the North Pole to receive the Second Race, and comprised the whole of what is now known as Northern Asia."—S.D. II. 6.

I

Iao – Greek—1. With the ancient Chaldeans and Phoenicians, the mystic symbol representing the Supreme, whose name is not to be named; 1 hence, also, the seven rays proceeding therefrom, the HEPTAKIS, or seven Nature Powers. 2. With the Gnostics, Jehovah. "Just as the Iao of the Mysteries was distinct from Jehovah, so also were the later Iao and Abraxas or Abrasax of some Gnostic sects identical with the God of the Hebrews, who was the same as the Egyptian Horus."—S.D. II. 496. TT

Incarnation – the spirit (MONAD) being veiled in the flesh (matter). See REINCARNATION. TT

Individual – The expression of the Higher Ego, or that which continues through a long series of incarnations, as distinguished from the personality, the expression of the Lower Ego 1 or that which endures but for one incarnation. See MANAS. TT

Indra – in the early Vedic period, the Supreme Deity as represented by the sky or the heavens—AKASHA. Later, Indra was looked to as subordinate to the TRIMURTI; the consummation of the DEVAS of the intermediate regions. "Indra is the St Michael of the Hindu Pantheon—the chief of the militant host."—S.D. II. 395. TT

Indriya or Indrya – Sanskrit – relating to Indra — 1. Power; capacity. 2. One of the senses or sense – organs. See JNANENDRIVAS and KARMENDRIYAS. 3. A sensation and its perception. 4. The astral UPADHI which receives sensation. TT

Initiation – the receiving of the higher knowledge and the powers that come therewith. "Initiation has to do with secret rites which are reserved for those only who have been prepared." *Theosophic Review.* There are said to be four great initiations before the soul may attain NIRVANA or liberation. The first of these—the SOHAN of the Buddhists, the PARIVRAJAKA of the Hindus takes place when the aspirant passes from the Probationary Path to the Path proper, a definitely accepted CHELA. With reference to initiations into the ancient mysteries, such as those of Bacchus and Eleusis, we have but fragmentary information. TT

Intuition – as used by Theosophists, this word generally signifies the direct speaking of the Higher Ego. TT

Inner Man – the Higher MANAS; the Higher Ego. TT

Io – With the Egyptians and Greeks, the Great Mother, the equivalent of Aditi, Isis, or Eve, the Mother of all the living; hence, also, the moon and the circle, as symbolizing the generative functions of the woman. TT

Isis – the Mother – divinity of the Egyptians, corresponding to the Aditi and Vach of the Hindus, the Io of the Greeks, or the Eva of the Chaldeans. In allusion to the mystery which she personifies, Isis is usually represented with face veiled. In front of her temple at Sais was written:—

"I am everything that hath been, that is, or that shall be; and no mortal hath ever yet removed the veil that shades my divinity from human eyes." The moon, or a circle, is the symbol of Isis. TT

Ishvara – Sanskrit – the Lord—1. The Supreme. 'ISHVARA' is that mighty Centre of Consciousness that exists unchanged in the bosom of the One Existence."—Evolution of Life and Form, 2. A Solar Logos. "The Lord of any Universe, of any system, is called ISHVARA."— *The Wisdom of the Upanishads*, 3. With the Vedantins, Cosmic Spirit; Atman. 4. The Lord of the Universe; Shiva. See "*Orpheus*" by G. R. S. Mead, TT

J
Jehovah – Hebrew—the tribal god of the Israelites, symbolized in his creative aspect by the moon. Esoterically considered, Jehovah is one of the ELOHIM, or Seven Creative Spirits. TT

Jivatma or Jivatman – Sanskrit – 1. The first coming forth of the Spirit; the Monad. 2. The Monad at any stage of its descent into the manifested worlds. Thus the JIVATMA may signify the ATMA – BUDDHI – MANAS, or Soul of man, or it may signify their reflection in the RUPA worlds below. TT

K

Ka – Sanskrit—Who?—1. In the Puranas; (a) the Inexplicable; the Unknown; (b) a name of Prajapati, the Creator; (c) any deity that is supreme to the mind of his worshipper. 2. In ancient Egypt, the astral body. TT

Kadmon – Hebrew—See ADAM – KADMON. TT

Kali Yuga – See Yuga.

Kalpa – Sanskrit—A period of activity or manifestation; a Day of Brahma (*q.v.*). "All beings . . . enter my lower nature at the end of a Kalpa: at the beginning of a Kalpa again 1 emanate them." — *Bhagavad Gita,* ix. 7. TT.

Kama – Sanskrit—1. Desire or passion, especially sex passion, in the abstract or as a personal god. 2. The fourth and highest principle of the quaternary or mortal man. "It is the life manifesting in the astral body and conditioned by it; it is characterised by the attribute of feeling, whether in the rudimentary form of sensation, or in the complex form of emotion, or in any of the grades that lie between."— *The Ancient Wisdom.* TT

Kama – manas—that blending of the mental and desire elements that forms the personality or common brain intelligence of the man. "The energies that express themselves through the lower kinds of mental matter are so readily changed by it into the slower vibrations that are responded to by astral matter that the two bodies are continually vibrating together, and become very closely interwoven." – The Ancient Wisdom. TT.

Karma – Sanskrit—1. Action, activity, movement; moral or Karman. Religious action. 2. That sequence of action generally known in the West as the Law of Cause and Effect. "It is man who plans and creates causes, and Karmic Law adjusts the effects, which adjustment is not an act, but is universal harmony, tending ever to resume its original position, like a bough which, bent too forcibly, rebounds with corresponding vigor." – S.D., ii. 319. 3. That which is the result of past cause or causes. Thus we speak of "good karma" and "evil karma," as the past actions have been good or evil; of "individual karma," of "national karma," of "collective karma," etc. Karma is also known as "physical," "astral," or "mental," as it works itself out in these respective worlds. See AGAMI KARMA, KRIYAMANA KARMA, PRARABDHA KARMA, SANCHITA KARMA. TT.

Kha – With the Egyptians, the physical body. TT

Kosmos – Greek—A spelling of Cosmos (q.v.). It may be noted that H. P. Blavatsky usually signifies the whole universe by Kosmos, and the solar system by Cosmos. TT.

Kriyashakti – 1. The creation of forms by means of thought; hence the power—divine or human—to manifest. "The mysterious power of thought which enables it to produce eternal, perceptible, phenomenal results by its own inherent energy."— S.D., I. 312. 2. The out – going or self – sacrificing powers of the Self or the Ego. TT

Krishna – In Hinduism: 1. the last incarnation of Vishnu. 2. The Second Aspect of the Trimurti; the Christos. TT.

Krita Yuga – See **Yuga.**

Kumaras – Sanskrit – youths—1. The four great Beings forming the highest in the occult hierarchy who help on the evolution of humanity. 2. One of the seven divisions of DHYAN CHOHANS 1, 3. The AGNISHVATTAS (q.v.); those having cosmic self – consciousness within the BUDDHIC World. TT

Kundalini – The coiled – up "serpent "—the latent divine power in man. The third stage of development is the awakening of the fiery Serpent— KUNDALINI—which is the Life that runs through the centres of these lotuses and unifies them, coordinating them into one harmonious whole. When this is done, the astral man is free." — "THE DREAMER." TT

Kundalini Shakti – The KUNDALINI power. "It is the universal life – principle which everywhere manifests in Nature. This force includes the two great forces of attraction and repulsion; electricity and magnetism are but manifestations of it."—S.D. I. 312. TT

Kurukshetra – Sanskrit – the field of the Kurus—1. The Armageddon or great battlefield, typifying the area of the conflict between the spirit and its encasement. "The Kurukshetra of the universe is man." Annie Besant. 2. The metaphor in Theosophy referring to the mythical Soul's battle to ultimately win and become the DIVINE MAN, or soul – infused personality. TT

L

Lama – Tibetan—A priest. TT

Lanoo (O'lano) – Tibetan—1. In Northern Buddhism, a CHELA or student of the esoteric doctrine. 2. used as a reference to the first – born Root Race; the 'Sons of Man.', pg. *SD, II.* TT.

Law of Cause and Effect—the Law of Cause and Effect is karma; operating in the realm of human life and bringing about adjustments between an individual and other individuals whom he has affected by his thoughts, emotions and actions. TT.

Lha – Tibetan – a spirit—In Northern Buddhism, high spiritual Beings; 1. SOLAR or LUNAR PITRIS; 2. the ASURAS; 3. the AGNISHVATTAS. TT.

Life – wave—an expression used by Theosophists to figure forth the descent of the Logos into the objective worlds. The Triune Deity is described as manifesting in three LIFEWAVES: —The First Life-wave is the outpouring of the Life of the Third Logos, the Brahmi of the Hindus, the Holy Ghost of the Christians. Sweeping downwards (or, more correctly, from within outwards), it endows the substance of the different worlds, "the fivefold field," with a simple capacity to respond to impulse or vibration (the TANMATRAS). The Life of the Second Logos, the Vishnu of the Hindus, the Christos of the Christians, then, in similar manner, floods the different planes, giving forth as emanations the DEVAS and the PITRIS, gathering the atoms into forms, forming stable centres which are slowly evolved by impact and response to impact into a consciousness of their own, and a yet more vivid consciousness, until they are ready for the descent of the THIRD LIFE – WAVE, that of the First Logos, Shiva, the Father, whereby they become self – conscious, and thus they enter the ranks of humanity.1. See "The Secret Doctrine", ii. 7. See "The Lost Lemuria" by W. Scott – Elliot.

Lemuria – the name given by Mme. Blavatsky to all the countries inhabited by the Third Root-race. The main continent of Lemuria is stated to have reached from the middle of the South Atlantic Ocean, across South Africa, Australia, New Zealand, and the greater part of the South Pacific. Further eastward of this was a large island continent stretching as far as, and including lands south of South America. Very nearly the whole of Europe and the greater part of Asia were, in this age, below the sea level. "Lemuria is said to have perished about 700,000 years before the commencement of what is now called the Tertiary Age."—S.D., II. 327. TT

Lemurians – The Third Root – race; the "Sweat-born" and the "Egg-born "of The Secret Doctrine. They were of gigantic size, androgynous or hermaphrodites during the earlier periods of the Race, but afterwards differentiating into distinctly male and female forms. The Race, as those later evolved, was separable into seven sub-races, but information sufficient to respectively characterize these has not yet been obtained. There are races presently in incarnation that retain the characteristics of the Lemurians.—*The Lost Lemuria.* TT

Logos – Greek – the Word—1. The mighty Being in whom, and by whom, the solar system exists. 2. The Deity of a PLANETARY CHAIN. See PLANETARY LOGOS. "With Himself He brings the fruits of a past Kosmos —the mighty spiritual Intelligences who are to be His co – workers and agents in the universe. . . . Highest of these are 'the Seven,' often Themselves spoken of as Logoi, since each in His place is the centre of a distinct department in the Kosmos, as the Logos is the centre of the whole." —*The Ancient Wisdom.* 1 See The Life – Waves, by "The Dreamer." TT.

Love – the action of light or radiation which is a transmutation in process of accomplishment with the passage across one state of being to another, through the agency of fire. An example is that spontaneous outflow of a loving heart and intelligent mind that characterizes those whose intuition is awakening to the call of the fifth kingdom in nature, the kingdom of souls.

http://www.lucistrust.org

Lucifer or Lucis – The great teacher H.P. Blavatsky, for whom Alice and Foster Bailey had enormous respect, sought to elicit a deeper understanding of the sacrifice made by Lucifer. The Baileys were serious students and teachers of Theosophy, a spiritual tradition which views Lucifer as one of the Solar Angels, those advanced Beings Who Theosophy says descended (thus "the fall") from Venus to our planet eons ago to bring the principle of mind to what was then animal – man. In the theosophical perspective, the descent of these Solar Angels was not a fall into sin or disgrace but rather an act of great sacrifice, as is suggested in the name "Lucifer" which means light – bearer. http://www.lucistrust.org

Lunar Pitris – Beings who have attained to so high a position in evolution on the preceding PLANETARY CHAIN—the Lunar — that they are now able to help on—"to father"—the evolution of humanity on this, the TERRENE CHAIN. The term, then, with this definition, includes the BARHISHADS and the LOWER DHYANIS or SOLAR PITRIS, but does not include the less advanced entities from the Lunar Chain, constituting the bulk of our present races, the seven classes of "LUNAR PITRIS" often spoken of by Mme. Blavatsky. For these Mrs. Besant has suggested the apt phrase "E – xlunar Monads", as avoiding confusion with the true PITRIS. TT

M

Maat – with the ancient Egyptians, KARMA or the just law. TT

Mahabhuta – 1. A great BHUTA or corporeal being. 2. Physical matter. TT

Maha Chohan – A DHYAN CHOHAN. TT

Maha – Manvantara — A thousand MAHA – YUGAS; a "Day of Brahma," i.e. 4320 million years. TT

Mahrajahs – The four great Beings, Kings of the DHYAN CHOHANS, who supervise the working out of the laws emanating from the "LORDS OF KARMA"; the MAHA-DEVAS, or DEVA-RAJAHS, presiding over the four cardinal points. TT

Mahat – Sanskrit – the Great One—Cosmic or Divine mind; the manifestation of the Third Logos on the third PLANE. TT

Mahatma or Mahatman – Sanskrit—great spirit—1. One who has attained NIRVANA, or liberation, but retains his physical body for the purpose of helping forward the progress of humanity. The word is the equivalent of the Buddhist ARHAT. See Master. 2. The Supreme. TT

Maha Vishnu – the Solar Logos. TT

Maha Yuga – see Yuga.

Maheshvara – Shiva. TT

Maitreya – Sanskrit – friendly—1. In the PURANAS, Brahma's "Body of Dawn." 2. In Hinduism, the term referring to the Master, Christ. TT.

Manas – Sanskrit mind—1. The world of mind or mental forms; the field of consciousness that lies between the BUDDHIIC and ASTRAL PLANES; MAHAT. 2. The mind of man, answering to the MAHAT of the cosmos. MANAS is known to Theosophists under two aspects, the HIGHER MIND, comprising the INDIVIDUALITY, and the LOWER MIND, comprising the PERSONALITY. The Higher Mind, involved with ATMA-BUDDHI, forms the microcosmic trinity or Self; the LOWER MIND, involved with KAMIC elements, forms the personal and desire nature of the man. The first is immortal; the second, mortal. TT

Manasic Plane – the Mental Plane; the Third World. See MANAS. TT

Manasaputras – Sanskrit – sons of mind—A comprehensive term for certain beings from a more advanced evolution than ours who " throw out sparks of mind," or incarnate on this globe in order that the upward progress of the human soul may be continued by its endowment with mind or the reasoning principles. It will thus be seen that the MANASAPUTRAS act as the medium for the THIRD OUT-POURING from the Logos, whereby the soul becomes self – conscious in the physical world, and the CAUSAL BODY is formed. The MANASAPUTRAS include the ASURAS, the AGNISHVATTAS, and the "Dragons of Wisdom" from the Venus Chain 1. TT

Mantra or Mantram – Sanskrit – speech—1. A form of words or syllables rhythmically arranged so that when sounded certain vibrations are generated, producing a desired effect on higher planes. But "in the great majority of cases the formula does nothing beyond strengthening the will of the person who uses it, and impressing upon the mind of the subject the result which it is desired to achieve." Withal "there is a much rarer type of mantram in which the sounds themselves produce a definite effect." —*Some Glimpses of Occultism*. 2. The Samhita or hymnal portion of the VEDA. TT

Manu – Sanskrit – thought—this word has been used with very varied connotations, but is correctly applicable to (I) the presiding Spirit—if personalized, the Creator, Ruler, and Guide—of a Race, a Round, or a Globe. I "Esoterically, every Manu, as an anthropomorphized patron of his special cycle (or Round) is but the personified idea of the Thought Divine . . . each of the Manus, therefore, being the special god, the creator and fashioner, of all that appears during his own respective cycle of being or MANVANTARA."—S.D., I. 93 – Each Round has two MANUS, a ROOT MANU and a SEED MANU. The names of these will be found in The Secret Doctrine.2. A MANVANTARA. TT

Manvantara – Sanskrit – MANU-ANTARA, the period between two MANUS—the cycle of manifestation as opposed to PRALAYA or non – manifestation. It includes the seven rounds of the great LIFE – WAVE of the Logos. The duration of the period, taking it as one – fourteenth of a "Day of Brahma", would be 308,571,428 years, and Mme. Blavatsky, in the Key to Theosophy, gives 308,448,000 years as "the reign of one Manu." Taking it, however, as 71 MAHA – YUGAS, the period would be 306,720,000 years. TT

Master – A Being who has attained to atmic or nirvanic consciousness. Theosophists so designate the Adepts or Mahatmas from whom they have their occult teachings. "The Masters are those who have passed through five great initiations, the four upon the path, and one beyond, which makes the Master."— Annie Besant. TT

Maya – Sanskrit – illusion—1. In its widest sense, MAYA, being the principle of form or limitation, may be said to include all manifestation, and so we have to go beyond manifestation to escape from it; but the word is generally used in a relative sense for phenomena or objective appearances that are created by the mind. "The nearer a body is to the Unknown Substance, the more it approaches Reality, as being the further removed from the world of Maya."—S.D., I. 169. "The term Maya, though sometimes used as a synonym for AVIDYA, is, properly speaking, applicable to PRAKRITI only."—The Theosophist. 2. The power of producing illusion. 3. The creative power by which the universe comes into manifestation. "Maya is conceived as a cosmic entity, a universal substance or sum of forces comprehending all conditioned powers, causes and effects. In itself it is unreal, opposed to the Real or Absolute Thought which informs it."—Lionel Burnett. TT

Mega-cosm – Greek – the great world—the world of the "Astral Light." TT

Meru, Mount – 1. In the Puranas, exoterically, the abode of the gods – the Olympus of the Greeks. 2. The sacred land at the North Pole; "the seed – vessel of the earth." TT

Microcosm – Greek—the reflection in miniature of the MACROCOSM. Thus, the atom may be spoken of as the "microcosm" of the solar system, its electrons moving under the same laws; and man may be termed the "microcosm" of the universe, since he has within himself all the forms and elements of that universe. TT

Monad – The one Self, or "Divine Spark," that gives the life, the fire, the consciousness to the form. Although one in essence, it is to be regarded as permeating all planes and kingdoms; thus we have the "mineral MONAD," the "vegetable monad," the "astral monad, etc. MONAD," the "vegetable monad," the "astral monad, etc." The Monads are not discrete principles, limited or conditioned, but rays from that one universal absolute Principle."—*S.D), ii. 176.* "It is called the Monad whether it be the Monad of spirit-matter, Atma, or the Monad of form, Atma-Buddhi, or the human Monad, Atma-Buddhi-Manas. In each case it is a unit, and acts as a unit, whether the unit be one-faced, two-faced, or three-faced."—*The Ancient Wisdom.* "As a well-made mirror produces a perfect image of an object, so is the human Spirit, ATMA-BUDDHI-MANAS, a perfect image of the Monad—is, indeed, the Monad himself veiled in denser matter." —*A Study in Consciousness.* TT

Monadic Essence – the atomic or innermost condition of the substance of a plane ensouled by the Second Life-wave. See ELEMENTAL ESSENCE. "We may define Monadic Essence ... as atomic matter ensouled by the life of the Second Logos; it is His clothing for the vivifying and holding together of forms."—*A Study in Consciousness.* TT

Mysteries – 1. Truths as presented to initiates—that is, in a form one or more degrees less veiled than as presented to the common people. 2. "Dramatic performances in which the mysteries of cosmogony and nature in general were personified by priests and neophytes, who enacted the parts of the various gods and goddesses." 1 TT

N

Naga – Sanskrit – serpent – 1. A common symbol for an ADEPT or INITIATE; one who has unified the spiritual and physical powers—generally spoken of as a "Serpent of Wisdom." "In the Secret Doctrine, the first Nagas—Beings wiser than serpents—are the "Sons of Will and Yoga," born before the complete separation of the sexes."—S.D. II. 191. 2. A DEMON or ASURA. The NAGAS are dwellers in the nether world (Patala), having human faces with the tails of serpents. 1 *Key to Theosophy.* TT

Nadi – Sanskrit—I. The channel or nerve for the conduction of a current. "A few of these Nadis are visible in the 'gross body,' e.g., the central canal of the spinal cord . . . but the rest, those that correspond to the nerves, are invisible." —Theosophical Review. 2. A current of life or energy. The nadis' condense to form the energy centres or chakras. TT

Nâga – Sanskrit., a serpent—1. A common symbol for an ADEPT or INITIATE; one who has unified the spiritual and physical powers—generally spoken of as a " Serpent of Wisdom." " In the Secret Doctrine, the first Nâgas—Beings wiser than serpents—are the " Sons of Will and Yoga," born before the complete separation of the sexes." 1 *Key to Theosophy.* S.D. ii. 191. 2. A Demon or Asura. The Nagas are dwellers in the nether world (PÂTÂLA), having human faces with the tails of serpents. TS

Nara – Sanskrit – the primordial man – 1. The Spirit from which comes man. 2. PARAMATMAN, or That from which the universe evolves. See NARAYANA. 3. "The waters," as the first manifestation of Nara. TT

Nature – spirits—ELEMENTAL. TT

Nephilim – Hebrew—Fallen angels; angels who descended from their high estate. (See Genesis VI – 4.) TT

Nirmanakayas – Sanskrit the sheaths of the NIRMANAS—1. The great Teachers of NIRVANIC spheres who guide the spiritual evolution of humanity, conveying the Wisdom from the Supreme to its unfoldment in man. Not merging completely in the Universal Consciousness, they are known as "Nirvanees with remains." 2. Adepts, "Lords of Compassion," who sacrifice their beatitude and voluntarily incarnate to help humanity. TT

Nirvana – Sanskrit – having life extinguished—the goal of the Path (q.v.); the final state of human evolution where divine wisdom is fully attained, and the consciousness expanded to embrace this Cosmos. "Nirvana is the heart of the universe, whence all its life – currents proceed. Hence the Great Breath comes forth, the life of all, and thither it is indrawn when the universe has reached its term. There is the Beatific Vision for which mystics long; there the unveiled Glory, the Supreme Goal." – *The Ancient Wisdom*. TT

O

Occultism – The science of the hidden—that is, of the kingdoms above (or within) the physical as manifested to the ordinary senses; the science of the Etheric, Astral, and Mental Worlds. TT

Occultist – One practicing, or engaged in the study of, occultism. TT

Odin – The Supreme Deity of Scandinavian mythology. TT

Odr – Norse—Mind; intelligence. TT

Om – the sacred word of the Hindus; the mystic monosyllable taken as a means to meditation; AUM. TT

Ond – Norse—Spirit. TT

Osiris – Greek—the first deity of the Egyptians, personifying the sun, and hence, also, fire. "Osiris is called in *The Book of the Dead*, 'Osiris, the double crocodile.' 'He is the good and bad principle; day and the night sun, the god and the mortal man."—S.D. II. 613. TT

P

Pairs of Opposites – the positive and negative principles by the cross – play of which life, sensation, consciousness, thought, and the self are evolved. Heat – cold, light – darkness, love – hate, may be instanced as "pairs of opposites." In the progress of the man, these have ultimately to be transcended. "Be thou . . . beyond the pairs of opposites." — Bhagavad Gita, ii. 45. "The delusive pairs of opposites." – Op. cit., vii. 28. The ultimate is in "opposites" are SAT and ASAT, Being and Non – being. Cf. the Gnostic term SYZYGY. TT

Path, The – in the representation of the growth of the soul, progress along a "path" is one of the oldest and most common of

metaphors, occurring in almost all mystic works. As used by
Theosophists, "the Path "—or the Path proper, to distinguish it from
the Probationary Path —signifies the course that is entered upon by
the chela after he has been accepted by a Master, and has passed the
first Initiation q.v.). It is divided into four stages, known to the
Hindus as the PARIVRAJAKA, the KUTICHAKA, the HAMSA,
and the PARAMAHAMSA (q.v.). The corresponding terms used by
the Buddhists are the SCROTAPATTI, the SAKRIDAGAMIN, the
ANAGAMIN, and the ARHAT. "The end of the Path is the threshold
of Nirvana."—*The Ancient Wisdom.* TT

Permanent Atom – an atom retained by the Reincarnating Ego
after the death of his vehicles. At the in drawing of the life from the
different bodies, a certain atom from each plane survives
disintegration, and is swept onward with the life. On this, the
permanent atom 2 is impressed the experiences, in essence, of the
body of which it has formed a part, so that, from it, the tone or
vibratory rate may be transferred to the new body when the ego
reincarnates. "These permanent particles are composed of three units,
a mental, an astral, and a physical. . . . After death these are stored up
in the causal body. At re – birth these are put out one after
another."—Theosophy and the New Psychology. "The permanent
atoms are the nuclei of the bodies, and are the expressions of the
centres of consciousness in their organic life—in their life of
manifestation and relation."—"THE DREAMER." TT

Personality – 1. The transitory expression of the Thinker—the
Individuality—on the Lower Mental, the Astral, and Physical Planes.
2. THE LOWER MIND. See MANAS. "Change, or the working of
consciousness in matter, fashions the mirror in which the changeless
"I" learns to know itself; for it connects up into a whole the
intellectual life of the physical man. And the act of reflection whereby
the ego becomes self – conscious produces in matter a consciousness
of physical personality, contrasting with that of an immaterial
(spiritual) individuality. In Theosophy, we call the ego 'THE
HIGHER MANAS,' and the personality 'the lower MANAS.'" —
Thos. Williams. TT

Pineal Gland – The Third Eye, gradually retreating inwards and
ceasing to function as the organ of sight, during the Fourth Race

became transmuted into the body known to physiologists as the "pineal gland." The powers of this body are—with few exceptions—at present latent in man; but with his further evolution, it is stated, they will become active, and the higher consciousness of the mental world will then be able to express itself through the physical brain. "The pineal gland becomes connected with one of the chakras in the astral body, and through that with the mental body, and serves as a physical organ for the transmission of thought from one brain to another."
—*A Study in Consciousness*. TT

Pitris – Sanskrit – forefathers, progenitors – The Beings who build for man (THE MONAD) the body whereby he may incarnate, and bring to him those principles of mind whereby the spiritual is brought into touch with the physical. We have thus two main classes of PITRIS, the BARHISHADS and the AGNISHVATTAS, the first, of whom there are four orders, having to do with the physical ancestry of man; the second, of whom there are three orders, having to do with his intellectual evolution. The term is also applied to the two orders of LOWER DHYANIS or SOLAR PITRIS, but the less progressed entities from the Lunar Chain, those who had not yet reached the individualized form, are best designated "EX-LUNAR MONADS." "One – third of the DHYANIS, i.e. the three classes of the ARUPA PITRIS . . . was doomed ... to be ... incarnated on earth."—S.D., ii. 98. **Note – The use of the term PITRIS, has been involved in much confusion. Owing partly to the wideness and looseness of its application, and partly to the very fragmentary nature of the information we have of those higher orders of beings to which it refers. Since the publication of *Mrs. Besant's Pedigree of Man*, however, an attempt is being made to reduce the ambiguity of its connotations and define its scope. TT

Pituitary Body – The rudiment of the organ known to physiologists as the "pituitary body " is supposed to have been a mouth, this becoming atrophied before the vertebrate stage of physical evolution is reached. It is active during the time of growth of the body, which growth it seems in the main to control. With the further evolution of man its office is also that of placing the astral and physical worlds *EN RAPPORT* so that, by its means, clairvoyant experiences may transmitted to the brain-consciousness. "The pituitary body is the organ of the psychic plane. Psychic vision is caused by the molecular motion of this body, which is directly connected with the optic nerve, and thus affects the sight and gives rise to hallucinations."—S.D.III., 548. TT

Plane – A field, or particular cosmic manifestation of the One Existence. Of these, in the esoteric doctrine, there are seven, each of the seven being again formed into seven, and each of these yet again into seven. The whole of the manifestation known as our PLANETARY CHAIN, with its seven planes, thus corresponds to one plane of the KOSMOS. "The process referred to as the ' Small Wheels '. . .takes place on the sixth region from above, and on the plane of the most material world of all in the manifested KOSMOS—our terrestrial plane. These seven wheels are our Planetary Chain."—S.D., I. 168. The different terrene planes— physical, astral, mental, etc.— are objectively conceived as substance at various rates of vibration, or—which is the same thing—of different densities. Subjectively conceived, a PLANE denotes a certain range or extent of consciousness. TT

Planetary Chain – A series of seven globes or worlds which form the field of evolution during the planetary cycle or MANVANTARA. The first three of these globes—generally known as A, B, and C— form a descending arc, the densest physical matter of the descent being reached in the fourth globe, D, of which our earth is an instance. The fifth globe, E, on the ascending arc (corresponding to C on the descending arc), usually belongs to the astral plane, and the sixth and seventh, F and G (corresponding to B and A on the descending arc), to the RUPA and ARUPA levels of the mental plane: these, therefore, are invisible to ordinary sight. "The globes in the arc of descent, and those in the arc of ascent, correspond with each other, those in the upward arc showing out in perfection that which those on the downward arc embryonically adumbrate, while the middle globe is the point of conflict and turning."—*The Pedigree of Man.* The complete evolution of our system comprises seven PLANETARY CHAINS successively brought forth, each chain being, as it were, a reincarnation of the preceding one. Three of these chains belong to the past; the fourth is the Terrene (earth), that of which the earth forms the fourth globe; the remaining three have yet to appear. TT

Planetary Logos – the great Being in whom, and through whom, a planetary chain exists. TT

Poseidonis – the island referred to by Plato under this name is stated to be the remnant of the ancient continent of Atlantis. Poseidonis "was submerged in the fourth and final great catastrophe of 9564 BCE."—The Story of Atlantis. TT

Pralaya – Sanskrit—The period when the life of a world, chain, or solar system is partially or wholly indrawn, activity or manifestation ceasing in part or in whole. The PRALAYA of a planet—the "winter" between the rounds of the Life-wave— is known as a "Minor PRALAYA"; the PRALAYA of a solar system is known as a "MAHA-PRALAYA "; and the PRALAYA of the Universe as a "KOSMIC PRALAYA." During the MINOR PRALAYAS, "the planets remain intact, though dead; just as a huge animal, caught and embedded in polar ice, remains the same for ages." S.D., I. 46. TT

Prana – Sanskrit – breath – 1. Cosmic life, manifesting on all planes; JIVA. "As, according to Hindu thought, there is but one Life, one Consciousness, everywhere, the word Prana has been used for the Supreme Self, the all – sustaining Breath. . . . Hence, that Life on every plane may be spoken of as the "Prana of the plane"; it becomes the life – breath in every creature."—A Study in Consciousness. 2. Specifically, the third of "the seven principles of man" the active power producing the vital phenomena. It is taken up by the Etheric Double from the Cosmic Life, to which it again returns on the death of the body. 3. One of the five "vital airs," or life principles, of the body. It is said to be located in the breast. TT

Pranayama – Sanskrit – 1. In yogism, the practice of controlling the breath. " – restraining the flow of the outgoing and incoming breaths, solely absorbed in Pranayama."—Bhagavad Gita, iv. 29. 2. The control of all the life-manifestations. "Pranayama is really the control ... of all the life-energies—the subdual of them all to the Self." *The Wisdom of the Upanishads.* TT

Prithivi – Sanskrit – the earth—the matter of the densest or physical plane; that TATTVA which forms the manifestation of the Third Logos on the physical plane. "That which is existence, reflecting itself in . . . Prithivi, shows forth what we call objective reality." *Evolution of Life and Form.* TT

Probationary Path – The first turning from the broad path of worldly desire; that which leads up to the Path proper. Four qualifications are defined by the YOGIS as being, in some measure, needful for one who determines to tread the "Probationary Path":—1. Discrimination between the real and the unreal, the transitory and the eternal – Sanskrit, VIVEKA. Indifference to external things – Sanskrit – VAIRAGYA. 3. Six mental acquirements – SHATSAMPATTI, that is to say:

   {a) Thought – control – Sanskrit, SHAMA.

   {b) Physical self – control – Sanskrit, DAMA.

   {c) Checking all sensual desire – Sanskrit, UPARATI.

   {d) Endurance; forbearance – Sanskrit – TITIKSHA.

   {e) Faith – Sanskrit – SHRADDHA.

   (f) Perfect mental equilibrium – Sanskrit – SAMADHANA.

   4. Aspiration, or desire for liberation – Sanskrit – MUMUKSHA. TT

Psychic – one who has the capacity to perceive etheric or astral forms; a clairvoyant or clairaudient. TT

Psychism – The manifestation of the powers of consciousness through organized matter. TT

Ptah – With the Egyptians, the Third Aspect of the Trinity; the Divine Spirit; the Creative Mind. "Ptah was originally the God of Death, of destruction, like Shiva. He is a Solar God only by virtue of the Sun's fire killing as well as vivifying."—S.D., I. 393. TT

Puranas – Sanskrit – ancient—Hindu Scriptures coming next in order of authority to the Vedas. There are eighteen different books, the teaching being thrown into dialogue form. TT

Puskara – Sanskrit – a lotus-flower—The Seventh DVIPA, or the land of the Seventh Root-race. It is supposed that it will arise where South America now is. TT

Q

Qabbalah – Hebrew – *Qabbālāh* [from *qābal* to receive, hand down] Also Cabala, Kabala, Kabbalah, etc. Tradition, that which is handed down; the theosophy of the Jews. Originally these truths were passed on orally by one initiate to chosen disciples, hence were referred to as the Tradition. The first one historically alleged to have reduced a large part of the secret Qabbalah of the Chaldees into systematic, and perhaps written, form was the Rabbi Shim'ôn ben Yohai, in the *Zohar*; but the work of this name that has come down to the present day — through the medieval Qabbalists — is but a compilation of the 13th century, presumably by Moses de Leon.

The principal doctrines of the Qabbalah deal with the nature of the divine incomprehensible All ('eyn soph); the divine emanations of the Sephiroth; cosmogony; the creation or emanation of angels and men, and of their destiny. The Jewish Qabbalah was derived from the Chaldean Qabbalah, and "mistaken is he who accepts the Kabalistic works of to – day, and the interpretations of the Zohar by the Rabbis, for the genuine Kabalistic lore of old! For no more to – day than in the day of Frederick von Schelling does the Kabala accessible to Europe and America, contain much more than 'ruins and fragments, much distorted remnants still of that *primitive system which is the key to all religious systems*' . . . The oldest system and the *Chaldean Kabala* were identical. The latest renderings of the *Zohar* are those of the Synagogue in the early centuries" (SD 2:461 – 2).

Blavatsky refers to a work no longer extant, the Chaldean Book of Numbers, as the basis for the Qabbalah. Tentative mention is also made of an alleged manuscript left by Count Saint – Germain giving keys for interpreting the Qabbalah.

"The kabalist is a student of 'secret science,' one who interprets the hidden meaning of the Scriptures with the help of the symbolical *Kabalah*, and explains the real one by these means. The Tanaim were the first kabalists among the Jews; they appeared at Jerusalem about the beginning of the third century before the Christian era. The books of *Ezekiel, Daniel, Henoch*, and the *Revelation* of St. John, are purely kabalistical. This secret doctrine is identical with that of the Chaldeans, and includes at the same time much of the Persian wisdom, or 'magic.' History catches glimpses of famous kabalists ever since the eleventh century. The Mediaeval ages, and even our own times, have had an enormous number of the most learned and intellectual men who were students of the *Kabala*...The most famous among the former were Paracelsus, Henry Khunrath, Jacob Bohmen, Robert Fludd, the two Van Helmonts, the Abbot John Trithemius, Cornelius Agrippa, Cardinal Nicolao Cusani,

Jerome Carden, Pope Sixtus IV., and such Christian scholars as Raymond Lully, Giovanni Pico de la Mirandola, Guillaume Postel, the great John Reuchlin, Dr. Henry More, Eugenius Philalethes (Thomas Vaughan), the erudite Jesuit Athanasius Kircher, Christian Knorr (Baron) von Rosenroth; then Sir Isaac Newton, Leibniz, Lord Bacon, Spinosa, etc., etc., the list being almost inexhaustible. As remarked by Mr. Isaac Myer, in his *Qabbalah* [p. 170], the ideas of the Kabalists have largely influenced European literature. 'Upon the practical Qabbalah, the Abbe de Villars (nephew of de Montfaucon) in 1670, published his celebrated satirical novel, "The Count de Gabalis," upon which Pope based his "Rape of the Lock." Qabbalism ran through the Mediaeval poems, the "Romance of the Rose," and permeates the writings of Dante.' No two of them, however, agreed upon the origin of the Kabala, the *Zohar, Sepher Yetzirah*, etc. Some show it as coming from the Biblical Patriarchs, Abraham, and even Seth; others from Egypt, others again from Chaldea. The system is certainly very old; but like all the rest of systems, whether religious or philosophical, the Kabala is derived directly from the primeval Secret Doctrine of the East; through the Vedas, the Upanishads, Orpheus and Thales, Pythagoras and the Egyptians. Whatever its source, its substratum is at any rate identical with that of all the other systems from the *Book of the Dead* down to the later Gnostics" (TG 167 – 8).

The Jewish Qabbalah even in its present partial or mutilated form is a more or less faithful echo of that once universal archaic wisdom – religion of mankind, which as the Qabbalah itself plainly states was originally delivered by "Divinity' to a select company of angels in Paradise," and from these angels – occult initiates or adepts – disseminated as the ages passed more or less faithfully among the different races of mankind. S.D.

Quaternary – The four lower aspects of man whose expression is known as the "Personality" {q.v.). "The Quaternary regarded alone, ere it is affected by contact with the mind, is merely a lower animal: it awaits the coming of the Mind to make it Man. . . .This Quaternary is the mortal part of man, and is distinguished by Theosophy as the personality."—Theosophical Manual I. See Seven Principles of Man. TT

R

Ra – In Egyptian theogony – 1. The Soul of the Universe. "Ra is shown, like Brahma, gestating in the Egg of the Universe."—S.D., I. 385. 2. The sun. TT

Race – See ROOT – RACE and SUB-RACE. TT

Rays, The Seven Solar – In the Vedas, the mystic expression of the seven creative energies of nature, personified as gods. They are named INSHUMNA, HARIKESHA, VISHVA-KARMAN, VISHVA-TRYARCHAS, SANNADHAS, SARVA-VASU, and SVARAJ. TT

Reincarnation – the coming back of the soul—the ATMA-BUDDHA-MANAS—to the physical world. It is a teaching of the oldest religions of the world, and accepted as a truth by Theosophists, that countless rebirths of the reincarnating ego are a necessity of its evolution. It is only when the ego has assimilated all the lessons of the physical worlds, and is free from all desires relating thereto, that MOKSHA, or liberation from this necessity, is attained. The doctrine differs from METEMPSYCHOSIS OR TRANSMIGRATION in that, in Reincarnation, the human soul can but reincarnate in a human body, never in a lower form. TT

Rishi – Sanskrit – 1. A generic name in India for a sage, or a teacher of great truths. "There were three classes of Rishis in India . . . The Royal or RAJARSHIS, kings and princes who adopted the ascetic life; the Divine or DEVARSHIS, or the sons of Dharma or Yoga; and the BRAHMARSHIS."— S.D.II., 527. 2. Specifically, the seven mind – born Sons of Brahma; the PRAJAPATIS. "The Rishis—the first group of seven in number— lived in days preceding the Vedic period . . . they may now be shown as something more than merely mortal philosophers."—S.D., III. 19. "The seven great Rishis, the ancient Four, and also the Manus, were born of MY nature and mind: of them this race was generated."—*Bhagavad Gita, x.* 6. 3. A MAHATMA OR ADEPT. The RISHIS, being "the progenitors of all that lives and breathes on earth," are often confounded on the one hand with the PITRIS 1, and on the other hand with the Manus. The RISHI is correctly spoken of as the Father of the sub-race; the Manu {q.v.} as the Father of the root-race. "There have been, and there will be, seven Rishis in every Root-race…just as there are fourteen Manus in every Round, the presiding Gods, the Rishis, and Sons of the Manus being identical."—S.D. II. 650. TT

Root Manu – a general term for the great Cause from which proceeds the human life and form for the Round of a Planetary Chain. "Just as each planetary Round commences with the appearance of a Root-Manu (Dhyan Chohan), and closes with a Seed-Manu, so a Root-and a Seed-Manu appear respectively at the beginning and the termination of the human period on any particular planet."—S.D. II. 322. TT

Root Race – The Secret Doctrine teaches that in this evolution or ROUND on this Planet the JIVATMA—the human soul—passes through seven main types or "Root-races." In the case of the two earliest of these, known as the "ADAMIC" and the " Hyperborean," the forms ensouled were astral and etheric respectively: " huge and indefinite " they were, with a low state of outward-going consciousness, exercised through the one sense (hearing) possessed by the First Race, or through the two senses (hearing and touch) possessed by the Second. But with the Third Race—the Lemurian —a denser and more human type was evolved, this being perfected in the Fourth or Atlantean Race. The Fifth Race, the Aryan, is now running its course on this globe concurrently with a large part of the Fourth Race and a few remnants of the Third. For it must be noted that, although each race gives birth to the succeeding race, the two will overlap in time, coexisting for many ages. 2. Of existing peoples, the Tartars, Chinese, and Mongolians belong to the Fourth Race; the Australian aborigines and Hottentots to the Third. See SUB – RACE. 1. See S.D., II. 382. 2. For instance, "the first two sub-races of the Atlanteans overlap the sixth and seventh sub-races of the Lemurians."—*Pedigree of Man*, p. 118. TT

Round – The great "Life-wave" from the Source of all Being, vivifying successively the seven globes that constitute a PLANETARY CHAIN, is spoken of technically as a "Round." As this Creative Energy passes on from one planet to another, so does that planet go into PRALAYA, and the next planet awakes, and its latent activities begin to manifest. Seven of these Rounds constitute a MANVANTARA. TT

Rupa – Sanskrit—A body or form as in the compounds KAMA RUPA, MAYAVI – RUPA, RUPA – DEVA, etc. But "We must remember that the principle of form is to be found in every stage of the manifested universe; and that when the phrase * the formless world ' is used, the word * formless ' is only true in relation to the worlds below the one so spoken of. All higher worlds are 'formless' regarded from below, that is, regarded by the organs of perception which are fitted for exercise in the lower world."—The Evolution of Life and Form. TT

S

Sabaoth – Hebrew – a host—1. A title of Jehovah. 2. Saturn. 3. According to Origen, the Genius of Mars. TT

Sadu – With the Chaldeans, elementals or genii. TT

Samadhi – **Sanskrit**—An ecstatic trance-like state of consciousness induced by concentration, in which the Yogi reaches the knowledge of the higher mental, or, perchance, even of the TURIYA state. See Yoga. "The state in which the ascetic loses the consciousness of every individuality, including his own."—Mme. Blavatsky. TT

Sanat Kumara – Sanskrit, the Lord of the World. www.lucistrust.org

Sankhya – One of the six Hindu SHASTRAS, or systems of intellectual and abstract philosophy, evolving the universe from substance (PRAKRITI) and spirit (PURUSHA OR ATMAN), the one non – existent save through the other. Differentiation is but in the seeming, and Deity, as Deity, is not recognized. Withal, the way of salvation for man lies in the knowledge of the One by means of the many; by the observance of certain principles, he eventually obtains liberation from SAMSARA, or the round of birth and death. The SANKHYA agrees with the Vedanta in being a synthetical system— the chief point of difference is that the Sankhya maintains that the two principles, PRAKRITI and PURUSHA, however far we may push them, still remain dual. This the Vedanta denies. TT

Sanna – One of the Buddhist SKANDHAS; abstract ideas or principles. TT

Sat-Chit-Ananda – Sanskrit – existence, mind, bliss – The TRIMURTI. Personalized, IT becomes SHIVA, BRAHMA, VISHNU. "The creative aspect is shown forth in Brahma. He expresses the universal mind, the divine Chit. The life which is in everything is Vishnu. He who is sometimes called the Destroyer, but is rather the Regenerator; MAHADEVA is Sat, or existence," – Four Great Religions. See Trimurti. TT

Sattva – Sanskrit – being; existence—1. The highest of the three GUNAS; harmony; light or truth; soothfastness. "A difficult word to translate: I am inclined to translate it as Harmony, for this reason, that, wherever there is pleasure, Sattva is present."— *Evolution of Life and Form*. 2. Atma – buddhi; the ANTAKARANA. 3. The real or essential. Also written as Satva, Satwa, Sattwa, and Sattwan. TT

Satya Yuga – See **Yuga.**

Seb – Egyptian – In Egyptian theogony, the equivalent of Cronos or Saturn. "Seb, the God of Time and of the Earth, is spoken of as having laid an egg, or the Universe." – S.D. I. 385. TT

Self, The – This word is used by Theosophists with three different connotations, the second and third expressing the same idea as the first, but with greater limitation, i ATMAN, the One Spirit in all. "I am the Self seated deep in every creature's heart. I am the beginning, the life, and the end of all existing things." – *Bhagavad Gita*, IX. 20. 2. The Higher Ego; the Thinker; the immortal man. 3. The Lower Ego. The first of these is spoken of as "The Self"; the second, as "The Higher Self"; and the third, as "The Lower Self." "And now thy Self is lost in Self; Thyself unto Thyself, merged in That Self from which thou first didst radiate." – *The Voice of the Silence*. TT

Sephira – Hebrew. With the Kaballists, the first emanation from AIN – SOPH; the equivalent of the HINDU VACH, the Gnostic SOPHIA, or the Christian Holy Ghost. "From within the Eternal Essence of Ain – Soph comes forth Sephira, the Active Power, called the Primordial Point and the Crown, Kether." —S.D., I. 378. TT

Sephiroth – Hebrew – numbers—With the Kabalists, the ten Emanations from AIN – SOPH, the Eternal. TT

Serpent – "The primitive symbol of the serpent symbolized Divine Wisdom and Perfection, and has always stood for psychical Regeneration and Immortality."—S.D., I. 102. T A widely adopted symbol for REASON, the characteristic endowment of man. See NAGA.

Seven Creative Hierarchies of Being – are the spiritual rulers of the planets. TT

Seven Principles of Man – in the earlier writings of the Theosophical Movement these principles were referred to as (1) ATMA, Spirit; (2) BUDDHI, spiritual soul; (3) MANAS, mind; (4) KAMA, feeling; (5) PRANA, life; (6) LINGA-SHARIRA, the etheric double; and (7) STHULA-SHARIRA, the physical body. But there is confusion here between "bodies" and "principles," between objective and subjective, and it would appear that it is to the fivefold universe —not to the sevenfold—that man, as thus described, is related. The analysis, then, is by no means satisfactory. Objectively considered, man is, perhaps, best described as consisting of a Mental Body (CAUSAL and MANASIC), an Astral Body, and a Physical Body (DENSE and ETHERIC). These correspond with, and are in relation to, "the three worlds"; and it is through, or by means of, these bodies that the "Principles," the JIVATMIC expression, manifest themselves. Higher than these three worlds, existence is ARUPA or formless, and the "Principles" are Divine rather than human. TT

Sishtas – Sanskrit term which means remainder or remnant. Those most evolved beings of any life-wave or kingdom, i.e. human kingdom, animal kingdom. The SISHTAS are the most enlightened beings that remain on the earth as its' representatives when the Monads of the highest order of beings of that kingdom move on to the nest succeeding globe, to next undergo experiences. GD.

Shambhala – "A very mysterious locality on account of its future associations." —Mme. Blavatsky. The residence of 'The Lord of the World', Sanat Kumara. TT, JHH.

Shangna Robe – In Buddhism, the initiation robe of the neophytes. "Metaphorically, the acquirement of Wisdom with which the Nirvana of destruction (of personality) is entered." —Mme. Blavatsky. TT

Shankara – Shiva. TT

Shankarshana – Cosmic life. TT

Shiva – generally considered as the Third Person of the Hindu Trinity. See TRIMURTI.

"He who is sometimes called the Destroyer, but is rather the Regenerator; He who is living Fire. . . ."—Four Great Religions.

Shravaka – Sanskrit – a hearer—A pupil. In Buddhism, a student of the teaching and one practiced in the four great truths. TT

Shveta – dvipa – Sanskrit – the white land)—1. In the PURANAS – Mount Meru. 2. A part of Atlantis; Ruta. TT

Siddha – Sanskrit – perfected—1. One having siddhis or occult powers. 2. A saint or yogi. 3. A Nirmanakaya. "The Siddhas are Nirmanakayas or the 'Spirits'— in the sense of an individual or conscious spirit—of great Sages from spheres on a higher plane than our own, who voluntarily incarnate in mortal bodies in order to help the human race." —S.D., II. 673. TT

Siirya – Sanskrit—1. The sun. SEE AGNI. 2. A Son of God. "Surya, the * Son,' who offers Himself as a sacrifice to himself." – S.D., III. 142. TT

Skandhas – 1. In Buddhism, the karmic results, the summing up of an incarnation, these results of the past prescribing the nature of the seed for the future lives in the body. "They are five in the popular, or exoteric, system of the Buddhists—i.e. RUPA, form or body, which leaves behind it its magnetic atoms and occult affinities; VEDANA, sensations, which do likewise; SANNA, or abstract ideas, which are the creative powers at work from one incarnation to another ; SAMKHARA, tendencies of mind; and VINNANA, mental powers."— Key to Theosophy. 2. A section or chapter of a book. TT

Sod – Hebrew – secret—Esoteric teaching or mysteries. TT

Sohan – In Buddhism: 1. the first great initiation, the aspirant becoming then an accepted chela. SROTAPATTI. 2. One of the four paths to NIRVANA. TT

Solar – as applied by occultists to any being or entity, indicates that that being has come into touch with the Higher Triad. Such a being is man. TT

Solar Angels, Angels, Returning NIRVANIS, Sons of God, AGNISHVATTAS – Solar angels who "fell to Earth" were rebellious, with their descent reflecting a mystery hinted at in the Scriptures, and "The Secret of the Ages" in Esoteric Psychology II, by A. Bailey, p. 93. Lucifer is the best known to us of the fallen angels. The secret is the mystery which lies behind the Plan of evolution because the solar angels' willingness to "fall"; being from Venus, being custodians of what we call the principle of Mind, bringing this as a pure gift to embryonic humanity and in so doing, sacrificing themselves to bring the "Light of the principle of Mind" to what was then animal man. This act marked the coming into action of the great Law of Duality by which matter, form; negative and passive, could be quickened by spirit. The act sacrifice at the dawn of human history is a thread woven throughout the great scriptures and mythologies of the world, so that like Prometheus, who stole "fire" or Mind for man, the solar angels chose to descend to Earth, assist in evolution by giving man a mental capacity with free will and providing humanity a choice of two paths, which must always be a choice for the human, who is guided by free will the and the capacity to make choices and to choose the higher way. The role of Guardian Angel was made possible by the sacrifice of the solar angels in their preservation of the principle of mind or, occultly, fire, through persistent repeated incarnations in form until animal man became thinking man and, finally, began to awaken to his true spiritual heritage: human and divine man. Thus the solar angel creates the form for the incarnating soul principle, the causal body, and it also withdraws that body at the fourth initiation, when the link between form and spirit has been permanently fused and the causal body is shattered. www.lucistrust.org

Solar Pitris – The name that has been given to the two classes of beings, the first of which, at the completion of the lunar cycle, had attained to the human kingdom, and the second of which was on the point of doing so. Progressed so far in their evolution that it was not needful for them to pass through the earlier rounds of the Terrene (Earth) Chain, they only enter this in the middle of the Fourth Round. "—the second division entered the humanity of earth after the separation of the sexes in the Third Race; the first division entered during the Fourth Race, the Atlantean."—*The Pedigree of Man.* TT

Solar Rays – See RAYS, THE SEVEN. Also known as the Lower Dhyanis. TT

Solomon's Seal – the symbolical interlaced triangles, as adopted by the Theosophical Society in its emblematical seal; called in India "the sign of Vishnu." TT

Soma – Sanskrit—I. The moon. 2. A plant used in sacrifices, and for making the "nectar of the gods." "In India the initiated received the Soma, sacred drink, which helped to liberate his soul from the body."— (S.I). III. 124. TT

Sons of Dhyana or Sons of Dharma – The Sons of Yoga. TT

Sons of Fire – 1. The first Seven Emanations of the Logos. 2. The AGNISHVATTAS: They "are 'the Sons of Fire' because they are the first Beings . . . evolved from primordial fire."— S.D.1. 114. 3. An order of the "Sons of Mind," coming from the Venus Chain, who manifested (by KRIYASHAKTI) on this globe as the Teachers of the infant humanity during the Third Race period. "Listen, ye sons of the Earth, to your Instructors, the sons of Fire."— *Stanzas of Dzyan.* 4. The SOLAR PITRIS. TT

Sons of Light – an analogue of the "Sons of Fire". TT

Sons of Mind – Mind – born Sons — The MANASAPUTRAS. The term has also been applied to the RISHIS, FRAJAPATIS, MANUS, KUMARAS, or other emanation of the Logos. TT

Sons of Wisdom – The MANASAPUTRAS (q.v.); more specifically, the AGNISHVATTA PITRIS. TT

Sons of Yoga – A phrase of general application to those Beings who come into manifestation more directly by means of the Divine Thought or Will. Specifically, the Sons of Yoga are the semi – astral beings of the early androgynous Third Race created by KRIYASHAKTI, or abstract meditation. See NAYA and RISHI. "It" [the Third Race] "created SONS OF WILL AND YOGA, by KRIYASHAKTI it created them, the Holy Fathers." —*Stanzas of Dzyan.* SONS OF DHYANA, SONS OF THE FIRE-MIST, are analogues. TT

Sophia – Greek—the Wisdom. It is a Gnostic term, the idea connoted being similar to that of the AKASHA of the occultist, or, when personalized, to that of the Holy Ghost of the early Christians. TT

Soul – as used by Theosophists, this word may be defined as Spirit manifesting objectively, that is, through substance of different grades. Thus, cosmically, it may be BUDDHI or the "Bliss-soul, "MAHAT or the "Intelligent Soul," or the "Astral Light," the "lowest division of the universal Soul." Microcosmically, it may be BUDDHI; it may be MANAS; or it may be KAMA. See SPIRIT. TT

Spirit – ATMAN; the supreme underlying KOSMIC Reality. "Matter is the vehicle for the manifestation of Soul on this plane of existence, and Soul is the vehicle on a higher plane for the manifestation of Spirit."—S.D., I. 80. TT

Srotapanna – Pali Canon – entering the stream—In Buddhism: 1. The first initiation; SOHAN. "Next, the condition of SROTAPANNA, in which, after seven births and deaths, a man becomes a Rabat."—Chinese Buddhism. 2. One of the four paths to NIRVANA. Also written SCROTAPANNA and SOTAPANNA.

Sub-plane—in the esoteric doctrine each plane contains seven sub-planes, the first or innermost of these being generally known as the atomic. The different sub – planes of the physical world have been generally termed the 1st ETHERIC OR ATOMIC; the 2nd ETHERIC or SUB-ATOMIC; the 3rd ETHERIC or SUPER-ETHERIC; the 4th ETHERIC or ETHERIC; gaseous; liquid; and solid. TT

Sub – race – the seven ROOT-RACES have each seven differentiations or Sub – races, and we have sufficient information with reference to the two last ROOT-RACES to enable us to define these. Thus the FOURTH ROOT-RACE is made up of the Rmoahal, the Tlavatli, the Toltec, the Turanian, the Semitic, the Akkadian, and the Mongolian SUB – RACES. See FIFTH ROOT-RACE. TT

Sura – Sanskrit – 1. A god or deva; specifically, those gods on the "right – hand path" in contradistinction to those on the "left hand path " – the ASURAS (q.v.)." The Third Race gave birth to the Fourth; the Sura became Asura." – *Stanzas of Dzyan*. 2. A sage. TT

Sutratma – Sanskrit – In the VEDANTIN system, while it has certain specific significations, the general idea conveyed by this term is that of a "thread" connecting the five different principles or KOSHAS. Essentially it is ATMA, and it is literally translated "the Thread – Self" or "the Thread – Soul"; for it is. 1. The HIGHER EGO, as that on which the fruits of the personalities of the different earth – lives are strung. 2. The MONAD, as that on which the unit of the experience of the descent into matter (the objective world) is strung. 3. The SECOND LOGOS, as that on which every living being is strung. "All the communication of the Monad with the planes below his own has been through the SUTRATMA, the life thread on which the atoms are strung. *A Study in Consciousness.* TT

Svabhava, Swabhava – Sanskrit – *Svabhāva*; from *sva* self + *bhū* to become, grow into. Self-becoming, self-generation, self-growing into something; the unfolding of the self or monadic essence by *inner* impulse, rather than by merely mechanical activity in nature — *self*-becoming or self-directed evolution. Each entity is the result of what it is in its own higher nature. "Its Swabhava can bring forth only that which itself is, its essential characteristic, its own inner nature. Swabhava, in short, may be called the essential Individuality of any monad, expressing its own characteristics, qualities, and type, by *self-urged evolution.* Consequently, each individual Swabhava brings forth and expresses as its own particular vehicles its various *swarupas*, signifying characteristic bodies or images or forms" (OG 166 – 7). The essential self, like a sun, sends a ray from itself into manifestation, and the vehicles formed by this ray express its own unique individual essence and path of evolutionary growth and experience. Every entity, in all ranges of its being, reflects its own essential individuality which is stamped on its inmost essence. A parallel concept is the stoic '*Spermatikoi Logoi*'; seed – reasons or – causes, "which were the fruits or results, the karmas, of former periods of activity. Having attained a certain stage of evolution, development, quality or characteristic; or individuality in the preceding Manvantara, when the next period of evolution came, they could produce nothing else but *that which they were themselves*, their *own inner natures*, as seeds do. The seed can produce nothing but what it itself is, what is in it; and this is the heart and essence of the doctrine of swabhava" (Fund 149). TS

Svastika, Swastika – Sanskrit – *Svastika*; An auspicious or lucky object; especially applied to the mystic symbol, a cross with four equal arms, the extremities of which are bent sharply at right angles, all in the same direction, marked upon persons and things in order to denote good luck, although originally the symbol had a far deeper significance. Sometimes the arms are bent to the left, sometimes to the right. The symbol is very widespread, and extremely ancient, engraved on every rock temple and prehistoric building in India, and wherever Buddhists have flourished, as well as in Greece, among the ancient Scandinavians, and in ancient America. It has been called the Jaina Cross; Fylfot, Mjolnir, or Thor's Hammer by the Scandinavian peoples; and in the Chaldean Book of Numbers the Worker's Hammer. TS

Sweat – born – an appellation of the Second and early Third Races from the Secret Doctrine. TT

Scythian – Greek – 1. Directed by the Greeks originally to various peoples, but most often to warlike Nomads of the Steppes, which is now southern Russia. 2. During the Roman Empire, applied to similar peoples in t northerly parts of Asia. 3. Blavatsky says they are late Atlantean sub-races (SD 2:774). TS

Sylphs—Spirits of the air; the highest class of Nature Spirits. See ELEMENTAL. TT

T

Taijas – Sanskrit – tejas or fire – 1. The radiant; the luminous. 2. That TATVA which forms the manifestation of the Third Logos on the mental plane; Agni. TT

Taijasa – Sanskrit – the shining – 1. With the Vedantins, the centre of Cosmic Consciousness from which emanate the Devas. 2. That reflection of the Self (JITVATMA) known as the KAMA-MANASIC centre; the SUKSHMA. The CHAKRAMS are its objective representation. "It is through this spiritual and intellectual Principle that man is united to his heavenly prototype; never through his lower inner self or astral body." – S.D, 3. Consciousness dealing with higher, or subjective, worlds. TT

Tanha – Sanskrit and Pali Canon—the desire for physical life or sentient existence; that which causes rebirth. "Question: What is the force or energy that is at work to produce the new being? Answer: TANHA—the will to live." – Buddhist Catechism. TT

Tanmatra or Tanmatram – Sanskrit – the measure of That – The first, and last, differentiation of universal indiscrete substance ; the manifestation of the Third Logos known as "the Divine Measure," since by it is the measure of their vibration given to the atoms or units of motion. The TANMATRAS, therefore, may be considered as the mode of manifestation, i.e. as that which proceeds from within outwards; and the five TANMATRAS, each with their seven sub – TANMATRAS, will represent for us the substance of the fivefold universe which forms the field for human evolution. "Each tattva has got for its ensouled life a TANMATRA or a modification of the Divine Consciousness. In each tattva, therefore, we have the Divine Consciousness as the central life, while the idea of resistance forms the outer wall."—"THE DREAMER." Vibration must "be determined by a law which, by limiting the vibratory possibilities, makes manifestation possible. This law is the TANMATRA." – *Theosophical Review.* TT

Tantra or Tantram – Sanskrit – the important, the essential – 1. A Hindu sacred and mystical book. Of these there are 160. The teaching is generally thrown into the form of a dialogue between Shiva and Durga, great prominence being given to the Shaktis or female energies of the deities. 2. Magical formulae as put in action. TT

Tao – Sanskrit – 1. Svabhavat is an equivalent, also the deep akasic abysses of the highest reaches of the cosmic anima mundi, manifesting periodically. 2. Chinese – The way, road, path; the Chinese treat of Tao in two aspects: the Tao of man (jen tao); and the Tao of the universe, which is again divided into two aspects, the Tao of heaven (t'ien tao) and the tao of earth (t'i tao). There is no supreme god in this system of philosophy, no Demiurge or maker of the cosmos: the yearly renovation of nature is due to the spontaneity of Tao. In the I Ching, Tao brings about the revolving mutations of the yin and yang: "there is in the system of mutations of nature; the Most Ultimate which produced the two Regulating Powers – the yin and yang, which produce the four shapes – the seasons." Hi-tsze. 3. With the Egyptian Gnostics, the genius of the Moon. TT, TS

Tattva – Sanskrit – "thatness," truth, reality – 1. Generally, the essential nature of things; the essential nature of the human soul as a mode of the Divine Consciousness. 2. Specifically, that fundamental law of substance, or that manifestation of the Third Logos, which is seen by us as the form of the atom or as the creation of the primary elements. "The Logos marks out, according to this divine measure [TANMATRA] the lines which determine the shape of the atom, the fundamental axes of growth, the angular relation of these, which determines the form.. . .These are, collectively, a TATTVA. "*A Study in Consciousness*. The five TATTVAS manifested are known to the MAHESVARAS as AKASHA, VAYU, TEJAS (or AGNI), APAS, and PRITHIVI (q.v). These constitute the planes of the Theosophist, and furnish the fivefold field for the evolution of man. The SANKHYA system has 25 TATTVAS, viz., AVYAKTA, BUDDHI, AHANKARA, MANAS, PURUSHA, the five TANMATRAS, the five MAHABHUTAS, as above, and the ten INDRYAS. See under these heads. TT

Tejas – Sanskrit – fire – SEE TAIJAS. TT

Terrestial Chain or Terrene – the Planetary Chain, of which the Earth is the lowest globe. TT

Tetrad or Tetraktis – Greek – four – the mystic square; the "Quaternary"; Man. TT

That – THE ONE EXISTENCE; the Absolute. "Then THAT vibrated motionless, one with Its' own glory; and beside THAT nothing else existed." – *Rig Veda.* "All comes forth from THAT; …in THAT, SAT, CHIT, and ANANDA have their root in unity, the One without a second; in THAT, unknown and unknowable, all is." – Four Great Religions. TT

Theosophy – Greek; Divine Wisdom – 1. "A name given by the Alexandrian philosophers to the ancient Wisdom – Religion, the Hidden Wisdom, in the third century A.D."2 2. That eternal revelation of the Divine Spirit which forms the source of all the religions, arts, and sciences of the world. Theosophy "is the one Truth which underlies all forms, all phenomena, all experience. Every system of religion arises from the attempt to formulate this underlying Truth, to give it definite expression in human language." – Wm. Kingsland. 1 Mme. Blavatsky. 2 *A Short Glossary,* by Annie Besant and H. Burrows. TT

Thoth – Thot – Hermes, God of Wisdom. In Egyptian cosmogony, the Divine Man; manifested Deity.1 the Atlantean Adept who came to Egypt and established the Ancient Wisdom after the deluge of Atlantis. TT

The Science of The Seven Rays – The cosmology of the Ageless Wisdom gives an explanation; to thereby grossly summarize and simplify: As part of the initial Plan, the One Life sought expansion.

Initially, that Life expressed in triple formation: as Life, Quality and Appearance, or Monad, Soul, and Personality; Will, Love, and Intelligence. The Seven Rays are the first differentiation of this threefold divinity; from three major rays, four minor rays unfold to reveal the sevenfold nature of divinity.

1st ray – The energy of Will, Purpose or Power, which is essentially the Will of Deity.

2nd ray – The energy of Love – Wisdom – the desire or love of Deity.

3rd ray – The energy of Active Intelligence or, to reverse it, intelligent activity.

4th ray – The energy of Harmony through Conflict.

5th ray – The energy of Concrete Knowledge or Science.

6th ray – The energy of Devotion or Idealism.

7th ray – The energy of Ceremonial Order.

http://www.lucistrust.org/

The One About Whom Not May Be Said – His Being is represented by our planet, the 4th in a series of Divine Expression and associated humanity, and has a specific relationship to the position of our solar system, in a series of solar systems, which constitute His expression. TG

Thread – self or Thread – soul – The Sutratma. TT

Tiamat – Chaldean – 1. The feminine power; *regarded as evil*, representing the Sea (**Mare, Mary**), the womb of life, which was the Chaldean serpent, slain by Bel, the chief deity. 2. In Babylon, Marduk replaces Bel. The mythologic serpent, described as the embodiment of evil; both physical and moral, was enormous – 300 miles long, moving in undulations 6 miles in height. When Marduk finally slew Tiamat he split the monster into two halves, using one as a covering of the heavens, so that the upper waters would not come down. Tiamat is cognate with the Babylonian Tiamtu, Tamtu, – the Ocean – rendered Thalatth by Berosus in his Chaldean cosmogony. There is here likewise the reference to the waters of wisdom, the divine wisdom and the lower wisdom of manifestation.

3. Blavatsky explains that the serpent **Tiamat is the Great Mother**, "the living principle of chaos. The struggle of Bel and then of Merodach, the Sun – god, with *Tiamat*, the Sea and its Dragon, a

'war' which ended in the defeat of the latter, has a purely cosmic and geological meaning, as well as an historical one. It is a page torn out of the History of the Secret and Sacred Sciences, their evolution, growth and death, *for the profane masses*. It relates first, to the systematic and gradual drying up of immense territories by the fierce Sun at a certain pre – historic period; one of the terrible droughts which ended by a gradual transformation of once fertile lands abundantly watered into the sandy deserts which they are now; and second, to the systematic persecution of the Prophets of the Right Path by those of the Left." (SD 2:503) TS

Tirnan – Oge – Irish – the Country of the Young, the Celtic paradise. See *Thrice – greatest Hermes,* by G. R. S. Mead and The Key to Theosophy by HBV. TT

Toltec – the Third Sub-race of the Fourth Root-race. 1. This people formed the supreme civilization reached in Atlantis. 2. The Toltec people migrated and civilized areas of Central America and were named after the sub-race of the Atlanteans. TT

Tree, Tree of Life – A variant of the cross or tau, to be considered in connection with the serpent which is wound round it. The two together symbolize the World Tree with the spiritual, intellectual, psychic, and psychological aggregate of forces encircling the World Tree and working in and through it – these forces often grouped in the Orient under the name of kundalini. In minor significance, the two together symbolize the life-waves, or any life-wave, passing through the planes, spirit circling through matter, Fohat working in the kosmos. Thus the tree symbol stands for the universe, and correspondentially for man, in whom the monadic ray kindles activity on the several planes; while the physiological key of interpretation applies to the analogies in the human body with its various structures through which play the pranic currents. The tree, by its form, represents evolution, for it begins with a root and spreads out into branches and twigs; only as applied to the kosmos the root is conceived to be on high and the branches to extend downwards. Thus, there is the Asvattha tree of India or Bodhi Tree, the Norse Yggdrasil, the Tree Ababel in the Koran, the Sephirothal Tree which is "Adam Qadmon."

In the Garden of Eden it is stated that there were two trees, the Tree of Life and the Tree of the Knowledge of Good and Evil, which signifies the two knowledges. It is said in Gnosticism that Ennoia (divine thought) and Ophis (serpent), as a unity, are the Logos; as separated they are the Tree of Life and the Tree of Knowledge, the former spiritual, the latter manasic. Adam eats the fruit of the Tree of Knowledge which means in one important allegory of human evolution that mankind after the separation of the sexes became endowed with manas, or that when humanity began to be endowed with dual manas, the rays then separated into the opposite sexes; and lest he should partake of the Tree of Life and become immortal, in the then imperfect state of evolution, he is turned out of Eden. It is stated that buddhi becomes transformed into the tree whose fruit is emancipation and which finally destroys the roots of the Asvattha, which here is the symbol of the mayavi life. This latter tree is also the emblem of secret and sacred knowledge, guarded by serpents or dragons; it may also refer to a sacred scripture. Dragons guarded the tree with the golden apples of the Hesperides; the trees of Meru were guarded by a serpent; Juno, on her wedding with Jupiter, gave him a tree with golden fruit, as Eve gave the fruit to Adam. Blavatsky says of Eve: "She it was who first led man to the Tree of Knowledge and made known to him Good and Evil; and if she had been left in peace to do quietly that which she wished to do, she would have conducted him to the Tree of Life and would thus have rendered him immortal." (Translated from the *La Revue Theosophique*, 1970, The Blue Lotus, 2:10. The Theosophical Review, Vol. 2, page 10. From Le Passe – Temps, Montbrison, France. THE BLUE LOTUS – 1970 – No. 1 to 12. Translation of 'The Theosophical Review' from 'The Blue Lotus'. AUDOIN (D.), GA BARBORKA, WHITE HR, HP BLAVATSKY Lucien BRET Th CHAPELLIER, E. Cusani, G. FARTHING, Ch GOSSELIN, Nine GRANDI, A. HERMANN or HERRMANN. N. KAUFFMANN, P. LAFLECHE, Ch. LALLEMAND, S. LANCRI, G. MONOD HERZEN Prof. BR Mullik Maria POTEL, V. RUSSEL, Hermine Sabetay, N. SRI RAM, G. TRIPET and VIA. Antiquated book information from http://www.abebooks.co.uk/.

Treta Yuga – See **Yuga**.

Triad – Atma – buddhi – manas is often referred to as the "Upper Triad." The "Lower (RUPA) Triad" may be considered as this trinity reflected in "The three worlds," physical, astral, and mental. TT

Tri – yana – Sanskrit – the three vehicles – The three degrees of Buddhahood, the SHRAVAKA, the BODHI-SATTVA, and the PRATYEKA – BUDDHA. TT

Trimurti – Sanskrit – assuming three aspects—The Hindu Triad, BRAHMA, VISHNU, SHIVA. "Vishnu represents the idea of evolution—the process by which the inner spirit unfolds and generates the universe of sensible forms .... Shiva represents the idea of involution, by which thought and the sensible universe are indrawn again into quiescence; and Brahma represents the state which is neither evolution nor involution, and yet is both—existence itself, now first brought into the region of thought through relation to Vishnu and Shiva". – Ed. Carpenter. See SAT – CHIT – ANANDA. TT

U

Upanishads – Sanskrit – esoteric doctrine – Mystical treatises on the VEDAS forming part of SHRUTI or the Revelation of Hinduism. The fundamental problems of the origin and nature of Deity, of the universe, of mind, and of matter are discussed. The UPANISHADS are said to be the source of all the six systems of Hindu philosophy. TT

V

Vaidhatra – Sanskrit – A son or emanation of Brahma known as SANAT – KUMARA. See Sanat Kumara. TT

Valhalla – Scandinavian – In Scandinavian mythology, the hall of the heroes slain in battle. TT

Vana – devatas – Sanskrit – Sprites or dryads of the woods. TT

Var – Scandinavian – Goddess of vows; ninth of the 14 goddesses; Asynjur of the Eddas: she hearkens to oaths and covenants, and takes vengeance on those who perjure themselves, avenging every breach of faith. Closely associated with her was the tenth goddess Vor, she who is wise and of a searching spirit; none can conceal anything from her. Both are classed as handmaidens of the goddess Freya or Venus. TS

Varuna – Sanskrit – the All – embracer – originally one of the three highest deities of the Hindus, "the Maker of Heaven and Earth, "VARUNA later became the God of the Waters. He or 'It' may be considered as the Ruler of the Water Elementals, or, abstractly, as the principle pervading the APAS – TATTVA, hence, the objective side of the KAMIC world. TT

Vayu – Sanskrit – 1. The air and wind and their personified principle, PAVANA. Vayu is one of the Vedic Trinity. 2. That TATTVA which forms the manifestation of the THIRD LOGOS on the BUDDHIC PLANE. 3. The Fire Deity that manifests as air. See Agni. 4. One of the five "airs" or life – principles of the body, viz. PRANA, APANA, SAMANA, UDANA, and VYANA. "There are two kinds of Vayu: 1 – PANCHIKRITA-VAYU, 'molecular air,' or compound gas, like the air of the atmosphere; and 2 – VAYU-ANMATRA, 'atomic air,' elementary gas, the substrate of the sensation of touch." *Theosophical Review.* TT

Veda – Sanskrit – knowledge – 1. The Hindu Scripture. It comprises the RIG – VEDA (the most ancient), the YAJUR-VEDA, the SAMA-VEDA, and the more modern ARTHARVA-VEDA. Each Veda has two portions, a SAMHITA, the MANTRAS, and a BRAHMANA or ceremonial exposition, both being SHRUTI or Divine Revelation. See VEDANTA. 2. Truth. "By the Vedas no books are meant. They mean the accumulated treasury of spiritual laws discovered by different persons in different times." TT

Vedanta – Sanskrit – the end of the Veda, or knowledge)—One of the six great systems of Hinduism, comprising three schools, the ADVAITA, the DVAITA, and the VISHISHTHADVAITA. Following the SANKHYA to a very great extent, it seeks a further cause of the manifested universe beyond the dual PURUSHA-PRAKRITI. This it finds in Deity (BRAHMAN), which, according to the ADVAITA, is one with the very Self in man, but, according to the DVAITA, a distinct Reality. The system is said to have been founded by Vyasa, and has as its greatest exponent SHANKARACHARYA. TT

Vishnu – Sanskrit – all – pervading—May be considered as the Second Person of the Hindu Trinity.1 See TRIMURTI. "The life which is in everything, the life which permeates, which sustains, the foundation of the universe ... is Vishnu, the All – Pervader, the sustaining life of God."—Annie Besant. In the Vedas, Vishnu is often identified with the sun, and, as the Father of the Adityas, becomes identical with BRAHMA. He has, according to the Brahmans, ten incarnations, viz.: MATSYA, the fish; KURMA, the tortoise; VARAHA, the boar NARASINHA, the man – lion; VAMANA, the dwarf; PARASHU – RAMA, Rama with the axe ; RAMA – CHANDRA, the hero of the RAMAYANA; BUDDHA, KRISHNA, and KALKI, who has yet to appear. See BRAHMA. TT

Vyasa – Sanskrit – one who distributes or diffuses knowledge, – A GURU. TT

W

Watcher – 1. A name for the celestial Beings (DHYAN – CHOHANS) who guide and supervise the manifestations of the Life of a Race, Planet, or ROUND. 2. The Monad. "The Watcher, or the Divine Prototype, is at the upper rung of the Ladder of Being; the Shadow (man) at the lower." —S.D., 1. 285. TT

White Magic – Magic used solely for the furtherance of the Divine Purpose, in contradistinction to Black Magic or sorcery. TT

Woden – See Odin. TT

Word, The – The Manifested Logos, sound being the first property of AKASHA (as in Akashic Record, the unmanifested. "The esoteric meaning of the word Logos—speech or Word, Verbum—is the rendering in objective expression, as in a photograph, of the concealed thought."—S.D., ii. 28. TT

Y

Yoga or Yogam – Sanskrit – union – A word of wide meaning; it is applied by the Hindus to almost any system by means of which it is believed the human soul or JIVATMA may emancipate itself from the MAYA of earth life, and attain to union with ISHVARA or the Universal Spirit. The ways and means of such union are of two main orders. In the one, HATHA – YOGA (q.v.), the devotee seeks to transcend the physical by reducing his own lives to impotency, Blavatsky stated that the Lemurians were perfecting HATHA YOGA; in the other, RAJA – YOGA (q.v.), the end is attained by an intensification of the consciousness by concentration and meditation. In the practice of yoga, generally, eight stages are enumerated by the Hindu philosophers: 1. Yama, restraint; forbearance. 2. NI – YAMA, religious observances. 3. ASANA, posture. 4. PRANA – YAMA, control of the breath. 5. PRATY – AHARA, restraint of the senses. 6. DHARANA, steadying the mind by concentration. 7. DHYANA, abstract contemplation. 8. SAMADHI, ecstatic meditation. See YOGA PHILOSOPHY. TT

Yoga – Sanskrit – *Hatha Yoga* and *Tantra Yoga* are the lowest forms of yoga and deal mainly with the body and lower mind. Since they do little or nothing to develop our higher nature they produce no lasting benefits, for it is only those things that can be recorded by our spiritual self that endure beyond death. The higher forms of yoga discipline include *Karma Yoga*: the yoga of action, comparable to what is known in the West as 'salvation by works', *Bhakti Yoga*: the yoga of love and devotion; similar to 'salvation by faith or love', *Jnana Yoga*: the yoga of wisdom or knowledge and *Raja Yoga*, literally the 'royal union'; the yoga of spiritual self – discipline and *Brahma Yoga*; the divine union', which is a synthesis of the best and purest practices in the other Yoga schools. Hatha Yoga is the teaching that growth of the soul is by means of the physical body, by the adoption of certain postures, by the regulation of the breath, or by other psycho – physical methods. "The theory of Hatha Yoga is includes the following: on the whole, it is easiest to begin development with the physical body, because then you are dealing with a thing of which you, at least, know something; that, starting with your physical body, you can bring it under control to a well – nigh incredible extent; that, as the physical body corresponds in its various parts to the organs of the higher bodies, it is possible to reach those organs of the higher bodies by stimulating the organs of the lower." – Theosophy and the New Psychology. TT, http://www.theosophy – nw.org/theosnw/path/oc – prat.htm

Yoga Philosophy – One of the six Hindu systems for the growth of the soul. As given forth by Patanjali, it is a deistic interpretation of the **Sankhya**; indeed, it is often considered to be but a subdivision of that system. But while the Yoga lays stress on religious practices, with the **Sankhya** wisdom is the *summum bonum*. Sir Edwin Arnold translates a passage from the **Bhagavad Gita** bearing on this point thus:—"There be two paths, Shown to this world; two schools of wisdom. First, The Sinkhya's which doth save in way of works, Prescribed by reason; next, the Yoga, which bids, Attain by meditation, spiritually; Yet these are one." TT

Yoni – Sanskrit – the womb – the female phallic symbol or power in nature, represented by an oval. It is worshipped by the Shaktis. TT

Yuga – Sanskrit – a generation—an age or cycle. According to the **MAHABHARATA,** our evolution is divided into four YUGAS, each of these YUGAS being preceded by a period called its **SANDHYA,** and followed by another period of equal length called its **SANDHYANSA.** The four YUGAS are known as: —**KRITA-YUGA,** called also **SATYA-YUGA,** or "The Golden Age," lasting until the middle of the Third Race —with its **SANDHYA** and **SANDHYANSA,** a period of 1,728,000 years. **TRETA-YUGA,** a period of 1,296,000 years. **DVAPARA-YUGA,** a period of 864,000 years. **KALI-YUGA,** the present, "The Black Age," a period of 432,000 years. These four YUGAS constitute a **MAHA-YUGA.** It will be understood that the YUGAS at any particular time are different for different races. 1 TT

1 – SANDHYA – the time period flowing each YUGA.

2 – SANDHYANSA – the time period flowing each SANDHYA, of equal length.

3 – KRITA YUGA or SATYA YUGA – 1.
2. "The Golden Age," lasting until the middle of the Third Race

4 – TRETA YUGA – a period of 1,296,000 years which follows the SANDHYANSA, a period   of 1,728,000 years.

5 – DVAPARA YUGA – a period of 864,000 years.

6 – KALI YUGA – a period of 432,000 years, which follows the DVAPARA YUGA.

7 – MAHA YUGA – these four YUGAS constitute a MAHA YUGA.

Yuga-kshaya, Yagantaka – The end of the YUGA. TT

Z

Zahir – In Islam, the manifested Logos. TT

Zeus – The main god over the gods on Mt. Olympus.

Janet Hizar Hansford

About the Author

Janet Hizar Hansford is a visionary author and scholar who dares to look at the genesis of this planet and the human being from reputable, non-traditional sources—ranging from obscure to fantastic- yet believable. Respectful of science, she reasons that this point of view only supplies partial answers, and falls short in answering the truly profound questions of human existence. History needs revisionist authors like Dr. Hansford! In the last century, a new breed of investigator has arisen from the ranks of scholarly explorers of our human heritage. These are the risk takers and the deep thinkers with a penchant for travel and independent inquiry. Anthrogenesis, her first book in this genre, brings forth unique gems of knowledge from the ancient literature, modern savants, and the inscrutable wisdom seekers of the early twentieth century. It contains nuggets of information from many areas, especially the ancient wisdom teaching of Theosophy, all fitting together to reveal a new picture of evolution and our place in the galaxy.

Dr. Hansford received her Ph.D. in 1988 in Clinical Psychology from William Lyon University, San Diego, California. She also holds an M.S. in Counseling Psychology from California State University, Fullerton and a B.S., with Honors, in Human Services from California State University, Fullerton. She is a trained 'Ericksonian' hypnotherapist and certified EMDR practitioner, licensed in California as a Marriage and Family Therapist. Dr. Hansford integrates mind-body healing practices such as sacred meditation, leading women's empowerment groups and vision quests, African dance and drumming, energy work, and spirit traditions with tribal indigenous peoples into her practice, while personally observing Jungian and the Eastern spiritual practices of Enlightenment. Now in Arizona, she practices as a Spiritual Advisor seeing clients, and lectures.

You may contact the author:

Email: dimpledoc@aol.com

Website: www.janethizarhansford.com

Anthrogenesis